# AN INTRODUCTION
*to the*
# NEW TESTAMENT

*Volume 2*
## THE PAULINE EPISTLES

# AN INTRODUCTION
*to the*
# NEW TESTAMENT

*Volume 2*

## THE PAULINE EPISTLES

*By*

D. EDMOND HIEBERT

MOODY PRESS
CHICAGO

Formerly entitled:
*An Introduction to the Pauline Epistles*



*Revised Edition*

**Second Printing, 1978**



All scripture quotations in this book are from the American Standard Version (1901), except where indicated otherwise.

The use of selected references from various versions of the Bible in this publication does not necessarily imply publisher endorsement of the versions in their entirety.

ISBN: 0-8024-4138-6

*Printed in the United States of America*

To

*my wife,*

*who cheerfully bears the added burdens laid upon her by the auditory handicap of her husband*

# CONTENTS


CHAPTER PAGE

Preface 9
Acknowledgments 11
1. A General Introduction to the Pauline Epistles 13
2. Suggested Study Procedure 25

*Part 1* ESCHATOLOGICAL GROUP

3. An Introduction to Group One 31
4. First Thessalonians 33
   *Introduction*
   *Outline*
   *Book List on 1 and 2 Thessalonians*
5. Second Thessalonians 54
   *Introduction*
   *Outline*

*Part 2* SOTERIOLOGICAL GROUP

6. An Introduction to Group Two 69
7. Galatians 71
   *Introduction*
   *Outline*
   *Book List*
8. First Corinthians 102
   *Introduction*
   *Outline*
   *Book List*
9. Second Corinthians 135
   *Introduction*
   *Outline*
   *Book List*
10. Romans 163
   *Introduction*
   *Outline*
   *Book List*

## *Part 3* CHRISTOLOGICAL GROUP


11. An Introduction to the Prison Epistles 205
12. Colossians 214
    *Introduction*
    *Outline*
    *Book List*
13. Philemon 240
    *Introduction*
    *Outline*
    *Book List*
14. Ephesians 253
    *Introduction*
    *Outline*
    *Book List*
15. Philippians 282
    *Introduction*
    *Outline*
    *Book List*


## *Part 4* ECCLESIOLOGICAL GROUP


16. An Introduction to the Pastoral Epistles 307
17. First Timothy 324
    *Introduction*
    *Outline*
    *Book List on the Pastoral Epistles*
18. Titus 340
    *Introduction*
    *Outline*
    *Book List*
19. Second Timothy 350
    *Introduction*
    *Outline*
    *Book List*

Bibliography 364
Index 378

# PREFACE

This book is intended as a guide for the systematic interpretation of Paul's epistles in the collegiate classroom, or for individual study. It is not a commentary on this section of Scripture, neither is it intended to displace the student's use of commentaries in studying these epistles. It is an outgrowth of years of college classroom exposition of the Pauline epistles, and is to aid the student's efforts in tracing the thought content of these profound writings.

The opening section of the book is an introductory survey of the Pauline epistles as a group. The brief section which follows, suggesting a study procedure, is to point out a fruitful method for the study of these letters. The epistles are then divided into four groups, arranged in chronological order. The material under each epistle consists of an Introduction, an Outline, and a Book List. The Introduction gives the necessary background materials for an intelligent study of the letters; the Outline is to guide the student in his mastery of the thought content of the epistles; the Book List points out the rich resources for an intensive exploration of the impenetrable depths of these matchless writings.

The Introductions aim to give a knowledge of the historical factors necessary for a proper understanding of the books. The usual points of introduction, such as the recipients of the letter, its occasion, the place, the purpose, etc., are presented in a nontechnical manner. I have not attempted to deal exhaustively with the critical problems of the epistles, nor have I advanced new and startling views or novel theories. I have given the student a brief introduction to these problems from the conservative viewpoint. Because of the divergent conclusions of the scholars on Pauline chronology, the dates assigned to the various epistles must be held as tentative.

Detailed outlines will guide the student to grasp the thought content. Favorable response to their use in the classroom emboldens me to present them in this way. I am not unmindful of the hazards involved in the attempt. I anticipate that the cry will be raised that the epistles are "excessively divided and subdivided." I am not implying that Paul composed these letters with these subdivisions consciously before his mind; yet a careful study of the epistles warrants the development of such detailed outlines. I am further aware that such detailed outlines inevitably reveal one's interpretation of difficult passages yet leave him without any means of justifying his views. No outline, however fully developed, can substitute for a personal study of the books themselves. The student must vitalize the outlines by personal study, investigation, and prayerful meditation.

The outlines are not to be thought of as final. Suggestions from many sources have entered into their development. The student is urged to study the outlines critically and to make improvements as he proceeds. If such a use of them brings the student to a fuller and truer understanding of these epistles, their purpose will have been fulfilled.

By themselves the outlines are cold and rather meaningless until they are vitalized through one's own study of Paul's letters. Here the use of interpretative volumes on the epistles comes in.

The Book Lists following the Outlines are meant to point out to the student something of the great variety of tools available to him for an intensive study of these profound writings. They constitute a selection from the vast numbers of available works in the field. Generally the Book Lists contain works that are more readily available. I hope that their diversity will meet the needs of different groups in systematic interpretation of the epistles.

My comments on the books in the lists are not critical reviews, but simply indications of the nature and scope of the books. In the case of the works covering more than one epistle, I have commented only when the book is first listed, in the order followed in this volume. A favorable comment on a volume does not imply endorsement of all its contents.

Nothing in this volume will dispense with the need for a personal study of the epistles themselves. I hope that this book will challenge readers to an intensive study of Paul's letters, which are among the richest and most profound writings in the world.

# ACKNOWLEDGMENTS

I OWE MUCH to many different sources, and I gladly acknowledge the application in this case of the words of the Lord: "Other men have labored, but you have reaped the results of their labors" (John 4:38, Williams). I wish also gratefully to record the inspiration and stimulation received from the various college students who have studied these epistles with me.

All Scripture quotations, unless otherwise indicated, are from the American Standard Version (1901), through the courtesy of the copyright holders, Division of Christian Education of the National Council of the Churches of Christ in the United States of America.

In the Introduction I have acknowledged by footnotes the sources of the materials drawn upon. Special acknowledgments are due to the following publishers for the use of their materials:

To Pickering and Inglis (London) for several brief paragraphs and sentences from *Know Your Bible, Volume II, The New Testament* by W. Graham Scroggie; to T. & T. Clark (Edinburgh) for several brief excerpts from R. D. Shaw's *The Pauline Epistles;* also James Moffatt's *Introduction to the Literature of the New Testament* and Ernest De Witt Burton's *A Critical and Exegetical Commentary on the Epistle to the Galatians;* to the University of London Press (London) for a sentence quotation or two from *An Introduction to the New Testament* by F. Bertram Clogg; to the Cambridge University Press (Cambridge) for a quotation from A. Plummer's *Second Epistle to the Corinthians (Cambridge Greek Testament)*, as well as from *The Epistles of Paul to the Colossians and to Philemon (Cambridge Greek Testament)* by A. Lukyn Williams; to Hodder and Stoughton for several brief quotations from several volumes of the *Moffatt New Testament Commentary.*

To the Lutheran Book Concern (Columbus, Ohio) for several brief quotations from the *Interpretations* of R. C. H. Lenski; to the University of Chicago Press (Chicago) for a few brief excerpts from Edgar J. Goodspeed's *An Introduction to the New Testament;* to the Columbia University Press (New York) for a few brief extracts from *The Literature of the New Testament* by Ernest Findlay Scott.

To the American Schools of Oriental Research (New Haven, Conn.) for some brief quotations from two articles appearing in *The Biblical Archaeologist.*

To the Gilmary Society (New York) for a few sentence references from *The Catholic Encyclopedia;* to the Wm. B. Eerdmans Publishing Co. (Grand Rapids) for some brief quotations from several articles in *The International Standard Bible Encyclopaedia.*

Where only a sentence or so has been quoted from a copyrighted volume, I have not thought it necessary to enumerate all such volumes here. All direct quotations are acknowledged in the footnotes of the text. Where any copyrighted material may have been used without proper acknowledgment, indulgence is craved for the oversight.

Various sources which can no longer be enumerated have entered into the author's development of the outlines of the epistles. The outlines were first developed for the author's own use in the classroom and without any thought of publication. Many different sources were consulted, assimilated, and incorporated into his own work. Stimulation and help from many sources is gratefully acknowledged.

I am grateful to two colleagues who read part of the manuscript and offered helpful suggestions.

# 1

# A GENERAL INTRODUCTION TO THE PAULINE EPISTLES

THE NEW TESTAMENT is striking in that practically one-third of its content is letters. Twenty-one of the twenty-seven books are epistles.[1] Of these twenty-one, thirteen bear the name of the apostle Paul. They form the bulk of the epistolary section of the New Testament. The remaining eight epistles, written by several different authors, constitute less than ten per cent of the New Testament.

## THE UNIQUENESS OF THE NEW TESTAMENT EPISTLES

In this prominent use of the epistolary form the New Testament is distinct from all the other sacred writings of the world. "The Scriptures of other oriental religions—the Vedas, the Zend Avesta, the Tripitaka, the Koran, the writings of Confucius—lack the direct and personal address altogether."[2] Pagan religions are ignorant of the new life in Christ that gave rise to the New Testament letters. The epistles unfold in terms of human experience the nature and processes of God's redemptive movements.

This characteristic is the unique glory of the New Testament. While the Old Testament contains numerous references to the use of letters and even preserves a few of them (cf. Jer. 29; Ezra 5:6-17), no books of the Old Testament are cast into the epistolary form. Says Bengel, "The epistolary form is a pre-eminence of the Scriptures of the New Testament as compared with those of the Old."[3]

1. "Twenty-one of the 27 N. T. books are epistles strictly. Three more are so in form: Luke, Acts, and Revelation addressed to the seven churches. Matthew, Mark, and John alone are not epistolary either in form or substance." A. R. Fausset, "Epistle," *Bible Cyclopaedia, Critical and Expository,* (1902), p. 210c.
2. Dwight M. Pratt, "Epistle," *The International Standard Bible Encyclopaedia,* (1939), Vol. II, p. 966a.
3. Quoted in Thomas Dehany Bernard, *The Progress of Doctrine in the New Testament,* (reprint, n.d.), p. 147.

The use of the epistle as a medium of revelation in the New Testament reveals the difference between the ages of law and grace. Under the legal dispensation the demands of God were set forth in legal documents, sealed with the direct authority of God; in the age of grace God further makes known His will to His children through loving letters of instruction and exhortation. The difference is aptly summarized by Heward when he remarks, "Statutory codes for subjects, letters of spiritual advice for sons."[4] Under the law, prophets delivered *oracles* to the *people,* solemnly setting forth their authoritative pronouncements with a "thus saith the Lord." With the inauguration of the age of grace, the apostles wrote *letters* to the *brethren* in a spirit of loving intimacy, setting forth the significance and implications of their new position in Christ. The New Testament use of the epistle as a vehicle of revelation emphasized the truth that now God's method is that of companionship rather than that of dictation. The revelation is made not so much in the way of information as in the way of education.

### The Fitness of the Epistle for Christian Revelation

The apostles' use of the letter to convey their teachings was eminently suited to the nature of Christianity. Christianity is basically a personal relationship between the individual and God through faith in Christ Jesus. The epistle readily lent itself to a free discussion of these personal relations in Christianity. It was likewise well adapted to an informal discussion of the fundamental theological doctrines which the readers had already accepted. Paul directed his epistles to converts who had already accepted Christ and His Gospel but whose lives revealed the need for further instruction in the outworkings of those truths in daily conduct.

The needs and capacities of the readers governed the contents of the epistle directed to them and influenced the application of the Gospel truths contained in it. In a letter Paul could treat important subjects with accuracy and fullness, and yet do so in immediate connection with actual life situations. His epistles are not abstract doctrinal dissertations on some particular aspect of the Christian faith. They were written to meet specific needs and were adapted to the occasion. The epistolary method enabled Paul to stress the truths of

4. Percy W. Heward, *God's Letters to His Church,* (1904), p. 7.

Christianity again and again in different contexts and with different applications, all according to the needs of his readers.

However, the use of the epistolary form, which places Paul on a level of companionship with his readers, does not rob these writings of their authority as Scripture. Everywhere in the lofty, unwavering testimony of the writer there is that sense of authority which gives these writings their force and finality. And the added fact of direct prophetic revelation in his epistles, furthering the progress of Christian doctrine, diffuses over them that certainty and majesty which stamps them as inspired Scripture.

### The Form of the Pauline Writings

There is a question whether Paul wrote letters or epistles. Adolf Deissman made a sharp distinction between the genuine letter and the literary epistle. The former he defined as being private and for particular eyes to read, whereas the latter was defined as a literary production more general in aim and intended for publication. Deissmann maintained that the writings of Paul had that spontaneousness and intimate, affectional personal element that marked them as genuine letters rather than epistles.[5] In the light of Deissmann's definition, the writings of Paul must be classified as letters. Obviously Paul did not compose theological treatises, intended for general consumption, under the guise of letters. Even when Paul wrote to a group of churches such as to the Galatians, or to an individual church, like Colossians, with explicit instructions that the epistle should be exchanged with the one from Laodicea (Col. 4:16), his writings contained the intimacy and spontaneity of the true letter. Under Deissmann's distinction, Romans comes the nearest to a true epistle.[6] He was correct in insisting that Paul's writings arose out of a definite historical situation and reveal the characteristics of a true letter.

The distinction, however, need not be too sharply drawn in regard to the Pauline writings in the New Testament. In common usage with regard to apostolic writings, the words *letter* and *epistle* are practically interchangeable, and there need be no misunderstanding when we continue to speak of the Pauline epistles. It must be admitted that there is in them a lofty spirit and tone that forever dis-

5. G. Adolf Deissmann, *Bible Studies,* (2d Ed., 1909), pp. 3-12, 42-49; also his *The New Testament in the Light of Modern Research,* (1929), pp. 28-31.
6. Everett F. Harrison, *Introduction to the New Testament,* (Revised Ed., 1971), pp. 256-258.

tinguishes them from the ordinary letter of that day. In the words of Pratt,

> The epistles of the N.T. are lifted into a distinct category by their spiritual eminence and power, and have given the word *epistle* a meaning and quality that will forever distinguish it from *letter*. In this distinction appears that Divine element usually defined as *inspiration:* a vital and spiritual enduement which keeps the writings of the apostles permanently "living and powerful," where those of their successors pass into disuse and obscurity.[7]

The numerous papyrus discoveries have further confirmed the evidence that the letters of that day adhered to a more or less fixed form. Examples of this form may be seen in the two letters of the book of Acts (Acts 15:23-29; 23:26-30). It was customary in that day for a writer to begin a letter with his own name and office, or other identification; then followed the name of the reader and a wish of some kind for the reader.[8] Paul follows this method; yet his rich Christian experience led him to expand this according to the genius of Christianity. Following his salutation, Paul makes it a practice to add a note of thanksgiving for the readers.[9] Then, in epistles dealing with theological problems, he launches into a doctrinal section, followed by a practical section; personal greetings and an autograph conclude the letter. However, when his primary purpose is personal or practical, the theological teaching comes in, for the most part, incidentally and by the way. A study of the outlines of the various epistles reveals a rich variation according to the occasion. Concerning the contents of Paul's writings, Findlay says,

> The contents of the epistles may be classified under the following heads,—as personal, theological, ethical, administrative, and devotional. These various topics and constituent elements run into each other and are combined in numberless ways. . . . But it is the proportion in which they are blended and the preponderance of the one constituent or the other which give to each epistle its distinctive complexion.[10]

7. Dwight M. Pratt, "Epistle," *International Standard Bible Encyclopaedia,* (1939), Vol. II, p. 967b. Italics in the original.
8. The order was: the writer's name in the nominative, the recipient in the dative, the greeting in the nominative, usually without any verb. Each or any of these three members of the salutation might be expanded at will.
9. Only Galatians contains no expression of thanks for the readers.
10. George G. Findlay, *The Epistles of Paul the Apostle,* (n.d.), p. 36.

### The Number of the Pauline Epistles

Thirteen of the New Testament epistles, nearly one-half the books in the New Testament, bear the name of the apostle Paul. In the order in which they appear in our New Testament they are Romans, 1 and 2 Corinthians, Galatians, Ephesians, Philippians, Colossians, 1 and 2 Thessalonians, 1 and 2 Timothy, Titus, and Philemon. The superscription to the Epistle to the Hebrews in the King James Version reads, "The epistle of Paul the apostle to the Hebrews." But these superscriptions are of late origin and are not found in the oldest manuscripts. Westcott and Hort, following the oldest manuscripts, give the simple title *Pros Ebraious* (To Hebrews).[11] The superscription attributing Hebrews to Paul embodies a later tradition concerning its authorship. The epistle itself is anonymous. While recognized as inspired, the question of the authorship of Hebrews has been in uncertainty from earliest times. In this study Hebrews is not included as one of the writings of the apostle, although Paul's influence upon it is evident.

That Paul wrote more than the thirteen epistles which we have in our Bible today is clear from references in them to letters now lost to us. In 1 Corinthians 5:9 Paul refers to a letter to Corinth which he had previously written to that church; therefore our so-called *First* Corinthians must be at least the second letter to that church. The expression "my letters" in 2 Corinthians 10:9 certainly has reference to more than two letters. In Colossians 4:16 reference is made to a letter "from Laodicea" which was to be read also in the Colossian church. While many scholars today hold that this has reference to our Ephesians, it may well refer to a lost letter. Ephesians 3:3 has sometimes been cited as another reference to a lost letter; yet this is not probable. When in 2 Thessalonians 3:17 Paul speaks of his own signature as the token of its genuineness "in every epistle," he must have reference to more than the two epistles to the Thessalonians which we now possess.

It seems obvious that Paul must have written many more letters than we now have. These would be called for by his ever-expanding sphere of labor. The farther he traveled and the more churches he founded, the larger his correspondence would become. He found it

11. Brooke Foss Westcott and Fenton John Anthony Hort, *The New Testament in the Original Greek*, (1935 reprint). So also all recent critical editions of the Greek Testament.

possible and necessary to keep in touch with his churches through his letters as well as through the visits of his helpers. When he sent his deputies to various churches it seems certain that he often must also have sent letters with them. His courtesy and gratitude for the many kindnesses shown him by the churches must have occasioned a number of letters, such as he once wrote to the Philippians (Phil. 4:10). Surely such correspondence seems to be included in his reference to the care of all the churches which came upon him daily (2 Cor. 11:28).

We need not be reluctant to accept the fact that a letter of the apostle Paul was permitted to perish. Lightfoot reminds us that many of the inspired words of the Lord Jesus Himself were allowed to go unpreserved.[12] In His superintending wisdom the Holy Spirit did not see fit to preserve for us all the words of Christ nor all the letters of the apostles in our New Testament Canon. But what we have is sufficient for our faith and practice. We must, however, point out that the earliest Church Fathers who quote from Paul's writings with acknowledgment cite only from letters that are in our New Testament.

## The Origin of the Pauline Epistles

Paul's epistles arose out of actual life situations and were intended to meet real needs and answer vital questions. They were not composed as abstract studies in theology, nor were they doctrinal treatises produced by an erudite, cloistered scholar; rather, the ready outpourings of an alert, compassionate pastoral heart. Again and again troublesome questions arose in the churches that called for Paul's help. Frequently believers failed to understand the implications of Christianity for their lives and engaged in practices that demanded the rebuke and correction of apostolic authority. Current heresies threatened inroads upon the young churches and called forth Paul's instruction and counsel. These churches looked to him for help and cherished his assistance, which was often given in the form of letters. At other times Paul heard good news or received tokens of affection from these churches; this caused him to write or express his joy and to give encouragement and exhortation.

12. J. B. Lightfoot, *Saint Paul's Epistle to the Philippians,* (1898), pp. 138-139.

## The Method of Composition and Transmission

1. *Composition.* Paul made it a practice to dictate his letters to an amanuensis (scribe), writing the concluding words himself. Tertius, the scribe to whom Paul dictated the Epistle to the Romans, even added a greeting of his own in the letter (Rom. 16:22). Paul's concluding words to his epistles constituted the evidence of their genuineness (2 Thess. 3:17; 1 Cor. 16:21; Col. 4:18). Apparently he adopted this method of authenticating his letters because of a case of forgery where someone had written a letter to the Thessalonians in Paul's name teaching that the Day of the Lord was already upon them (2 Thess. 2:1-2, Gr.).

Various conjectures have been advanced as to why Paul usually did not write his letters with his own hand. It has been thought that he dictated because of imperfect eyesight, or that he lacked the ready ability to write rapidly the Greek characters, or that the rough work of tent-making had affected his fingers to such an extent that he found writing a difficult task. The reason for his method is nowhere stated. But obviously it was the convenience of the method. Competent scribes were available, and probably many churches had professional scribes whom Paul could employ. They could easily take his dictation, perhaps even use a form of shorthand.[13] Then, this method relieved Paul of the labor of writing and left his mind free to concentrate on developing the thought and the manner of its expression.

The epistles bear obvious traces of dictation. Shaw says,

> We feel we are all the time listening to a *speaker*—one whom we may imagine walking up and down his room, while the pen of the shorthand writer flies swiftly over the parchment to keep pace with the utterance. All the Epistles have this air of being spoken, reported, and passed on without much revisal.[14]

Yet we must not assume that his letters were dashed off without preparation. They reveal careful planning. A close study reveals a careful choice of words in the development of his subject. In epistles like

13. "Shorthand was in use among the Romans at least from the time of their occupation of Palestine, and among the Greeks it goes back to considerably earlier time." E. F. Harrison, *Introduction to the New Testament,* (Revised Ed., 1971), p. 254. See Richard N. Longenecker, "Ancient Amanuenses and the Pauline Epistles," *New Dimensions in New Testament Study,* ch. 18, edited by Richard N. Longenecker and Merrill C. Tenney, (1974).
14. R. D. Shaw, *The Pauline Epistles,* (4th Ed., 1924 reprint), p. 10. Italics in original.

Romans and Ephesians the course of the argument must have been fully worked out before pen was put to paper.

We must also remember that Paul prepared his epistles to be read aloud to the congregations (cf. 1 Thess. 5:27; Col. 4:16). This very fact necessitated writing with care and in language of a certain dignity and elevation. "Ever and again they contain passages of lofty eloquence, which cannot be fully appreciated until we hear them read out by a finished speaker.[15]

2. *Transmission.* After a letter had been composed, there remained the problem of its transmission. This was not as simple a matter as it is for us today. Paul's letters were taken by a special courier or sent along with some friend who was traveling to that city. Travel was extensive in the reign of the emperors, no doubt because of the security afforded by the forces of Rome and because of the network of well-built Roman roads. But the postal system established by the Emperor Augustus was a state service, and private messages had to be conveyed by private messengers.[16] Paul usually used one of his helpers as his courier (cf. Col. 4:7-8; Eph. 6:21-22; Phil. 2:25-28).

## The Order of the Pauline Epistles

The epistles of Paul may be studied in either one of two different orders. They may be studied in their present canonical order, or in their chronological order.

1. *Canonical order.* It is obvious that the present order of these epistles was determined by the length of the epistle. The longest, Romans, stands first; and the shortest, Philemon, stands last. The letters addressed to churches appear in the order of their length, and the epistles to individuals follow in the same order. This fact has caused some critics to declare that the present order is haphazard and destitute of any real significance.

Others, however, maintain that the present order is not haphazard, but has real meaning and value. It is pointed out that the present order is the order of logical instruction. Thus Bernard says,

> The Pauline Epistles appear, with very small variation, to have been

15. Ernest Findlay Scott, *The Literature of the New Testament,* (1948 reprint), p. 109.
16. George Hope Stevenson, "Postal Service (Roman)," in *The Oxford Classical Dictionary,* (1957 reprint), p. 723; M. Luther Stirewalt, Jr., "Paul's Evaluation of Letter-Writing," in *Search the Scriptures,* edited by J. M. Myers, O. Reimherr, and H. N. Bream, (1969), pp. 183-190.

> habitually ranged in that order in which we read them now; and it is one which on the whole, and in a certain measure, produces the effect of a course of doctrine. They fall naturally into groups, which stand, relatively to each other, in the places which they ought to occupy for purposes of progressive instruction.[17]

Under this viewpoint it is logical that Romans with its clear doctrine of justification should stand first. That is where a course in divine instruction must begin. And it is equally fitting that the two Thessalonian epistles should come last in the group addressed to churches, since they are chiefly occupied with the second coming of Christ, the natural climax of the Christian life.

Again, it has been said that the present order of the epistles addressed to churches corresponds to the order of experience. It corresponds to God's threefold classification of men given in 1 Corinthians 2:14-3:1.[18] Romans, coming first, is addressed to the *natural* man, and sets before him the Gospel of salvation as the answer to his needs. The next three epistles, 1 and 2 Corinthians and Galatians, are addressed to local churches and deal with the problems and perplexities of the *carnal* man. His problems, both doctrinal and practical, are revealed and answered in these epistles. The next three, Ephesians, Philippians, and Colossians, portray the position and privilege of the *spiritual* man. They are addressed to the individual saints "in Christ" who find their life in Him and rise superior to local circumstances. The Thessalonian epistles, again addressed to a group, picture the hope and end of the Church of Christ here on earth.

If such an interpretation of the present order of the epistles of Paul be thought somewhat artificial, it should be remembered that the sum of truth is always greater than the value of its separate parts. At any rate, the present order of the epistles cannot be condemned as meaningless.

2. *Chronological order.* These epistles may also profitably be studied in their chronological order, as near as that can be determined. This order of study "reveals the development of the Apostle's thought and the sequence of the circumstances which made the Let-

17. Thomas Dehany Bernard, *The Progress of Doctrine in the New Testament,* (n.d.), p. 157.
18. See Norman B. Harrison, *His Very Own,* (1930), pp. 9-10, or Harrison, *His Book, or Structure in Scripture,* (1936), pp. 84-89.

ters necessary."[19] To see them in their chronological setting is to add much to a clearer and fuller understanding of them.

The chronological order of the epistles can be determined with a fair degree of accuracy in the light of the Acts. It must be said, however, that the place of Galatians is quite uncertain in such an arrangement. These letters were written over a period of about fifteen years, from various places and under varying circumstances. It is generally held that all of them must be dated after the beginning of the second missionary journey.

On the basis of the chronological order, some persons attempt to trace the doctrinal development in Paul's thinking. But this does not yield significant results. "The development which manifests itself in the sequence of his Epistles is rather in the mode of presenting the Gospel than in its essential conceptions."[20] It must be remembered that they are all the products of the years of Paul's spiritual maturity. He had been a Christian for more than fourteen years before any of them was written (cf. Gal. 2:1). That certain thoughts which are prominent in the later epistles are absent in the earlier epistles does not mean that they had not been present to his mind at the earlier stage. It simply means that the circumstances when writing the earlier epistles did not call them forth.

### The Grouping of the Pauline Epistles

Paul's letters have been classified in different ways. From the standpoint of their destination they have been grouped as "Church Epistles" and "Personal Epistles." This is the arrangement followed in our Bible. Of the thirteen epistles, nine are addressed to a church or a group of churches, while four are addressed to individuals. Churches in the following places were recipients of letters: one to Rome, two to Corinth, one to the group of churches in Galatia, one to Ephesus (although a number of modern scholars hold that this is really a circular letter to the churches of the province of Asia), one to Philippi, one to Colossae, and two to Thessalonica. Four are addressed to individuals: two to Timothy, one to Titus, and one to Philemon. However, because of the importance of the letters to Timothy and Titus for church life, this distinction is not of much significance.

19. W. Graham Scroggie, *Know Your Bible, A Brief Introduction to the Scriptures, Volume II, The New Testament,* (n.d.), p. 98.
20. R. D. Shaw, *The Pauline Epistles,* (4th Ed., 1924 reprint), p. 6.

The epistles may also be grouped in relation to Paul's first Roman captivity: before, during, and after that event. This gives us six epistles before the imprisonment: 1 and 2 Thessalonians, Galatians, 1 and 2 Corinthians, and Romans; four during the imprisonment: Colossians, Philemon, Ephesians, and Philippians; and three following the first imprisonment: 1 Timothy, Titus, and 2 Timothy.

On this view the four epistles written during the imprisonment are designated "the prison epistles." The term "pastoral epistles" is now commonly employed to designate the three letters following the first Roman imprisonment, since they were written to men who stood in positions of ecclesiastical responsibility. Lange insisted that Philemon is "a decided pastoral,"[21] yet few today would agree in including Philemon under the term "pastoral epistles."

The common practice is to make a fourfold classification by dividing the six epistles before the imprisonment into two distinct groups. This fourfold grouping is supported not only by questions of chronology but also by the character and contents of the epistles. This classification was popularized by J. B. Lightfoot and others. The accompanying table shows the grouping and the order of the epistles here used.

THE FOUR GROUPS OF EPISTLES

| *Group* | *Books* | *Time Written* | *Characteristics* |
|---|---|---|---|
| I | 1 Thessalonians | During second tour | Eschatological |
| | 2 Thessalonians | During second tour | (Coming of Christ) |
| II | Galatians | Second or third tour | Soteriological |
| | 1 Corinthians | Third tour | (Cross of Christ) |
| | 2 Corinthians | Third tour | |
| | Romans | Third tour | |
| III | Colossians | First imprisonment | Christological |
| | Philemon | First imprisonment | (Character of Christ) |
| | Ephesians | First imprisonment | |
| | Philippians | First imprisonment | |
| IV | 1 Timothy | After 1st imprisonment | Ecclesiological |
| | Titus | After 1st imprisonment | (Church of Christ) |
| | 2 Timothy | During 2nd imprisonment | |

21. John Peter Lange, *The Epistle to the Romans,* (1950 reprint), p. 16. See also J. J. Van Oosterzee, "Philemon," Lange's *Commentary,* p. 1.

There is no question concerning the order of the groups, although there is some doubt as to the exact order within the various groups, especially in groups II and III. The question of the chronological position of Galatians has called forth the widest diversity of opinion. Because of its similarity to Romans, Lightfoot and others have placed it on the third missionary journey, shortly before the writing of Romans. Advocates of the *South-Galatian* theory generally place it earlier, some even insisting that it was written before the Thessalonian epistles. No other Pauline epistle is capable of being given such a wide range of datings within the framework of Acts as Galatians.

The order in group III turns around the question of the position of Philippians. That it stands alone in the group is evident, but scholars are not agreed as to whether it should be placed first or last in the group.

The fourth group has been the subject of much controversy. Liberal scholars, denying their genuineness, have placed the date of these epistles long after the death of Paul. Conservative scholars, accepting them as of Pauline origin and composition, have always placed them toward the close of the Apostle's life. The conservative position is finding increasing acceptance in recent scholarship.

### The Value of the Pauline Epistles

The Pauline epistles form one of the inestimable treasures of the Christian Church. Serious and prolonged study of them only increases one's appreciation of their matchless value for the Church and the individual believer. Much has been written in praise of these epistles, and no tribute paid them is too high. The following words are from Philip Schaff, in his monumental *History of the Christian Church:*

> Tracts for the times, they are tracts for all times. Children of the fleeting moment, they contain truths of infinite moment. They compress more ideas in fewer words than any other writings, human or divine, excepting the Gospels. They discuss the highest themes which can challenge an immortal mind. . . . And all this before humble little societies of poor, uncultured artisans, freedmen and slaves! And yet they are of more real and general value to the church than all the systems of theology from Origen to Schleiermacher.[22]

Or, we may add, Barth or Bultmann.

22. Philip Schaff, *History of the Christian Church,* (1910), Vol. I, p. 741.

# 2

# SUGGESTED STUDY PROCEDURE

THE PAULINE EPISTLES demand and are eminently worthy of the most serious and prolonged study. Only a patient, painstaking mastery of their contents will give one an adequate appreciation of their abiding value and impenetrable depths. The most fruitful method for mastering the contents of these epistles is to concentrate upon one at a time until it truly becomes one's own. To be most effective, such a concentrated study of an individual epistle should be preceded by a reasonably adequate acquaintance with the background story as found in the Old Testament and the Gospels, and especially in the Acts. An individual book of the Bible is always of greater significance when seen in its proper relation to the whole.

1. Read the epistle *straight through* at one sitting. Seek to follow the train of thought as you read. Then read it again, and yet again. The more often it is read the better.[1] If you wish, read different versions after the epistle has been read several times in one's study Bible.[2] Only such a direct reading and rereading of these profound writings will enable you to gain a mastery of them. Information about the great classics of art or literature cannot replace a direct acquaintance with them. Neither does the reading of expositions on the Pauline epistles eliminate the need for a personal reading and rereading of them. Those who have gained a mastery of these profound books have been persistent readers of them.[3]

1. After two or three readings it may be well to use a different edition of the Biblical text lest the very familiarity of the arrangements of the very words on the page dull the freshness of the impression.
2. Such as J. N. Darby, Montgomery, Weymouth, Williams, Berkeley Version, New American Standard Bible, New International Version; also translations in other languages which the student knows.
3. It is said of that great expositor G. Campbell Morgan that "he set for his own standard the reading of a book fifty times before putting pen to paper in preparation." Jill Morgan, *A Man of the Word, Life of G. Campbell Morgan*, (1951), p. 164.

The idea in this repeated reading of the epistle is first of all to get a clear impression of its general contents and character. The effort should be to get a bird's-eye view of the entire epistle. Then concentration upon minor divisions and smaller details will follow. The student is not ready for a detailed study of the epistle until he is thoroughly conversant with the general thought trend and feeling of the book. And this can only be gained by a repeated, prayerful reading of the epistle.

We would urge the student who does not use the original Greek to use a copy of the American Standard Version (1901) for his detailed study. It is the best substitute for a knowledge of the original language available to the English reader. This version has been criticized for its close adherence to the order and structure of the original Greek. Because of its attempt to reproduce the original as closely as possible, this translation admittedly does not have quite the smooth flow of language characteristic of the King James Version (1611). Weigle words this criticism as follows:

> The major defect of the English Revised Version and of its variant, the American Standard Version, is that these are literal, word-for-word translations, which follow the order of the Greek words wherever possible, rather than the order which is natural to English.[4]

Yet this very so-called defect makes it all the more valuable to the student who wishes to get as close as possible to the exact thought and expression of the original without a knowledge of the original language. The accurate student must ever bear in mind that these epistles were originally written in Greek and not in English.[5]

2. Notice the *setting* of the epistle in its own group. As indicated in the General Introduction, the Pauline epistles naturally fall into

4. Luther A. Weigle, and members of the Revision Committee, *An Introduction to the Revised Standard Version of the New Testament,* (1946), p. 53.
5. The Revised Standard Version (1946; 1952) is an attempt to return, at least in a measure, to the classic style of the King James. While this translation has definite value for the student for comparative purposes, we feel that as a vehicle for the careful study of the epistles of Paul it cannot replace the more literal American Standard Version or the New American Standard Bible. Since the Revised Standard Version is quite free to break up the longer Greek sentences into a number of shorter, more idiomatic English sentences, it often fails to reveal the true connection of the thought as well as does the American Standard Version with its more literal order and sentence structure. It is much to be regretted that it omits all indications of added words in its text, thus giving the student no clue to words that have actually been added by the translators. Perhaps this is due to the fact that some of its renderings are very loose, amounting practically to a paraphrase rather than a strict translation.

four groups, each group having its own general theme and characteristics. Notice the epistles belonging to the group and the characterization of that group. Then read the introduction to that group. For example, if 1 Thessalonians is the epistle being studied, notice that, with 2 Thessalonians, it belongs to the *first* group and that as the first member of the group it is the earliest epistle of Paul which we have. Notice further that the two epistles of this group are characterized by their eschatological emphasis. Observe what is said concerning the order of these epistles.

3. Study the *Introduction* to the epistle Before reading the Introduction, read the epistle once more to find all available information concerning the author, the readers, the occasion, the place of composition, and purpose of the epistle. To be most profitable it is urged that the student note on a sheet of paper with the appropriate heading all the information found under these various points. Thus, on a sheet labeled "Author" any information found as to who the author was, where he was, the circumstances under which he wrote, the time he wrote, and so on, should be recorded. The same should be done for the other topics as the material is discovered in the reading. Following this personal study concerning the matters of introduction, turn to the Introduction to the epistle and read it to supplement the materials you have gathered.

4. Notice the *Outline* of the epistle following the Introduction. At first notice the main divisions of the epistle and mark them in the margins of your study Bible. With these main divisions in mind reread the epistle in the light of these divisions. Then notice the main subdivisions under each section and seek to recall the contents of the section in the light of the Outline. With the Outline of the section open before you, read that portion of the epistle again.

To illustrate from the Outline of 1 Thessalonians: notice that the first verse constitutes the Salutation, while the last three verses of the epistle form the Conclusion. Then notice that the epistle is divided into two main sections, the Personal and the Practical. Note the verses in each division and mark them in the margin of your Bible. Then notice that the first main division is divided into three sections, noticing the name and the verses included under each. Mark these divisions likewise in the margin. Then with the outline before you, read the section again in the light of the detailed Outline.

5. Make a *verse-by-verse* study of the epistle. Having gained a general acquaintance with the epistle as a whole through your repeated readings of it, and having noticed the various larger divisions of the epistle, you are now ready to make a detailed study of the epistle. Make an individual study of each verse as you go. Notice the force and meaning of the exact words and phrases used. Study the verse in the light of its context and notice the connection with what has gone before. Seek to gain all the information and light that you can from the passage for yourself. Such personal, independent study is of vital importance in the development of your abilities as a student of Scripture. Keep the results of this study in notes and comments on each section as it is studied.

Following your own study of the text, turn to a good exposition or commentary on the epistle and profit by the labors of others on it. A list of books for further study follows the outline for each epistle. It is well to supplement your own notes with the material thus discovered. Such a recording of your findings not only makes your study more meaningful but also preserves it for future use.

6. Meditate upon and *digest* the *results* of your study. This is of great importance for lasting results in the life of the student. Much Bible study is of little consequence because the material studied is not prayerfully assimilated for personal living. The ultimate aim of Bible study is not an informed intellect but a transformed personality.

Such persistent study, under the guidance of the Holy Spirit, brings lasting benefit to the student. Not only does it provide valued mental discipline and treasured information, but it will feed the soul. You will find that Paul's epistles have an increasing charm and spiritual dynamic little suspected before. The more these letters are studied, the more one will realize that they warrant lifetime study.

# *Part 1*

# ESCHATOLOGICAL GROUP

1 Thessalonians

2 Thessalonians

# 3

# AN INTRODUCTION TO GROUP ONE

THE TWO EPISTLES to the young church in Thessalonica, written from Corinth on the second missionary journey, constitute the Eschatological Group among the Pauline epistles. Both give great prominence to the doctrine of Christ's second coming. Unlike the second group, they contain no formal consideration of the doctrine of salvation; the thought is rather that of the personal return of the Saviour. Practically the entire contents of these two epistles are related to this glorious truth.

1 and 2 Thessalonians are generally regarded as Paul's earliest extant writings. 2 Thessalonians was written soon after the first letter and supplements its eschatological teaching. While some would date Galatians even earlier than these books, we believe that Galatians comes a little later and holds the first position in the second group.

A few scholars have attempted to reverse the accepted order of these epistles. But their arguments for this view are not convincing. They claim that 2 Thessalonians betrays all the characteristics of a first epistle. But 2 Thessalonians 2:15 refers to an epistle already received by the Thessalonians. Some think that Paul's words in 1 Thessalonians 4:10-12 contain a reference to the fuller instructions already given in 2 Thessalonians 3:6-15. But this is unnatural and overlooks the fact that the development of the trouble in Thessalonica made necessary the more explicit instructions in the Second Epistle. The criterion of genuineness given at the end of 2 Thessalonians (3:17) is quite groundless if this is Paul's first epistle to the Thessalonians, but it is psychologically valid if it comes after 1 Thessalonians. There is nothing in 1 Thessalonians to presuppose a previous letter of the character of 2 Thessalonians. On the other hand, there is a logical order and development if the traditional order of these epistles is accepted. As Neil says,

> In each of the topics dealt with—persecution, Second Advent, idleness—there is an obvious intensification of the difficulties, and development of the situation, as described in the first letter, which make any alteration of the sequence impossible.[1]

The relation of these two epistles to each other Gloag states as follows:

> The First Epistle describes how the Thessalonians received the Word of God, whilst the Second Epistle mentions their progress in faith, love, and patience. The First Epistle treats of the uncertainty of the advent; the Second Epistle corrects the misapprehension of the Thessalonians concerning that uncertainty. The First Epistle adverts to the spirit of disorder, the germs of which the apostle saw in the Thessalonian Church; the Second Epistle rebukes this spirit still more sharply, as these germs had developed and borne pernicious fruit. The First Epistle had given the Thessalonians commandments to be obeyed; and, in the Second Epistle, the apostle exhorts them to hold the traditions which he had delivered to them, whether by word or his Epistle.[2]

The present order of the Thessalonian epistles may be accepted without any misgivings or uncertainty.[3]

1. William Neil, "The Epistle of Paul to the Thessalonians," *Moffatt Commentary* (1950), p. xx.
2. P. J. Gloag, "II Thessalonians," *Pulpit Commentary*, (1950 reprint), pp. v-vi.
3. For the canonical order see Theodor Zahn, *Introduction to the New Testament*, (1909), Vol. I, pp. 231-232; Leon Morris, "The First and Second Epistles to the Thessalonians," *New International Commentary on the New Testament*, (1959), pp. 37-41; Donald Guthrie, *New Testament Introduction*, (Revised Ed., 1970), pp. 575-578. For the reverse order see T. W. Manson, *Studies in the Gospels and Epistles*, (1962), pp. 266-278; R. Gregson, "A Solution to the Problems of the Thessalonian Epistles," *The Evangelical Quarterly*, Vol. XXXVIII, No. 2, April-June 1966, pp. 76-80.

# 4

# FIRST THESSALONIANS

## An Introduction to 1 Thessalonians

The hope of the Redeemer's return has well been called the pole-star of the Christian Church. That it is so held forth in the New Testament is beyond dispute. And the First Epistle to the Thessalonians is unique in that it contains one of the fullest elaborations of this hope of the Church to be found in the New Testament.

### THE CITY OF THESSALONICA

1. *Location.* The city of Thessalonica was a large and prosperous seaport, situated on the northernmost point of the Thermaic Gulf; it was a short distance east of the mouth of the Axius river. In Paul's day it was one of the most important cities in the Roman province of Macedonia. It has been one of the chief cities of Macedonia from Hellenistic times down to our own day. The name of an earlier town at that place, Therma or Therme, may have been derived from the warm mineral springs which still exist in the vicinity. On the southwestern horizon is the cloudy height of Mount Olympus, the fabled home of the Greek gods.

2. *Name.* The place came into prominence about 315 B.C. when Cassander, the son-in-law of Philip of Macedon, enlarged and strengthened it by concentrating the population of several neighboring villages at that place. He renamed it Thessalonica in honor of his wife, the half-sister of Alexander the Great. This name, in the shortened form of Salonika, it retains to this day.

3. *Prominence.* Thessalonica rapidly became a place of importance and wealth. Its advantageous position at the head of the Thermaic Gulf made it an important seat of commerce. Its position on the

famous Egnatian Way, commanding the entrance to two great inland districts, likewise enhanced its power. The Egnation Way, from the Adriatic to the Hellespont, brought Thessalonica into direct contact with the stream of continual traffic between Rome and the eastern provinces. Cicero spoke of it as "lying in the lap of the empire."

4. *Political status.* The political fortunes of Thessalonica further augmented its importance. After the battle of Pydna (168 B.C.), when the Romans divided the conquered kingdom of Macedonia into four republics, Thessalonica was made the capital of the second division. In 146 B.C., when the territory of Macedonia was organized into a single province, it became the residence of the Roman governor and capital of the whole province. In the civil war between Caesar and Pompey, Thessalonica took the senatorial side and formed one of Pompey's chief bases (49-48 B.C.), but during the final struggles of the Roman republic, in 42 B.C., it stood on the side of Anthony and Octavian. Augustus rewarded the loyalty of Thessalonica by making it a "free city."[1] As such it was self-governing in all of its internal affairs. It had no garrison of Roman soldiers. Citizens had the right of holding assembly and appointing magistrates. The members of the supreme board of magistrates at Thessalonica bore the somewhat unusual title of "politarchs" and seem to have been five or six in number.[2] Luke's accuracy in the use of this title was once questioned, but Luke has been triumphantly vindicated by the discovery of inscriptions of it.[3]

5. *Inhabitants.* The majority of the Thessalonians were native Greeks. Because of the political status of the city, it retained its essential Greek character. A sprinkling of Romans and Orientals lived there, and because of the attractive commerce at Thessalonica, there was a large Jewish colony in the city. The activity and influence of this Jewish community may be seen in the large number of Gentile "God-fearers" who frequented their synagogue, having become dissatisfied with their pagan religions.

1. M. N. Tod, "Thessalonica," *International Standard Bible Encyclopaedia* (1939), Vol. V, p. 2970b.
2. George Milligan, *St. Paul's Epistles to the Thessalonians,* (1952 reprint), p. xxiii, note 3.
3. Ernest DeWitt Burton, "The Politarchs," *The American Journal of Theology,* No. 2 (1898), pp. 598-632; Merrill F. Unger, *Archaeology and the New Testament,* (1962), pp. 228-229.

THE CHURCH IN THESSALONICA

1. *Origin.* The church in Thessalonica owed its origin to the work of Paul and his helpers in that city on the second missionary journey. Luke describes the beginnings of the church in Acts 17:1-10. It was the second city in Macedonia to receive the Gospel from Paul. While at Troas he had received the "Macedonian call" (Acts 16:9-10), and in response to it the missionary party had immediately crossed over into Macedonia and begun work in Philippi, resulting in the establishment of the Philippian church. After having been shamefully beaten and imprisoned at Philippi, Paul and Silas proceeded westward along the Egnatian Way.[4] They passed through the ancient cities of Amphipolis and Appolonia, since apparently there were no synagogues there, and arrived at Thessalonica a hundred miles from Philippi. The size and importance of Thessalonica, as well as the fact that it had an important synagogue, made Paul eager to plant the Gospel in that city.

Following his custom, Paul began work in Thessalonica in the Jewish synagogue. For three successive Sabbaths he preached the Gospel to these Jews, basing his appeal on the Old Testament Scriptures. By his quotations from them and his exposition of them he proved that the promised Messiah, for whom the Jews had been taught to look, was "to suffer, and to rise again from the dead." Following this exposition, he showed that the historical Jesus, whom he had come to proclaim, was indeed the fulfillment of these prophecies.

From the charge that was made against him before the magistrates, as well as from the contents of the two letters to the Thessalonians, it appears that Paul laid considerable stress on the doctrine of the Kingdom of God and its final establishment by the personal appearing of the risen and exalted Christ.

The result of this synagogue ministry Luke states as follows:

> And some of them were persuaded, and consorted with Paul and Silas; and of the devout Greeks a great multitude, and of the chief women not a few (Acts 17:4).

Some Jews were won through Paul's preaching. Aristarchus, who afterwards proved a true and helpful comrade to the Apostle (Acts 27:2; Col. 4:10-11), seems to have been among them. But the ma-

4. It has been thought that Timothy remained at Philippi with Luke for a while and rejoined Paul at Beroea.

jority of the converts were from "the God-fearers" who had been attracted to the synagogue by the ethical monotheism of the Jews. Likewise the wives of a good number of the leading Thessalonian citizens were among those won to the Gospel.

2. *Membership.* From Luke's account it appears that the majority of the Thessalonian church were from among the "God-fearers" who had frequented the synagogue; but the epistle seems to indicate that the majority were converts from pure heathenism. They are described as those who "turned unto God from idols, to serve a living and true God" (1:9; cf. 2:14-16).[5] Ramsey, on the basis of Codex D compared with A, would amend the text of Acts 17:4 to read, "many of the God-fearing *proselytes,* and a great multitude of the Greeks."[6] Then verse 4 would indicate a wider sphere of influence and would account for the mass of Gentiles that seem to be so prominent in the epistle. The emendation is attractive but lacks manuscript authority.

The reason for the large number of Gentile converts was that the apostle carried on a mission directly among them when the synagogue was closed to him. Paul's success among the "God-fearers" in the synagogue naturally aroused the opposition of the unbelieving Jews, and after three weeks the synagogue doors were closed to him. As in other places, this apparently caused Paul to turn directly to the Gentiles in Thessalonica for an extensive ministry among them. It was during this ministry that the majority of the converts from heathenism were won.

3. *Length of stay.* The length of Paul's stay at Thessalonica has been variously estimated. Luke mentions only a period of three weeks in connection with the work at Thessalonica. Is it to be inferred that this is the total length of the apostle's stay at Thessalonica? Lenski thinks that his stay covered little more than four weeks.[7] However, others feel that these three weeks have reference only to the synagogue ministry at Thessalonica and that the actual stay was considerably longer. It has been asserted that the results achieved demand a period longer than three weeks. But it is never safe to say

5. But R. C. H. Lenski, *Interpretation of the Acts of the Apostles* (1934), asserts that "both passages apply to Greek proselytes, and do not demand only converts from paganism," p. 688.
6. W. M. Ramsay, *St. Paul the Traveller and the Roman Citizen,* (1896), pp. 226-227, 235-236.
7. R. C. H. Lenski, *Interpretation of St. Paul's Epistles to the Colossians, to the Thessalonians, to Timothy, to Titus and to Philemon,* (1937), p. 214.

that certain results could not have been achieved in such a short time. More substantial arguments have been advanced for a longer stay. Paul reminds the Thessalonians that he had supported himself by manual labor while there (2:9). Gloag holds that "it was his custom to do so only when his residence in any city was prolonged."[8] It may, however, simply show that Paul was preparing to stay a good while in Thessalonica. More to the point is the information found in the letter to the Philippians that his Philippian converts sent him an offering twice while he was in Thessalonica (Phil. 4:16). That this has reference to the period when the Thessalonian church was founded is confirmed by the Apostle's statement that it was "in the beginning of the Gospel" (Phil. 4:15). These repeated gifts of money from Philippi, a hundred miles away, would definitely imply that the stay must have been more than the three weeks mentioned by Luke. Moffatt says, "Two or three months possibly may be allowed for this fruitful mission at Thessalonica."[9] Ramsay is even willing to allow six months for the work there.[10]

4. *Opposition.* The unbelieving Jews, who jealously watched Paul's success among the Gentiles, finally launched an attack on the work which drove Paul from the city. Spurred on by their jealousy, these Jews resorted to the ignoble strategy described by Luke:

> But the Jews, being moved with jealousy, took unto them certain vile fellows of the rabble, and gathering a crowd, set the city on an uproar; and assaulting the house of Jason, they sought to bring them forth to the people (Acts 17:5).

Fortunately the intended victims were abroad or well hidden and could not be located by the mob. Not to be frustrated in their purpose,

> They dragged Jason and certain brethren before the rulers of the city, crying, These that have turned the world upside down are come hither also; whom Jason hath received: and these all act contrary to the decrees of Caesar, saying that there is another king, *one* Jesus (Acts 17:6-7).

That was an ugly charge. Many a man in that day was ruined by

8. P. J. Gloag, "I Thessalonians," *Pulpit Commentary,* (1950 reprint), p. v.
9. James Moffatt, "First and Second Epistles to the Thessalonians," *Expositor's Greek Testament,* (n.d.), Vol. IV, p. 3.
10. W. M. Ramsay, *St. Paul the Traveller and the Roman Citizen,* (1898), p. 228.

such a charge. The magistrates did not dare to treat it lightly. Doubtless they had some knowledge concerning the new teaching.[11] They seem to have been rather favorably disposed to the missionaries. Their settlement of the case was shrewd. "When they had taken security from Jason and the rest, they let them go" (Acts 17:9). The accused were charged with the responsibility that the trouble would not be repeated. This settlement inflicted no injury on the missionaries or their sureties, and at the same time it satisfied the accusers, and safeguarded the magistrates against suspicion of condoning treason.[12]

This settlement, however, made it impossible for the missionaries to remain there any longer. Their presence would endanger their converts, for the Jews would be sure to raise another uproar if they remained. In agreement with their converts, Paul and Silas that night left Thessalonica under cover of darkness. Diverging from the Egnatian Way, they traveled some forty miles southwest to Beroea, where they had an effective ministry among the Jews until their work was again interrupted by the vicious Jews from Thessalonica. Leaving Silas and Timothy at Beroea, some of the brethren from there brought Paul all the way to Athens. There Paul remained alone waiting for his helpers to join him.

### THE OCCASION FOR 1 THESSALONIANS

Having experienced the implacable hatred of the Thessalonian Jews even at Beroea, Paul was rightly concerned about the welfare of the Thessalonian believers. He could well imagine the kind of treatment they would receive from the enemy. And he had apparently heard that the persecution there was continuing. Hence he was filled with great concern for his Thessalonian converts, from whom he had been so suddenly and prematurely separated.

From Paul's statement in 1 Thessalonians 3:1 it seems evident that Silas and Timothy did come to Athens while Paul was there.[13] His concern for the Thessalonians caused Paul to send Timothy back to Thessalonica to establish them and comfort them concerning their

11. Compare the statement about the numerous converts "of the chief women." Acts 17:4.
12. Ramsay calls the settlement "the mildest that was prudent in the circumstances." W. M. Ramsay, *St. Paul the Traveller and the Roman Citizen* (1898), p. 230.
13. William Paley, *Horae Paulinae,* (n.d.), ch. IX, No. 4, showed that although Acts "does not expressly notice this arrival, yet it contains intimations which render it extremely probable that the fact took place."

faith (1 Thess. 3:1-2). If Timothy remained at Philippi until he rejoined Paul at Beroea, this would explain why Timothy was sent, since he would be personally unknown to the malicious Jews of Thessalonica. Perhaps Silas was sent back to Philippi at this time. While they were gone, Paul moved on to Corinth. Here they found Paul on their return (Acts 18:5).

Paul's suspense concerning the Thessalonians was ended by the return of Timothy and his report concerning them. It has been suggested that Timothy also brought a letter from the Thessalonians themselves addressed to Paul.[14] If so, it is strange that Paul made no reference to it. The report of Timothy was the immediate occasion for the writing of this epistle (3:6-7). Since it was impossible for him to revisit the Thessalonians personally (2:18), he resorted to the writing of this letter as a substitute for a personal visit.

### THE PLACE AND DATE OF 1 THESSALONIANS

1. *Place.* Corinth is generally accepted as the place from which Paul wrote 1 Thessalonians. The subscription in the King James Version reads, "The First Epistle to the Thessalonians was written from Athens." Though such a note is found in some old manuscripts, it is evidently a mistake. It records a tradition that evidently arose out of a misunderstanding of Paul's words, "We thought it good to be left behind at Athens alone" (3:1). But Paul's statement has reference to a past event and "indirectly implies that the Apostle was not at Athens when he wrote these words."[15] These subscriptions were not written by Paul and are not authoritative.

From the epistle we know that it was written when Timothy returned to Paul from his visit to Thessalonica (3:6-7). Paul sent Timothy back from Athens (3:1-2), but from Acts 18:5 we know that he and Silas rejoined Paul at Corinth. Since the epistle is in the name of all three, they were together at the time of the writing. This places them at Corinth during the early part of Paul's mission there. It was therefore during early months of the work at Corinth that 1 Thessalonians was written.

2. *Date.* The actual date assigned to 1 Thessalonians will be determined by the date assigned to the proconsulship of Gallio at Cor-

14. David Smith, *The Life and Letters of St. Paul,* (n.d.), p. 152; D. Edmond Hiebert, *The Thessalonian Epistles,* (1971), p. 21.
15. P. J. Gloag, "I Thessalonians," *Pulpit Commentary,* (1950 reprint), p. viii.

inth. The reference to Gallio's proconsulship of Achaia provides a historical landmark in the ministry of Paul at Corinth. A mutilated inscription discovered at Delphi names Gallio as proconsul and associates him with the twenty-sixth acclamation of Claudius as emperor.[16] Available information thus locates Gallio in Corinth between January 25 and August 1, 52. Assuming that he took office in midsummer, he arrived in Corinth July 51. This date is widely accepted today. But others hold that it is about a year too early. Thus Lenski points out that imperial orders made the time of leaving Rome April 1, later April 15, and holds that his arrival should be dated May 52, rather than 51.[17] This places Gallio at Corinth about ten months later.

Acts implies that Paul was hauled before Gallio shortly after his arrival. The date would therefore be either July 51 or May 52. The length of Paul's ministry at Corinth at the time has been estimated from six months to a year and a half.[18] A year seems most probable. Since Paul wrote 1 Thessalonians soon after commencing work at Corinth, the epistle may be dated in late summer or early fall of either A.D. 50 or 51. Whatever the exact date, we do know that it was written within some twenty years after the death of Christ.

3. *Bearer.* The epistle contains no indication as to how it was sent to Thessalonica. But doubtless it was carried by a personal courier or a friend who was traveling to that city. It was perhaps from this messenger on his return that Paul received the news which led to the writing of the Second Epistle.

### THE PURPOSE OF 1 THESSALONIANS

When Paul received the information concerning the Thessalonians from Timothy, he at once wrote this letter out of the gratitude of his heart. It reveals the affectionate nature of the apostle and portrays the intimate relations that he had with his converts. His purpose in writing the epistle may be summarized as follows.

1. *Commendation.* He wrote to express his joy and appreciation

16. For the inscription and discussion see F. J. Foakes Jackson and Kirsopp Lake, editors, *The Beginnings of Christianity,* (1966), Vol. V, pp. 460-464; C. K. Barrett, *The New Testament Background: Selected Documents,* (1961), pp. 48-49.
17. R. C. H. Lenski, *The Interpretation of St. Paul's Epistles to the Colossians, to the Thessalonians, to Timothy, to Titus, and to Philemon,* (1937), p. 215.
18. R. C. H. Lenski, *Loc. cit.;* Werner Georg Kümmel. *Introduction to the New Testament,* (1966), p. 180.

that they had remained true to the Gospel under severe testing. It caused him to give thanks and to take courage (3:7-9). Although he had forewarned them of coming persecution (3:4), still he was greatly relieved to know that they had not failed under the actual test (3:6). He commended them that they had become an example to others in the steadfastness of their faith (1:7) as well as in their brotherly love (4:9-10).

2. *Vindication.* Along with the good news from Thessalonica, Timothy had to report the fact that certain slanders and insinuations against the Apostle were being circulated in Thessalonica to harass the Christians. Paul found it necessary to use the first half of the epistle to defend himself against these calumniations. This defense of himself must have been personally distasteful to the Apostle, but it was necessary not for his own sake but for the sake of his converts. "He was the first Christian the Thessalonians had ever seen. He and his friends practically represented the Christian faith."[19] If therefore the enemies of Christianity could shake the faith of his converts in the Apostle's moral integrity, and publicly discredit him, their faith would be practically destroyed. In these attacks, apparently of Jewish origin,[20] the attempt was to class Paul with the wandering, mercenary, religious impostors who plied their arts on the gullible people of the day. The enemies declared that Paul was proclaiming his new doctrine for what he could get out of it. No doubt they would point to the fact that on several occasions while there in Thessalonica he had received money from his dupes at Philippi. It was such slanders that caused the Apostle to rehearse again the nature of his ministry among them (2:1-12). He reminded them of the sufferings for the Gospel he had previously experienced at Philippi. In spite of these sufferings, the marks of which were still plainly evident when he had arrived, he had preached to them with pure motives. He also recalled to them the fact that he had worked to maintain himself while there. He had been chargeable to none of them, for he had not been dominated by mercenary motives.

Again, the enemies would insist that Paul was just a sly, unscrupulous fellow who left his followers in the lurch and fled when difficulties

19. James Moffatt, "The First and Second Epistles to the Thesalonians," *Expositor's Greek Testament,* (n.d.), Vol. IV, p. 7.
20. George Milligan, *St. Paul's Epistles to the Thessalonians,* (1952 reprint), pp. xxxi-xxxii.

arose. If he was what he claimed to be, why did he not come back? They implied that he was afraid to come because of what might happen to him. These falsehoods Paul met by stating his relations to the Thessalonians since his forced separation from them (2:17–3:13). He greatly desired to revisit them; in fact he had made two separate attempts to return but had been prevented. Because of his desire to re-establish contact with them, he had sent Timothy back to them to encourage and strengthen them and to get information about them.

These attacks on his character, which caused the Apostle to open up his heart to the Thessalonians, must have been personally very distasteful to him, but they have brought great gain to us. These passages of indignant protest and intimate self-revelation have given us an open view into the very heart of the Apostle. These insinuations "against Paul's character were like torches flung at an unpopular figure; they simply served to light up his grandeur."[21]

3. *Admonition.* Along with the good report about the steadfast endurance of the Thessalonians under persecution, Paul learned that they were not free from the temptation to immoral practices so prevalent among the heathen (4:1-8). It is not said that they were actually guilty of serious moral failure, but the Apostle felt it needful to give them some practical moral admonitions, knowing the temptations to which they were constantly exposed.

A growing lack of respect for their leaders also needed correction. Doubtless while still there Paul had arranged for spiritual leaders in the church. From Acts 14:23 we see that Paul wisely did not leave his converts without the needed organization and leadership. Perhaps some of the earliest converts, or at any rate some with recognized gifts, came into the position of spiritual leaders in the life and worship of the congregation. But there were some who were developing a spirit of insubordination toward these spiritual leaders. Under the pretense of edifying others, they had become unruly. Paul sought to correct this condition by giving them some pointed admonitions (5:12-14).

4. *Revelation.* Certain doctrinal matters also called for an authoritative word from the Apostle. Apparently they had developed an erroneous idea as to the relation between the resurrection of the

21. James Moffatt, "The First and Second Epistles to the Thessalonians," *Expositor's Greek Testament,* (n.d.), Vol. IV, p. 6.

dead and the reign of Christ. They seem to have thought that those who are alive at the coming of the Lord will have a great advantage over those who have died. They thought that the living would be allowed to see His glory and to participate in His reign while the dead would slumber through these great events. Some of their loved ones had died, with the result that they were greatly distressed about them. In writing this epistle Paul took occasion to correct this misconception among the Thessalonians. He gave them the glorious revelation concerning the true relation of the living and the dead to the second coming of Christ which we find in 4:13-18.

### THE CHARACTERISTICS OF 1 THESSALONIANS

1. *Self-revelation.* 1 Thessalonians is one of the most personal of the letters of Paul. In it the real Paul stands out clearly before us in all the charm of his rich and varied personality. "This Letter," says Scroggie, "more than any other of Paul's, is characterized by simplicity, gentleness, and affection."[22] In it we see the warm outpouring of a tender pastoral heart in loving affection toward those he loves and longs to help. He records his intense affection for his young converts (2:7-8), his desire for their sympathy and prayers (5:25), his keen sensitiveness as to what others are saying about him (2:1-12), his longing for their spiritual progress (3:11-13), and his fierce indignation against those who are hindering the cause of Christ (2: 15-16). The epistle reveals his tact in dealing with his converts. Although he found it necessary to give blunt warnings, he wisely precedes these by a recognition of the good qualities of the brethren.

2. *Doctrinal content.* It is a mistake to assert that this epistle is devoid of doctrinal content. While assuredly it does not contain the elaborate doctrinal developments of Galatians, Romans, or Ephesians, it nevertheless has a definite doctrinal background. Because of the nature of the circumstances which called forth this epistle, there was no need for a formal elaboration of these doctrines. Such clear-cut statements of doctrine were usually not given until some situation had arisen that called them forth. The purpose of the epistle was practical rather than doctrinal.

But the epistle does reveal a rich doctrinal background. Scofield says, "The Epistle is incidentally most interesting as showing the

22. W. Graham Scroggie, *Know Your Bible, A Brief Introduction to the Scriptures, Volume II, The New Testament,* (n.d.), p. 108.

richness in doctrine of the primitive evangelism." He thinks that it reveals that during Paul's brief ministry at Thessalonica he "taught all the great doctrines of the Christian faith," and Scofield lists no less than eleven of them.[23]

Kerr remarks that the frequent use of *Lord* as applied to Jesus is "especially noticeable" while Milligan regards it as "the distinctive Name of these Epistles."[24] It is a clear testimony to the firm faith in the deity of Jesus Christ that prevailed in the Early Church. In full agreement with this is the fact that in 3:11 Paul explicitly directs his worship to Jesus along with the Father.

The doctrine of the second coming is prominent in this epistle. Each of the five chapters ends on the note of the Lord's return (1:10; 2:19; 3:13; 4:16-17; 5:23).[25] The clear revelation of the Lord's coming for His Church (4:13-18) has been of special interest and inspiration to the Church down through the centuries.

Of interest is the observation that this epistle does not contain a single direct quotation from the Old Testament.

3. *Witness value.* Because of its early date this epistle bears striking witness to the content of the earliest Gospel. Written little more than twenty years after the resurrection of Christ, it proves that the teachings of Christianity root directly back to the divine self-revelation made in Christ Jesus. It proves that the picture of Christ given in the four Gospels is not the devout fabrication of hero-worshiping souls during the latter part of the first century. This epistle bears solid witness to the truthfulness of the Gospel message. Walker has aptly summarized this in the following words:

> When we remember that Paul was converted more than fourteen years before the writing of the Epistle, and that he tells us that his conversion was of such an overwhelming nature as to impel him in a straight course from which he never varied, and when we note that at the end of fourteen years Peter and John, having fully heard the Gospel which he preached, had no corrections to offer (Gal. 1:11-2:10, esp. 2:6-10), we see that the view of Christ and His message

23. C. I. Scofield, *The Scofield Reference Bible,* (1917), p. 1267, Introduction to 1 Thessalonians, and note 1.
24. John H. Kerr, *An Introduction to the New Testament* (1931 reprint), p. 106; George Milligan, *St. Paul's Epistles to the Thessalonians,* (1952 reprint), p. 136.
25. For a devotional study of these five references see Herbert Lockyer, "The Second Advent in the Thessalonian Epistles," *Our Hope,* Oct. 1952, pp. 232-236; or Lockyer, *Selected Scripture Summaries, Volume Two,* (1975), pp. 126-134.

given in this Epistle traces itself back into the very presence of the most intimate friends of Jesus.[26]

This brief and informal communication from the apostle Paul to his troubled Thessalonian converts is therefore rightly regarded as a priceless heritage of the Christian Church.

## An Outline of 1 Thessalonians

### THE SALUTATION (1:1)

1. The Writers
2. The Readers
3. The Greeting

### I. PERSONAL: PERSONAL RELATIONS TO THE THESSALONIANS (1:2–3:13)

1. The thanksgiving for them (1:2-10)
   a. The character of the thanksgiving (2)
   b. The grounds for the thanksgiving (3-10)
      1) Because of their Christian virtues (3)
      2) Because of their divine election (4-7)
         a) The assurance as to their election (4)
         b) The reasons for the assurance (5-7)
            (i) The preaching to them (5)
            (ii) The response by them (6-7)
      3) Because of the reports of others concerning them (8-10)
         a) The spread of the Gospel from them (8)
         b) The contents of the reports about them (9-10)
            (i) The success of the work among them (9a)
            (ii) The change reported in them (9b-10)
2. The relations while being with them (2:1-16)
   a. The ministry among them (2:1-12)
      1) The circumstances of the ministry (1-2)
         a) Negative—It was not ineffective (1)
         b) Positive—It was with boldness and amid conflict (2)
      2) The motives of the ministers (3-4)
         a) Negative—The denial of impure motives (3)
         b) Positive—The work in God-approved motives (4)

26. Rollin Hough Walker, "Thessalonians, The First Epistle of Paul to the," *International Standard Bible Encyclopaedia,* (1939), Vol. V, p. 2966b.

3) The conduct of the messengers (5-12)
   a) The description of their conduct (5-8)
      (i) Negative—What their conduct was not like (5-6)
      (ii) Positive—What their conduct was like (7-8)
   b) The Thessalonians' confirmation of the conduct (9-12)
      (i) Their memory of the work done among them (9)
      (ii) Their testimony of the workers' conduct (10-12)
         (a) The personal conduct of the workers (10)
         (b) The workers' relation to the converts (11-12)

b. The thanksgiving for their reception of the Gospel (2:13-16)
   1) The nature of their reception of the Word (13)
   2) The result of their reception of the Word (14-16)
      a) They became imitators of the Judean churches (14a)
      b) They entered the fellowship of suffering for the Word (14b-16)
         (i) The suffering as similar to that of the Judean churches (14b)
         (ii) The description of the Jewish persecutors (15-16)

3. The relation since being separated from them (2:17-3:13)
   a. The desire to revisit them hindered (2:17-20)
      1) The frustrated yearning to see them again (17-18)
      2) The expression of affection for them (19-20)
   b. The sending of Timothy to visit them (3:1-5)
      1) The circumstances in sending Timothy (1)
      2) The characterization of the one sent (2a)
      3) The purpose in sending Timothy (2b-4)
         a) To stabilize them in their faith (2b)
         b) To prevent their being lured from the faith by tribulation (3-4)
      4) The motive of Paul in sending Timothy (5)
   c. The effect of Timothy's report about them (3:6-13)
      1) The contents of Timothy's report (6)
      2) The reaction to Timothy's report (7-10)
         a) It brought comfort and encouragement (7-8)

b) It evoked thanksgiving and prayer for them (9-10)
(i) The thanksgiving before God because of them (9)
(ii) The prayer in regard to them (10)
3) The contents of the prayer for them (11-13)
a) The God addressed in the prayer (11a)
b) The petitions made in the prayer (11b-13)
(i) That God may make a way for the writers to them (11b)
(ii) That they may grow in love (12-13)

II. PRACTICAL: INSTRUCTIONS IN DOCTRINE AND LIFE (4:1–5:25)
1. The exhortations concerning Christian living (4:1-12)
a. The exhortation to advance in God-pleasing conduct (1-2)
1) The attitude in making the exhortation (1a)
2) The contents of the exhortation (1b)
3) The reminder of such previous charges (2)
b. The exhortation to sanctification (3-8)
1) The basis for the exhortation (3a)
2) The application of the exhortation (3b-6a)
a) To abstain from fornication (3b-5)
(i) Positive—How to act (4)
(ii) Negative—How not to act (5)
b) To abstain from defrauding the brother (6a)
3) The reasons for the exhortation (6b-8)
a) Because sin brings God's vengeance (6b)
b) Because it is in accord with God's call (7)
c) Because rejection of it is rejection of God (8)
c. The exhortation to brotherly love and ministry (9-12)
1) The commendation of their love (9-10a)
a) The acknowledgment of their mutual love (9a)
b) The reasons for their mutual love (9b-10a)
2) The exhortation to abounding love and industry (10b-12)
a) The exhortation to further abounding in love (10b)
b) The exhortation to be industrious (11-12)
(i) The contents of the exhortation (11a)
(ii) The reminder of such past charges (11b
(iii) The reasons for the exhortation (12)

2. The instruction concerning the dead in Christ (4:13-18)
   a. The need for proper instruction concerning the dead (13)
   b. The relation of the dead to the returning Christ (14-15)
      1) The basis for the relationship (14a)
      2) The statement of the relationship (14b-15)
         a) The dead in Christ will be brought with Him (14b)
         b) The living will not precede the dead in Christ (15)
   c. The manner and results of Christ's coming (16-17)
      1) The manner of His coming (16a)
      2) The results at His coming (16b-17)
         a) The dead shall be raised first (16b)
         b) The living shall be caught up (17a)
         c) The believers shall be forever with the Lord (17b)
   d. The comfort in these words to be utilized (18)
3. The exhortation to watchfulness in view of the Lord's coming (5:1-11)
   a. The uncertainty of the time of His coming (1-2)
      1) Their lack of need for instruction concerning the time (1)
      2) Their knowledge concerning the manner of His coming (2)
   b. The result of this uncertainty for the unprepared (3)
   c. The effect of this uncertainty upon believers (4-11)
      1) The position and nature of believers (4-5)
      2) The exhortation to believers to be prepared (6-8)
         a) The exhortation to watchfulness (6-7)
         b) The exhortation to be spiritually armored (8)
      3) The salvation appointed for the believer (9-10)
      4) The exhortation to mutual edification (11)
4. The instructions for church discipline (5:12-15)
   a. The instructions concerning their spiritual leaders (12-13)
      1) They are to recognize their leaders (12)
      2) They are to esteem their leaders (13a)
      3) They are to be at peace among themselves (13b)
   b. The instructions concerning faulty members (14-15)
      1) They are to help and encourage the needy (14)
      2) They are to promote right relations among the members (15)

5. The instructions for holy living (5:16-25)
   a. The principles for holy living (16-22)
      1) The principles of the inner life (16-18)
         a) The triplet of commands (16-18a)
         b) The reason for the commands (18b)
      2) The principles for assembly life (19-22)
         a) The negative commands for the assembly (19-20)
         b) The positive commands for the assembly (21-22)
   b. The prayer for their entire sanctification (23-24)
      1) The God addressed in the prayer (23a)
      2) The request for them in the prayer (23)
      3) The assurance of the answer to the prayer (24)
   c. The request for prayer for the writers (25)

THE CONCLUSION (5:26-28)

1. The salutation (26)
2. The adjuration (27)
3. The benediction (28)

## A Book List on 1 and 2 Thessalonians

Auberlen, C. A., and Riggenback, C. J., "The Two Epistles of Paul to the Thessalonians," Lange's *Commentary on the Holy Scriptures.* Translated from the German, with additions by John Lillie. Grand Rapids: Zondervan Publishing House (1950 reprint).

Valuable textual exegesis with an abundance of ethical, homiletical, and practical material added, much of which is definitely dated. A conservative Lutheran commentary. The additions by the translator add to the value of the work.

Bailey, John W., and Clarke, James W., "The First and Second Epistles to the Thessalonians," *The Interpreter's Bible.* Vol. 11. New York: Abingdon Press (1955).

Uses the Authorized and Revised Standard versions texts. In keeping with the format of the series, the material is divided into two parts, exegetical and expository notes. The work of two capable American liberal scholars.

Best, Ernest, "A Commentary on the First and Second Epistles to the Thessalonians." *Harper's New Testament Commentaries.* New York: Harper & Row (1972).

Based on the author's own translation. This verse-by-verse critical commentary, the work of a British liberal scholar, holds that both epistles were written by the same author "who was probably Paul but may have been Silvanus or Timothy." Seeks to view the letters in the light of the possible influence of Gnosticism and allied movements. Pays attention to grammatical, linguistic, and textual matters.

Bicknell, E. J., "The First and Second Epistles to the Thessalonians." *Westminster Commentaries.* London: Methuen & Co. (1932).

Uses the English Revised Version. The introduction supports the authenticity of both epistles as well as their present order. A careful paraphrase follows the biblical text section by section. The exegetical notes, verse by verse, are rather brief, with added excursuses at points of special importance. Anglican, with some liberal leanings.

Denney, James, "The Epistles to the Thessalonians," *The Expositor's Bible.* Vol. VI. Grand Rapids: Wm. B. Eerdmans Pub. Co. (1943 reprint).

A vigorous and informative homiletical exposition by a noted Scottish theologian of the past generation.

Ellicott, Charles J., *A Critical and Grammatical Commentary on St. Paul's Epistles to the Thessalonians.* Andover, Mass.: Warren F. Draper (1864).

Greek text. First published in 1861, this noted, scholarly, highly technical treatment of these epistles is still of value for the advanced student. Places strong emphasis on grammatical matters.

Erdman, Charles R., *The Epistles of Paul to the Thessalonians.* Philadelphia: The Westminster Press (1935).

A brief yet quite thorough and easily read evangelical exposition by a noted Presbyterian professor and author.

Findlay, G. G., "The Epistles to the Thessalonians." *Cambridge Greek Testament for Schools and Colleges.* Cambridge: University Press (1904).

Greek text. A careful exposition of the text of these epistles, giving attention to technical matters, together with practical insights.

Frame, James Everett, "A Critical and Exegetical Commentary on the Epistles of St. Paul to the Thessalonians." *The International Critical Commentary.* New York: Charles Scribner's Sons (1912).

Greek text. An important grammatical and exegetical study of these epistles. Weakest in its handling of doctrinal and eschatological matters.

Hendriksen, William, "Exposition of I and II Thessalonians." *New Testament Commentary.* Grand Rapids: Baker Book House (1955).

An up-to-date, scholarly exposition of the Thessalonian epistles by a noted evangelical scholar in the Reformed tradition. Each chapter is concluded with a doctrinal summary of its contents.

Hiebert, D. Edmond, *The Thessalonian Epistles. A Call to Readiness.* Chicago: Moody Press (1971).

Uses the American Standard Version. A full exegetical treatment of these epistles on the basis of the original but suited to the English reader. Premillennial.

Hogg, C. F., and Vine, W. E., *The Epistles to the Thessalonians, with Notes Exegetical and Expository.* Grand Rapids: Kregel Publications (1959 reprint).

An analysis of the Greek text for the English student, with valuable word studies. A good combination of careful exegesis and warm devotional study. The work of two British Plymouth Brethren scholars, the volume sets forth a post-tribulational return of Christ.

Horne, Charles M., "The Epistles to the Thessalonians. A Study Man. ual." Shield Bible Study Series. Grand Rapids: Baker Book House (1961).

A brief, well-outlined study guide by an evangelical Bible teacher. The work is based on a study of the original but suited to the lay Bible student.

Kelcy, Raymond C., "The Letters of Paul to the Thessalonians." *The Living Word Commentary.* Austin, Texas: R. B. Sweet Co. (1968).

The Revised Standard Version is printed at the top of the page. The work of a conservative scholar belonging to the Churches of Christ; the commentary brings out the force of the original for the common reader. Amillennial.

Lenski, R. C. H., *The Interpretation of St. Paul's Epistles to the Colossians, to the Thessalonians, to Timothy, to Titus, and to Philemon.* Columbus, Ohio: Lutheran Book Concern (1937).

Prints the author's own quite literal translation as the basis for the exposition. A monumental exegetical study of these epistles by an accomplished conservative Lutheran scholar. Amillennial.

Lünemann, Gottlieb, "Critical and Exegetical Handbook to the Epistles of St. Paul to the Thessalonians." H. A. W. Meyer's *Critical and Exegetical Commentary on the New Testament.* Translated from the German by Paton J. Gloag. Edinburgh: T. & T. Clark (1884).

Greek text. A thorough exposition of these epistles by a scholarly German professor of the past century. One of the justly celebrated older commentaries, with ample presentation of varying views on all important points. Dated but still of value for those familiar with the Greek or desiring the views of scholars of the past.

MacDonald, William, *Letters to the Thessalonians.* Kansas City, Kans.: Walterick Publishers (1969).

A detailed outline is given at the beginning of each of the sections into which the epistles are divided, followed by concise verse-by-verse comments. Suited to the lay Bible student. Premillennial, pretribulational viewpoint.

Milligan, George, *St. Paul's Epistles to the Thessalonians.* Grand Rapids: Wm. B. Eerdmans Pub. Co. (1952 reprint).

Greek text. A noted critical study by a pioneer authority in the papyri. Has much valuable material in the introduction and the added notes.

Moore, A. L., "1 and 2 Thessalonians." *The Century Bible. New Series.* London: Thomas Nelson & Sons (1969).

A concise verse-by-verse commentary by an evangelical British scholar. Makes frequent reference to the Greek, given in transliterated form.

Morris, Leon, "The Epistles of Paul to the Thessalonians." *The Tyndale New Testament Commentaries.* Grand Rapids: Wm. B. Eerdmans Pub. Co. (1957).

Uses the King James Version as the basis for the exposition. A clear verse-by-verse interpretation by a noted Australian evangelical scholar. Well suited to the lay reader. Amillennial.

———, "The First and Second Epistles to the Thessalonians." *The New International Commentary on the New Testament.* Grand Rapids: Wm. B. Eerdmans Pub. Co. (1959).

A scholarly work by a noted evangelical scholar, displaying a wealth of learning. Presents the meaning of the original without demanding a knowledge of the Greek. The interpretation is in the Reformed tradition.

Neil, William, "The Epistle of Paul to the Thessalonians." *The Moffatt New Testament Commentary.* London: Hodder and Stoughton (1950).

Uses the Moffatt translation but is based on an independent study of the original. A stimulating work by a liberal British scholar. Weak in its handling of the eschatological passages.

Plummer, Alfred, *A Commentary on St. Paul's First Epistle to the Thessalonians.* London: Robert Scott (1918).

——, *A Commentary on St. Paul's Second Epistle to the Thessalonians.* London: Robert Scott (1918).

While not as full as the author's excellent work on the Gospel of Luke, these volumes provide a critical exegetical unfolding of these epistles. Greek words are often quoted but generally in parentheses, so that the non-Greek reader can readily profit from these volumes.

Ryrie, Charles Caldwell, "First and Second Thessalonians." *Everyman's Bible Commentary.* Chicago: Moody Press (1959).

A brief, well-outlined treatment of these epistles by a noted conservative seminary professor. Well adapted as a first volume for the study of these letters. Premillennial.

Stevens, William Arnold, "Commentary on the Epistles to the Thessalonians," *An American Commentary.* Philadelphia: The American Baptist Publication Society (1890, reprint, n.d.).

Uses the King James and English Revised versions. A significant interpretation by a recognized Baptist New Testament scholar of the past century.

Ward, Ronald A., *A Commentary on First and Second Thessalonians.* Waco, Texas: Word Books (1973).

Based on the Revised Standard Version, this verse-by-verse exposition seeks to bring out the message of these letters as well as to relate them to the life of the modern Church. Has sections on the theology of each epistle. The work of an evangelical Anglican scholar.

# 5

# SECOND THESSALONIANS

## An Introduction to 2 Thessalonians

Second Thessalonians, the second member of the Eschatological Group among the Pauline epistles, advances the teaching concerning the second coming of Christ. Like other New Testament "second" epistles, it forms a logical sequel to the first. Its teaching concerning the second coming does not contradict that found in the First Epistle, as is sometimes asserted; it supplements it.

### THE AUTHENTICITY OF 2 THESSALONIANS

1. *Evidence.* The external evidence in favor of the authenticity of 2 Thessalonians is earlier and even stronger than that for 1 Thessalonians. It is quoted more frequently by the Early Church Fathers than is the First Epistle. The passage about "the man of sin" (2:1-12) made a strong impression on the Early Church and frequent reference was made to it. Polycarp seems to quote from the epistle, though anonymously. Justin Martyr alludes to it. Irenaeus is the first to mention it directly by name. It is quoted by Clement of Alexandria and by Tertullian as by the apostle Paul. It is found in the Muratorian Canon, the Syriac, Vulgate, and Old Latin versions, and in Marcion's Canon. It has a recognized place in every subsequent list of New Testament books. Attestations come from every section of the Christian Church. The manuscript evidence for 2 Thessalonians is the same as that for 1 Thessalonians.

The internal evidence for the Pauline authorship of this epistle is likewise strong. Twice the writer refers to himself as Paul (1:1; 3:17). The general contents are definitely Pauline. In the words of Neil, "In respect of vocabulary, style, and fundamental theological assumptions, the second letter is as Pauline as the first."[1] The resemblances between the two epistles are obvious. The two are practically identical in their prayers (1 Thess. 3:11-13; 5:23; 2 Thess. 2:16-17; 3:16), thanksgiving (1 Thess. 1:2-3; 2 Thess. 1:3), and transitions (1 Thess. 4:1; 2 Thess. 3:1). Drum asserts that "two-thirds of 2 Thessalonians is like to 1 Thessalonians in vocabulary and style."[2] The Pauline imprint on 2 Thessalonians is stated as follows by Gloag:

> The character of Paul is impressed upon this Epistle: his lively sympathy with his converts, his gratitude to God for the increase of their faith and love, his joy in their spiritual welfare, his tenderness when censuring them, his assertion of his apostolic authority, his reference to his former instructions, his request for an interest in their prayers,—all these characteristics of the apostle are found in this Epistle.[3]

2. *Objections.* The genuineness of 2 Thessalonians was never questioned until the radical German criticism of the past century brought it under attack.[4] All objections to the epistle proceed on internal grounds, and generally they start from the assumption of the authenticity of 1 Thessalonians. Objections have been raised on the basis of its doctrinal contents as well as its literary relationships to 1 Thessalonians.

Doctrinally, the passage that has offended most is the eschatological section about "the man of sin" (2:1-12). It has been declared impossible that Paul should have written this fantastic prophecy. It is asserted that the eschatology of this section is un-Pauline and contradicts Paul's teaching in 1 Thessalonians. In 1 Thessalonians Paul says that the parousia is imminent (4:14–5:3), but in 2 Thessalonians the writer denies this and teaches that the "apostasy" and the revelation of "the man of sin" must first occur (2:1-12). Starting from this alleged incompatibility of 2 Thessalonians 2:1-12 with 1 Thessalonians, the critics postulated that this passage about "the man of sin" was really a later interpolation into a genuine Pauline epistle.

1. William Neil, "The Epistle of Paul to the Thessalonians," *Moffatt Commentary,* 1950), p. xxi.
2. Walter Drum, "Thessalonians, Epistles to the," *The Catholic Encyclopaedia,* (1940), Vol. XIV, p. 632a.
3. P. J. Gloag, "The Second Epistle of Paul to the Thessalonians," *Pulpit Commentary,* (1950 reprint), pp. i-ii.
4. For a list of the critics see George Milligan, *St. Paul's Epistles to the Thessalonians,* (1952 reprint), p. lxxviii.

But it was soon evident that the passage forms the very reason for the epistle and that the whole book must stand or fall with it. And so the whole letter was brought under question.[5] But the attempt to prove the epistle a forgery raises more problems than it solves.[6] One of the serious objections raised is that a spurious epistle should be accepted as genuine shortly after Paul's death. Further, the necessity of producing a satisfactory explanation for such a letter offers a greater problem than the traditional view.[7]

It is generally admitted today that it is not impossible that the same man could have written both epistles. Some critics, not governed by a high view of Biblical inspiration, suggest that it shows what a confused maze of eschatological conceptions could co-exist in the same person at one time.[8] Others suggest that it is not necessary to attempt to reconcile the two pictures; as a wise and practical man, Paul felt free to alter his position under the stress of circumstances.[9] But the conservative Christian, holding to a high view of inspiration, sees no need to resort to such explanations. He believes that both epistles can be fully accepted as they stand. The simplest explanation seems to be that both letters are accurate, but that they have reference to different phases of the second coming.[10]

The tendency of recent criticism is to reverse the earlier evaluation as to the genuineness of the eschatological passage in chapter two. It is now felt that this section offers no argument against the Pauline authorship of the epistle, but rather that it is, if anything, the part of the letter most likely to be genuine. Hausrath conjectured that the rest of the epistle was really a later scaffolding built around the original Pauline passage in 2:1-12.

The critics' emphasis has shifted rather to the problem of the literary relationship of the two letters. Some say that the tone and style of the epistle militates against its genuineness.

5. One suspects that a primary motive of these critics was the desire to get rid of the supernatural, and since this passage about "the man of sin" is undeniably prophetic in character, it must be eliminated.
6. See William Neil, "The Epistle of Paul to the Thessalonians," *Moffatt Commentary,* (1950), p. xxiv.
7. See Arthur S. Peake, *A Critical Introduction to the New Testament,* (1919), p. 16, for an evaluation of two suggested explanations.
8. See reference by George Milligan, *St. Paul's Epistles to the Thessalonians,* (1952 reprint), p. lxxxvi, note 1.
9. Edgar J. Goodspeed, *An Introduction to the New Testament,* (1937), p. 19.
10. W. Graham Scroggie, *Know Your Bible, A Brief Introduction to the Scriptures, Volume II, The New Testament,* (n.d.), p. 114.

Certain critics hold that the tone of the two books is vastly different. The First Epistle is characterized by a warmth and glowing affection for the readers, while the Second is rather chilly and officially formal. But the formality of 2 Thessalonians turns largely on the use of certain phrases (cf. 1:3; 2:13) and is largely apparent. But warm and personal passages are not wanting (1:11; 2:16-17; 3:3-5). A change in the mood of the same writer and changed circumstances among the Thessalonians could account for the difference in tone.

Again, it is said that the very similarity of the two epistles suggests the work of a clever imitator. Would it be likely that a writer of Paul's mental stature should write two letters in terms so similar and after so short an interval to the same church? The great similarity of the two epistles in plan and language, it is asserted, suggests that someone familiar with 1 Thessalonians used it as a model by which to compose 2 Thessalonians. The similarity of the two letters is striking, but we must not forget the existence of even more notable parallelism in Ephesians and Colossians. It may be pointed out that apart from the greetings and farewells and general framework, which might be expected to reveal such likenesses, the actual parallelism between 1 and 2 Thessalonians does not extend to more than one-third of their whole contents.[11] And, further, the actual parallelisms in language are often not drawn from corresponding sections of the epistles but from the two epistles as a whole. While the resemblance between the two present an interesting literary problem, they do not militate against the Pauline authorship of the Second Epistle. Zahn has suggested that the similarities may be due to the fact that Paul read again the preliminary draft copy of his First Letter before writing the Second.[12]

Again it is said that while the First Epistle suggests a Gentile audience, the Second suggests an audience well acquainted with Jewish tradition and Old Testament phraseology (cf. 1:6-10; 2:1-12). But the Thessalonian Christians, familiar with the eschatological truths in 1 Thessalonians, and reminded of the teaching the Apostle had given them while yet with them (2 Thess. 2:5), would find little more in 2 Thessalonians of a distinctly Jewish flavor.

3. *Conclusion.* Recent criticism, after a century of speculation,

11. See George Milligan, *St. Paul's Epistles to the Thessalonians,* (1952 reprint), pp. lxxxi-lxxxv.
12. Theodor Zahn, *Introduction to the New Testament,* (1909), Vol. I, p. 250.

has worked itself around again to practically the traditional position as to the authorship of 2 Thessalonians.[13] The critical attempts to discredit the Pauline authorship of the epistle have proved to be ineffectual. Accordingly Walker says,

> There is today a manifest tendency among all scholars, including those in the more radical camps, to return to the traditional position concerning the authorship.[14]

Thus Moffatt, himself by no means a conservative, says,

> It is fair to say that almost every one of the features which seem to portray another physiognomy from that of Paul can be explained, without straining the evidence, upon the hypothesis that he wrote the epistle himself (so most recent editors.)[15]

And so once more the position of conservative Christianity stands vindicated.

### THE OCCASION FOR 2 THESSALONIANS

The immediate occasion for the writing of 2 Thessalonians was the nature of the further information about the Thessalonians received by Paul. We have no knowledge as to who the bearer of the First Epistle was. Whoever he was, he probably remained at Thessalonica long enough to notice the effect of the First Epistle and to get an insight into the spirit and conditions of the Thessalonian church. Subsequent contacts through messengers are also possible.

The report received concerning the developments at Thessalonica contained both favorable and unfavorable elements. The Thessalonians had made progress in their faith and love (1:3). They had remained firm under repeated outbreaks of persecution (1:4). Also their distress about the death of their loved ones had been relieved by the teachings of the First Epistle. But their excitement relative to the second coming had been intensified. They were agitated by the view "that the day of the Lord is already here" (2 Thess. 2:2, Gr.).[16] Thinking that they were already in "the day of the Lord"

13. See William Neil, *The Epistle of Paul to the Thessalonians,* (1950), pp. xxiii-xxvi for the course in the cycle of criticism.
14. Rollin Hough Walker, "Thessalonians, The Second Epistle of Paul to the," *International Standard Bible Encyclopaedia,* (1939), Vol. V, p. 2968b.
15. James Moffatt, *An Introduction to the Literature of the New Testament,* (1949 reprint), p. 79.
16. So rendered in the translations of Moffatt, Weymouth, and Williams and similarly in most recent versions.

just preceding His return, they were looking for the immediate return of Christ. This expectancy of a speedy coming of the Lord had even caused some of them to give up their accustomed occupations. This leisure time had led some of them to become busybodies, interfering with those who wanted to work (3:10-12). It was the report of these conditions in the Thessalonian church that called forth this epistle.

### THE PLACE AND DATE OF 2 THESSALONIANS

1. *Place.* Like the First Epistle, this one was written in Corinth. The names of Paul, Silas, and Timothy are again associated in the salutation (1:1). Hence they were together at the time of its composition. From Acts 18:5 we know that they were together at Corinth, but following the Corinthian mission we know of no place where these three men were together again. Silas drops entirely out of the story of Acts after this time. The place definitely appears to be Corinth.

Seemingly a few months elapsed between the writing of the two epistles. Circumstances at Thessalonica apparently had not changed very much. The church still experienced persecution (1:4). Yet time enough had passed to permit the problem of idleness, already touched upon in the First Epistle (1 Thess. 4:11-12), to develop into rather serious proportions (3:6-15). And sufficient time must be allowed for the messenger to observe conditions and results or for later reports of developments to be received.

In this epistle Paul requests that the Thessalonians pray for him that he "may be delivered from unreasonable and evil men" (3:2). This suggests that Paul was anticipating opposition to himself and his work at Corinth. His active ministry among the Gentiles in Corinth angered the Corinthian Jews. Apparently Paul feared a repetition of experiences at Thessalonica and was thinking of leaving the city before the trouble broke out. But the Lord gave him definite directions to remain in the city with the assurance that he would not be harmed (Acts 18:9-10). The trouble finally did erupt under Gallio (Acts 18:12-17), but the outcome was a confirmation of the promise of the Lord to Paul. The epistle obviously belongs to the time before the trouble flared up.

2. *Date.* The exact date for 2 Thessalonians will vary with that

assigned to the First Epistle. If the First Epistle is dated as written in the late summer of A.D. 50 or 51, then this epistle may be dated during the fall or early winter of A.D. 50 or 51.

### THE PURPOSE OF 2 THESSALONIANS

Paul wrote this epistle in response to the conditions reported in the Thessalonian church. With his usual tact he commends what is praiseworthy in them but faithfully rebukes the wrong.

1. *Commendation.* The Apostle takes the occasion to commend the Thessalonians for their remarkable progress in their faith and love (1:3). He encourages them by informing them that he is using their steadfastness and faith under persecution as a stimulus to other churches (1:4). He offers them comfort and encouragement in their afflictions by reminding them of the glorious future that awaits them when the Lord shall come in judgment upon the persecutors (1:5-12).

2. *Corrections.* The primary reason for writing, however, lay in the rapid development of two dangerous tendencies in the church which needed correction. The first of these was doctrinal, the other practical.

The Thessalonian church was being greatly agitated by the teaching, promulgated by certain ones in their midst, that "the day of the Lord is already here" (2:2, Williams). They were being told that they were in that terrible time, "the day of the Lord," depicted in the Old Testament in connection with the coming of the Lord. And their persecutions seemed to confirm the view that they were already in that period of trial and anguish. The Apostle appeals to them by the very hope of "our gathering together unto him" (2:1), not to allow themselves to be shaken or troubled. This hope, which he had set before them in the First Epistle (4:13-18), had not yet been fulfilled. That was the first phase of the Lord's coming and was imminent. But the other phase of the Lord's coming, that connected with "the day of the Lord," was not yet present, since two events had to precede it: the apostasy and the manifestation of "the man of sin" (2:3). Therefore they need not be disturbed by thinking that they already were in that fearful time, "the day of the Lord."

Out of this doctrinal error a practical difficulty had arisen. Some of the members, convinced that the end was near, had given up their daily occupations and were living in idleness. Spending their time in propagating their views, these idlers were living off of others and were causing trouble. Paul had already touched upon the problem in his First Epistle (4:11-12), hoping that the admonition would keep the tendency from developing into anything serious. But the situation, aided by the doctrinal perversion spreading among them, had grown steadily worse. To meet this danger, Paul rebukes these idlers and instructs the church as to its attitude toward them (3:6-15).

### THE CHARACTERISTICS OF 2 THESSALONIANS

1. *Contents.* Of Paul's nine letters to churches, this is the shortest. Only the Letter to Titus and the little note to Philemon are briefer.

The three short chapters of this epistle contain no less than four prayers for the readers (1:11-12; 2:16-17; 3:5; 3:16). There is further the Apostle's request for the prayers of the readers on his behalf (3:1).

Like 1 Thessalonians, this book, although largely occupied with eschatological teaching, does not contain a single direct quotation from the Old Testament.

The concluding section on practical Christian duties (3:5-15) is a "weighty passage on dutifulness, attending to one's present responsibility, doing the work which lies to one's hand, free from religious excitement and intrusive curiosity."[17] The reaction of the Apostle reveals his good sense and sound judgment. He does not allow his hope of the future to blind him to everyday duties. His incisive rule, "If any will not work, neither let him eat" (3:10), gives the first clear statement of the principle that honest work is one of the elements of Christian living.

Of interest is Paul's mark of authentication for his letters—the signature in his own hand (3:17). Apparently this method was adopted to safeguard his churches against the possible danger of being misled by letters claiming to be from him.

2. *Prophecy.* The most noted characteristic of this epistle is the famous eschatological passage in chapter two (2:1-12). This passage is distinctive in the Pauline writings. Nowhere else does the author give us such a detailed prophecy of end-time events. Its interpretation has been the occasion for great differences of opinion.[18] How-

17. W. Graham Scroggie, *Know Your Bible, A Brief Introduction to the Scriptures, Volume II, The New Testament,* (n.d.), p. 115.
18. For an historical survey of views see George Milligan, *St. Paul's Epistles to the Thessalonians,* (1908; 1952 reprint), pp. 166-173.

ever, because the passage is obscure to us today does not necessarily mean that it was obscure to the original readers. It must be remembered that the Apostle had given them previous instructions on this subject which are not preserved for us (2:5). Rather than giving them something entirely new, he was recalling what he had already given them.

The prophecy about "the man of sin" has been differently viewed. Two prominent interpretations may be mentioned. There is the view which identifies the man of sin with the papacy. According to this view the "temple of God" (2:4) is the Church in which the Pope, claiming to be the vicar of Christ, shows himself off that he is God. The apostasy, already working in apostolic days, as it developed more and more, made the full development of the papacy possible. This has been the prevalent view among Protestants generally since the Reformation.

This view is not without its serious difficulties. It was quite natural that the Reformers, locked in fierce conflict with the papal forces, should come to this conclusion; to them the identification seemed quite obvious. But in the light of subsequent history the identification is beset with difficulty. The popes have never claimed for themselves exclusive divine honor (2:4). "No pope 'is called God' nor 'worshipped' as God, but each declares himself to be the 'vicar' of Christ and only as such infallible in matters of religion."[19] Again, Paul presented the rise of the Man of Sin as the sign of the nearness of the Lord's return. But if the Man of Sin has already been on the scene for hundreds of years, the prophecy consequently has failed of the significance which Paul attached to it. It also makes the Man of Sin a succession of persons rather than one person as the passage suggests.

The more probable view is that this wicked person is the final, personal embodiment of the principle of lawlessness. This principle of lawlessness was already at work in Paul's day (2:7) and was bringing suffering upon the Thessalonian church in the form of persecution. During the course of history this principle has manifested itself in many historical characters. It will find its final, Satan-inspired manifestation (2:9) in the personal "Antichrist" of Scripture who will be destroyed by the personal return of Christ (2:8).

19. Charles R. Erdman, *The Epistles of Paul to the Thessalonians,* (1935), p. 89.

The reference to the "restrainer" (2:6-7) has likewise produced varied views. This restraining power on "the mystery of lawlessness" has been identified with the Roman Empire and the emperor; more generally, it has been equated with the restraining influences of civil society as such. Others suggest that the restrainer is God and that which restrains is the operation of His varied providences. A popular view is that the restraining power is the Holy Spirit ("the one restraining," verse 7) working in and through the Christian Church ("that which restraineth," verse 6).[20]

As the Eschatological Group, both of these epistles contain a remarkable passage about the second coming of Christ (1 Thess. 4:13-18; 2 Thess. 2:1-12). It has been asserted that these two passages definitely contradict each other. It is said that the first teaches the imminence of Christ's return, while the other teaches that some definite events must precede the return.

The difficulty lies not in any actual contradiction between these two remarkable passages but in a failure to notice their differences. Each has a different aspect of the second coming in view. The New Testament distinguishes two phases of His coming: His coming *for* His saints, when the dead in Christ shall be raised and the living caught up to meet Him in the air (1 Thess. 4:13-18). This is often referred to as the Rapture, the "catching up" of the Church. The second phase is His coming to earth in glory *with* His saints to judge the wicked and to destroy the Man of Sin. This is set forth in 2 Thessalonians 1:7-10; 2:1-12.

The aspect of the second coming presented is in accord with the occasion of each epistle. When these differences are recognized added light is shed on them. In comparing 1 Thessalonians 4:13-18 with 2 Thessalonians 2:1-12, Scroggie says:

> The first of these is for the comfort and encouragement of Christ's saints, and the second tells of coming judgment on Christ's foes; the first relates to the Church, and the second, to the world: the first speaks of the *Parousia* (iv. 15), and the second, of the *Apocalupsis* (1. 7): the first reveals that Christ will come to the *air*, and the second, that He will come to the *earth:* the first points to "the Day of Christ" (cf. Phil. i. 10), and the second, to "the Day of the Lord"

20. F. W. Grant, *The Numerical Bible, Being a Revised Translation of the Holy Scriptures with Expository Notes—Acts to 2 Corinthians,* (1901; reprint, n.d.), p. 438-439.

(ii. 2 R.V.). Failure to distinguish these viewpoints will result in much confusion.[21]

All prophecy of the future is to be a present light in dark places, to guide the feet of His saints in the path of God (2 Peter 1:19). A reverent study of this epistle will contribute toward that end.

## An Outline of 2 Thessalonians

THE SALUTATION (1:1-2)

1. The writers (1a)
2. The readers (1b)
3. The greeting (2)

I. THE COMFORT GIVEN THEM IN THEIR AFFLICTION (1:3-12)

1. The thanksgiving for their growth and steadfastness (3-4)
   a. The nature of the thanksgiving (3a)
   b. The reasons for the thanksgiving (3b)
   c. The effect upon the writers (4)
2. The encouragement in view of Christ's return (5-10)
   a. The indication of God's righteous judgment (5)
   b. The revelation of God's righteous judgment (6-8)
      1) The outcome of the judgment (6-7a)
      2) The circumstances attending the judgment (7b)
      3) The subjects of the judgment (8)
   c. The consequences of God's righteous judgment (9-10)
      1) The eternal punishment of the lost (9)
      2) The glorification of God in His saints (10)
3. The prayer for them in their affliction (11-12)
   a. The nature of the prayer (11a)
   b. The substance of the prayer (11b)
   c. The purpose of the prayer (12)

21. W. Graham Scroggie, *Know Your Bible, A Brief Introduction to the Scriptures, Volume II, The New Testament,* (n.d.), p. 114. Italics in original. See also William MacDonald, *What's the Difference?*, (1975), pp. 15-21; Everett F. Harrison, "Rapture," in *Baker's Dictionary of Theology* (1960); John F. Walvoord, *The Rapture Question,* (1957; 1972 reprint); George E. Ladd, *The Blessed Hope* (1956).

## II. THE EVENTS PRECEDING THE DAY OF THE LORD (2:1-12)

1. The exhortation to calmness about the day of the Lord (1-3a)
   a. The subject matter of the exhortation (1)
   b. The contents of the exhortation (2)
      1) The mental attitude prohibited (2a)
      2) The teaching contradicted (2b)
   c. The warning against being beguiled (3a)
2. The indication of the preceding events (3b)
3. The instruction about the Man of Sin (4-12)
   a. The self-exaltation of the Man of Sin (4)
   b. The reminder of past instructions on the subject (5)
   c. The restraint upon the mystery of lawlessness (6-7)
      1) "That which restraineth" (6)
      2) "One that restraineth now" (7)
   d. The manifestation of the lawless one (8a)
   e. The destruction of the lawless one (8b)
   f. The power of the lawless one over the lost (9-12)
      1) The source of his power (9a)
      2) The description of his power (9b-10a)
      3) The subjects under his power (10a)
      4) The reason for his power over the lost (10b-12)
         a) The guilt of the lost (10b)
         b) The judgment upon the lost (11-12)

## III. THE RENEWED THANKSGIVING AND PRAYER FOR THEM (2:13-17)

1. The thanksgivng because of God's choice of them (13-14)
   a. The nature of the thanksgiving (13a)
   b. The ground for the thanksgiving (13b-14)
2. The exhortation to steadfastness (15)
3. The prayer for their comfort and stability (16-17)
   a. The ones to whom the prayer is directed (16)
   b. The contents of the prayer (17)

IV. THE EXHORTATIONS TO PRACTICAL CHRISTIAN DUTIES (3:1-15)

1. The request for their prayers (1-2)
   a. The request for the liberty of the Gospel (1)
   b. The request for the safety of the messengers (2)
2. The confidence concerning their progress (3-5)
   a. The description of the confidence concerning them (3-4)
      1) That God will keep them (3)
      2) That they will be obedient to the instructions (4)
   b. The prayer for their growth in love and patience (5)
3. The command to discipline the disorderly (6-12)
   a. The authority in giving the command (6a)
   b. The contents of the command to the church (6b)
   c. The apostolic example behind the command (7-9)
      1) The duty of imitating his example (7a)
      2) The description of the example (7b-9)
         a) Negative—The conduct denied (7b-8a)
         b) Positive—The conduct affirmed (8b-9)
   d. The previous expression of the command (10)
   e. The information necessitating the command (11)
   f. The command to the disorderly (12)
4. The exhortation to the loyal members (13-15)
   a. The exhortation to continued well-doing (13)
   b. The exhortation concerning the disorderly (14-15)
      1) The action toward such a one (14)
      2) The attitude toward such a one (15)

THE CONCLUSION (3:16-18)

1. The prayer (16)
2. The authentication (17)
3. The benediction (18)

A BOOK LIST ON 2 THESSALONIANS

(See the Book List under 1 Thessalonians.)

*Part 2*

# SOTERIOLOGICAL GROUP

Galatians

1 Corinthians

2 Corinthians

Romans

# 6

# AN INTRODUCTION TO GROUP TWO

In a very real sense the four epistles which compose the second group among the Pauline epistles constitute the very heart of the Gospel. Known as the Soteriological Group, these important epistles deal with the question of salvation. In a distinctive sense they are the epistles of the cross and were written from the standpoint of Calvary. Their distinctive theme is the atonement of Christ. They proclaim the message of a free and full salvation through faith in the crucified and risen Christ.

Because of the work of the Judaizers in the Early Church, the question of the way of salvation soon blazed forth in all its intensity. It was fanned into white heat by the admission of Gentiles into the Church in large numbers through the work of Paul. Paul taught that salvation was by faith in Christ alone, but the Judaizers insisted upon the addition of works of law. At the Jerusalem Conference (Acts 15) the Judaizers were defeated in their effort to fasten the bonds of Jewish legalism upon the Gospel. Nevertheless they persisted in hounding the steps of Paul, seeking to inoculate his converts with their legalistic teachings. These epistles are the outcome of that controversy.

In Galatians Paul defends his Gospel of justification by faith against the attacks of the Judaizers. In it he refutes their efforts to pervert the doctrine of salvation. Galatians is the monument of the emancipation of Christianity from Judaism. In 1 Corinthians Paul overcomes the dangers which threaten the Gospel, dangers springing up because of the practical perversion of the Gospel by the inconsistent conduct of its adherents. He shows that the doctrine of justification by faith has its salutary effects on the ethical, social, and ecclesiastical problems of the believers. In 2 Corinthians Paul defends the Gospel by refuting the Judaistic attempt to pervert it through an attack upon the character of its chief exponent. They were seeking to undermine the Gospel of justification by faith by undermining and discrediting the character of Paul as its messenger. Paul's intimate self-revelations refute the chicanery of the enemies and leave the Gospel of grace triumphant. In Romans, the fourth epistle of the group, we have a calm, logical, noncontroversial exposition of the doctrine of salvation in its wider reaches and ramifications. In it the Apostle presents God's method of salvation by faith in the light of man's universal need, the purposes of God with Jew and Gentile, and the practical effects of that salvation on the daily life of the believer.

Findlay states the value of these four epistles in the following paragraph:

> It is difficult to exaggerate the importance which belongs to these four epistles in the defence and confirmation of the Gospel—alike in face of sacerdotal and Romish perversions and of rationalistic denials of its truth. They furnish us with an impregnable fortress of our faith, planted in the midst of the New Testament; and they supply a fixed starting-point and indubitable test for the examination of all questions touching the origin and nature of Christianity, and the history of the apostolic age.[1]

The four epistles of this group are the four longest of Paul's writings. They constitute nearly sixty per cent of all the material from Paul in the New Testament.

There has been considerable diversity of opinion as to the exact place of Galatians in this group. Because of its remarkable affinity to Romans, it has generally been placed next to Romans, near the end of the third missionary journey. The more recent tendency, because of the impact of the *South-Galatian* theory, is to place it before the Corinthian epistles, hence first in the group. The question of the place of Galatians in this group is intimately related to several critical problems connected with the epistle.

1. George G. Findlay, *The Epistles of Paul the Apostle,* (n.d.), pp. 69-70.

# 7

# GALATIANS

## An Introduction to Galatians

The Epistle to the Galatians may well be called the *Magna Charta* of Christian liberty. Buried for a thousand years under Catholic legalism, the truths of this epistle came to life again with the Protestant Reformation. Under Luther this book again became the battle cry for Christian liberty. His *Commentary on Galatians* was the manifesto which launched the movement to recover for Christians "the liberty wherewith Christ hath made us free" (Gal. 5:1, A.V.). Luther considered Galatians in a special sense his own.[1] He loved this epistle because he had to fight Paul's battle for the liberty of the Gospel all over again. "The Epistle to the Galatians is the charter of Evangelical Faith."

### THE CHARACTER OF THE GALATIAN CHURCHES

1. *Unity.* This letter was addressed to "the churches of Galatia" (1:2). Galatians is the only Pauline epistle that is specifically addressed to a group of churches.[3] Conditions in these churches enabled Paul to address them as a unit. They were all the fruit of a single mission (3:1-3; 4:13-14), and all were affected by the same disturbance (1:6-7; 5:7-9). There was not time for individual letters, so he addressed a circular letter to them all.

2. *Founder.* Throughout the book Paul assumes the position of the founder of the churches. He directly addresses them as his spiritual children (4:19-20) and clearly states that he brought the Gospel

1. "The Epistle to the Galatians is my Epistle; I have betrothed myself to it; it is my wife."—Luther.
2. G. G. Findlay, "The Epistle to the Galatians," *Expositor's Bible*, (1903), p. 4.
3. Cf. 2 Cor. 1:1, "with all the *saints* that are in the whole of Achaia." If Ephesians is a circular letter, it is not so addressed.

to them (1:8, 11). He began work among them while he was suffering from some physical affliction (4:13). His evangelization of them was characterized by a vivid preaching of the crucified Christ (3:1) and the empowering ministry of the Holy Spirit (3:2, 5). The message was confirmed by miracles in their midst (3:5).

3. *Reception.* The Apostle's reception by the Galatians was warm-hearted and affectionate. Their relation to him was of a peculiarly tender nature. They received his message with great enthusiasm (4:12-15). They did not despise him because of his infirmity but received him with great respect and reverence ("as an angel of God," 4:14). Because of their love for him they stood ready to make drastic sacrifices for him ("would have plucked out your eyes and given them to me," 4:15). They willingly endured persecution for their faith (3:4). The Apostle remained with them long enough to see that they "were running well" (5:7).[4]

4. *Composition.* The Galatian churches were composed predominantly of converts from among the Gentiles. Before their conversion they had been idolaters (4:8). The attempt to have them receive circumcision likewise shows their Gentile background (5:2; 6:12). But there was a minority of Jewish converts in the churches (3:27-29). Throughout the epistle Paul takes for granted that the readers are familiar with Old Testament history (4:21-31; 3:7-9), the law (3:10-12), and the prophets (4:27). This familiarity with the Old Testament has been taken to imply that the members had been attendants at the Jewish synagogues. It must be remembered, however, that all Christians, whether Jewish or Gentile, would naturally turn to the Hebrew Scriptures for further knowledge and grounding in their faith.

### THE MEANING OF "GALATIA"

1. *Twofold usage.* When Paul wrote this epistle the term *Galatia* was used in two different senses. It was used in an *ethnographic* sense to designate the territory inhabited by the Galatian or Celtic people in north-central Asia Minor. These were Celtic tribes which had migrated into Asia Minor from ancient Gaul. In 390 B.C. a wave of these Gauls attacked Rome and nearly destroyed that rising republic.

4. This observation of their progress apparently was confirmed by a second visit to them.

In 281 B.C. another movement eastward, with the objective of finding a new home for the overcrowded Gauls, poured into Macedonia and Greece. After ravaging Macedonia they were routed at Delphi and were forced to withdraw from Greece and soon after from Macedonia. They erected a kingdom in Thrace called Thyle and soon crossed the Hellespont into Asia. Upon entering Asia Minor they ravaged the peninsula as far as the Taurus mountains. Their ravages, however, were checked by the surrounding kings, and the invaders were confined to that central part of Asia Minor which received the permanent name of Galatia. In 189 B.C. the Romans, by a single campaign under the Roman Consul Cn. Manlius Vulso, subjugated the Galatians to Rome. They were permitted to retain their independence and continued to be governed by their own princes. The boundaries of their territory varied from time to time. When Amyntas, the last king of the Galatian tribes, was killed in war in 25 B.C., Augustus converted his kingdom into a Roman province called Galatia. Besides the territory originally called Galatia, the Roman province included Isauria, part of Lycaonia, the southeastern district of Phrygia, and a portion of Pisidia. Because of these additions, the name Galatia, in the new *political* sense, embraced a larger area than the name in the *ethnographic* sense. The name Galatia continued in popular usage to denote the territory in the northern part of the province originally occupied by the Gauls. Thus the term came to acquire a twofold significance.

2. *Paul's usage.* When Paul addressed "the churches of *Galatia*" (1:2), in which sense was he using the term? It may bear either the *ethnographic* or the *political* connotation. There is disagreement among the scholars as to his precise meaning. According to the older view the term denotes the northern section of the province, the region around Ancyra, Pessinus, and Tavium which was called Galatia after the invasion of the Gauls. The more recent view is that Paul is using the term in the *political* sense and that it is equally applicable to the mixed population of the southern part of the province.

It is clear that Luke in the Acts, when speaking of Asia Minor, usually employs the old ethnographic names without regard to the boundaries of the Roman provinces. Thus he speaks of Lycaonia, Mysia, Phrygia, and Pisidia, all old territorial names and not Roman provinces. Paul's usage, however, seems to be different. A study of Paul's practice leads Zahn to conclude that "Paul never uses any but the provincial name for districts under Roman rule, and never employs territorial names which are not also names of Roman provinces."[5] Thus he speaks of Achaia, Arabia, Asia, Cilicia, Dalmatia, Illyricum, Judea, Macedonia, Spain, Syria and, of course, Galatia. Some scholars contend that some of these terms Paul seems to use in their popular ethnographic sense rather than in their strictly political sense.[6] Burton thinks that this contention cannot be positively demonstrated.[7] The fact that Paul uses no terms that are definitely ethnographic and nonpolitical, and that there is no clear case of the ethnographic rather than the political meaning in terms that have a double significance, robs the objection of its force.

3. *Rival theories.* This ambiguity as to the meaning of *Galatia* is reflected in the two theories as to the location of the Galatian churches, known respectively as the *North-Galatian* and the *South-Galatian* theories.

The *North-Galatian* theory holds that Paul founded these churches in ethnic, that is, northern Galatia on the second missionary journey. It points to Acts 16:6 as the time of their founding and holds that he revisited them on the third journey (18:23). Ancyra, Pessinus, and Tavium, and perhaps even Julipolis, are named as the cities where these churches were located. This location was taken for granted without discussion by the ancient interpreters of the epistle. It is held by many modern scholars.[8] This view was very attractively presented by J. B. Lightfoot in his commentary on the epistle.[9]

The *South-Galatian* theory holds that these churches were located in southern Galatia and must be identified with the churches established by Paul and Barnabas during the first missionary journey, as recorded in Acts 13:13–14:23. On his second journey Paul revisited

5. Theodor Zahn, *Introduction to the New Testament,* (1909), Vol. I, p. 175. See also Donald Guthrie, *New Testament Introduction,* (Revised Ed., 1970), p. 454.
6. Cf. A. Lukyn Williams, "The Epistle of Paul the Apostle to the Galatians," *Cambridge Greek Testament,* (1910), pp. xix-xxi; Werner Georg Kümmel, *Introduction to the New Testament,* (1966), p. 192.
7. Ernest De Witt Burton, *A Critical and Exegetical Commentary on the Epistle to the Galatians,* (1950 reprint), pp. xxv-xxvi.
8. It is popular in France and Germany. See L. Cerfaux, "The Epistle to the Galatians," *Introduction to the New Testament,* A. Robert and A. Feuillet, editors, (1965), p. 402; Alfred Wikenhauser, *New Testament Introduction,* (1963), p. 374.
9. J. B. Lightfoot, *Saint Paul's Epistle to the Galatians,* (1910 reprint), pp. 1-56.

these churches and from there went on to Europe. This view was first proposed by J. J. Schmidt in 1748, but it received only scattered support until it was championed by the voluminous writings of W. M. Ramsay. Ramsay, an authority on the history and archaeology of Asia Minor, was definitely led to espouse this position through his researches in that region. Since the opening of the present century the *South-Galatian* theory has been making rapid gains and an ever increasing number of scholars accept it as the more probable view.[10]

### THE VISITS OF PAUL TO GALATIA

Before considering the claims of these rival views, it will be well briefly to review Luke's account of Paul's visits to the province of Galatia. Such a visit was made on each of his three journeys.

1. *First journey.* On the first journey Paul and Barnabas, leaving Syrian Antioch, passed through the island of Cyprus, entered the province of Pamphilia, and without a preaching ministry there, passed on into the interior of Asia Minor (Acts 13:4-14). Their work of establishing churches at Antioch of Pisidia, Iconium, Lystra, and Derbe is adequately described in Acts 13:14—14:21. From Derbe they retraced their steps to organize the churches which they had founded (14:21-24), spoke "the word in Perga" of Pamphilia (14:24), and returned to Syrian Antioch (14:26). All scholars are now agreed that the cities of Pisidian Antioch, Iconium, Lystra, and Derbe were in the province of Galatia, and that the term *Galatians* would properly apply to them also. The southern part of the province was composed of three ethnographic regions, Lycaonia in the southeastern part, Pisidia to the west of it, and Phrygia to the north of Pisidia, part of it in the province of Galatia but the major portion of it in the province of Asia. "Antioch the Pisidian" (Greek) was not really in Pisidia but on its border and apparently was a Phrygian city.[11] Iconium was likewise a Phrygian city. Lystra and Derbe belonged in the ethnographic section of Lycaonia. Only part of Lycaonia was in Galatia, the remainder being in the Kingdom of Antiochus.[12]

10. "In America and Britain the South Galatian theory is popular." William David Davis, "Paul the Apostle," in *Twentieth Century Encyclopedia,* Lefferts A. Loetscher, editor, (1955), Vol. II, p. 854. "Most modern scholars lean to the South Galatian theory." Donald Guthrie, *New Testament Introduction,* (Revised Ed., 1970), p. 457.
11. W. M. Ramsay, *St. Paul the Traveller and the Roman Citizen,* (1896), p. 124.
12. R. C. H. Lenski, *The Interpretation of the Acts of the Apostles,* (1934), p. 562.

2. *Second journey.* Upon leaving Syrian Antioch on the second journey, Paul and Silas passed "through Syria and Cilicia, confirming the churches" (15:41). They revisited the churches of Derbe and Lystra. Here Paul found Timothy, circumcised him, and took him along as his assistant (16:1-3). In view of Paul's announced intention to revisit "every city wherein we proclaimed the word of the Lord" (15:36), it seems certain that they also visited Iconium and Pisidian Antioch, delivering the decrees of the Jerusalem Conference and strengthening the churches (16:4-5). On leaving Pisidian Antioch the missionaries were minded to enter the new field of Asia to the west of them but were forbidden to do so by the Spirit. Having been forbidden to preach in Asia,[13] they turned north and went "through the *region of Phrygia and Galatia*" (16:6). Although the expression is differently interpreted, it seems best to hold that both names are adjectives and that the whole phrase refers to territory which was partly in Phrygia and partly in Galatia, both terms being ethnographically understood.[13a] It is clear that they entered the region of northern Galatia. Burton thinks that their route ran a little east of north from Pisidian Antioch, perhaps touching Pessinus itself.[14] The intention of the missionaries was to enter the province of Bithynia, but again the Spirit did not permit (16:7). Turning west they skirted Mysia and came down to Troas on the Aegean Sea, where the call to Europe was received (16:8-9).

According to the *North-Galatian* theory, a great preaching mission was carried on in northern Galatia, the missionaries making a great swing east, even as far as Tavium. It is even assumed by some that the winter was passed in this work of evangelism in northern Galatia.[15]

Advocates of the *South-Galatian* theory object to this assumption of a protracted mission in this region. It is pointed out that Luke does not even suggest that any preaching was done, much less that a number of churches were founded. If they went as far as Tavium, Luke might at least have hinted at the fact of such a preaching tour.

13. The aorist participle expresses causative, antecedent action. Cf. R. C. H. Lenski, *Ibid.*, p. 637.
13a. Robert G. Hoerber, "Galatians 2:10 and the Acts of the Apostles," *Concordia Theological Monthly* 31 (August 1960):486 and references in footnotes.
14. Ernest De Witt Burton, *A Critical and Exegetical Commentary on the Epistle to the Galatians*, (1950 reprint), p. xli.
15. George G. Findlay, *The Epistles of Paul the Apostle*, (4th Ed., n.d.), p. 13, also p. 120.

The tone of the whole passage sounds much more like a forced march than a long protracted missionary tour.

3. *Third journey.* Paul again entered the province of Galatia on his third journey. On leaving Syrian Antioch, he "went through the *region of Galatia, and Phrygia,* in order, establishing all the disciples" (18:23). While the scholars differ again on the meaning of the expression, here also it seems best to understand both Galatia and Phrygia in the ethnic sense.[16] In Acts 19:1 the route of Paul seems to be summarized in the words, "Paul having passed through the *upper country* came to Ephesus." The *North-Galatian* theory again postulates a great swing through northern Galatia. The *South-Galatian* theory finds no reasons for such a detour, since no church had been established there on the second journey. Burton holds that the expression "the upper country" is "generally and probably rightly understood of the highlands of Asia in contrast with the coast plain."[17]

### THE LOCATION OF THE GALATIAN CHURCHES

The question of the location of the Galatian churches is one of several perplexing problems of this epistle. Both the *North-* and the *South-Galatian* locations for these churches have their ardent supporters.

1. *North Galatia.* Advocates of this view point to the fact that this is the unanimous view of the Church Fathers. But, say the opponents, this is due to the fact that "during the second century, the term Galatia ceased to bear the sense which it had to a Roman in the first century."[18] In the second century the province was again restricted to ethnic Galatia and the double meaning of the term disappeared. The Patristic commentators, writing after that date, interpreted the term in the light of their own day.

In Acts Luke speaks of Antioch as Pisidian, and of Lystra and Derbe as Lycaonian; the inhabitants of these cities were not Galatians. To have called them Galatians, say the North-Galatian advocates, would have been tactless on the part of Paul. But it is answered that because of its political usage, the term *Galatians* need not imply Celtic origin. In fact it is hard to conceive of a more suitable form of

16. So F. F. Bruce, *The Acts of the Apostles,* (1951), p. 350.
17. Ernest De Witt Burton, *A Critical and Exegetical Commentary on the Epistle to the Galatians,* (1950 reprint), p. xxxix.
18. W. M. Ramsay, *The Church in the Roman Empire Before A.D. 170,* (1919), p. 111.

address to apply to the dwellers in south Galatia, with their mixed background, than the term Galatians. Instead of the term being displeasing to these southern inhabitants of the province, Shaw feels rather that it would be very pleasing to them since it recognized them as part of the great and popular Roman Empire.[19] Paul as a Jew was not ashamed to be known as a Roman citizen.

Lightfoot thought that the fickleness of the Galatians, asserted by Julius Caesar and others, was illustrated in the sudden change in the Galatians to which the epistle bears witness (1:6) and confirmed the Gallic origin of the readers.[20] But in spite of the glowing pages of Lightfoot, this argument can no longer be regarded as having real force. Warmheartedness and fickleness seem equally to have characterized the Lycaonians.[21] The numerous vices rebuked in the epistle (5:19-21) were not peculiar to the Galatians, but must be charged to mankind generally. Ramsay's studies led him to the conclusion that the people of southern Galatia were more apt to change suddenly than the Gauls in the north. The Gauls were proud and independent, and kept their own religion and language, and even laws, under the Roman rule.[22]

Lightfoot thought that from the analogy of Luke's use of ethnographic terms it was highly probable that Paul likewise, because of his knowledge of the region, would use the term *Galatia* in its popular rather than its official and political sense.[23] But Luke's usage of the term cannot be used to prove Paul's usage of it. Paul elsewhere seems always to use the provincial rather than the ethnographic terms. This was definitely in accordance with Paul's habit of thinking and working in terms of Roman provinces in his evangelistic campaigns. Certainly Peter used the term in the political sense, since he employed it in a list with four other names all of which designate provinces (1 Peter 1:1).

2. *South Galatia.* Advocates of the *South-Galatian* theory hold that this view fits in perfectly with what we know about the founding of churches in the province of Galatia. We know all about the churches in southern Galatia; why then postulate the existence of

19. R. D. Shaw, *The Pauline Epistles,* (4th Ed., 1924 reprint), p. 93.
20. J. B. Lightfoot, *Saint Paul's Epistle to the Galatians,* (1910 reprint), pp. 14-16.
21. Cf. Acts 14:6-18 with 14:19-20.
22. W. M. Ramsay, "Galatia," *International Standard Bible Encyclopaedia,* (1939), Vol. II, p. 1155b.
23. J. B. Lightfoot, *Saint Paul's Epistle to the Galatians,* (1910 reprint), pp. 19-20.

churches in north Galatia of which we have no record and whose very existence is in doubt? In view of the large space that Luke gives to the southern churches, and none to the northern, is it reasonable to think that Paul would write thus to churches whose very existence Luke does not even imply? *North-Galatian* advocates reply that Paul may well have written to these southern churches but his letters to them have not been preserved, or that the conditions in these churches may not have called for a letter. On the other hand, Lightfoot admits that it is strange that not a single name of a person or place in connection with the Apostle's preaching in northern Galatia has been preserved in either Acts or the Galatian epistle.[24]

*South-Galatian* advocates assert that when Paul preached in Galatia the northern part was still mainly Celtic and pastoral with comparatively little commerce and few roads, while southern Galatia had flourishing cities and a steady stream of commerce along the important highway that runs through that section.[25] Was it likely that Paul would go up over difficult and dangerous terrain to this rougher northern section when sick? To this it is replied that northern Galatia was not undeveloped and backward as this implies. It was by no means inaccessible by road; there were regular roads from either Iconium or Antioch to Pessinus.[26] Desiring to enter Bithynia for Gospel labors, Paul would not be deterred by any rough or unfrequented path. And the sickness he mentions (4:13) may well have occurred after he was in the region. The sickness also creates a problem for the South-Galatians.

Ramsay contended that the reference to Paul's sickness did fit Paul's preaching in south Galatia. He suggested that when Paul landed at Perga a siege of chronic malaria fever forced him to leave the low country and go into the highlands of Antioch to seek recovery in its bracing climate. Here he recovered from the attack, but the Galatians saw the repulsive effects of it.[27] But it is difficult to see, declares the rebuttal, how this supposition fits in with the vigorous ministry in south Galatia which Luke presents (Acts 13:13–14:23). Further, the journey of a hundred miles from Perga to Antioch would

24. *Ibid.*, p. 21.
25. Frederic Rendall, "The Epistle of Paul to the Galatians," *Expositor's Greek Testament*, (n.d.), Vol. III, p. 128.
26. James Moffatt, *An Introduction to the Literature of the New Testament*, (1949 reprint), p. 97.
27. W. M. Ramsay, *St. Paul the Traveller and the Roman Citizen*, (1896), pp. 94-97.

be one that a fever-stricken patient would be very unlikely to undertake.[28]

The mention of Barnabas as though well known to the readers accords best with the South-Galatian position, since he was not with Paul when the journey through northern Galatia was made and hence would be unknown to the Galatians. But the epistle does not say that he was personally known to them. In 1 Corinthians 9:6 and Colossians 4:10 he is mentioned as a Christian worker of repute among believers generally.

In 1 Corinthians 16:1 Paul says that the Galatian churches had a share in the offering for the Judean saints. Yet they were not represented by the group taking the collection to Jerusalem (Acts 20:4) if they were in north Galatia. Gaius and Timothy in the group were from the southern churches. But the inference that Gaius and Timothy would represent the southern churches is not certain. In the list Achaia has no representative at all, yet it is certain that Corinth had a share in the offering.

If the Galatian churches were located in northern Galatia, how are we to explain the fact that the Judaizers, coming from Jerusalem and pursuing the steps of Paul, passed by these southern churches? Is it conceivable that they would leave untouched these churches, situated on important highways, and go into the pastoral sections of northern Galatia?

3. *Conclusion.* While the evidence for either view is not conclusive, it seems to us that the balance of probability is in favor of the *South-Galatian* theory. While this position is steadily growing in popularity, it must be admitted that the *North-Galatian* theory is arguable and has its able defenders. Fortunately, neither the value of the epistle or its interpretation is seriously affected by the question. It is not a liberal versus conservative controversy. It is rather a question of historical and biographical interest.

### THE OCCASION FOR GALATIANS

1. *Changed attitude.* The Epistle to the Galatians was called forth by the startling report to Paul that a sudden and drastic change of attitude toward him and his Gospel had taken place among the Galatians. At the beginning their attitude toward him had been of a

28. George G. Findlay, "Galatians, Epistle to the," *The International Standard Bible Encyclopaedia,* (1939), Vol. II, p. 1161b.

tender and affectionate character. But this had suddenly been changed under the influence of some false teachers among them. They were coming to give adherence to another gospel (1:7). Having begun in the Spirit, they were now being led to turn to the law for perfection (3:3). They were being urged to accept circumcision (5:2-4) and to observe Jewish days and seasons (4:10). They were coming to think rather disparagingly of their founder, even questioning his apostolic authority (1:1; 2:1-11). Dissension and conflicts among them had resulted (5:15).

2. *Cause.* The reason for this sudden change on the part of the Galatians was the intrusion of an alien propaganda into their midst. This propaganda was introduced by the arrival of some Jewish-Christian teachers who probably came from Jerusalem and seem to have claimed the authority of the Jerusalem leaders.[29] In the letter Paul carefully distinguishes these teachers from the Galatians to whom he is writing (1:7-8; 3:1; 4:17; 5:12). They worked within the framework of the Christian church and claimed to be Christians, acknowledging Jesus as Messiah. But while they professed to accept Christ, yet in theory and practice they tended to minimize and neutralize Him. They robbed Christ of His uniqueness by putting other things on a level with Him as necessary to salvation. They gave the Galatians to understand that Christianity was but the logical development of the hopes of Judaism. While Christianity had introduced much that was new, it yet did not abrogate the distinctive rites of the Jewish religion. It followed that circumcision as the initiatory rite was necessary for the Christian (5:2; 6:12), and this involved the necessity of keeping the Mosaic law (4:21) with all its rites and ceremonies (4:10). Only through the door of Judaism could Gentile converts enter the Kingdom of God. Since this teaching was contrary to what the Galatians had received from Paul, it was necessary for these teachers to seek to undermine and destroy, if possible, the authority and influence of Paul.

3. *Paul's reaction.* Paul was amazed and profoundly disturbed by these sudden developments (1:6). He recognized that it put in jeopardy not only his entire Galatian ministry, but, if this teaching

29. The suggestions of some recent scholars that the troublers were Gentile "Judaizers" or Gnostics are unconvincing. See Werner Georg Kümmel, *Introduction to the New Testament* (1966), pp. 193-195; Donald Guthrie, *New Testament Introduction* (Revised Ed., 1970), pp. 466-468.

could be established, it would undermine the entire Gospel as he preached it. The presence of these Judaizers in Galatia clearly revealed that they were not willing to abide by the decision reached at the Jerusalem Conference (Acts 15; Gal. 2:1-10). Apparently sensing such a danger, on his second visit to Galatia Paul had cautioned the Galatians against it (1:9; 5:3; 4:16). But now the danger had struck, threatening to engulf and destroy his work. Because circumstances made it impossible for Paul to go to the scene, he wrote this letter (4:20).

### THE DATE AND PLACE OF GALATIANS

1. *Date.* There is no evidence which makes it possible to determine with certainty the exact date of the epistle. The best that can be done is to fix certain limits within which it was written.

As is evident from the Acts narrative, the date is affected by the view taken of the location of the churches. On the *North-Galatian* theory it could not have been written until some time after Acts 16:6, and more probably not until after Acts 18:23. If the *South-Galatian* theory is adopted, a much longer period is opened up for a possible date. Advocates of this theory have assigned Galatians to almost every conceivable date between the end of the first missionary journey and the latter part of the third. There are, however, certain indications which seem definitely to limit this range.

The expression "so quickly" in Galatians 1:6 cannot be used as an argument for an early dating of the epistle, as though it were written soon after their conversion. It points not to the time of their conversion but to the swiftness of the change in the Galatians.

The phrase *to proteron* (4:13) is generally taken to prove that Paul had visited the Galatians twice before writing. It is true that in Koine Greek the expression may simply mean "formerly," rather than "the first time." But in view of the fact that in 1:9 and 5:3 Paul speaks of having given them certain warnings, it seems simplest to suppose that two visits to them had been made. We accept this interpretation. Then on the *North-Galatian* theory the epistle could not have been written until after Acts 18:23. On the *South-Galatian* theory it must then be placed after the visit mentioned in Acts 16:6. The explanation of some that these two visits can be accounted for by the assumption that Paul distinguished between his first visit to the South-Galatian churches and the return trip on the same journey (Derbe getting only one visit!) cannot be accepted.[30] In Acts 15:36 Paul looks back to the journey through southern Galatia as one event.

The events recorded in the first two chapters offer further time limitations. The visit to Jerusalem mentioned in Galatians 1:18-19, and dated three years after his conversion, is by common consent identified with the visit mentioned in Acts 9:26-30. The differences in the accounts illustrate the differing purposes of the two narratives. There is less agreement as to the identification of the visit mentioned in Galatians 2:1-10. Dated as being "after the space of fourteen years," it came at least fourteen years after his conversion, or quite probably, fourteen years after the first visit. Is this visit to be identified with the "famine visit" in Acts 11-12 or with the visit to the Jerusalem Conference in Acts 15? The former view opens up a date before the Jerusalem Conference; the latter view forbids it.

Blunt, Garvie, Mackenzie, Duncan, F. F. Bruce, Tenney, and Hoerber[31] hold that Galatians 2:1-10 must be equated with the visit of Acts 11-12. It is argued that in Galatians Paul is building his case upon the rarity of his contacts with Jerusalem, hence he could not have failed to mention the "famine visit" if it was not the visit of Galatians 2:1-10. To do so would have laid him open to the charge of dishonesty and deception. It may be answered that Paul's purpose did not require him to enumerate all his visits to Jerusalem, only those pertinent to his argument. The Apostle's account stresses not his visits to Jerusalem as such but rather his independence of the older apostles. It is doubtful if he saw any of the apostles on that visit, since the relief fund, the specific motive for the visit, was delivered to the "elders" (Acts 11:30). With the persecution raging in Jerusalem, it would have been an inopportune time for Paul to advance his claims. Moe further points out that it would not have been in

30. Douglas Round, *The Date of St. Paul's Epistle to the Galatians,* (1906), pp. 9, 35-36; T. Henshaw, *New Testament Literature in the Light of Modern Scholarship,* (1957), p. 218.
31. A. W. F. Blunt, "The Epistle of Paul to the Galatians," *The Clarendon Bible,* (1950 reprint), pp. 77-84; E. H. Pearce and A. E. Garvie, *The Study Bible, Galatians,* (n.d.), pp. 123-128; W. Douglas Mackenzie, "Galatians and Romans," *The Westminster New Testament,* (1912), pp. 22-32; George S. Duncan, "The Epistle of Paul to the Galatians," *The Moffatt New Testament Commentary,* (1948), pp. xxii-xxvi; F. F. Bruce, "Commentary on the Book of the Acts," *New International Commentary on the New Testament,* (1954), pp. 244, 298-300; Merrill C. Tenney, *New Testament Survey,* (1961), p. 267; Robert G. Hoerber, "Galatians 2:1-10 and the Acts of the Apostles," *Concordia Theological Monthly* 31 (August 1960):482-491.

good taste "if, immediately after Paul and Barnabas had presented the gift of the Gentile Christians, the pillars of the mother congregation should have enjoined upon them for the future to remember the poor in the mother congregations."[32] Harrison notes a chronological difficulty in this identification."[33] The death of Agrippa I is established at A.D. 44; Acts 12:1 links the famine visit with the persecution and death of Agrippa, while Paul in Galatians 2:1 dates the visit as after fourteen years, either from the previous visit mentioned or, possibly, his conversion. If we subtract either seventeen years or fourteen years from A.D. 40, the resultant date in either case is too early for Paul's conversion. Findlay also maintains that if we synchronize Paul's statements of time in Galatians 1 and 2 about his visits to Jerusalem with the statement about the rule of Aretas in Damascus (2 Cor. 11:32-33), the identification of Galatians 2:1-10 with Acts 11-12 is excluded because of insufficient time.[34] Moffatt points out that this proposed identification "makes the burning question of circumcision for Gentile Christians emerge in an acute shape some time before the period of Acts 15—a view for which there is no evidence in Acts, and against which the probabilities of the general situation tell heavily."[35] Stein feels that this view is not in harmony with Luke's presentation of Barnabas in Acts 11-12 as the leader of the relief party since in Galatians 2:1-10 Paul clearly is the recognized leader.[36] Guthrie notes that this identification raises serious difficulty in understanding on what basis the Jerusalem leaders recognized and confirmed Paul's apostleship to the Gentiles (Gal. 2:7-9).[37] At that time Paul had not yet been on any of his missionary journeys. The preaching mentioned in Galatians 1:23, or his work in the Antioch church, would not have offered sufficient evidence for his distinctive field.

On the other hand, scholars like Lightfoot, Beet, Rendall, Williams, Hendrickson,[38] and others make a strong case for the identification of

32. Olaf Moe, *The Apostle Paul, His Life and His Work,* (1950), p. 153.
33. Everett F. Harrison, *Introduction to the New Testament,* (1971), p. 277.
34. George G. Findlay, "Galatians, Epistle to the," *International Standard Bible Encyclopaedia,* (1939), Vol. II, p. 1160b.
35. James Moffatt, *An Introduction to the Literature of the New Testament,* (1949 reprint), p. 92.
36. Robert H. Stein, "The Relationship of Galatians 2:1-10 and Acts 15:1-35; "Two Neglected Arguments," *Journal of the Evangelical Theological Society,* Vol. 17, No. 4, Fall 1974, pp. 241-242.
37. Donald Guthrie, *New Testament Introduction,* (Revised Ed., 1970), p. 464.
38. J. B. Lightfoot, *Saint Paul's Epistle to the Galatians,* (1910 reprint), pp. 123-132; Joseph Agar Beet, *A Commentary on St. Paul's Epistle to the Galatians,* (1885), pp. 188-191; Frederic Rendall, "The Epistle of Paul to the Galatians," *The Ex-*

Galatians 2:1-10 with Acts 15. Admittedly the two accounts differ remarkably. But when we remember the distinctive purpose and viewpoint of each account, the differences, like those in the first visit, are not so improbable. Acts gives the historical account from the standpoint of the organic development of the Church, while Paul narrates his personal defense of his authority and apostleship. The accounts seem best harmonized by the view that in Acts we have the record of two public sessions and in Galatians the record of a further private meeting with the Jerusalem leaders coming between Acts 15:5 and 6.[39] This identification seems to us to be the most probable. It seems to have been the earliest identification. It is the view of Irenaeus in his work *Against Heresies*.[40]

Objection is made to this identification on the grounds that Paul makes no mention of the decrees of the council in this epistle. If the council had already taken place, why, it is asked, did not Paul settle the question easily by quoting the decision of the conference, as Acts 16:4 states that he actually did on his second visit to Galatia? The fact that Paul makes no mention at all of the decision of the Jerusalem Conference is remarkable, but we find the same silence concerning the decision of the Conference in his other epistles where reference to the matter might have been expected (cf. I Cor. 8; Rom. 14). That Paul does not mention the decrees to the Galatians may well be due to the fact that they were already familiar with them (Acts 16:4). But since his delivery of the decrees, the situation had changed. As Purves observes, "The Judaizers themselves had violated the compact by denying the freedom from the law which the council had granted, and the whole discussion had reverted to the original question of circumcision."[41] In dealing with the problem, Paul therefore "appeals to general principles and to his own independent apostolic authority."[42] Fausset points to a further reason with his observation that "the decree did not go the length of his position, it merely did not

*positor's Greek Testament,* (n.d.), Vol. III, pp. 141-144; A. Lukyn Williams, "The Epistle of Paul the Apostle to the Galatians," *Cambridge Greek Testament,* (1910), pp. 145-147; William Hendriksen, "Exposition of Galatians," *New Testament Commentary,* (1968), pp. 69-74.

39. J. B. Lightfoot, *Saint Paul's Epistle to the Galatians,* (1910 reprint), pp. 125-126.
40. Irenaeus, "Against Heresies," Bk. III, 13. 3. *The Ante-Nicene Fathers,* (1950 reprint), Vol. I, p. 437.
41. George T. Purves, *Christianity in the Apostolic Age,* (1955 reprint), p. 153.
42. J. S. Howson, "Galatians," *The Speaker's Commentary, New Testament,* (1881), Vol. III, p. 511.

impose Mosaic ordinances, but he here maintains the Mosaic institution itself is at an end."[43]

The identification of Galatians 2:1-10 with Acts 15 carries with it the conclusion that Galatians was written after the Jerusalem Conference. Since Paul had already made two visits to Galatia when he wrote, the time of writing must be somewhere after the visit of Acts 16:6 on the second journey.

But where does Paul's collision with Peter at Antioch (Gal. 2:11-14) fit into the picture? The event itself is undated. The most natural view is to take it as following the events of Galatians 2:1-10. Turner, however, has reversed the chronological order and identifies the "certain from James" (Gal 2:12) with the "certain men" who came to Antioch from Judea (Acts 15:1), thus making the event precede the Jerusalem Conference.[44] While the language of Galatians does not necessarily prohibit such an arrangement, "it does distinct violence to the psychological probabilities of the situation."[45] It seems most natural to assign it to the period of time which Paul and Barnabas spent at Antioch following the conference (Acts 15:30-36).

But did it occur before the second missionary journey? Some would place it before the beginning of the third journey, feeling that otherwise it would make Peter yield on the morrow after the conference. But Peter's action was only a temporary defection when he was carried away by old feelings and attitudes against his more reasoned convictions. It is said that to place it before the second journey does not give the Judaizers enough time to recover from the defeat at the Jerusalem Conference. But their very actions suggest that they would soon formulate their strategy and lose little time in putting it into operation, realizing that the longer they waited, the harder would the achievements of Paul be to overcome. Their first point of attack in their crafty and persistent campaign against Gentile liberty would be to attempt to set up a separate church table for the circumcision at Antioch. The Jerusalem Conference did indeed settle the question of law-keeping for the Gentiles, but it left untouched this matter of law-keeping as regards Jewish Christians. Peter did not realize the implications of his action, but Paul saw the danger from the outset.

43. A. R. Fausset, "Paul," *Bible Cyclopaedia, Critical and Expository*, (1902), p. 545c.
44. C. H. Turner, "Chronology of the New Testament," Hastings *Dictionary of the Bible*, (1899), Vol. I, p. 424a.
45. Ernest De Witt Burton, *A Critical and Exegetical Commentary on the Epistle to the Galatians*, (1950 reprint), p. li.

He resisted it at Antioch and seems to have warned the Galatians on his second visit to them. Apparently the incident was occasioned by the same general movement that later came to Galatia. In citing this incident to the Galatians, Paul was holding up a mirror in which they might see themselves.

The evidence thus suggests that Galatians was written some time after Paul had made his second visit to the Galatian churches. A more precise dating depends on the place of origin assigned to it.

2. *Place.* On the *North-Galatian* theory the place of origin may be at Ephesus, during Paul's ministry there of nearly three years, or either in Macedonia or in Corinth on the third journey, near the time of Romans.

On the *South-Galatian* theory two different places are suggested. Ramsay,[46] Goodspeed,[47] and others would place it at Syrian Antioch at the close of the second journey. This view is possible. It allows sufficient time for the work of the Judaizers. It accounts for his use of the word Antioch without any further word of explanation and gives the account of his experience with Peter its most natural setting. But if Paul was at Antioch when the startling news came, what would keep him from going to Galatia at once as he said he wished he could (Gal. 4:20)?

The other view is to place it at Corinth on the second journey. Zahn,[48] Rendall,[49] and Lenski[50] hold that it was written during the early part of Paul's stay at Corinth, before the arrival of Silas and Timothy (Acts 18:5), thus making it the earliest of the Pauline epistles. This, however, seems to leave too little time for the Judaizers to get in their work. Others, like Allen and Grensted,[51] feel that it is more probably to be dated some time after the Thessalonian epistles. It would allow Paul time to gather a band of adherents at Corinth (Gal. 1:2), would allow sufficient time for the work of the Judaizers, and give time for the messengers to come to Corinth from Galatia

46. W. M. Ramsay, *St. Paul the Traveller and the Roman Citizen,* (1896), pp. 189-192.
47. Edgar J. Goodspeed, *An Introduction to the New Testament,* (9th impression, 1948), p. 26.
48. Theodor Zahn, *Introduction to the New Testament,* (1909), Vol. I, pp. 193-199.
49. Frederic Rendall, "The Epistle of Paul to the Galatians," *Expositor's Greek Testament,* (n.d.), Vol. III, pp. 144-147.
50. R. C. H. Lenski, *The Interpretation of St. Paul's Epistles to the Galatians, to the Ephesians, and to the Philippians,* (1937), pp. 13-15.
51. Willoughby C. Allen and L. W. Grensted, *Introduction to the Books of the New Testament,* (3rd Ed., 1936 reprint), p. 138.

upon hearing of his work there. Since the Lord had definitely instructed Paul to remain at Corinth (Acts 18:9-10), this would account for his inability to go to Galatia personally to deal with the defection. This view seems to us the most probable. The epistle would then be dated in the spring of A.D. 52.

### THE PURPOSE OF GALATIANS

1. *Vindication.* Because of the Judaizers' attacks made upon him as an apostle, Paul first of all defended his apostolic call and authority. This had to be established before his doctrine of salvation by faith could be authenticated. He devotes the first two chapters to his vindication by showing how he got his Gospel, how the Jerusalem leaders confirmed his Gospel, and how he rebuked the inconsistency of the very apostle to whom the Judaizers appealed for their authority.

2. *Exposition.* Having verified his apostolic authority, in the next two chapters Paul sets forth an exposition of the Gospel of justification by faith as he held it and had taught it to the Galatians. A reasoned, comprehensive presentation of that Gospel in the light of the Old Testament would be its best defense.

3. *Morality.* Paul further purposed to exhibit that the life of Christian liberty does not mean a life of lawlessness or license. His opponents had attacked his Gospel by declaring that his removal of the restraining law from the life of the Christian promoted lawlessness and invited license and unrestrained lust (5:13-25). Paul urges them to maintain their liberty in Christ (5:1), to beware of the forces threatening to destroy that liberty (5:2-12), and to practice living a life governed by love and guided by the Holy Spirit (5:13-25). Such a life bears the fruit of the Spirit, bears the burdens of the weak and needy, and never grows weary of doing good to all men (5:16–6:10). The truth of justification by faith logically leads to a life of good works.

### THE CHARACTERISTICS OF GALATIANS

1. *Value.* The Epistle to the Galatians gives an inimitable picture of the apostle Paul. It "displays, within a brief compass, all the qualities most characteristic of Paul—his courage, his tenderness, his

earnestness and sincerity, his burning devotion to Christ."[52] Goodspeed points out the distinctiveness of this epistle as follows,

> Paul's letters are probably the most extraordinary letters in the world, but none of them is more remarkable than Galatians. Its vigor, variety, audacity, and self-revealing frankness, together with its deep and direct insight into religious truth, put it in a class by itself among the books of the New Testament.[53]

Galatians is one of the fundamental documents of the Christian faith. It is the classic vindication of the Gospel of justification by faith. Its impact upon the faith of the Church is inestimable.

2. *Tone.* Galatians is an epistle of conflict. Paul attacks with his very first words (1:1-5). Its tone of severity is characteristic. The readers are never addressed as "saints in Christ." There is not a word of praise for the readers, not even thanksgiving for them. It is the only Pauline epistle that contains no thanksgiving for the readers. But the severity is mingled with appeals of touching affection (4:12-15, 19-20). Thus as Alford says,

> It unites the two extreme affections of his remarkable character: severity, and tenderness: both, the attributes of a man of strong and deep emotion.[54]

3. *Unity.* The epistle is distinguished by its rigid adherence to its purpose. The Galatian defection centered around two points, the denial of his authority and the repudiation of his Gospel of justification by faith. This double aspect is pursued throughout the epistle, receiving summary statement in the very salutation (1:1-5).

4. *Handwritten.* Galatians is the only epistle in which Paul calls attention to his handwritting. The concluding paragraph begins thus: "Notice the large letters I am making in writing to you with my own hand" (6:11, *The Twentieth Century New Testament*). Paul is not exclaiming about the size of the epistle, as the King James assumes. It is rather a reference to the size of the letters he is making. Many scholars, assuming that Paul uses the epistolary aorist, think that he writes only the concluding seven verses. Paul usually employed an amanuensis for his letters and added only the closing words

52. Ernest Findlay Scott, *The Literature of the New Testament,* (1932), p. 152.
53. Edgar J. Goodspeed, *An Introduction to the New Testament,* (9th impression, 1948)), pp. 26-27.
54. Henry Alford, *The Greek Testament,* (1958), Vol. III, p. 4 Proleg.

with his own hand (Rom 16:22; 1 Cor. 16:21; Col. 4:18; 2 Thess. 3:17). But since Paul seems never to employ the aorist to designate the writing of only a few concluding words, it seems best to view this as a statement that Paul is writing the whole epistle with his own hand and that all was written in large script.[55] That very fact constituted an eloquent testimony to them of his deep concern for them and his intense yearning to rescue his erring children.

### An Outline of Galatians

THE INTRODUCTION (1:1-10)

1. The salutation (1-5)
   a. The writer (1-2a)
      1) Paul, the Apostle (1)
      2) The brethren with him (2a)
   b. The readers (2b)
   c. The greeting (3-5)
      1) The contents of the greeting (3a)
      2) The source of the grace and peace (3b-4)
      3) The doxology (5)
2. The rebuke (6-10)
   a. His astonishment at their fickleness (6-7)
      1) The reason for the astonishment (6)
      2) The explanation of the departure (7)
   b. His assertion about its seriousness (8-9)
      1) The seriousness asserted (8)
      2) The seriousness reaffirmed (9)
   c. His attitude in the matter (10)

I. PERSONAL: THE VINDICATION OF HIS APOSTOLIC AUTHORITY (1:11–2:21)

1. How he got his Gospel (1:11-24)
   a. The origin of his Gospel through revelation (11-12)
      1) The assertion as to its nature (11)
      2) The manner of its reception (12)
   b. The previous conduct of the one given the revelation (13-14)
      1) The manner of his former life known to them (13a)

55. So Mill, Ewald, Hofman, Eadie, Zoeckler, Clemen, Huxtable, Ellicott, S. J. Turner, Zahn, Lenski, Wuest, and others.

2) The description of his former life (13b-14)
   a) In relation to the Church of God (13b)
   b) In relation to Judaism (14)

c. The description of the revelation received (15-17)
   1) The source of the revelation (15)
   2) The subject of the revelation (16a)
   3) The purpose of the revelation (16b)
   4) The response to the revelation (16c-17)

d. His independence of the Jerusalem apostles (18-24)
   1) The first visit to Jerusalem (18-20)
      a) The time of the visit (18a)
      b) The purpose of the visit (18b)
      c) The duration of the visit (18c)
      d) The scope of contacts during the visit (19-20)
   2) The subsequent absence from Jerusalem (21-24)
      a) The place of his withdrawal (21)
      b) The lack of acquaintance with the Judean churches (22)
      c) The response of the churches to reports about him (23-24)

2. How his Gospel was confirmed by the apostles at Jerusalem (2:1-10)
   a. The circumstances of its presentation to them (1-2)
      1) The journey to Jerusalem (1-2a)
      2) The presentation made at Jerusalem (2b)
   b. The outcome of his presentation of his Gospel to them (3-10)
      1) The maintenance of his position, as seen in Titus (3)
      2) The conflict with the false brethren (4-5)
         a) The presence of the false brethren (4)
         b) The refusal to yield to their demands (5)
      3) The approval of his Gospel by the Jerusalem leaders (6-10)
         a) Their failure to add anything to his Gospel (6)
         b) Their approval of his Gospel in full (7-10)
            (i) The basis of their approval (7-9a)
            (ii) The expression of their approval (9b)
            (iii) The one request with their approval (10)

3. How he rebuked Peter's inconsistent conduct (2:11-21)
   a. The circumstances when giving the rebuke (11-13)
      1) The fact of his rebuke of Peter (11)
      2) The reason for his rebuke of Peter (12)
      3) The effect of the inconsistent conduct of Peter (13)
   b. The justification for giving the rebuke (14-21)
      1) His question of rebuke to Peter (14)
      2) His explanation of his doctrinal position (15-21)
         a) The insufficiency of the law (15-18)
            (i) The discovery of believing Jews about justification (15-16)
            (ii) The rejection of a conclusion from Peter's action (17)
            (iii) The significance of a return to law-works (18)
         b) The new life in Christ (19-21)
            (i) The effect of the law led to the new life (19)
            (ii) The nature of the new life (20)
            (iii) The grace of God nullified by law-keeping (21)

II. DOCTRINAL: THE EXPOSITION OF JUSTIFICATION BY FAITH (3:1—4:31)

1. The elaboration of the doctrine of justification (3:1—4:7)
   a. The nature of justification as by faith, not law (3:1-14)
      1) The inconsistency of their conduct (1-5)
         a) The question about their turning from the crucified Christ (1)
         b) The question about the beginning of their Christian life (2)
         c) The question about their method of perfection (3)
         d) The question about their sufferings as believers (4)
         e) The question about the basis of God's work among them (5)
      2) The example of Abraham's justification (6-9)
         a) The means of Abraham's justification (6)
         b) The identity of the sons of Abraham (7)
         c) The announcement to Abraham concerning Gentile justification by faith (8)
         d) The sharers in the blessings of Abraham (9)

- 3) The deliverance from law-works through Christ (10-14)
  - a) The curse upon those under law-works (10)
  - b) The inability of law-works to justify (11-12)
  - c) The deliverance from the curse through Christ (13-14)
    - (i) The fact of our deliverance through Christ (13a)
    - (ii) The means of our deliverance from the curse (13b)
    - (iii) The purpose in our deliverance from the curse (14)

b. The limitations of the law and its relations to faith (3:15–4:7)

- 1) The covenant with Abraham unaltered by the law (3:15-18)
  - a) The illustration of a man's covenant as binding (15)
  - b) The fact illustrated is the divine promise to Abraham (16)
  - c) The application of the principle of an unalterable covenant (17-18)
    - (i) The law did not alter the promise (17)
    - (ii) The inheritance is not through law but promise (18)
- 2) The true place and purpose of the law (3:19-29)
  - a) The temporary nature of the law (19-20)
    - (i) The reason for the adding of the law (19a)
    - (ii) The time limit for the law (19b)
    - (iii) The manner of the establishment of the law (19c-20)
  - b) The inability of the law to produce life (21-22)
    - (i) The law not contrary to the promise (21a)
    - (ii) The law unable to produce life (21b)
    - (iii) The Scripture shut up all to faith in Christ (22)
  - c) The law as a child-leader to Christ with His blessings (23-29)
    - (i) The old position under law (23-24)
      - (a) The position of confinement under law (23)
      - (b) The function of the law as child-leader to Christ (24)

(ii) The new position in Christ (25-29)
(a) The nature of the new position (25-26)
(b) The entry into the new life (27)
(c) The effect of the new life (28)
(d) The fulfillment of the promise to Abraham (29)
3) The contrasted position under law and faith (4:1-7)
a) The illustration of the position of the heir as a minor (1-2)
b) The application of the illustration to believers (3-6)
(i) The condition of bondage as minors (3)
(ii) The position as free sons through God's Son (4-6)
(a) The sending of the Son of God (4-5)
(b) The sending of the Spirit of God (6)
(iii) The conclusion for the believer (7)
2. The appeal for them to drop their legalism (4:8-31)
a. The acceptance of Jewish legalism is a return to bondage (8-11)
1) Their past condition of bondage (8)
2) Their present deliverance from bondage (9a)
3) Their legalism as a return to bondage (9b-10)
4) Their action a cause of concern to him (11)
b. The appeal from his relations to them (12-20)
1) The appeal for them to adopt his position (12a)
2) The reminder of his past relations to them (12b-14)
3) The change in their relation to him (15-18)
4) The travail he is undergoing for them (19-20)
c. The appeal from the two contrasted covenants (21-31)
1) The question to those desiring to be under law (21)
2) The story of Abraham's two sons (22-23)
3) The allegorical interpretation of the story (24-30)
a) The two mothers representing two covenants (24a)
b) The description of the two covenants (24b-28)
(i) The one representing a covenant of bondage (24b-25)
(ii) The other representing a covenant of freedom (26-28)

c) The expulsion of the slave woman and her son (29-30)
4) The conclusion from the story (31)

III. PRACTICAL: THE LIFE OF CHRISTIAN LIBERTY (5:1–6:10)

1. The call to maintain their Christian liberty (5:1)
2. The peril to Christian liberty (5:2-12)
   a. The peril to them in circumcision (2-6)
      1) The consequences of accepting circumcision (2-4)
         a) It renders Christ useless to them (2)
         b) It makes a man debtor to do the whole law (3)
         c) It severs them from Christ (4a)
         d) It constitutes a fall from grace (4b)
      2) The attitude of the true believer (5-6)
   b. The condemnation of the false teacher (7-12)
      1) The explanation for their defection (7)
      2) The characterization of the teaching (8-9)
      3) The condemnation of the one troubling them (10-12)
         a) The confidence he has in them (10a)
         b) The troubler will bear his judgment (10b)
         c) The refutation of charges that he preaches circumcision (11)
         d) The wish that these teachers would go to the consistent end (12)
3. The life of Christian liberty (5:13–6:10)
   a. It is directed by love (5:13-15)
      1) The believer called to liberty (13a)
      2) The use of Christian liberty (13b)
      3) The fulfillment of the law through love (14)
      4) The results of the lack of love (15)
   b. It is a walk in the Spirit, not in the flesh (5:16-25)
      1) The command to walk by the Spirit (16)
      2) The conflict between the Spirit and the flesh (17-18)
      3) The contrasted products of the flesh and the Spirit (19-23)
         a) The works of the flesh (19-21)
         b) The fruit of the Spirit (22-23)
      4) The persons living by the Spirit (24-25)

c. It is a life of mutual burden-bearing (5:26–6:10)
1) The burden of moral faults (5:26–6:5)
a) The warning against wrong attitudes towards others (5:26)
b) The attitude of humility in restoring the fallen (6:1)
c) The duty of mutual burden-bearing (2)
d) The proper attitude toward self (3-5)
2) The burden of temporal needs (6-10)
a) The exhortation to communicate with their teachers (6)
b) The law of the spiritual harvest (7-8)
c) The encouragement to well-doing (9-10)

THE CONCLUSION (6:11-17)

1. His reference to his large letters (11)
2. His rebuke of his adversaries (12-13)
3. His confidence in the cross (14-16)
   a. His glorying only in the cross (14a)
   b. His crucifixion through the cross (14b)
   c. His evaluation of things through the cross (15)
   d. His benediction upon those accepting this principle (16)
4. His marks of apostleship (17)

THE BENEDICTION (6:18)

## A Book List on Galatians

Beet, Joseph Agar, *A Commentary on St. Paul's Epistle to the Galatians.* 1885. London: Hodder and Stoughton (5th Ed., n.d.).

A verse-by-verse interpretation by a Wesleyan theologian of the past century. Provides doctrinal summaries as a contribution toward systematic theology. Holds to the North-Galatian theory and thinks the "Lord's brothers" were the sons of Joseph by a former marriage. Concludes with special studies relating Galatians to Acts, Romans, James, and I John.

Bligh, John, *Galatians in Greek: A Structural Analysis of St. Paul's Epistle to the Galatians with Notes on the Greek.* Detroit: University of Detroit Press (1966).

A detailed examination of each word and phrase of the Greek text, together with a structural analysis of the epistle. Finds unparalleled literary symmetry in Galatians. Holds its structure proves that Paul wrote Galatians with great care, not in haste as is often thought.

———, "Galatians. A Discussion of St. Paul's Epistle." *Householder Commentaries*. London: St. Paul Publications (1969).

An extensive work by an accomplished Roman Catholic scholar. Prints the author's own translation. Adopts the South-Galatian view and assigns the letter to the third missionary journey but postulates that 2:15-5:13 was actually composed by Paul some years before. The commentary, presented in question-and-answer form, does not take up philological matters dealt with in the volume above, but seeks to elaborate the theology of Paul. Heavy use is made of Philo as well as ancient, medieval, and modern commentators on Galatians. Irenic in spirit.

Bring, Ragnar, *Commentary on Galatians*. Translated by Eric Wahlstrom. Philadelphia: Muhlenberg Press (1961).

A critical commentary by a Swedish Lutheran professor which concentrates on the logical implications of Galatians. Divides the epistle into two major divisions: 1:6-5:12 dealing with Paul's understanding of law and Gospel; 5:13-6:10 presenting Paul's view of Christian ethics. Does not believe that Galatians and Acts can be harmonized.

Brown, John, *An Exposition of the Epistle of Paul the Apostle to the Galatians*. (1853). Evansville, Ind.: The Sovereign Grace Book Club (1957).

A thorough exposition by a Scottish professor of the past century. Still of significant value for the expository preacher. Unfortunately Brown's introduction to Galatians has been omitted in this edition.

Burton, Ernest DeWitt, "A Critical and Exegetical Commentary on the Epistle to the Galatians." *The International Critical Commentary*. Edinburgh: T. & T. Clark (1921).

An exhaustive study of the Greek text by a noted liberal scholar. Offers summaries of previous views and gives special attention to grammatical and linguistic matters. Makes important word studies. Favors the South-Galatian theory and equates Acts 15 with Galatians 2 but holds that Acts is "inaccurate."

Calvin, John, "The Epistles of Paul to the Galatians Ephesians, Philippians and Colossians." *Calvin's Commentaries*. Translated by T. H. L. Parker. Editors, D. W. and T. F. Torrance. Grand Rapids: Wm. B. Eerdmans Pub. Co. (1965).

A fresh translation of these expositions by the prince of Reformation expositors. Valuable for insights into Reformation day views.

Cole, R. Alan, "The Epistle of Paul to the Galatians." *Tyndale New Testament Commentaries.* Grand Rapids: Wm. B. Eerdmans Pub. Co. (1965).

A readable conservative interpretation providing a concise unfolding of the teaching of the letter. Maintains a good balance between lexical comments and discussions of a more theological nature. Examines different interpretations in a non-dogmatic spirit. Favors the South-Galatian theory.

Duncan, George S., "The Epistle of Paul to the Galatians." *The Moffatt New Testament Commentary.* London: Hodder and Stoughton (1934).

Uses the Moffatt Translation, but offers an independent study of the original. A clear, thorough exposition which approaches Galatians from a historical point of view but brings out the essential meaning of the epistle. Advocates the South-Galatian view and equates Galatians 2 with Acts 11.

Eadie, John, *Commentary on the Epistle of Paul to the Galatians.* (1869). Grand Rapids: Zondervan Publishing House (reprint of 1894 edition, n.d.)

Greek text. A thorough, very helpful exposition for those knowing Greek, but due to its age lacks the insights of more recent investigation. Supports the North-Galatian theory; has an extended note on the identity of James, the Lord's brother (pp. 57-100).

Erdman, Charles R., *The Epistle of Paul to the Galatians.* Philadelphia: The Westminster Press (1930).

A brief, careful, readable exposition by a conservative Presbyterian professor. Well suited to the average lay Bible student.

Findlay, G. G., "The Epistle to the Galatians," *The Expositor's Bible.* Grand Rapids: Wm. B. Eerdmans Pub. Co., Vol. V (1943 reprint).

An exhaustive exposition by a conservative scholar of the past century. Contains much relevant material in spite of its age.

Guthrie, Donald, "Galatians." *The Century Bible. New Series.* London: Thomas Nelson & Sons (1969).

Based on the Revised Standard Version. A 50-page introduction adequately discusses various introductory problems. Leans to the South-Galatian theory and an early date for Galatians. The phrase-by-phrase interpretation provides a conservative unfolding of the teaching and dynamic faith of Paul. Appendixes on the centrality of

Christ in Galatians and the source of opposition at Galatia add to the value.

Hendriksen, William, "Exposition of Galatians." *New Testament Commentary*. Grand Rapids: Baker Book House (1968).

A full treatment by a conservative scholar in the Reformed tradition. The introduction presents a unique treatment of the North-South-Galatian controversy. Holds to the South-Galatian view. Contains much practical matter.

Hogg, C. F., and Vine, W. E., *The Epistle of Paul the Apostle to the Galatians, with Notes Exegetical and Expository*. (1922). London: Pickering & Inglis (reprint, n.d.).

A careful conservative interpretation which places emphasis upon the meaning of the original to bring out the full thought of the epistle. Valuable word studies and doctrinal summaries unfold the epistle for the English reader.

Johnson, Robert L., "The Letter of Paul to the Galatians." *The Living Word Commentary*. Austin, Tex.: R. B. Sweet Co. (1969).

Comments based on the Revised Standard Version but brings out the force of the original. The variant views concerning introductory matters receive fair presentation, but the viewpoint adopted is conservative. Leans to the South-Galatian view and equates Galatians 2 with Acts 15.

Lenski, R. C. H., *The Interpretation of St. Paul's Epistles to the Galatians, to the Ephesians, and to the Philippians*. Columbus, Ohio: Lutheran Book Concern (1937).

Prints the author's own literal translation. A scholarly, full, and very satisfactory interpretation by a conservative Lutheran scholar. A strong defense of the South-Galatian theory.

Lightfoot, J. B., *Saint Paul's Epistle to the Galatians, A Revised Text with Introduction, Notes and Dissertations*. (1865). Grand Rapids: Zondervan Publishing House (1966 reprint).

A classic commentary on the Greek text of Galatians with valuable linguistic insights. Thoroughly grounded in classical Greek, some of Lightfoot's views need some modification in the light of recent Koine studies. Presents a strong defense of the North-Galatian view. Three important dissertations comprise a third of the volume.

McDonald, H. D., *Freedom in Faith, A Commentary on Paul's Epistle to the Galatians*. London: Pickering & Inglis (1973).

Prints the Revised Standard Version. A non-technical, verse-by-verse commentary by a conservative English scholar and intended for the average Christian who desires to come to grips with the New Testament teaching of the believer's freedom in faith. No discussion of introductory problems.

Ramsay, William M., *A Historical Commentary on St. Paul's Epistle to the Galatians.* (1899). Grand Rapids: Baker Book House (1965).

The major emphasis is on the background for the epistle. The author used his vast knowledge of the historical and archaeological backgrounds of Asia Minor to support his strong defense of the South-Galatian view. Identifies Galatians 2 with Acts 11 and thinks that Paul's thorn in the flesh was malaria.

Ridderbos, Herman N., "The Epistle of Paul to the Churches of Galatia." *The New International Commentary on the New Testament.* Grand Rapids: Wm. B. Eerdmans Pub. Co. (1953).

A non-technical exposition of the text of Galatians with grammatical and lexical matters kept to the footnotes. Accepts the South-Galatian theory and an early date for the epistle. A conservative treatment by a Dutch Reformed scholar.

Stamm, Raymond T., and Blackwelder, Oscar Fisher, "The Epistle to the Galatians," *The Interpreter's Bible.* New York: Abingdon-Cokesbury Press (1953).

A thorough liberal exposition by two American Lutheran scholars. The introduction and exegesis by Stamm, the exposition by Blackwelder. Stamm accepts the South-Galatian theory as the "better working hypothesis" and holds that Paul was fighting on two fronts in Galatians—against the Judaizers and against the antinomians who wanted to abandon the Old Testament altogether.

Stott, John R. W., *The Message of Galatians.* London: Inter-Varsity Press (1968).

A valuable series of nineteen expository messages on Galatians by a conservative Anglican scholar-preacher.

Tenney, Merrill C., *Galatians: The Charter of Christian Liberty.* Grand Rapids: Wm. B. Eerdmans Pub. Co. (1950).

Not a commentary in the usual sense, but an invaluable aid to help the student grapple personally with the text. Excellent as illustrating various methods of Bible study. Provides much helpful material for the actual interpretation of Galatians.

Vos, Howard F., "Galatians, A Call to Christian Liberty." *Everyman's Bible Commentary.* Chicago: Moody Press (1971).

A readable unfolding of the message of Galatians, stressing the need for biblical "freedom." A conservative exposition, well suited to the lay Bible student.

Williams, A. Lukyn, "The Epistle of Paul the Apostle to the Galatians." *Cambridge Greek Testament for Schools and Colleges.* Cambridge: University Press (1910).

A scholarly, independent elucidation of the Greek text.

Wilson, Geoffrey B., *Galatians. A Digest of Reformed Comment.* Edinburgh: The Banner of Truth Trust (1973).

A concise verse-by-verse treatment, freely quoting various writers to present the view of Reformed interpreters of Galatians. Well suited to the lay reader.

Wuest, Kenneth S., *Galatians in the Greek New Testament for the English Reader.* Grand Rapids: Wm. B. Eerdmans Pub. Co. (1944).

A simplified commentary on the original text carried over into English for the student who does not know Greek; presents an expanded translation and exegetical comments and word studies.

# 8

# FIRST CORINTHIANS

## An Introduction to 1 Corinthians

We possess more detailed information about the actual conditions within the church at Corinth than about any other church in the New Testament. The picture given us of this church shows that even apostolic churches were not perfect churches. Our picture of the Corinthian church is drawn, not by an enemy of the church, but by the founder of that church himself, as contained in his two epistles to that church which have been preserved for us.

### THE CITY OF CORINTH

1. *Location.* The city of Corinth was situated near the southern end of the narrow isthmus which connects the Grecian Peloponnesus with the continent. At the southern edge of the city towered the famous Acrocorinthus, a rocky eminence rising from the plain almost perpendicularly to a height of over one thousand eight-hundred feet. Its summit, a space some half-mile square, was sufficiently broad to accommodate a considerable town. Because of the abundance of water there and the protection offered by the isolated mountain, a settlement was early begun at the site of Corinth. Because of its strategic position, Corinth had the unique distinction of having a gulf on two sides; to the west stretched the Corinthian Gulf, while the Saronic Gulf lay eastward from the city. On the eastern horizon, some forty-five miles distant, the Acropolis of rival Athens was clearly visible.

2. *History.* Although the Corinth in which Paul worked was a comparatively new city, it had a long and illustrious past. Archaeological excavations have revealed that the site of Corinth was one of

the first regions of Greece to be inhabited.[1] Corinth was an important city during the days of Homer, who spoke of it as "wealthy Corinth." Aided by its geographic location, Corinth rivaled in importance other Greek centers such as Athens, Thebes, and Sparta. Corinth was long the implacable foe of powerful Athens. Although continually prominent among the city-states of Greece, Corinth never held the first place till the last days of Greek freedom. After the Greeks lost their independence in the battle of Chaeroneia in 338 B.C., Philip II of Macedon and his son, Alexander the Great, made Corinth the seat of a new Hellenic League. The struggle of the Greeks to throw off the yoke of Macedon led to the intervention of Rome and the eventual enslavement of all the Greeks. With the Roman victory Corinth fell. In 146 B.C. the Roman general Lucius Mummius plundered the city of its treasures, equal to those of Athens, and completely destroyed it to crush all Greek aspirations to independence.

After the site of ancient Corinth had lain in ruins for a hundred years, the practical eye of Julius Caesar recognized the beauty and importance of the place. In 46 B.C. he sent a colony of veterans and freedmen to the place and rebuilt Corinth as a Roman colony. The re-founded city was named Colonia Laus Julia Corinthiensis. A new era of phenomenal growth and prosperity ensued. The Emperor Augustus made Corinth the capital of the Province of Achaia, and Corinth became the residence of the proconsul. Under Augustus and his successors, Corinth was rebuilt on the lines of a Roman city. Its official language was Latin, but the common speech of its mixed population was Greek. When Paul visited the city, a little more than a hundred years after its restoration, it was the metropolis of the Peloponnesus.

3. *Commerce.* The position of Corinth gave it command over two different streams of commerce. Its location at the head of the Corinthian isthmus gave it control over the only route for merchandise between the peninsula and the mainland of Greece. Because of its proximity to the Corinthian as well as the Saronic gulfs, it largely commanded the trade between Asia and Italy. Corinth had the rare fortune of having three harbors in its vicinity to foster its commercial interests. Its harbor on the Corinthian Gulf, looking toward the west,

1. See Oscar Broneer, "Corinth: Center of St. Paul's Missionary Work in Greece," *The Biblical Archaeologist,* Dec. 1951, pp. 78-96, for the history and archaeology of Corinth.

was Lechaeum, a short distance north of the city. On the Saronic Gulf, some seven miles east of the city, was the port of Cenchreae, while the port of Schoenus was situated a few miles north of Cenchreae. It thus commanded most of the traffic between the Ionian and the Aegean seas. Strabo accurately summed up the situation when he said,

> Corinth is called "wealthy" because of its commerce, since it is situated on the Isthmus and is master of two harbors, of which the one leads straight to Asia, and the other to Italy; and it makes easy the exchange of merchandise from both countries that are so far distant from each other.[2]

Since the journey around Cape Malea, the southernmost promontory of Greece, was a detour of two hundred miles and a perilous adventure, most merchants chose to unload their goods at one of the Corinthian ports. The cargoes were then carried across the isthmus and reloaded at the other port. Arrangements were contrived whereby small vessels were hauled across the isthmus by means of a ship tramway with wooden rails. Large vessels could not be accommodated and had to go around. The desirability of cutting a canal across the isthmus was recognized by such notables as Alexander the Great, Julius Caesar, and Nero. In A.D. 66 Nero actually began the construction of such a canal by digging the first dirt with a golden spade and set six thousand young Jews, recently captured by Vespasian in the Jewish War, at work to excavate it, but the attempt was abandoned. It was not until modern times that a canal was finally cut across the isthmus. During 1881-1893 the present four-mile canal was cut across the isthmus at the narrowest point.

4. *Inhabitants.* The population of Corinth in Paul's days was quite cosmopolitan. The Roman colonists whom Julius Caesar had planted at Corinth formed the basis for the dominant Roman minority. As a colony the city was quite thoroughly Roman. Varied nationalities, however, mingled in Corinth. There were many native Greeks in the city, and they left their own mark upon the life in Corinth. Its money-making opportunities attracted a large colony of Jews. Its cosmopolitan character is described by Beet:

2. Strabo, *Geography*, VIII, vi, 20. Quoted from Jack Finegan, *Light from the Ancient East*, (1946), p. 279.

> In Corinth, a Roman colony and the capital of a Roman province, the political capital of Greece, having a Jewish synagogue, and seated on two seas as the centre of the commerce of the eastern Mediterranean, we have an epitome of the civilized world in the days of Paul.[3]

Because it was a seaport and emporium of commerce, many classes and nationalities mingled in Corinth. Through its streets thronged travelers and traders and agents of vice from almost every known country. As in every large city, great wealth and extreme poverty existed side by side. At the time of Paul's visit to the city its population was somewhere between six and seven hundred thousand, of whom approximately two-thirds were slaves. The resultant social life in Corinth revealed the usual degrading characteristics of such a city. Shaw says:

> At night its streets were hideous with the brawls and lewd songs of drunken revelry. In the daytime its markets and squares swarmed with Jewish pedlars, foreign traders, sailors, soldiers, athletes in training, boxers, wrestlers, charioteers, racing-men, betting-men, courtesans, slaves, idlers and parasites of every description—a veritable pandemonium![4]

5. *Culture.* Unlike Athens, its famous neighbor, Corinth never became famous for its philosophers. Yet it cultivated various arts. Its pottery was shipped into all parts of the Mediterranean world. It became famous for its Corinthian brass, and Corinthian capitals and pillars are still known in architecture. The Corinthians prided themselves on their ability to adorn their city and the various temples with artistic embellishments. Corinth also produced a number of noted painters. While the Corinthians did not distinguish themselves in the field of literature, they did produce a goodly number of statesmen of importance. The Corinthians prided themselves on their interest in "knowledge" and philosophical pursuits, yet with the majority this interest was quite shallow and superficial.

After the restoration of Corinth the Isthmian games were revived. "Next to the Olympic Games, which were held every four years, the celebrations at the Isthmia were the most splendid and best attended

3. Joseph Agar Beet, *A Commentary on St. Paul's Epistles to the Corinthians,* (1882), p. 16.
4. R. D. Shaw, *The Pauline Epistles,* (1924 reprint), p. 130.

of all the national festivals of Greece."[5] Preparations for these games, which were held every two years, began months ahead and proved a rich source of profit to the vendors and entertainers from Corinth. The contests were held in the Isthmian stadium near the port of Schoenus on the Saronic Gulf.

6. *Morals and religion.* Corinth was a wicked city, even as large cities in the Empire went. The term "a Corinthian" meant a profligate, and "to Corinthianize" meant to engage in prostitution. In the Greek plays Corinthians were usually represented as drunkards.

The immorality of Corinth was fostered by the degrading worship of the goddess Aphrodite, the goddess of love. In the old city of Corinth, situated on the topmost peak of Acrocorinthus, was a magnificent temple to this goddess with a thousand female *Hieroduli* (consecrated prostitutes) for the free use of the visitors to the temple. The worship of Venus (the Roman counterpart of the Greek Aphrodite) was restored in the new Corinth, although we have no account of the females in connection with the new temple.

With the restoration of Corinth the worship of most of the ancient gods was also restored. The temples of various other gods were located in the city, such as Athena, Apollo, Poseidon, Hermes, and others. There was also a Pantheon, or temple of All the Gods. The temple of Aesculapius, the god of healing, was surrounded by a number of buildings designed for the use of the patients coming there. These accommodations provide an excellent illustration of a pagan hospital.[6] There were also temples to foreign cults, such as the Egyptian gods Isis and Serapis.

"East and west mingled their dregs of foulness in the new Gomorrah of classic culture, and the orgies of the Paphian goddess were as notorious as those of Isis or of Asherah."[7] Money was freely spent in Corinth for sinful pleasures by those who had come for a moral holiday. The flourishing of both eastern and western religions in Corinth furthered rather than hindered its moral corruption.

A residence of more than a year and a half at Corinth gave the apostle Paul an opportunity to see the degradation of paganism at

5. Oscar Broneer, "Corinth: Center of St. Paul's Missionary Work in Greece," *The Biblical Archaeologist,* Dec. 1951, p. 95. Cf. Broneer, "The Apostle Paul and the Isthmian Games," *The Biblical Archaeologist,* Feb. 1962, pp. 2-31.
6. Oscar Broneer, "Corinth: Center of St. Paul's Missionary Work in Greece," *The Biblical Archaeologist,* Dec. 1951, pp. 83-88.
7. F. W. Farrar, *The Life and Work of St. Paul,* (1889), p. 316.

first hand. It was while at Corinth, during the third missionary journey, that he painted the dark picture of paganism found in the first chapter of Romans.

THE CHURCH IN CORINTH

1. *Origin.* The apostle Paul was the founder of the church in Corinth (1 Cor. 3:6, 10; 4:15). The historical account of its origin is found in Acts 18:1-18. Paul was on his second missionary journey. He had established several churches in Macedonia, but persecution had driven him to Athens. After a brief and not too successful work in Athens, Paul came to Corinth. Here he found Aquila, one of his own countrymen, recently banished from Rome because of the edict of Claudius against the Jews. Since both were tent-makers by trade, Paul accepted the hospitality of Aquila and Priscilla and labored with them. Out of this partnership of work sprang a lasting partnership of faith.[8]

Apparently Paul at first considered his stay at Corinth only a temporary sojourn. He was waiting for the coming of his helpers with the information that he might return to the unfinished work in Macedonia.[9] While thus laboring and waiting, he made use of the opportunity offered him in the Jewish synagogue to proclaim the message of Christ to the Jews and the Greeks who attended.

With the coming of Silas and Timothy the situation was changed. Timothy brought information about the Thessalonian church and the report caused Paul to write First Thessalonians to his harassed converts. A few months later, when additional information concerning the Thessalonians was received, the Second Epistle was written. A number of scholars hold that the Epistle to the Galatians was also written during the time of this ministry at Corinth; some scholars place Galatians even before the Thessalonian Letters.

With the coming of his helpers Paul "held himself [middle voice] to the Word" (Acts 18:5, Gr.) and began an intensive, full-time ministry in Corinth. Silas apparently had brought an offering from the church at Philippi (2 Cor. 11:8-9; Phil. 4:15) which relieved the Apostle of the necessity of manual labor and freed him for an active campaign. This intensified effort to convince the Jews that Jesus was

8. It is impossible to decide the question as to whether or not Aquila and Priscilla were Christians before they met Paul; probably they were.
9. David Smith, *The Life and Letters of St. Paul,* (n.d.), pp. 151-152.

the Messiah resulted in fierce opposition on their part. With his converts Paul withdrew from the synagogue and established an independent work nearby in the house of Titus Justus, one of the Greek converts who had attended the synagogue. Among Paul's converts were some Jews, notably Crispus, the ruler of the synagogue, but the larger number of the converts were Greek proselytes. These Greek converts, by their social position and family connections, formed a bridge of access to the rest of the Gentile community. A large and fruitful ministry was carried on in Corinth (Acts 18:8).

The success of this Gentile ministry in Corinth aroused the fierce anger of the Jews. Paul feared a repetition of troubles with these Jews such as he had experienced in Thessalonica and was thinking of leaving the city to spare his followers the resultant persecution. But in a vision at night the Lord told Paul to remain in Corinth and assured him of great success and protection (Acts 18:9-10). Encouraged by these assurances, the Apostle settled down for a protracted ministry in Corinth.

The trouble with the Jews that Paul had feared finally flared into the open when Gallio, the new proconsul, arrived in Corinth. The new proconsul, the elder brother of the famous Seneca, was renowned for his gentleness and amiability. Seeking to take advantage of the new governor, the Jews rose up against Paul and, bringing him before the judgment seat, accused him of teaching a way of worship contrary to the law. Realizing that it was a religious argument and as such not in the sphere of his functions as a Roman judge, Gallio resolutely refused to take the case and summarily dismissed the court. When the Jewish leader, Sosthenes, refused to leave as directed, Gallio ordered his lictors to clear the court, and they "beat him before the judgment-seat."[10] This refusal of Gallio to act against Paul left him free to continue his work "yet many days" at Corinth before he decided to leave (Acts 18:18).

This reference to Gallio provides a historical landmark for the date of Paul's ministry at Corinth. The date for the accession of Gallio to the proconsulship of Achaia was fixed by the discovery of a mutilated inscription at Delphi in 1908 which associated him with the twenty-sixth acclamation of Claudius. On the basis of this inscription it is

10. See R. C. H. Lenski, *Interpretation of the Acts of the Apostles,* (1934), pp. 755-757, on the common view that the Gentile crowd beat Sosthenes.

generally held that the office of Gallio dated from A.D. July 51 to July 52. Paul apparently had already been in Corinth a year and a half when Gallio arrived. On the basis of these figures, Paul came to Corinth at the beginning of the year A.D. 50. Lenski, however, contends, this is about a year too early since Gallio would assume office in May rather than in July. He holds that "Gallio must have arrived in Corinth before May 1 of the year 52."[11] Accordingly he places the arrival of Paul in Corinth in the fall of A.D. 51. David Smith also accepts this figure.[12] (See the discussion and sources cited on p. 40.)

2. *Membership.* When Paul departed from Corinth he left a church with a good-sized membership. The members had a varied background—Greeks, Romans, Jews, and perhaps some other nationalities. While some Jews had been won (Acts 18:8), the majority of the members were from the Gentiles (1 Cor. 12:2). It is of interest to note that a number of the Corinthian Christians had Roman names.[13] But the characteristics of the church as such would suggest that the majority were Greeks.

While there were a few of noble rank in the church, the majority of the members were from humbler stations in life (1 Cor. 1:26-31). These latter doubtless came "from dockyards, potteries, and brass-foundries, from poor shopkeepers, bakers, brokers, fullers, and stray waifs in the motley crowds of Corinth."[14] Marked social differences existed in the membership; it included slaves as well as freedmen (7:21-22; 12:13). Economic differences likewise were present; a few were wealthy, but the majority were poor (11:21-22). Some of them had a deeply sinful past (6:9-11).

The Corinthian church, planted in a notoriously wicked city, inevitably exhibited many characteristics of its environment. The influences of heathen Corinth were not immediately overcome by the members. Some of the old moral habits and practices crept into the church and became the cause for apostolic concern (5:9; 5:1-2). The intellectual faults of the Greek race also manifested themselves in the life of the church. Says Findlay,

11. R. C. H. Lenski, *Ibid.*, p. 750.
12. David Smith, *Life and Letters of St. Paul,* (n.d.), p. 651.
13. Cf. Crispus and Gaius (1 Cor. 1:14), Fortunatus (16:17), Tertius and Quartus (Rom. 16:22-23), and Titus Justus (Acts 18:7).
14. James Moffatt, "First Epistle of Paul to the Corinthians," *Moffatt Commentary,* (n.d.), p. xix.

> Among so many freshly awakened and eager but undisciplined minds, the Greek intellectualism took on a crude and shallow form; it betrayed a childish conceit and fondness for rhetoric and philosophical jargon (1. 17, ii. 1-5, etc.), and allied itself with the factiousness that was the inveterate curse of Greece. The Corinthian talent in matters of "word and knowledge" ran into emulation and frivolous disputes.[15]

Aware of the Greek fondness for oratorical eloquence, the Apostle in carrying on the mission at Corinth deliberately chose not to preach to them "with excellency of speech or of wisdom" (2:1) in order that their faith "should not stand in the wisdom of men, but in the power of God" (2:5). Using great simplicity of speech, he preached to them "Jesus Christ, and him crucified" (2:2). This attitude of the Apostle was later turned against him by his enemies at Corinth (2 Cor. 10:10).

3. *Contacts with Apollos.* Some time after Paul's departure, Apollos, an Alexandrian Jew, "an eloquent man . . . and . . . mighty in the scriptures" (Acts 18:24), arrived at Corinth. His eloquent ministry proved a great blessing to the Corinthian church, for he effectively watered the seed that Paul had planted (I Cor. 3:6).

It must not be thought, however, that Apollos simply took over the work of Paul at Corinth. The ministry of Apollos was not restricted to the Corinthian church. From Luke's account it is apparent that his ministry was valuable to the Christians in that his was largely a defensive ministry. This eloquent man rendered a great service to the believers in Achaia in that "he powerfully confuted the Jews, *and that* publicly, showing by the scriptures that Jesus was the Christ" (Acts 18:28).

### THE OCCASION FOR 1 CORINTHIANS

It would appear that our First Corinthians was not occasioned by a single event but rather by a series of events which had a cumulative effect, ultimately determining the final form of the letter.

1. *Preliminary causes.* The preliminary causes for the writing of 1 Corinthians lie in Paul's contacts with the Corinthians after his departure from Corinth. When Paul left Corinth he took his friends Aquila and Priscilla as far as Ephesus, where they remained while he

15. G. G. Findlay, "The First Epistle of Paul to the Corinthians," *Expositor's Greek Testament,* (n.d.), Vol. II. p. 731.

went on to Jerusalem (Acts 18:18-22). Paul returned to Ephesus on his third missionary journey for a ministry of three years (Acts 19:10; 20:31). Since Ephesus was in constant ship communications with Corinth, Paul had means of keeping in touch with the Corinthian church. Several traces of these contacts have survived.

Paul apparently visited Corinth during his Ephesian ministry. Acts does not mention it, but it seems implied from 2 Corinthians 12:14 and 13:1-2 where Paul speaks of coming to Corinth a "third time." This visit gave him an insight into tendencies in the church. The time was probably before he wrote 1 Corinthians, but modern scholars generally place it after.[16] If connected with 2 Corinthians 2:1, Paul's experiences there proved painful to him.

In 1 Corinthians 5:9 reference is made to a letter which he had already written to the Corinthians. Our First Corinthians, therefore, is at least the second letter by the Apostle to this church. In this lost letter Paul dealt with problems in the church. One of the points of the letter was to give them instruction concerning their attitude toward fornicators. His instructions in that letter apparently were misinterpreted, and Paul found it necessary in 1 Corinthians to correct the misunderstanding.

Further, in 1:11 Paul tells the Corinthians that he has received information about their church factions from members of the household of Chloe. This information would add to his concern about conditions in the church at Corinth.

These points of information about the Corinthian church caused Paul to send Timothy to Corinth by way of Macedonia (Acts 19:21-22; 1 Cor. 4:17). As his personal representative, Timothy was to remind the Corinthians of Paul's life and teaching concerning the life in Christ. However, further contacts with the Corinthian church led Paul to write 1 Corinthians before Timothy had time to get to Corinth. Accordingly, in the epistle Paul exhorts the Corinthians to make Timothy feel at ease while with them and to send him back to him (16:10-11).

First Corinthians 16:12 indicates that Apollos was at Ephesus when Paul wrote. Just when he had left Corinth is not clear. He probably left when he became unintentionally involved in their party factions

16. Donald Guthrie, *New Testament Introduction,* (Revised Ed., 1970), pp. 427-429.

(1 Cor. 1:12). He would be able to confirm the reports Paul had received.

2. *Immediate occasion.* Not long after the departure of Timothy, Paul was gladdened by the arrival of three messengers from the Corinthian church, Stephanas, Fortunatus, and Achaicus (1 Cor. 16:17). They provided the direct contact with the Corinthian church that he had desired. It seems that they brought a letter from the church asking the Apostle's advice concerning certain problems that perplexed them (7:1; 8:1; 12:1; 16:1).

The coming of this delegation with the letter from the Corinthian church was the immediate occasion for the writing of 1 Corinthians. In writing the letter, however, the Apostle did not confine himself to the problems that had been presented to him by the church but also dealt with other problems that demanded attention.

### THE PLACE AND DATE OF 1 CORINTHIANS

1. *Place.* The epistle was written from Ephesus, as is clear from 16:8-9. Paul told the Corinthians that he was planning on staying "at Ephesus until Pentecost." He planned on visiting them after having passed through Macedonia, before going to Jerusalem with the offering being raised in his various churches (16:3-7; Acts 20:3). The place is also evident from the greetings sent from "the churches of Asia" as well as from Aquila and Priscilla who were living at Ephesus (Acts 18:26).

From Acts 19 it is apparent that 1 Corinthians was written near the close of Paul's ministry at Ephesus. Further, from his use of the Passover imagery in 1 Corinthians 5:6-8 it seems to have been written near the Passover season.

The subscription in the King James Version, following the *Textus Receptus,* reads, "The first Epistle to the Corinthians was written from Philippi by Stephanas, and Fortunatus, and Achaicus, and Timothy." This place-location is plainly a mistake. Probably the designation is due to a misunderstanding of Paul's words in 1 Corinthians 16:5, "For I pass through Macedonia." But Paul's use of the present tense in this verse is not a statement of history but a statement of his plans. These subscriptions are of late origin and are not authoritative.

2. *Date.* While scholars are in general agreement that this epistle was written in the spring of the last year of Paul's ministry at Ephesus, they are not in agreement as to the specific date. Some would make

the date as early as A.D. 53, while others place it as late as 58. Moffatt says it was "not earlier than 55 and not later than 57."[17] The preponderance of opinion is in favor of placing the date at A.D. 57. This is the date that seems most probable to us.

3. *Bearer.* There is no mention of the person who was the bearer of this epistle. It is obvious that Timothy was not the bearer, since Paul's instructions in the letter make it evident that he did not expect Timothy to arrive there until after they had received the letter (1 Cor. 16:10-11). Paul desired to have Apollos go to Corinth, but for some reason, possibly for fear that his presence might aggravate the party spirit in the church, he declined to go at that time (1 Cor. 16:12). It is probable that the delegation from Corinth (1 Cor. 16:17) took this letter with them when they returned home.

### THE PURPOSE OF 1 CORINTHIANS

From a study of its contents it is plain that Paul's purpose in writing this epistle was twofold, to correct the disorders existing in the church and to answer the questions that they had submitted to him. His method is to alternate between the faults of the church and his replies to their questions. Since their questions did not cover all the problems, the Apostle also included other matters that required his attention. The alternation between the two purposes in the epistle is evident.

1. *Church faults* (1:10–6:20). The first four chapters are devoted to the problem of their church factions, knowledge concerning which he had received from the house of Chloe (1:11). This is followed in the next two chapters by two matters that reveal moral delinquency in the church. The first of these is the case of gross immorality (5:1-13). The other is their litigations before pagan courts (6:1-11). Both of these problems arise out of their failure to apprehend the Christian truth concerning the sanctity of the body (6:12-20).

2. *Replies to questions* (7:1–11:1). With chapter seven the Apostle turns to the questions which they have submitted to him. The first question that he deals with concerns various aspects of the problem of marriage and celibacy (ch. 7). Next he gives an elaborate answer to the problem of eating meats sacrificed to idols (8:1–11:1).

3. *Church faults* (11:2-34). With 11:2 he again reverts to serious

17. James Moffatt, "The First Epistle of Paul to the Corinthians," *Moffatt Commentary,* (n.d), p. xv.

faults in the church about which he has been informed. First he deals with the problem of the behavior of the women in the worship service (2-16), and then he takes up the matter of their disorders in connection with the Lord's Supper (17-34).

4. *Reply to questions* (12:1–14:40). Chapters 12 to 14 are written in reply to their question about spiritual gifts. Recognizing their rich endowment of spiritual gifts (ch. 12), he shows that they must be governed by love (ch. 13) and points out that the two outstanding gifts, tongues and prophecy, must be used for the edification of all (ch. 14).

5. *Doctrinal fault* (15:1-58). He had heard that some among them are questioning the teaching about the resurrection of the body (15:12) and accordingly launches into an elaborate discussion of the matter.

6. *Reply to questions* (16:1-14). He had previously urged them to participate in the offering that was being raised for the saints in Judea. He now answers their question as to procedure in making up the offering.

The remainder of the concluding chapter is given over to an announcement of his plans of travel and other personal matters. In writing this epistle, Paul resisted the temptation to visit the Corinthians "with a rod" (4:21) and sought instead to give them an opportunity to correct these evils themselves. He therefore deliberately changed his plans to visit them in order to give them time to work out the difficulty. He studiously avoided the appearance of attempting to "have lordship over" their faith (2 Cor. 1:15-24).

### THE CHARACTERISTICS OF 1 CORINTHIANS

1. *Contents.* Of all the New Testament epistles only Romans is longer than 1 Corinthians. A glance at the outline of 1 Corinthians impresses one with the variety of subjects discussed. This varied material is dealt with in an orderly and logical manner that makes it comparatively easy to follow the line of thought.

Belonging to the Soteriological Group among the Pauline epistles, it is an illustration of the truth that no area in the believer's life is exempt from the salvation that is in Christ Jesus. "This is the epistle of the cross in its social application."[18] It reveals the burning desire

18. G. G. Findlay, "The First Epistle of Paul to the Corinthians," *Expositor's Greek Testament,* (n.d.), Vol. II, p. 739.

of the Apostle that the cross of Christ shall be applied to every problem in the Christian life. The intention of the epistle is intensely practical.

While the primary intention of the epistle was practical rather than doctrinal, yet it contains several passages of greatest doctrinal significance. The treatment of the Lord's Supper (11:17-34) is the fullest in the New Testament. The twelfth chapter contains a very valuable discussion concerning the local church as the Body of Christ, revealing that in essence it is "an organism rather than an organization."[19] Chapter 15 is an exhaustive development of the doctrine of the resurrection. The famous "hymn of love" in chapter 13 is the classic statement of the subject. F. F. Bruce remarks, "Above all, this letter emphasizes the surpassing power and worth of the love of God in human life; Christianity may survive in the absence of many valuable things, but it will die if love is absent."[20]

There are, further, a number of shorter passages of great doctrinal importance, such as the passage on the reactions to the word of the cross revealing human destiny (1:18-25), or the revelation that God will apply the fire test to the work of the builder (3:12-15).

2. *Style.* Williams says that the language of 1 Corinthians "is the simplest and most direct found in Paul's epistles."[21] The sentences are not as involved and complicated as in Galatians, 2 Corinthians, or Ephesians. Alford pays tribute to the language of this epistle in the following words:

> In style, this Epistle ranks perhaps the foremost of all as to sublimity, and earnest and impassioned eloquence. . . . About the whole Epistle there is a character of lofty and sustained solemnity,—an absence of tortuousness of construction, and an apologetic plainness, which contrast remarkably with the personal portions of the second Epistle.[22]

In this book some of the most sublime passages flow forth without effort as the Apostle pursues his purpose, and that in a letter in which he entirely repudiates all attempts at rhetoric as utterly inconsistent

19. C. K. Barrett, "A Commentary on the First Epistle to the Corinthians," *Harper's New Testament Commentaries,* (1968), p. 23.
20. F. F. Bruce, "Corinthians, First Epistle to the," *The Zondervan Pictorial Encyclopedia of the Bible,* (1975), Vol. I, p. 972.
21. Charles B. Williams, *An Introduction to New Testament Literature,* (1929) pp. 128-129.
22. Henry Alford, *The Greek Testament,* (1958), Vol. II, pp. 56-57 Proleg.

with the simplicity of the Gospel (2:1-5). This epistle offers a beautiful illustration of the unconscious character of true eloquence.

3. *Revelations.* This book is remarkable for the revelations that it makes both of the writer and the readers. It gives a remarkable revelation of Paul's self-control amid distressing conditions, and his practical wisdom in meeting such conditions. Paul wrote this epistle, he tells us, "out of much affliction and anguish of heart . . . with many tears" (2 Cor. 2:4).[23] Yet in writing it he restrained his feelings and wrote with a dignity and calm well calculated to achieve his purpose. It also reveals his practical wisdom in dealing with the most complex and perplexing problems in the Christian life. The answers given in this epistle reveal him to be a real spiritual statesman with profound wisdom and insight.

The letter also contains a distressing revelation of the interior life of an apostolic church. It forever dissipates the dream that churches founded and nurtured by the apostles were in an exceptional condition of holiness of life or purity of doctrine. Out of the sins and shortcomings of the Corinthian church our sovereign God has seen fit to give us one of the priceless treasures of the New Testament.

## An Outline of 1 Corinthians

THE INTRODUCTION (1:1-9)

1. The salutation (1-3)
   a. The writers (1)
   b. The readers (2)
   c. The greeting (3)
2. The thanksgiving (4-8)
   a. The nature of the thanksgiving (4a)
   b. The basis for the thanksgiving (4b)
   c. The object of the thanksgiving (5-8)
      1) The thanksgiving for their past enrichment (5-6)
      2) The thanksgiving for their present condition (7-8)
3. The affirmation (9)

23. This assumes that the reference is to our canonical 1 Corinthians, a view with which many modern scholars do not agree. See Donald Guthrie, *New Testament Introduction,* (Revised Ed., 1970), pp. 429-430. In support see Philip E. Hughes, "Paul's Second Epistle to the Corinthians," *The New International Commentary on the New Testament,* (1962), pp. 54-57; R. C. H. Lenski, *The Interpretation of St. Paul's First and Second Epistle to the Corinthians,* (1935), pp. 896-900.

I. CONCERNING CHURCH FACTIONS (1:10–4:21)

1. The reaction to the report of their factions (1:10-17)
    a. The appeal for Christian unity (10)
    b. The source of his information about their factions (11)
    c. The nature of their factions (12)
    d. The absurdity of their factions (13)
    e. The basis for their factions not in his work there (14-17)
        1) His work was not one of form (14-16)
        2) His work was preaching the Gospel (17)

2. The arguments against church factions (1:18–4:5)
    a. Their inconsistency with the nature of the Gospel (1:18–3:4)
        1) The Gospel is not worldly wisdom (1:18–2:5)
            a) The proof from the reactions to the Gospel (1:18-25)
                (1) The reaction to the cross reveal human fate (18)
                (2) The futility of worldly wisdom for salvation (19-21)
                    (a) The cross set aside human wisdom (19-20)
                    (b) The cross as the means of salvation (21)
                (3) The crucified Christ as God's wisdom and power (22-25)
                    (a) The types of worldly wisdom (22)
                    (b) The message of divine wisdom (23-25)
                        (i) The subject of Christian preaching (23a)
                        (ii) The reactions to the Christian message (23b-24)
                        (iii) The proof of God's superiority (25)
            b) The proof from the makeup of the church (1:26-31)
                (1) The recipients of God's call (26-29)
                    (a) The kind of whom not many are called (26)
                    (b) The things God does choose (27-29)
                (2) The significance of Christ to the called (30-31)
            c) The proof from his work among them (2:1-5)
                (1) The attitude in giving them God's message (1-2)
                (2) The manner of his work among them (3-4)
                (3) The purpose of his work among them (5)

2) The Gospel is heavenly wisdom (2:6–3:4)
  a) The recipients of this wisdom (2:6a)
  b) The nature of this wisdom (2:6b-12)
    (1) Negative—It is not the wisdom of this world (6b)
    (2) Positive—It is God's wisdom in a mystery (7-12)
      (a) It was previously hidden, but in God's plan (7b)
      (b) It was unknown to worldly wisdom (8-9)
      (c) It is revealed through the Spirit (10-12)
  c) The apprehension of this wisdom (2:13–3:4)
    (1) The manner of its transmission (2:13)
    (2) The people apprehending this wisdom (2:14-16)
      (a) The inability of the natural man (14)
      (b) The apprehension of the spiritual man (15-16)
    (3) The hindrances to its apprehension (3:1-4)
      (a) The fact of their carnality (1-3a)
      (b) The evidence of their carnality (3b-4)

b. Their inconsistency with the true view of ministers (3:5–4:5)
  1) The ministers as laborers in God's field (3:5-9)
    a) The function of ministers (5)
    b) The work of each under God's direction (6-7)
    c) The work and reward of the minister (8)
    d) The summary of the teaching (9)
  2) The ministers as builders of God's sanctuary (3:10-23)
    a) The work of the builder will be tested (10-15)
      (1) The foundation for the building (10-11)
      (2) The testing of the builder's work (12-15)
        (a) The building materials used (12)
        (b) The revelation of the work by fire (13)
        (c) The results of the fire test (14-15)
    b) The destruction of God's sanctuary divinely punished (16-17)
    c) The admonition concerning their view of ministers (18-23)
      (1) The false view is based on worldly wisdom (18-21a)

(2) The true view realizes that all are their possession (21b-23)
3) The ministers as stewards of the mysteries of God (4:1-5)
a) The view to be taken of ministers (1)
b) The demand for faithfulness in the steward (2)
c) The Lord as the Judge of His steward (3-4)
d) The appeal to withhold judgment till the Lord comes (5)
3. The Apostle's appeal to the Corinthians (4:6-21)
a. The application of the argument to their divisions (6-13)
1) The purpose in the application (6)
2) The failure to recognize talents as gifts (7)
3) The resultant false self-estimation (8)
4) The contrasted experiences of the apostles (9-13)
a) The lowly position of the apostles (9)
b) The contrast between them and the Corinthians (10)
c) The description of their labors and experiences (11-13)
b. The appeal to them to follow his example (14-17)
1) His aim in writing to them (14)
2) His relation to them as their spiritual father (15-16)
3) His reason for the sending of Timothy to them (17)
c. The warning that their attitude will determine his action (18-21)
1) The puffed-up attitude of some (18)
2) The fact of his coming to Corinth (19-21)

II. CONCERNING MORAL DELINQUENCIES IN THE CHURCH (5:1–6:20)

1. The case of gross immorality (5:1-13)
a. The discipline of the incestuous person (1-8)
1) The nature of the sin (1)
2) The failure of the church to act (2)
3) The judgment of the guilty person (3-5)
a) The judgment of the Apostle in his absence (3)
b) The formal judgment to be passed on him (4-5)
4) The appeal to the church to act (6-8)
a) The rebuke of their attitude (6)

b) The appeal to remove the evil (7a)
c) The argument from their position (7b-8)
b. The general principle in handling such cases (9-13)
1) The interpretation of his former instructions (9-11)
a) The contents of the instructions (9)
b) The meaning of the instructions (10-11)
2) The call to act upon this principle (12-13)
2. The evil of their litigations before pagan courts (6:1-11)
a. The brazenness of their litigations (1)
b. The reasons for settling their grievances in the Church (2-6)
1) Because of the Church's future work of judging (2-3)
2) Because their lawsuits set up unqualified judges (4-5a)
3) Because it shows the Church's failure to exercise judgment (5b-6)
c. The results of their litigations (7-8)
d. The warning against unrighteousness (9-11)
1) The exclusion of the unrighteous from the Kingdom (9-10)
2) The position of the redeemed as inconsistent with sin (11)
3. The sanctity of the body (6:12-20)
a. The limitation upon Christian liberty (12)
b. The application of the principle in two areas (13-14)
1) The application to foods (13a)
2) The application to sex (13b-14)
c. The sanctity of the body to prevent its sinful use (15-20)
1) The nature of the believer's body forbids fornication (15)
2) The contrast between the two unions (16-17)
3) The admonition to flee fornication (18a)
4) The nature of the sin of fornication (18b)
5) The Christian view and use of the body (19-20)

III. CONCERNING MARRIAGE (In Answer to Their Letter) (7:1-40)

1. The problem of marriage and celibacy (1-9)
a. The approval of the celibate life (1b)
b. The instructions concerning the married life (2-6)
1) The reason for the preferability of marriage (2a)

2) The nature of the marriage relation (2b)
3) The duties in the marriage relation (3-4)
4) The mutual regulation of sex relations (5-6)

c. The recognition of both marriage and celibacy as proper (7)
d. The advice of the Apostle to the unmarried (8-9)

2. The problem of marriage and separation (10-16)
   a. The charge to Christian couples (10-11)
      1) The authority for the charge (10a)
      2) The contents of the change (10b-11)
   b. The charge to those of mixed marriages (12-16)
      1) The nature of the charge (12a)
      2) The contents of the charge (12b-16)
         a) The separation not to be caused by the believer (12b-14)
            (i) The duty of the believing partner (12b-13)
            (ii) The reason for the duty (14)
         b) The separation when caused by the unbeliever (15-16)
3. The Christian life and one's earthly station (17-24)
   a. The basic principle of life for the convert (17)
   b. The application of the principle to life (18-24)
      1) The principle applied to former religious distinctions (18-20)
         a) The attitude toward these religious distinctions (18)
         b) The reason for the attitude suggested (19)
         c) The restatement of the principle (20)
      2) The principle applied to the social status of believers (21-24)
         a) The illustrations of social status (21-22)
         b) The true position for believers (23)
         c) The restatement of the principle (24)
4. The advice concerning the unmarried (25-40)
   a. The advice concerning virgins (25-35)
      1) The nature of his advice to them (25)
      2) The substance of his advice to them (26-27)
      3) The hard times as the reason for the advice (28-31)
         a) The entry into marriage is not wrong (28a)
         b) The entry into marriage increases one's cares (28b)

c) The Christian to be free from domination by temporal things (29-31)
4) The resultant freedom as the advantage in the advice (32-34)
a) The statement of his desire for them (32a)
b) The contrasted cares of the single and the married (32b-34)
5) The motive in giving the advice (35)
b. The advice to parents of marriageable daughters (36-38)
1) The conditions when marriage should be permitted (36)
2) The conditions when permission to marry should not be given (37)
3) The assertion that both are proper (38)
c. The advice to widows (39-40)

## IV. CONCERNING FOOD OFFERED TO IDOLS (8:1–11:1)

1. The relationship of love to knowledge (8:1-13)
a. The need for love with knowledge (1-3)
b. The consideration of the claim to liberty through knowledge (4-8)
1) The truth in their argument for liberty to eat (4-6)
a) The fact that an idol has no real existence (4)
b) The fact that Christians recognize only one God (5-6)
2) The danger to the weak brother in their argument (7)
3) The fact that food does not determine relation to God (8)
c. The warning against causing the weak brother to sin (9-12)
1) The warning to those with knowledge (9)
2) The illustration of the effect of his knowledge (10)
3) The consequences of acting on his knowledge (11-12)
d. The voluntary restriction of personal liberty (13)
2. The Apostle's example of the voluntary restriction of liberties (9:1-27)
a. His authority as an apostle (1-3)
b. His rights as an apostle (4-12a)
1) The indication of the rights being claimed (4-6)
2) The recognition of these rights in other fields (7)

3) The justification of his claim to these rights (8-12a)
  a) The justification from Scripture (8-10)
    (i) The questions about these rights (8)
    (ii) The quotation about these rights (9a)
    (iii) The directive applied to the worker's right (9b-10)
  b) The justification from his labors among them (11-12a)

c. His reasons for waiving these rights (12b-23)
  1) Because he would not hinder the Gospel (12b-14)
    a) The fact that he waived these rights (12b)
    b) The reason for not using his rights (12c)
    c) The validation of these rights (13-14)
  2) Because it gives him a ground for boasting (15-18)
    a) The fact that he waived these rights (15a)
    b) The determination not to use these rights (15b)
    c) The ground for his glorying explained (16-18)
      (i) The compulsion upon him to preach the Gospel (16)
      (ii) The condition under which he labors (17)
      (iii) The determination to get a reward (18)
  3) Because it enables him to win more to Christ (19-23)
    a) The statement of his principle of action (19)
    b) The illustration of the principle in conduct (20-22)
    c) The motive for his conduct (23)

d. His appeal for them to follow his example (24-27)
  1) The appeal to them to run victoriously (24-25)
  2) The Apostle's example of exercising self-control (26-27)

3. The history of Israel a warning against abuse of liberty (10:1-13)
  a. The reminder of Israel's history (1-5)
    1) The privileges of Israel (1-4)
    2) The fate of Israel (5)
  b. The warnings from the history of Israel (6-11)
    1) The lessons contained in Israel's history (6-10)
      a) The general warning against lusting (6)
      b) The specific instances from their example (7-10)
    2) The significance of Israel's experiences (11)

c. The consequent admonitions to those under testing (12-13)
1) The admonition to realize the danger of falling (12)
2) The encouragement to those being tempted to fall (13)

4. The appeal to avoid idolatry as inconsistent with Christianity (10:14-22)
a. The admonition to flee from idolatry (14)
b. The argument to the strong against participation (15-20)
1) The recipients of the argument (15)
2) The illustrations of the significance of participation (16-18)
a) The participation in the Lord's Supper (16-17)
b) The participation in the Old Testament sacrifices (18)
3) The application of the principle to idol feasts (19-20a)
4) The reasons for avoiding idolatry (20b-22)

5. The summary of general principles for governing their conduct (10:23–11:1)
a. The statement of basic considerations (23-24)
1) The limitations upon Christian liberty (23)
2) The proper consideration for others (24)
b. The instructions concerning meats sold for food (25-30)
1) The instructions to those eating at home (25-26)
2) The instructions to those eating out with unbelievers (27-30)
a) The normal attitude to be assumed (27)
b) The circumstances under which to refrain from eating (28-30)
c. The concluding admonitions on the subject (10:31–11:1)
1) The admonition to do all to God's glory (31)
2) The admonition to maintain proper relations to all men (32-33)
3) The admonition to follow the apostolic example (11:1)

V. CONCERNING DISORDERS IN PUBLIC WORSHIP (11:2–14:40)

1. The consideration of the veiling of women (11:2-16)
a. The apostolic praise for their obedience (2)
b. The argument from the principle of subordination (3-6)

1) The statement of the principle of subordination (3)
2) The application of the principle of subordination (4-6)
   a) The principle applied to the man (4)
   b) The principle applied to the woman (5-6)

c. The enforcement of the principle of subordination (7-15)
1) The enforcement from the creative relation (7-12)
   a) The statement of the creative relation (7-10)
   b) The mutual relation in the Lord (11-12)
2) The enforcement from the instinct of propriety (13-15)
   a) The questions about propriety (13-14)
   b) The assertion about the woman's hair (15)

d. The termination of the argument (16)

2. The disorders in connection with the Lord's Supper (11:17-34)

a. The Corinthian disorders at the Lord's Supper (17-22)
1) The withholding of the apostolic praise (17)
2) The nature of their disorders (18-21)
   a) The report of their divisions in the Church (18-19)
   b) The description of their disorders at the Lord's Supper (20-21)
3) The rebuke for their disorders at the Lord's Supper (22)

b. The institution of the Lord's Supper (23-26)
1) The revelation concerning the Lord's Supper (23a)
2) The manner of institution of the Lord's Supper (23b-25)
3) The meaning of the Lord's Supper (26)

c. The consequences of disorderly participation in the Lord's Supper (27-32)
1) The significance of participation in an unworthy manner (27)
2) The procedure for participation in a worthy manner (28)
3) The result of participation in an unworthy manner (29-32)
   a) The statement of the result (29)
   b) The manifestations of the result (30)
   c) The obviation of the result (31)
   d) The divine intention in the result (32)

d. The suggestions for observing the Lord's Supper (33-34a)

e. The further ordering upon his arrival (34b)

3. The problem concerning spiritual gifts in the Church (12:1–14:40)

- a. The rich endowment of the gifts (12:1-31)
  - 1) The test of the Spirit (1-3)
    - a) The apostolic desire for them to be informed (1)
    - b) The reminder of their past condition (2)
    - c) The test for one speaking in the Spirit (3)
  - 2) The diversity of the gifts (4-11)
    - a) The common source behind the diversity (4-6)
    - b) The purpose of the gifts (7)
    - c) The examples of the diverse gifts (8-10)
    - d) The Spirit as the source of all gifts (11)
  - 3) The nature of the Body of Christ (12-13)
    - a) The unity of the Body (12)
    - b) The entrance into the Body (13)
  - 4) The harmony in the Body (14-26)
    - a) The structure of the Body as of many members (14)
    - b) The disruption of the harmony in the Body (15-24a)
      - (i) The disruption through the self-depreciation of the members (15-20)
        - (a) The illustration of the broken harmony (15-16)
        - (b) The correction of the disruption (17-20)
          - (aa) The corrective questions (17)
          - (bb) The corrective facts (18-20)
      - (ii) The disruption through depreciation of other members (21-24a)
        - (a) The illustrations of the depreciation (21)
        - (b) The correction of the depreciation (22-24a)
    - c) The realization of the harmony of the Body (24b-26)
  - 5) The identification of the Body (27)
  - 6) The differing functions of the members (28-31)
    - a) The varied functions enumerated (28)
    - b) The distribution of the functions (29-30)
    - c) The attitude enjoined upon the members (31)
- b. The vitalization of the gifts (13:1-13)
  - 1) The necessity for love in the exercise of the gifts (1-3)
    - a) The need for love with the gift of tongues (1)
    - b) The need for love with superior gifts (2)
    - c) The need for love with benevolence (3)

- 2) The characteristics of love (4-7)
  - a) The essential nature of love (4a)
  - b) The negative characteristics of love (4b-6a)
  - c) The positive characteristics of love (6b-7)
- 3) The permanence of love (8-13)
  - a) The assertion of love's permanence (8a)
  - b) The comparison of love with passing things (8b-12)
    - (i) The examples of passing things (8b)
    - (ii) The reason for their cessation (9-10)
    - (iii) The illustration from personal development (11)
    - (iv) The appliction of the illustration (12)
  - c) The superiority of love among permanent things (13)

c. The proper use of the gifts (14:1-40)
- 1) The comparative value of tongues and prophecy (1-25)
  - a) The comparison of their value in the Church (1-19)
    - (i) The advice concerning spiritual gifts (1)
    - (ii) The argument concerning tongues and prophecy (2-6)
      - (a) The contrasted nature of the two (2-4)
      - (b) The argument from the contrast (5-6)
    - (iii) The teaching concerning tongues through illustrations (7-13)
      - (a) The illustrations from musical instruments (7-9)
        - (aa) The illustrations used (7-8)
        - (bb) The application made (9)
      - (b) The illustrations from different voices (10-13)
        - (aa) The illustration used (10-11)
        - (bb) The exhortation made (12-13)
    - (iv) The Apostle's use of tongues and prophecy (14-19)
      - (a) His determination to use both in worship (14-15)
      - (b) His reminder that edification is the aim (16-17)
      - (c) His preference for prophecy in the Church (18-19)

b) The comparison of the function to non-believers (20-25)
(i) The appeal for mental maturity (20)
(ii) The sign value of tongues and prophecy (21-22)
(iii) The effect of tongues and prophecy on non-believers (23-25)
(a) The effect of tongues (23)
(b) The effect of prophecy (24-25)
2) The orderly employment of tongues and prophecy (26-36)
a) The principle of orderliness in worship (26)
b) The specific instructions concerning their services (27-36)
(i) The instructions as to tongues and interpretation (27-28)
(ii) The instructions as to prophecy and revelation (29-33a)
(a) The orderly procedure in prophesying (29)
(b) The self-control in the use of prophecy (30-33a)
(iii) The restrictions on women in the worship service (33b-36)
(a) The restriction placed on women (33b-34)
(b) The provision for their information (35)
(c) The rebuke to the Corinthian arrogance (36)
3) The concluding statements (37-40)
a) The authentication of the instructions (37-38)
b) The concluding admonitions on the subject (39-40)

VI. CONCERNING THE RESURRECTION (15:1-58)

1. The Gospel of Christ's resurrection (1-11)
a. The proclamation and reception of the Gospel (1-2)
b. The essential nature of the Gospel (3-4)
c. The witnesses to the resurrection of Christ (5-10)
d. The summary statement of the section (11)
2. The necessity of Christ's resurrection (12-34)
a. The necessity of His resurrection for salvation (12-19)

- 1) The denial of a resurrection by some of them (12)
- 2) The consequences of the denial of a resurrection (13-19)
  - a) The first series of consequences of the denial (13-15)
  - b) The second series of consequences of the denial (16-18)
  - c) The summary statement of the consequences (19)

b. The necessity of His resurrection in God's program (20-28)
- 1) The historic pledge for the program (20)
- 2) The divine provision to achieve the program (21-22)
- 3) The divine order in the program (23-28)
  - a) The resurrection of Christ as the firstfruits (23a)
  - b) The resurrection of those who are Christ's at His coming (23b)
  - c) The final consummation of the program (24-28)
    - (i) The nature of the consummation (24a)
    - (ii) The conditions for the consummation (24b-26)
    - (iii) The personal subjection of the Son (27-28)

c. The necessity of His resurrection for present Christian conduct (29-34)
- 1) The question concerning baptism for the dead (29)
- 2) The question concerning the jeopardizing of our lives (30-34)
  - a) The consequent foolishness of such conduct (30-32)
  - b) The rebuke deserved by them (33-34)

3. The prospect of the Christian's resurrection (35-57)

a. The nature of the resurrection body (35-49)
- 1) The objector's questions about the resurrection body (35)
- 2) The answer concerning the resurrection body (36-49)
  - a) The analogy of the resurrection (36-41)
    - (i) The illustration from the plant (36-38)
    - (ii) The variety in the work of God (39-41)
      - (a) The varieties of flesh (39)
      - (b) The varieties of bodies (40-41)
  - b) The application to the resurrection body (42-49)
    - (i) The contrast between the natural and spiritual body (42-44)
    - (ii) The contrast between the first and the last Adam (45-49)

(a) The statement of the contrast (45)
(b) The order of the two (46)
(c) The details in the contrast (47-49)

b. The change that produces the resurrection body (50-57)
   1) The condition necessitating the change (50)
   2) The nature of the change (51-52)
      a) The revelation concerning the change (51a)
      b) The description of the change (51b-52)
   3) The imperative of the change (53)
   4) The triumph of the resurrection change (54-57)
      a) The victory over death (54)
      b) The challenge to vanquished death (55-56)
      c) The source of the victory (57)

4. The concluding appeal for steadfastness (58)

## VII. CONCERNING PRACTICAL AND PERSONAL MATTERS (16:1-24)

1. The instructions for raising the collection (1-4)
   a. The instructions also given to the Galatian churches (1)
   b. The method to be used in the collecting of the money (2)
   c. The transmission of the collection (3-4)
2. The information concerning contemplated visits to Corinth (5-12)
   a. The communication concerning his own visit to them (5-9)
      1) His plans for coming to Corinth (5-7)
         a) The route he will travel (5)
         b) The time he intends to stay (6)
         c) The reason for the plans (7)
      2) His present tarrying at Ephesus (8-9)
   b. The instructions concerning the visit of Timothy (10-11)
   c. The information concerning a visit of Apollos (12)
3. The concluding admonitions to the Corinthians (13-14)
4. The acknowledgment of the representatives from Corinth (15-18)
   a. The appeal concerning the house of Stephanas (15-16)
   b. The statement about the coming of the three representatives (17-18)

5. The concluding salutations (19-24)
   a. The salutations from others (19-20)
      1) The salutations from those with him (19-20a)
      2) The mutual salutations to be given (20b)
   b. The salutation from Paul himself (21-24)
      1) The authentication (21)
      2) The double warning (22)
      3) The benediction (23)
      4) The affection (24)

## A Book List on 1 Corinthians

Barclay, William, "The Letters to the Corinthians," *The Daily Study Bible.* Philadelphia: The Westminster Press (1956).

Uses author's own translation. Especially valuable for the historical background material presented. Good word studies and various illustrations.

Barrett, C. K., "A Commentary on the First Epistle to the Corinthians." *Harper's New Testament Commentaries.* New York: Harper & Row (1968).

A fresh translation by the author. A thorough and valuable modern treatment of I Corinthians with special attention to the Greek text. The work of a capable critical exegete whose low view of inspiration allows him to disparage the historical evidence for Christ's resurrection and stamp Paul's picture of the eschatological end as "mythological."

Beet, Joseph Agar, *A Commentary on St. Paul's Epistles to the Corinthians.* London: Hodder and Stoughton (1882).

A clear and full interpretation by a British Methodist scholar of the past century. Its doctrinal summaries are intended as a contribution to systematic theology.

Boyer, James L., *For a World like Ours. Studies in I Corinthians.* Grand Rapids: Baker Book House (1971).

A well-outlined, brief exposition intended to guide laymen in the study of this letter. A stimulating conservative interpretation by a professor of Greek and New Testament. Divides the letter into its natural divisions, with questions for discussion at the end of each section. Includes maps and some photographs of scenes of historical significance in connection with Corinth.

Bruce, F. F., "1 and 2 Corinthians," *New Century Bible, Based on the Revised Standard Version.* London: Oliphants (1971).

A verse-by-verse analysis of the English text, always related to the Greek. Offers a structural analysis of the epistles. Valuable discussion of modern views concerning the "Corinthian correspondence." Frequent references in the discussion to further literature.

Edwards, Thomas Charles, *A Commentary on the First Epistle to the Corinthians*. London: Hodder and Stoughton (1885).

Greek text. An exhaustive exposition by an independent, evangelical British scholar of the past century.

Erdman, Charles R., *The First Epistle of Paul to the Corinthians*. Philadelphia: The Westminster Press (1928).

A brief conservative exposition by a Presbyterian professor of the past generation. Well adapted to the non-professional Bible student.

Findlay, G. G., "The First Epistle of Paul to the Corinthians," *The Expositor's Greek Testament*. Vol. II. (1900). Grand Rapids: Wm. B. Eerdmans Pub. Co. (reprint, n.d.).

A thorough commentary on the Greek text by an evangelical Methodist scholar of the past generation. Characterized by a thorough grasp of Pauline thought in the epistle. For the advanced student.

Godet, F., *Commentary on the First Epistle of St. Paul to the Corinthians*. Translated from the French by A. Cusin. Two vols. Grand Rapids: Zondervan Publishing House (1957 reprint of the 1886 edition).

An exhaustive technical commentary by a conservative French scholar of the past century. Valuable for its exegesis and warm spiritual views but weak and out of date in matters of textual criticism.

Goudge, H. L., "The First Epistle to the Corinthians." *Westminster Commentaries*. London: Methuen & Co. (Revised Ed., 1911).

A very helpful commentary aimed at meeting the needs of the theological student and the clergy by an evangelical British scholar. Various added notes supplement the concise comments on the individual verses.

Grosheide, F. W., "Commentary on the First Epistle to the Corinthians." *The New International Commentary on the New Testament*. Grand Rapids: Wm. B. Eerdmans Pub. Co. (1953).

An informative exposition by a Dutch scholar in the Reformed tradition holding that the main thrust of the epistle is against the spiritually proud who insist on their own right. Not up to the standard of excellence of other volumes in this series.

Heading, John, *First Epistle to the Corinthians*. Kilmarnock, Scotland: John Ritchie (1965).

A thorough, verse-by-verse conservative exposition with emphasis on the structural organization of the epistle. Holds that Paul's speaking in tongues meant his use of Greek. Premillennial in its eschatology. Refreshingly independent, the work of a British Plymouth Brethren minister of the Word.

Hodge, Charles, *An Exposition of the First Epistle to the Corinthians.* (1857). Grand Rapids: Wm. B. Eerdmans Pub. Co. (1950 reprint).

A comprehensive verse-by-verse exposition by a noted Calvinistic theologian of the past century. Valuable for its doctrinal emphasis.

Ironside, H. A., *Addresses on the First Epistle to the Corinthians.* New York: Loizeaux Brothers (1952).

A series of 39 expository addresses by a well-known Bible teacher-pastor covering the entire epistle. Practical and informative lectures with numerous pertinent illustrations. Premillennial in emphasis.

Kelly, William, *Notes on the First Epistle of Paul the Apostle to the Corinthians with a New Translation.* (1882). London: G. Morrish (reprint, n.d.).

An independent, conservative exposition by a Plymouth Brethren scholar of the past century. The footnotes deal mostly with manuscript evidence for variant textual readings.

Kling, Christian Friedrich, "The Epistles of Paul the Apostle to the Corinthians." John Peter Lange, *Commentary on the Holy Scriptures.* Translated from the German, with additions, by D. W. Poor (1868). Grand Rapids: Zondervan Publishing House (reprint, n.d.).

A voluminous conservative Lutheran exposition. The epistles are divided into convenient paragraphs, with the material under each section appearing in three parts, exegetical and critical, doctrinal and ethical, homiletical and practical. Contains much rich ore to be mined by those willing to dig into its closely printed pages.

Lenski, R. C. H., *The Interpretation of St. Paul's First and Second Epistle to the Corinthians.* Columbus, Ohio: Lutheran Book Concern (1935).

Uses the author's own literal translation. A monumental work (1,383 pages) of evangelical scholarship by an Amillennial Lutheran scholar. Offers many significant word studies in unfolding the meaning of the epistles. Strongly defends the unity of 2 Corinthians. Indispensable for the serious student.

Luck, G. Coleman, "First Corinthians," *Everyman's Bible Commentary.* Chicago: Moody Press (1958).

A clear, non-technical study of the epistle, concentrating on major thoughts, problem passages, and practical applications. Well suited for home Bible-study classes or other adult groups.

Moffatt, James, "The First Epistle of Paul to the Corinthians." *The Moffatt New Testament Commentary.* New York: Harper & Brothers (n.d.).

Based on Moffatt's own translation. A critical exposition by a liberal British scholar of note. Helpful for its treatment of critical problems raised by a close study of the text.

Morgan, G. Campbell, *The Corinthian Letters of Paul. An Exposition of I and II Corinthians.* New York: Fleming H. Revell (1956).

Carefully outlined pulpit expositions by a noted expository preacher. Reflects the fervent devotional approach of the preacher in dealing with the problems that plague the Church.

Morris, Leon, "The First Epistle of Paul to the Corinthians." *The Tyndale New Testament Commentaries.* Grand Rapids: Wm. B. Eerdmans Pub. Co. (1958).

Based on the King James text. A compact, accurate, verse-by-verse exposition, always related to the Greek, by a well-known conservative scholar. Well suited to the church Bible teacher.

Robertson, Archibald, and Plummer, Alfred, "A Critical and Exegetical Commentary on the First Epistle of St. Paul to the Corinthians." *The International Critical Commentary.* 2d Ed. (1914). Edinburgh: T. & T. Clark (1953 reprint).

Greek text. Important introduction and a very thorough treatment of the Greek text, bringing out its finer shades of meaning. Essential for the careful student of the original text.

Shetler, Sanford G., "Paul's Letter to the Corinthians 55 A.D." *Compact Commentary Series.* Harrisonburg, Va.: Christian Light Publications (1971).

Uses the King James Version. A brief exposition from a firm conservative viewpoint. The concise treatment is specially suited to the lay reader. As a member of the Mennonite brotherhood, the author devotes 25 of 150 pages to 1 Cor. 11:1-16 concerning the veiling of women, which is accepted as a universal teaching for all the Church.

Vine, W. E., *1 Corinthians.* London: Oliphants (1951).

Uses the English Revised Version. A verse-by-verse exposition, always relating to the Greek text, by a late British Plymouth Brethren scholar. Combines scholarly insight with simplicity of diction and spiritual warmth. Does not deal with introductory problems.

# 9

# SECOND CORINTHIANS

## An Introduction to 2 Corinthians

Second Corinthians is the most autobiographical of all of Paul's epistles. In it he bares his heart and life as in none of his other writings. This prominent personal element in 2 Corinthians makes it especially valuable for an understanding of the character of the Apostle. Yet its very wealth of personal references creates difficulty for the interpreter.

### THE UNITY OF 2 CORINTHIANS

It is the unity of 2 Corinthians, rather than its authenticity, that is brought into question by the critics. The Pauline authorship of 2 Corinthians in its entirety has been all but universally accepted.[1] External evidence amply asserts it. The contents of the epistle are so manifestly Pauline in character as to compel its acceptance as such. But on the question of the unity of the epistle, modern scholarship is sharply divided. With no other Pauline epistle does the critical dexterity in the speculative dissection of Biblical documents come into fuller operation than in 2 Corinthians.

1. *Phenomena.* The common view of Christendom has always been that the epistle is a unity. Not until modern times has this view been challenged. In 1776 Semler hit upon the idea that the last four chapters were not an integral part of the epistle. This hypothesis, however, did not attract serious attention until much later. But today the various hypotheses have exhausted about every possibility.

The external evidence is wholly against any dissection of the letter. No manuscript, version, or Church Father gives any indication that

1. Only the radical Dutch school of critics has rejected it.

the epistle ever existed in a form which lacked part of the present epistle or that any one of its parts ever existed apart from the rest. 2 Corinthians reveals nothing of the textual phenomena seen in connection with Romans 15 and 16 or John 7:53–8:11. All attacks upon the unity of 2 Corinthians are based solely upon internal grounds.

Even a casual reading of 2 Corinthians reveals that the epistle consists of three main parts, each clearly marked off from the other. The first seven chapters contain the Apostle's defense of his conduct and his ministry. The second unit, chapters 8 and 9, deals with the offering being raised by the Apostle in his churches for the poor saints in Judea. Chapters 10 to 13 form the third segment of the epistle and contain the great invective of the Apostle against his enemies and their followers. The distinctness of these three sections has always been recognized, yet it is the very distinctness of these parts that has given rise to an avalanche of hypotheses as attempts to explain the phenomena.

2. *Critical theory.* The divergent views of the scholars about 2 Corinthians arise out of the attempt to bridge the gap between the First and the Second Epistle. That this is no simple task is readily admitted. Plummer pictures it thus:

> The transition from the region of 1 Corinthians to that of 2 Corinthians has been compared to the passage from the clear, if somewhat intricate, paths of a laid-out park into the obscurity of a trackless forest. The vegetation is still much the same; but it is no longer easy to find one's way through it.[2]

It is evident from a reading of 2 Corinthians, especially the last four chapters, that since the writing of 1 Corinthians there has been a great increase in the opposition to Paul's authority at Corinth. But the events connected with this increased opposition are not so clear. The only event in the interval between the two epistles that can be established without any possibility of dispute is the visit of Titus to Corinth to rectify the situation by inducing the rebellious party to submit (2 Cor. 2:12-13; 7:6-15). But from the text of 2 Corinthians several other events have been postulated.

In the effort to reconstruct the course of events between the two epistles, the critical theory posits the ocurrence of several other hap-

2. A. Plummer, "The Second Epistle of Paul the Apostle to the Corinthians," *Cambridge Greek Testament,* (1912), p. xiv.

penings. Here only the general positions in the critical theory can be indicated without giving all the variations in the hypotheses.[3]

From 2 Corinthians 12:14 and 13:1 it is correctly inferred that at the time Paul wrote 2 Corinthians he was going to Corinth for the *third* time. The question is when the second trip was made to Corinth. Acts is silent about that trip. The traditional view placed this second visit before the writing of 1 Corinthians, but recent scholars generally place this visit between First and Second Corinthians.[4] Paul made this visit, it is held, because a serious crisis had arisen in the Corinthian church which Timothy, sent there by Paul, had been unable to handle. Judaizing emissaries from Palestine had arrived and were fomenting opposition to Paul (2 Cor. 10:7; 11:23, etc.). From Ephesus Paul made a short and painful visit to Corinth during which he was grossly insulted by some Corinthian (2 Cor. 2:1; 12:14; 2:5-8; 7:12). This hypothesis is erected on the inference contained in Paul's statement in 2:1 that he is determined "not to come *again* to you with *sorrow*" and on the belief that the offender of 2 Corinthians 2:5-11 is not the incestuous person of 1 Corinthians 5:1-8. Unable to cope with the situation, it is held, perhaps because of sickness, Paul hurried back to Ephesus deeply grieved.

From Ephesus, the theory continues, Paul sent Titus back to Corinth with a severe letter (2 Cor. 2:3-4; 7:8, 12). This "tear letter" is postulated from Paul's statement in 2 Corinthians 2:4, "For out of much affliction and anguish of heart I wrote unto you with many tears." This intermediate letter is necessary since the critics cannot see these tears in our 1 Corinthians. It is categorically asserted that "1 Corinthians is not the letter written with many tears."[5] *One* main topic of this letter, it is held, was the Apostle's demand that the Corinthian church should punish the insulting offender.[6]

Two views as to the fate of this severe letter are held. One view is

3. See the position as presented by A. Plummer, "The Second Epistle of Paul the Apostle to the Corinthians," *Cambridge Greek Testament,* (1912), pp. xiv-xx; xxxiv-xliv; R. H. Strachan, *The Second Epistle of Paul to the Corinthians,* (1935), pp. xiv-xxii, xxxix-xl; Edgar J. Goodspeed, *An Introduction to the New Testament,* (1937), pp. 55-68; T. Henshaw, *New Testament Literature in the Light of Modern Scholarship,* (1957), pp. 241-247.
4. Kirsopp Lake and Silva Lake, *An Introduction to the New Testament,* (1938), p. 120; Werner Georg Kümmel, *Introduction to the New Testament,* (1966), pp. 207-208.
5. Edgar J. Goodspeed, *An Introduction to the New Testament,* (1937), p. 57.
6. A. Plummer, "The Second Epistle of Paul the Apostle to the Corinthians," *Cambridge Greek Testament,* (1912 reprint), p. xv.

that this letter, like the one before 1 Corinthians, has been entirely lost. Others insist that a considerable portion of this letter is preserved for us in 2 Corinthians 10:1–13:10. This latter view, of course, splits the unity of 2 Corinthians.

It is this severe letter, we are told, that Paul regretted writing and the possible outcome of which caused him such great mental distress (2 Cor. 7:5-9). It was the report of the favorable effect of this severe letter that caused Paul to write his fourth letter to the Corinthians, namely the first nine chapters of our 2 Corinthians.

Some critics make a further attack on the unity of 2 Corinthians by insisting that 2 Corinthians 6:14–7:1 is an interpolation. It is then held to be a fragment of an earlier letter, perhaps part of the letter mentioned in 1 Corinthians 5:9.[7]

3. *Reactions.* Admittedly the effort to reconstruct the background for 2 Corinthians is beset with difficulties. Yet one cannot help but feel that this complex reconstruction of events is based upon a number of ingenious suppositions that are incapable of proof.

It seems that the logical procedure would be to attempt to explain, as far as possible, the Second Epistle in the light of the First. The effort to understand the events between the two epistles should be based on the assumption of the close connection between the two. Instead of manufacturing new cases and diverse situations from the casual references in 2 Corinthians, it is natural and justifiable to try to explain the Second Letter, as far as possible, out of the First. Of the relationship between the two epistles Denney says,

> This close connection is not a hypothesis, of greater or less probability, like so much that figures in Introductions to the Second Epistle; it is a large and solid fact, which is worth more for our guidance than the most ingenious conjectural combination.[8]

Instances of this close connection may be noted. Thus, the events described in 2 Corinthians 1:8-10; 2:12-13 attach themselves immediately to the situation described in 1 Corinthians 16:7-9. Paul was at Ephesus when the First Epistle was written. According to the

7. See R. H. Strachan, "The Second Epistle of Paul to the Corinthians," *Moffatt Commentary,* (1935), p. xv, following the lead of James Moffatt in *The New Testament, A New Translation,* (n.d.), p. 274, note. Or Ernest Findlay Scott, *The Literature of the New Testament,* (1932), pp. 130, 131.
8. James Denney, "The Second Epistle to the Corinthians," *Expositor's Bible,* (1903), p. 1.

plan announced in 1 Corinthians, he proceeded to Troas, but due to the non-appearance of Titus, he could not rest, so went on to Macedonia. There Titus met him with the welcome news that caused the writing of 2 Corinthians.

More explicit is the connection between 2 Corinthians 1:13-17, 23 and 1 Corinthians 16:5-6. Previous to 1 Corinthians Paul had announced his intention of giving Corinth a double visit while on his way to and from Macedonia. But the troubled conditions in Corinth caused him to change the plans for their sake. This change in plans, announced in 1 Corinthians 16:5, was seized upon by his critics as a sign of fickleness. Accordingly, in the Second Epistle Paul found it necessary to defend himself against the charge and to explain the reasons for the change in plans (2 Cor. 1:23–2:4).

Denney further cites a number of close correspondences between the two epistles and concludes by saying,

> The coincidences in detail would be very striking under any circumstances; but in combination with the fact that the two Epistles, as has just been shown by the explanation of the change of purpose about the journey, are in the closest connection with each other they seem to me to come as nearly as possible to demonstration.[9]

If this close connection between the two epistles can be accepted, it removes the ground for most of the hypothetical reconstructions of the critical view. Then the letter to which Paul refers in 2 Corinthians 2:4 and 7:8, 12 is our First Corinthians. Likewise the offender in 2 Corinthians 2:5-11 and 7:12 is then to be identified with the offender of 1 Corinthians 5:1-8.

But the critics assert that the letter mentioned in 1 Corinthians 2:4 cannot be our 1 Corinthians. Paul says that he wrote it "with many tears," but the critics fail to find the tears in 1 Corinthians of which Paul speaks. They assert that the contents of that epistle cannot be described as having been particularly painful to Paul or hurtful to the Corinthians' feelings.[10] Therefore another letter, a severe letter, must be postulated. But this is a failure to understand the true nature of 1 Corinthians. While it is true that the tears do not lie openly on the surface of 1 Corinthians, conditions in Corinth, as revealed in that

9. *Ibid.*, p. 3.
10. Edgar J. Goodspeed, *An Introduction to the New Testament*, (1937), p. 57. For the different views see Donald Guthrie, *New Testament Introduction*, (Revised Ed., 1970), pp. 429-438.

epistle, were sad enough to depress the heart of any spiritual Christian, to say nothing of the heart of Paul who had founded the church and whose whole heart was wrapped up in its welfare. In writing the epistle Paul deliberately restrained his tears in order calmly to deal with the problems. Bernard holds that the body of the letter proper is to be found in the first six chapters, since the remainder of the epistle is largely taken up with answering the questions of the Corinthians. The faults rebuked in these early chapters deeply grieved the heart of the Apostle.

> It is in these earlier chapters that we are to look for traces of mental anguish and depression, and I hold that they are plainly there to be found, and that the note of identification afforded by 2 Cor. ii. 4 is answered by such passages as I Cor. iii. 12-15, iv. 11-13, v. 1-6, vi. 5, 9, 11.[11]

The critics object to this identification on the basis of 2 Corinthians 7:8 by saying that it is inconceivable that the Apostle should have regretted writing such a monument of Christian truth as the First Epistle. But as Hughes correctly points out, that is to misread the nature of Paul's stated regret.

> Paul does not say that he regretted the *writing* of the letter, as though he wished it had remained unwritten, distressing though its composition and despatch must have been to him. It was a letter that had to be written if he was to be a faithful father in God to the Corinthians. What he *does* say is that he regretted the *sorrow* which that letter had at first caused them: parental love does not rejoice in the sorrow which necessary correction brings; but the correction itself is not a matter for regret.[12]

This revelation of his own feelings was proof of his own fatherly concern for his Corinthian "problem children."

Refusing to accept 1 Corinthians as the letter referred to many of the critics point to 2 Corinthians 10:1–13:10 as this severe letter. If, as is held, this severe letter was occasioned by the insult that Paul experienced at Corinth on his second visit there, one of the objects of Paul in writing it must have been to insist on the punishment of

11. J. H. Bernard, "The Second Epistle to the Corinthians," *Expositor's Greek Testament,* (n.d.), Vol. III, pp. 13-14.
12. Philip E. Hughes, "Paul's Second Epistle to the Corinthians," *The New International Commentary on the New Testament,* (1962), pp. xxix-xxx. Italics in original. See also pp. 270-271.

the offender. But chapters 10:1—13:10 have no reference whatever to such an offender. Rather, they "are wholly taken up with what the Apostle means to do when he comes to Corinth the third time; they refer not to this (imaginary) insolent person, but to the misbelieving and the immoral in general."[13] To retort, as is sometimes done, that these chapters are not the whole of the original letter is simply an attempt to support one unproven assumption with another equally gratuitous.

On the assumption of the close relation between the two epistles, the reference in 2 Corinthians 7:12 to the person "that did the wrong" and he "that suffered the wrong" will be the son and the father in 1 Corinthians 5:1. But the critics deny the identification. They cannot imagine that Paul would speak of a great sin and crime, like that of the incestuous person, in language such as he employs in 2 Corinthians 2:5-11, 7:12. Thus Peake insists that "if we identify the offender in the two Epistles, the grossness of the offense seems to be passed over altogether too lightly in the Second."[14] But this fails to perceive the entire situation. Paul's demand for the excommunication of the incestuous person had been the test case for the loyalty and obedience of the Corinthian church. His great anxiety had been to awaken the sleeping conscience of the Corinthian church and to induce them to exercise their power of spiritual discipline. The letter had produced the desired effect and the offender had been excommunicated. He had become penitent. The desired result had been achieved in regard to the church as well as the guilty individual. The Apostle accordingly now asks the church to lift the ban imposed on the offender, "lest by any means such a one should be swallowed up with his overmuch sorrow" (2 Cor. 2:7). Paul is guarding against the opposite danger of hopeless despair in his case and the evil effect it would have on the church. The view that the offenders in the two epistles are to be identified seems more probable than the hypothesis which must manufacture an entirely new episode for the Second Epistle. From the similarity of the language employed in both epistles concerning the offender Bernard makes a strong case for the identity of the two.[15]

13. James Denney, "The Second Epistle to the Corinthians," *Expositor's Bible,* (1903), p. 6.
14. Arthur S. Peake, *A Critical Introduction to the New Testament,* (1919), p. 34.
15. J. H. Bernard, "The Second Epistle to the Corinthians," *Expositor's Greek Testament,* (n.d.). Vol. III, pp. 14-16.

For the conservative student the most serious objection to this hypothetical reconstruction of events is the effort to dissect this epistle. In the face of all textual evidence to the contrary, we are asked to believe that 2 Corinthians is the result of the union of two, or even three or more fragments of Pauline letters, arbitrarily run together to form a new epistle. If such were the case it is passing strange that not the slightest trace of it has been left in literature. The hypothesis rests upon an improbable assumption. We are solicited to believe that chapters 10-13, as an independent letter, lost their opening pages in such a way as to leave no mutilated sentence. Then the first nine chapters, as another independent letter, lost their ending in such a way as to leave no mutilated sentence, so that the two fragments could readily be run together. The probabilities for such an event are very small indeed. To evade this difficulty Strachan blandly postulates an editor who felt "himself free to restore, where necessary, grammatical connections."[16] Or again the explanation is just reversed by postulating that when the Pauline epistles were edited for the Canon, the letter found in chapters 10-13 was stripped of its opening and added to the later and larger one (chs. 1-9) to make a single writing similar in length to 2 Corinthians.[17] To all such hypothetical juggling we would reply with the words of Cartledge,

> If several letters could have been jumbled into one letter, we cannot have a very high regard for the accuracy of what we have; our view of inspiration would have to be lowered a bit.[18]

We are told that the difference in tone between chapters 1-9 and 10-13 makes it impossible to believe that the two parts originally formed one letter. It is asserted that the unity of the epistle as it stands "is psychologically impossible."[19] Admittedly the sudden change in tone at chapter 10 poses a real problem concerning its unity. To seek to deny or minimize the fact, would be futile and unwise. But who will determine what is "psychologically impos-

16. R. H. Strachan, "The Second Epistle of Paul to the Corinthians," *Moffatt Commentary,* (1935), p. xxi.
17. James Moffatt, *An Introduction to the Literature of the New Testament,* (1949 reprint), p. 121; Floyd V. Filson and James Reid, "The Second Epistle to the Corinthians," *The Interpreter's Bible,* (1953), Vol. X, p. 271.
18. Samuel A. Cartledge, *A Conservative Introduction to the New Testament,* (1938), p. 103.
19. Edgar J. Goodspeed, *An Introduction to the New Testament,* (1937), p. 59.

sible"? The criteria of the critics inevitably are subjective in nature and variable in application. But having set up their subjective standards they do not hesitate to eliminate certain sections of Scripture, of lesser or greater extent, because they do not conform to their principles of probability. In 2 Corinthians this principle is brought into operation on a large scale. Lenski tartly remarks:

> The critics propose to tell us what Paul could and what he could not write in this Epistle. In their minds all of this is settled by such canons as they are pleased to set up, and as critics they propose to hew to the line. So much the worse for us, if we do not agree and applaud![20]

Rather than summarily rejecting the unity of the epistle, the effort should be made to follow the mind of the Apostle in the composition of it. An attentive reading of the epistle as we have it today leaves one with the impression of an order that is both natural and logical. Zahn states this order thus:

> In spirit the reader follows Paul from Ephesus through Troas to Macedonia (chaps. i-vii); then he lingers with him for a moment in the Churches of Macedonia (chaps. viii-ix.); finally, he is led to the consideration of conditions in the Church at Corinth from the point of view of Paul's coming visit there. The three sections of the letter treat respectively, the immediate past with its misunderstandings and explanations, the present with its practical problems, and the near future with its anxieties.[21]

When thus read as a whole the gulfs between the three sections do not seem to be as impossible as the critics think. The change in tone in the last section is indeed unexpected but not necessarily impossible psychologically for Paul. Cambier remarks,

> Paul is not above all a theologian who constructs well balanced expositions; he is a religious leader who is very practical, and a good organizer. Having proved his affection (1-7), he also knows how to defend his rights (10-13). Those at whom he aims are not only the Judaizing intruders, but the ensemble of the faithful who let themselves be swayed by these "super-apostles" and are tempted to disregard the authority of their apostle and father. He also speaks to

20. R. C. H. Lenski, *The Interpretation of St. Paul's First and Second Epistle to the Corinthians,* (1935), p. 822.
21. Theodor Zahn, *Introduction to the New Testament,* (1909), Vol. I, p. 312.

them directly when challenging them, while he speaks of the Judaizing missionaries in the third person (10, 11-12; 11, 13-15, 20, 22f.)[22]

It has been pointed out that there is a similar change of tone in Demosthenes' oration "On the Crown." In the first part he speaks in a calm, deliberate tone, but after a while "words of bitter mockery gush forth impetuously like a thundershower."[23] Does that mean that we have two different orations patched together? Alford remarks,

> On the principle which these critics have adopted, the first Ep. to the Cor. might be divided into at least eight separate epistles, marked off by the successive changes of subject.[24]

The question of the unity of 2 Corinthians is still hotly debated. Thrall concludes that "the evidence is very evenly divided" and asserts that a definite decision "is difficult to reach."[25] Hughes notes that during "recent years, to impugn the unity of 2 Corinthians was to be very much in the fashion; but now a swing back to the traditional view of the letter's integrity is noticeable" and cites a number of contemporary scholars in its favor.[26] We unhesitatingly accept the real unity of 2 Corinthians.

### THE APOSTLE'S RELATIONS WITH THE CORINTHIAN CHURCH

It may be desirable to tabulate our reconstruction of the probable sequence of events in the Apostle's relations with the Corinthian church. This reconstruction is tentative and proceeds upon the assumption of the close relation of the two epistles to the Corinthians.

1. The founding of the Corinthian church by the Apostle on the second missionary journey (Acts 18:1-18).

2. The three years' ministry of Paul at Ephesus during the third missionary journey (Acts 19:1-20; 20:31).

3. The brief visit of Paul to Corinth from Ephesus (2 Cor. 12:14; 13:1).

4. The sending of Titus to Corinth to inaugurate the collection (2 Cor. 8:6, 10; 1 Cor. 16:1).

22. J. Cambier, "The Second Epistle to the Corinthians," *Introduction to the New Testament,* A. Robert and A. Feuillet, editors, (1965), p. 439.
23. Heinrich August Wilhelm Meyer, *Critical and Exegetical Hand-Book to the Epistles to the Corinthians,* (1884), p. 414, quoting from Hug's *Einleitung.*
24. Henry Alford, *The Greek Testament,* (1958), Vol. II, p. 58 Proleg.
25. Margaret E. Thrall, "The First and Second Letters of Paul to the Corinthians," *The Cambridge Bible Commentary,* (1965), p. 10.
26. Philip E. Hughes, "Paul's Second Epistle to the Corinthians," *The New International Commentary on the New Testament,* (1962), pp. xxi-xxii.

5. The writing of a lost letter to Corinth (1 Cor. 5:9). (Points 4 and 5 may well relate to the same time.)

6. The information about church factions at Corinth received from members of the household of Chloe (1 Cor. 1:11).

7. The sending of Timothy to Corinth by way of Macedonia (1 Cor. 4:17; 16:10-11; Acts 19:21-22).

8. The arrival of the three delegates from Corinth with the letter from the Corinthian church (1 Cor. 16:17; 7:1; 8:1; 12:1).

9. The writing of our *1 Corinthians* at Ephesus (1 Cor. 16:8).

10. The arrival at Corinth of the Judaizers from Palestine and their fomenting of opposition to Paul (2 Cor. 3:1; 10:12-18; 11:1-23).

11. The return of Timothy from Corinth to Paul at Ephesus (2 Cor. 1:1, 3-12).

12. The sending of Titus to Corinth from Ephesus with plans for him to meet Paul at Troas (2 Cor. 2:12-13; 7:6-7).

13. The arrival of Paul at Troas, his restlessness and departure into Macedonia (2 Cor. 2:12-13).

14. The arrival of Titus in Macedonia and Paul's relief at the report of Titus (2 Cor. 7:6-7).

15. The writing of our *2 Corinthians* from Macedonia (2 Cor. 7:5-15).

16. The return of Titus to Corinth with 2 Corinthians to complete the raising of the collection (2 Cor. 8:6, 16-18).

17. The later visit of Paul to Corinth for three months (Acts 20:3).

18. The writing of *Romans* at Corinth (Rom. 15:22-29; 16:1, 23). The tranquil atmosphere of Romans reveals that the Corinthian troubles were successfully settled.

### THE OCCASION FOR 2 CORINTHIANS

It seems that Timothy did arrive in Corinth from Macedonia as Paul had expected him to (1 Cor. 16:10-11). If Timothy did not arrive in Corinth as announced it seems inevitable that an explanation and apology would have been found in 2 Corinthians. If Paul felt it necessary to defend his own change of plans in visiting Corinth, it seems that Timothy's failure to come as announced would have furnished the adversaries another ground for their charge of fickleness. Apparently Timothy's report of conditions in Corinth caused Paul to send Titus to Corinth to deal with the situation, with instructions to rejoin the Apostle at Troas by way of Macedonia (2 Cor.

2:12-13). The uproar at Ephesus, caused by Demetrius (Acts 19:23-41), perhaps hastened Paul's departure from the city (Acts 20:1). Paul proceeded to Troas as planned and waited for the coming of Titus. Although Paul found an open door to preach at Troas, the failure of Titus to come caused him such anxiety concerning affairs at Corinth that he had no heart to carry on the work there (2 Cor. 2:12-13). Anxious to meet Titus, he sailed for Macedonia where he encountered new causes for distress (2 Cor. 7:6). He waited there long enough to ascertain the mind of the Macedonian churches and partially to make up the collection there for the Judean saints (2 Cor. 8:1-5). At last Titus arrived with his report from Corinth. The report was generally favorable as to the reaction of the church, but Titus had to advise Paul of the persistence of a small minority opposition, apparently inspired by the presence of some Judaizers from Judea. This statement of affairs by Titus furnished the immediate occasion for the writing of 2 Corinthians.

### THE PLACE AND DATE OF 2 CORINTHIANS

1. *Place.* From the epistle itself we know that 2 Corinthians was written from Macedonia (2:13; 7:5-7). At precisely what place in Macedonia is not stated. It is generally assumed that the place was Philippi. The subscription in the King James Version, based on some early manuscripts, asserts this view: "The Second Epistle to the Corinthians was written from Philippi, a city of Macedonia, by Titus and Lucas." Alford, however, questions this traditional view concerning the place of writing and points rather to Thessalonica. He believes that Paul's reference to "the grace of God which hath been given in the churches of Macedonia" (8:1) indicates that the Apostle had not been stationed at Philippi only. Since Paul had been so eager to revisit the Thessalonian church, Alford feels that Thessalonica must have been visited and would be more likely as the place of composition.[27] All that can be said with certainty is that II Corinthians was written on the third missionary journey while Paul was visiting one of the Macedonian churches which he had founded during the second journey.

2. *Date.* When we accept the view of the close relation of the Second Epistle to the First, it is evident that only a few months, rather

27. Henry Alford, *The Greek Testament,* (1958), Vol. II, pp. 59-60 Proleg.

than a year or more, elapsed between their composition. The First Epistle was written near the Easter season of A.D. 57. Leaving Ephesus around Pentecost, Paul tarried for some time at Troas, then went on to Macedonia. He was visiting the churches in Macedonia when Titus came from Corinth with his report that occasioned this letter. Thus this epistle seems to have been written during the late summer or autumn of the year A.D. 57. Following the writing of 2 Corinthians Paul continued his ministry in Macedonia which seems to have carried him as far as the borders of Illyricum (Rom. 15:19).[28] The three months of that winter were spent in Corinth (Acts 20:3).

3. *Bearer.* The bearer of 2 Corinthians was Titus. Paul sent him back to Corinth with this letter, accompanied by two other brethren, to complete the offering that had been started in Corinth a year ago (2 Cor. 8:16-24; 8:10).

### THE PURPOSE OF 2 CORINTHIANS

1. *Vindication.* The one predominant purpose of Paul in writing this entire epistle is to re-establish fully his apostolic authority in the Corinthian church. Other purposes apparent in the epistle are subservient to this. Meyer states it thus:

> The aim of the Epistle is stated by Paul himself at xiii. 10, viz. to put the church before his arrival in person into that frame of mind, which it was necessary that he should find, in order that he might thereupon set to work among them, not with stern corrective authority, but for their edification. But in order to attain this aim, he had to make it his chief task to elucidate, confirm, and vindicate his apostolic authority, which, in consequence of his former letter, has been assailed still more vehemently, openly, and influentially by opponents. For, if that were regained, his whole influence would be regained; if the church were again confirmed on this point, and the opposition defeated, every hindrance to his successful personal labour amongst them would be removed. With the establishment of his apostolic character and reputation he is therefore chiefly occupied in the whole Epistle; everything else is only subordinate, including a detailed appeal respecting the collection.[29]

28. M. N. Tod, "Illyricum," *The International Standard Bible Encyclopaedia,* (1939), Vol. III, pp. 1149b-1150a.
29. Heinrich August Wilhelm Meyer, *Critical and Exegetical Hand-Book to the Epistles to the Corinthians,* (1884), p. 411.

This effort to vindicate his apostolic authority, personally distasteful to him (2 Cor. 12:11) had been made necessary by the development of determined opposition in the church. It apparently was fostered by certain agitators who had invaded the Corinthian church, apparently since the writing of 1 Corinthians. Their precise identity has been disputed.[30] That they were Hebrews is certain (11:22), but it has been questioned whether they were Judaizers from Palestine, such as had invaded the Galatian churches, or Hellenistic Jews of the Dispersion who were tinged with Gnostic views. The former has been the generally accepted view, although it is true that the teachings of the Judaizers are not formally refuted in this epistle. It is clear that they were intruders from without (3:1; 10:13-15), made special claims to superior apostolic authority (11:5, 22; 12:11), prided themselves on their Jewish distinctives (11:22), were overbearing in their attitudes (11:20) and libertine in their relations (6:14–7:1; 12:21). They preached a different gospel (11:3-4) and strongly opposed Paul by attacking his person (10:1, 10; 11:6), his teaching (10:12-18; 11:7-12; 2:17), and his veracity (1:15-18; 10:9-11; 12:16-19). Their teaching and conduct showed that they were false apostles, ministers of Satan (11:13-15).

In the last section of the epistle (chs. 10-13) Paul turns his full attention to the refutation of these charges. In the first section (chs. 1-7) he touched on them only as they came into the line of his thought. In it he proved to his converts the sincerity and purity of his motives. Now his concern is also to nullify the influence of these agitators over the Corinthians. It is his complaint against the Corinthians that they have allowed themselves to be misled by such men. He fears what he will find upon coming to Corinth if their deliverance from this influence is not realized (12:19–13:10).

2. *Minor purposes.* A few minor purposes are also apparent in the writing of the epistle. It offers him an opportunity to express his great joy over the fact that the Gospel has been triumphant in Corinth in the face of the powerful forces that sought to destroy it (2:14-17). He also uses the occasion to offer the church some needed

30. See T. Henshaw, *New Testament Literature in the Light of Modern Scholarship* (1957 reprint), pp. 240-241; Werner Georg Kümmel, *Introduction to the New Testament,* (1966), pp. 208-210; Philip E. Hughes, "Paul's Second Epistle to the Corinthians," *The New International Commentary on the New Testament* (1962), pp. 356-358; Donald Guthrie, *New Testament Introduction,* Revised Ed., pp. 422-424.

instruction in regard to the penitent offender (2:5-11). And now that things are again moving forward in Corinth he takes the opportunity to set in motion again the movement for the collection (chs. 8-9). In view of the fact that the Judaizers were seeking to discredit the Apostle and to disrupt his work at Corinth as well as elsewhere, Paul felt all the more keenly the desirability of carrying through the collection for the poor saints in Judea. Such an offering, he felt, was the best refutation of the charges advanced by the enemies that Paul and his Gentile churches were hostile to the Jewish brethren in Judea.

### THE CHARACTERISTICS OF 2 CORINTHIANS

1. *Style.* The language of the epistle reveals that it was written during a time of intense emotional stress. "The broken constructions and frequent anacolutha," says Bernard, "show that it was written at a time of mental agitation and excitement."[31] The epistle is marked with boundless variety, yet it is intensely Pauline. Its contents shift rapidly from one character to another. "Consolation and rebuke, gentleness and severity, earnestness and irony, succeed one another at very short intervals and without notice."[32] Williams points out that "there is a constant mixing of metaphors, as treasure in earthen vessels; the spiritual body compared to a house that clothes the soul, etc."[33]

2. *Contents.* Since emotions are not concerned with logical order, it is not surprising that this has been termed the least systematic of all of Paul's writings. The thread of the epistle is historical, but it is interwoven with extended disgressions. "The whole letter," says Bengel, "reminds us of an itinerary, but interwoven with the noblest precepts."[34] It reflects the various stations in Paul's journey, and his very emotions at each place are revealed. It indicates his troubles at Ephesus (1:8), the anxiety at Troas (2:12-13), the exultant triumph experienced in Macedonia (2:14; 7:6-7), and his concern about conditions at Corinth upon his arrival (13:1, 10). Thus the epistle contains a remarkable self-revelation of the Apostle's inner life. "It is the most personal letter in the canon of the New Testament."[35]

31. J. H. Bernard, "The Second Epistle to the Corinthians," *Expositor's Greek Testament,* (n.d.), Vol. III, p. 30.
32. Henry Alford, *The Greek Testament,* (1958), Vol. II, p. 61 Proleg.
33. Charles B. Williams, *An Introduction to New Testament Literature,* (1929), p. 143.
34. Quoted from F. W. Farrar, *The Life and Work of St. Paul,* (1889), p. 408.
35. Charles B. Williams, *An Introduction to New Testament Literature,* (1929), p. 142.

The epistle gives us some interesting information about Paul that would otherwise have been lost to us. From 11:32-33 we learn that the Jews enlisted the aid of the Ethnarch of Damascus in their effort to apprehend Paul in that city. His experience of being caught up into Paradise (12:1-4) he mentions here for the first time after fourteen years, and then only because it is forced out of him. Here only do we have an account of his "thorn in the flesh" (12:7-9). The marvelous catalog of his experiences given in 11:23-28 reveals clearly how much there was in the arduous life of the Apostle that remains entirely unknown to us.

Although the letter is predominantly personal, it contains some very important doctrinal teachings. One of the great treasures of Christian literature is the extended passage on the nature of the Christian ministry (2:12–6:10). More in detail, mention may be made of the contrast between the two covenants (3:4-18); the blindness of the world to the glory of the Gospel (4:3-6); the hope of the beyond (5:1-9); the judgment seat of Christ (5:10-11); the message of reconciliation (5:18-20); and the substitutionary work of Christ (5:21). Of abiding value are the various references to the person and work of Satan (2:10-11; 4:3-4; 11:3, 14-15; 12:7-9). Important in its contemporary implications is the passage on the nature of the world and the duty of the believer to separate from it (6:14–7:1). The subject of Christian giving finds no more elaborate and valuable exposition anywhere in Scripture than that found in Chapters 8 and 9.

3. *Value.* The epistle has abiding value for the theologian, the student of the life of Paul, as well as the minister of the Gospel. The doctrinal truths embedded in the epistle will always call for the close study of the theologian. The student of the life of Paul finds in it an intriguing yet often baffling source of information concerning the Apostle. Evangelistic preaching has drawn heavily upon the contents of this epistle for its messages. In a volume of sermons on this epistle, Ockenga asserts that this is "one of the most evangelistic books in the Bible. Preaching through it will result in the salvation of many souls."[36]

It is of value and lasting interest to compare the two epistles to the Corinthian church. They are closely related to each other, yet they

36. Harold J. Ockenga, *The Comfort of God, Preaching in Second Corinthians,* (1944), p. 7.

are very different from each other. The comparison of the two is aptly given by Scroggie in the following paragraph:

> The First gives insight into the character and condition of the early Churches; the Second, into the life and character of the Apostle Paul. The First is objective and practical; the Second is subjective and personal. The First is systematic; the Second is not. The First is deliberate; the Second is impassioned. The First warns against Pagan influences; the Second against Judaic influences. The two together are valuable beyond all estimate for an understanding of the problems of first century Christians, and for an appreciation of the greatest missionary of the Christian era.[37]

### An Outline of 2 Corinthians

THE INTRODUCTION (1:1-11)

1. The salutation (1-2)
   a. The writers (1a)
   b. The readers (1b)
   c. The greeting (2)
2. The thanksgiving (3-11)
   a. The values from the experience of suffering (3-7)
      1) The praise to the God who comforts (3-4a)
      2) The reason for the divine comforting (4b)
      3) The means of the divine comforting (4c)
      4) The experience of the comfort from God (5)
      5) The values of the apostolic experience (6-7)
   b. The nature of the experience of suffering (8-11)
      1) The danger of death in which he was (8)
      2) The effect of the sentence of death in him (9)
      3) The deliverance by God (10)
      4) The fellowship with him through prayer (11)

I. CONSOLATION: PAUL'S TRIALS AND COMFORTS AS A PREACHER (1:12–7:16)

1. Explanation: The personal vindication (1:12–2:11)
   a. The sincerity of his conduct (1:12-14)
      1) The manner of his life (12)
      2) The assertion about his letters (13-14)

37. W. Graham Scroggie, *Know Your Bible, A Brief Introduction to the Scriptures, Volume II, The New Testament,* (n.d.), pp. 142-143.

b. The explanation of the change of plans (1:15–2:4)
   1) The defense of his dependableness (1:15-22)
      a) The nature of the original plan (15-16)
      b) The answer to the charge of fickleness (17-22)
         (1) The indication of the charge of fickleness (17)
         (2) The refutation of the charge of fickleness (18-22)
            (a) The denial based on God's faithfulness (18)
            (b) The Christ preached to them is faithful (19)
            (c) The fulfillment of God's promises in Christ through him (20)
            (d) The work of God in him as His instrument (21-22)
   2) The reasons for the change in plans (1:23–2:4)
      a) The change was made for their sake (1:23-24)
      b) The change was made for his own sake (2:1-4)
         (1) His personal determination in not coming (1-2)
         (2) His purpose when he wrote to them (3-4)
            (a) The purpose in regard to himself (3)
            (b) The purpose in regard to them (4)
c. The advice concerning the repentant offender (2:5-11)
   1) The nature of the offense (5)
   2) The nature of the action now advised (6-8)
      a) The sufficiency of the punishment given (6)
      b) The attitude to be taken to the repentant one (7-8)
   3) The reason for the action urged (9-11)
      a) His demand for action was a test of obedience (9)
      b) His forgiveness should prompt their forgiveness (10-11)

2. Exposition: The nature of the ministry (2:12–6:10)
   a. The triumph of the ministry (2:12-17)
      1) The anxiety he experienced at Troas (12-13)
      2) The triumph experienced in Christ (14-17)
         a) The thanksgiving for the triumph (14a)
         b) The part of the ministers in the triumph (14b-16a)
         c) The sufficiency for this ministry (16b-17)
   b. The accreditation of the ministry (3:1-3)
      1) The questions concerning their recommendation (1)
      2) The nature of their recommendation (2-3)

c. The glory of the ministry (3:4-18)
   1) The ministry is empowered of God (4-6)
   2) The ministry exceeds in glory (7-11)
      a) The ministry has greater glory (7-9)
         (i) The glory of the two ministries (7-8)
         (ii) The superior glory of the ministry of righteousness (9)
      b) The ministry has permanent glory (10-11)
   3) The ministry bestows glory (12-18)
      a) The apostolic boldness (12-13a)
      b) The veil of the Mosaic ministry (13b-15)
      c) The means of the removal of the veil (16)
      d) The results of the removal of the veil (17-18)
d. The perseverance of the ministry (4:1—5:10)
   1) The perseverance amid blindness to the Gospel (4:1-6)
      a) The sincerity of the workers (1-2)
      b) The blindness of the lost (3-4)
      c) The light of the Gospel ministry (5-6)
   2) The perseverance amid suffering (4:7-15)
      a) The vessels holding the treasure (7)
      b) The experiences of suffering (8-12)
         (i) The description of the suffering (8-9)
         (ii) The purpose of the suffering (10-12)
      c) The secret of victory amid suffering (13-15)
         (i) The possession of an intense faith (13)
         (ii) The knowledge of a glorious hope (14)
         (iii) The attitude of self-forgetfulness (15)
   3) The perseverance inspired by hope (4:16—5:10)
      a) The inspiration of hope in this life (4:16-18)
         (i) The present experience of renewal (16)
         (ii) The comparison of present affliction and future glory (17-18)
      b) The contemplation of the future life (5:1-10)
         (i) The assurance concerning the two houses (1)
         (ii) The desire inspired by hope (2-4)
            (a) The statement of the desire (2-3)
            (b) The restatement of the desire (4)
         (iii) The experienced verification of the hope (5)
         (iv) The present attitude because of the hope (6-8)

(v) The aim inspired by the hope (9-10)
e. The motivation of the ministry (5:11-17)
1) The indication of the motives (11-15)
a) The motive from the fear of the Lord (11)
b) The motive of unselfish concern for others (12-13)
c) The motive from the love of Christ (14-15)
2) The results of the new life (16-17)
f. The message of the ministry (5:18-21)
1) The preparation of the messengers (18-19)
a) The divine source of all things (18a)
b) The divine work in the messengers (18b)
c) The divine work of reconciliation in Christ (19a)
d) The divine commission to the messengers (19b)
2) The work of the messengers (20-21)
a) The position of the messengers (20a)
b) The plea of the messengers (20b)
c) The basis for the message (21)
g. The summary concerning the ministry (6:1-10)
1) The position of the ministers (1a)
2) The plea of the ministers (1b-2)
3) The conduct of the ministers (3-10)
a) Negative—What their conduct is not (3)
b) Positive—What their conduct is like (4-10)
(i) The statement of the conduct (4a)
(ii) The elaboration of the conduct (4b-10)
(a) As to physical sufferings (4b-5)
(b) As to personal characteristics (6-8a)
(c) As to paradoxical experiences (8b-10)
3. Exhortation: The consequent appeals (6:11—7:4)
a. The appeal for sympathy (6:11-13)
b. The appeal for separation (6:14—7:1)
1) The command of separation (6:14a)
2) The arguments for separation (6:14b-16)
a) The questions as to the incongruity (14b-16a)
b) The assertion as to the believer's nature (16b)
3) The restatement of the appeal for separation (6:17—7:1)
a) The Old Testament statement (6:17-18)
b) The apostolic application (7:1)

c. The appeal for affection (7:2-4)
4. Recognition: The effect of his former letter (7:5-16)
a. The suspense endured in Macedonia (5)
b. The comfort experienced with the coming of Titus (6-15)
1) The comfort derived from the news of Titus (6-12)
a) The description of the comfort (6-7)
(i) The source of the comfort in God (6a)
(ii) The means of the comfort (6b-7a)
(iii) The effect of the comfort (7b)
b) The interpretation of their grief (8-11)
(i) The Apostle's attitude toward their grief (8-9)
(a) His past regret at grieving them (8)
(b) His present joy at their godly repentance (9)
(ii) The nature of their grief (10-11)
(a) The effects of the two kinds of sorrow (10)
(b) The results of their own grief (11)
c) The purpose he had in his letter to them (12)
2) The comfort experienced from the joy of Titus (13-15)
a) The cause for the added joy (13)
b) The confirmation of his boasting to Titus (14)
c) The reaction of Titus to their obedience (15)
c. The Apostle's assurance concerning them (16)

II. SOLICITATION: PAUL'S PLEA CONCERNING THE COLLECTION (8:1–9:15)
1. Example: The giving of the Macedonians (8:1-6)
a. The explanation concerning their giving (1)
b. The circumstances of their giving (2)
c. The manner of their giving (3-4)
d. The method of their giving (5)
e. The result of their giving (6)
2. Exhortation: The appeal for Christian giving (8:7-15)
a. The appeal to abound in "this grace also" (7)
b. The motives prompting such giving (8-12)
1) The motivation in their love (8-9)
a) The purpose is to test their love (8)
b) The impetus for their love (9)

2) The motivation in their willingness to give (10-12)
  a) The opportunity to fulfill their willingness (10)
  b) The appeal to complete the doing (11)
  c) The basis for acceptableness in giving (12)
c. The principle underlying the collection (13-15)

3. Commendation: The approval of the messengers (8:16-24)
   a. The coming of Titus to Corinth (16-17)
   b. The brethren accompanying Titus to Corinth (18-22)
      1) The brother being sent with Titus (18-19a)
      2) The explanation about the ministration (19b-21)
      3) The brother being sent with them (22)
   c. The recommendation of the messengers (23)
   d. The admonition to the Corinthians (24)
4. Explanation: The reason for sending the messengers (9:1-5)
   a. The situation in Achaia relative to the collection (1-2)
   b. The purpose in sending the brethren about the collection (3-4)
      1) The statement of the purpose (3)
      2) The indication of the motive (4)
   c. The commission to the brethren concerning the collection (5)
5. Results: The blessings of liberality (9:6-15)
   a. The viewpoint in Christian giving (6)
   b. The spirit in Christian giving (7)
   c. The results of liberality in giving (8-14)
      1) The added blessing of God on the giver (8-11)
         a) The thing God is able to do (8-9)
         b) The thing God will do (10-11)
      2) The thankful reaction of those receiving the gift (12-14)
         a) The nature of this ministry of giving (12)
         b) The reaction of the recipients of the gift (13-14)
            (i) Their thanksgiving to God (13)
            (ii) Their regard for the givers (14)
   d. The thanksgiving for God's inexpressible gift (15)

III. VINDICATION: PAUL'S DEFENSE OF HIS APOSTOLIC AUTHORITY (10:1–13:10)

1. Power: The Apostle's divine authority (10:1-18)

a. His appeal to the church (1-6)
   1) The basis for his appeal (1)
   2) The contents of his appeal (2)
   3) The description of his warfare (3-6)
      a) The nature of his warfare (3)
      b) The weapons of his warfare (4)
      c) The course of battle in the warfare (5-6)
b. His answer to a misled member (7-11)
   1) The appeal to them to consider reality (7a)
   2) The challenge to a misled member (7b)
   3) The verification of his authority (8-9)
   4) The indication of the criticism (10)
   5) The warning to "such a one" (11)
c. His appraisal of the claims of the false teachers (12-18)
   1) The absurd boasting of the false teachers (12)
   2) The justified boasting of the Apostle (13-16)
      a) The standard of measurement to be used (13)
      b) The actual achievement to be measured (14-16)
         (i) The nature of the achievement (14)
         (ii) The plans based upon that achievement (15-16)
   3) The final test for boasting (17-18)

2. Apostleship: The Apostle's foolish boasting (11:1–12:13)
   a. His request to be permitted to boast (11:1-4)
      1) The statement of the request (1)
      2) The reasons for the request (2-4)
         a) His personal concern for them (2)
         b) His anxious fear concerning them (3-4)
            (i) The nature of his fears (3)
            (ii) The grounds for his fears (4)
   b. His refutation of personal inferiority (11:5-15)
      1) The general statement of his position (5)
      2) The specific areas of refutation (6-15)
         a) The refutation as to his preaching (6)
         b) The refutation concerning his gratuitous service (7-15)
            (i) The stinging question concerning his free service (7)
            (ii) The objective facts about his ministry to them (8-9a)

(iii) The abiding determination as to this position (9b-10)
(iv) The compelling motive for his free service (11-15)
(a) Negative—Not because of lack of love (11)
(b) Positive—To cut off occasion to the false teachers (12-15)
(aa) The statement of the purpose (12)
(bb) The character of the false teachers (13)
(cc) The explanation for their practice (14-15)

c. His grounds for boasting (11:16—12:10)
1) The preparation for the foolish boasting (11:16-21)
a) The reluctance to boast (16-17)
(i) The view to be taken of his boasting (16)
(ii) The level taken in the boasting (17)
b) The compulsion for the boasting (18)
c) The consolation in his boasting (19-21a)
d) The determination likewise to use boasting (21b)
2) The first round of foolish boasting (11:22-33)
a) The boasting as to the flesh (22)
b) The boasting concerning service (23-29)
(i) His position of superiority (23a)
(ii) His evidence for his superiority (23b-29)
(a) The general assertion (23b)
(b) The specific instances (24-29)
c) The boasting concerning his weakness (30-33)
(i) His weakness as the subject of boasting (30)
(ii) His assertion of his truthfulness (31)
(iii) His illustration of his weakness (32-33)
3) The second round of foolish boasting (12:1-10)
a) His feeling about his boasting (1)
b) His boasting about visions (2-5)
(i) The mention of the experience (2-4)
(ii) The attitude toward the experience (5)
c) His boasting in his weakness (6-10)
(i) The explanation of his attitude (6)

(ii) The description of his weakness (7-9a)
(iii) The attitude taken toward his weakness (9b-10)

d. His boasting in retrospect (12:11-13)
   1) The feeling about the boasting (11a)
   2) The cause for the boasting (11b-13)
      a) Their failure to commend him (11b)
      b) Their obligations to commend him (11c-13)

3. Arrival: The Apostle's impending visit to Corinth (12:14–13:10)
   a. His gratuitous service to them (12:14-18)
      1) His assertion about his free service upon arrival (14a)
      2) His reasons for his attitude (14b)
      3) His willingness to be spent for them (15)
      4) His refutation of a slander against him (16-18)
         a) The indication of the slander (16)
         b) The refutation of the slander (17-18)
   b. His fear about conditions at his coming (12:19-21)
      1) The correction of their false impression (19)
      2) The contents of his fears about them (20-21)
         a) The resultant disappointment to him and them (20a)
         b) The presence of definite evils among them (20b)
         c) The personal sorrow at unrepented sins (21)
   c. His procedure at his coming (13:1-4)
      1) The investigation which he will make (1-2)
      2) The proof that will be given them (3-4)
   d. His final appeal to the Corinthians (13:5-10)
      1) The appeal to them for self-testing (5-6)
      2) The prayer of the Apostle for them (7-9)
      3) The purpose of his letter to them (10)

THE CONCLUSION (13:11-14)

1. The exhortation (11)
2. The salutations (12-13)
3. The benediction (14)

## A Book List on 2 Corinthians[1]

Barrett, C. K., "A Commentary on the Second Epistle to the Corin-

1. See also the book list under 1 Corinthians for works covering both epistles.

thians." *Harper's New Testament Commentaries.* New York: Harper & Row (1973).

Prints author's own translation. A thorough treatment by a noted critical scholar, based on the original text and manifesting an impressive knowledge of contemporary literature and research. While rejecting a radical partition theory, he holds that there was an interval between the writing of the first nine and the last four chapters. Barrett accepts the reconstruction of events between our First and Second Corinthians which postulates a sorrowful intermediate visit to Corinth and the writing of a severe letter before our Second Corinthians. Maintains that it is the Christology which holds our canonical epistles together.

Bernard, J. H., "The Second Epistle of Paul to the Corinthians," *The Expositor's Greek Testament.* Vol. III. Grand Rapids: Wm. B. Eerdmans Pub. Co. (reprint, n.d.).

Greek text. A critical commentary defending the integrity and unity of 2 Corinthians and insisting on a close relation between our Corinthian epistles. The work of a brilliant Anglican churchman of the past generation.

Denney, James, "The Second Epistle to the Corinthians," *The Expositor's Bible.* Vol. V. Grand Rapids: Wm. B. Eerdmans Pub. Co. (1943 reprint).

A thorough, reverent exposition, characterized by clarity of thought, evangelical warmth, and freshness of expression.

Erdman, Charles R., *The Second Epistle of Paul to the Corinthians.*[2] Philadelphia: The Westminster Press (1929).

Filson, Floyd V., and Reid, James, "The Second Epistle to the Corinthians," *The Interpreter's Bible.* Vol. 10. New York: Abingdon Press (1953).

Prints the King James and Revised Standard versions in parallel columns at top of the page. Introduction and exegesis by Filson, the exposition by Reid. A thorough treatment by two liberal American scholars. Accepts Pauline authorship of the epistle but rejects its unity, holding that chapters 10-13 are a part of a "stern letter" prior to 2 Cor. 1-9.

Goudge, H. L., "The Second Epistle to the Corinthians." *Westminster Commentaries.* London: Methuen & Co. (1927).

Heading, John, *Second Epistle to the Corinthians.* Kilmarnock, Scotland: John Ritchie, (1966).

2. When an author's work on both epistles appears in two separate volumes, comments generally are given only in the book list under 1 Corinthians.

Hodge, Charles, *An Exposition of the Second Epistle to the Corinthians.* Grand Rapids: Wm. B. Eerdmans Pub. Co. (1860; 1950 reprint).

Hughes, Philip Edgcumbe, "Paul's Second Epistle to the Corinthians." "*The New International Commentary on the New Testament.* Grand Rapids: Wm. B. Eerdmans Pub. Co. (1962), 508 pp.

A thorough exposition of 2 Corinthians, strongly defending the unity of the epistle. An outstanding volume in this significant series, and one of the very best single-volume conservative commentaries on this epistle.

Ironside, H. A., *Addresses on the Second Epistle to the Corinthians.* New York: Loizeaux Brothers (1939).

Kelly, William, *Notes on the Second Epistle of Paul the Apostle to the Corinthians, with a New Translation.* London: G. Morris (1882; reprint, n.d.).

Luck, G. Coleman, "Second Corinthians." *Everyman's Bible Commentary.* Chicago: Moody Press (1959).

Menzies, Allan, *The Second Epistle of the Apostle Paul to the Corinthians.* London: Macmillan and Co. (1912).

Uses the Greek and an original translation on facing pages. A thorough introductory discussion of Paul's relations to the Corinthians between our 1 and 2 Corinthians. Defends the unity of 2 Corinthians. Concise, valuable verse-by-verse comments.

Meyer, J. P., *Ministers of Christ. A Commentary on the Second Epistle of Paul to the Corinthians.* Milwaukee: Northwestern Pub. House (1963).

Greek text. A thorough interpretation by an evangelical Lutheran theologian. Aims at presenting a clear understanding of Paul's thought and the situation out of which the epistle arose. Holds to the unity of 2 Corinthians and a close connection with the first epistle.

Moule, Handley C. G., *The Second Epistle to the Corinthians. A Translation, Paraphrase, and Exposition.* Edited with appendixes by A. W. Handley Moule. Grand Rapids: Zondervan Publishing House (1962).

A devotional interpretation published posthumously. A welcome addition from a conservative Anglican churchman of the past generation. Similar to the author's devotional *Studies in Ephesians, Philippians, and Colossians.*

Plummer, Alfred, "A Critical and Exegetical Commentary on the Second Epistle of St. Paul to the Corinthians." *The International Critical Commentary*. Edinburgh: T. & T. Clark (1915).

An exhaustive commentary on the Greek text. Plummer insists on Pauline authorship of the entire book but holds that chapters 10-13 form a separate letter. Important for the Greek student.

———, "The Second Epistle of Paul the Apostle to the Corinthians." *Cambridge Greek Testament for Schools and Colleges*. Cambridge: University Press (1912).

Greek text with critical notes. Plummer asserts the genuineness of 2 Corinthians yet argues strongly against its unity. Insists that the offender in 2 Corinthians 2:5-11 cannot be the incestuous person of 1 Corinthians 5:1-8. Asserts that the historical treatment of the doctrine of the trinity begins with 2 Corinthians 13:14.

Strachan, R. H., "The Second Epistle of Paul to the Corinthians." *The Moffatt New Testament Commentary*. New York: Harper & Brothers (1935).

The text, in the Moffatt translation, arranged on the basis of the radical partition theory. A thoroughly liberal interpretation. Denies that the doctrine of the trinity is found in the Bible and questions the preexistence of Christ.

Tasker, R. V. G., "The Second Epistle of Paul to the Corinthians." *The Tyndale New Testament Commentaries*. Grand Rapids: Wm. B. Eerdmans Pub. Co. (1958).

A perceptive, concise interpretation by a British evangelical scholar. Maintains the unity and integrity of the epistle. Holds that Paul's "thorn in the flesh" refers not to physical affliction but to adversaries.

# 10

# ROMANS

## An Introduction to Romans

The Epistle to the Romans is acknowledged to be one of the most profound books in existence. Its impressive grandeur and impenetrable depths make it one of the most highly prized parts of Holy Scripture. It has very appropriately been termed the Cathedral of the Christian faith. It was not without adequate reason that this matchless epistle was assigned the first position among the Pauline writings in our New Testament Canon. It forms one of the major bulwarks of evangelical Christianity.

### THE CITY OF ROME IN A.D. 58.

1. *Importance.* As the capital of the fourth world empire, Rome was the largest and most important city in the world at the time. From it went forth the powers that held the vast Roman Empire under control. All roads ran to and from Rome. The influence of Rome was upon all men. And certainly the apostle Paul was not unaware of the strategic importance of the city in his vision of world evangelization. The latter part of the Acts definitely reveals the influence of Rome on the thinking and planning of the Apostle.

2. *Rule.* When the Epistle to the Romans was addressed to the saints resident in the world capital, Rome was experiencing the better days of the earlier years of Nero's reign (A.D. 54-68). The Empire was enjoying one of its happiest periods since the death of Augustus. This was largely due to the wise administration of Seneca and Burrus.[1] Although corruption and injustice lurked in many places, the government of the provinces was generally fair and just. The rule of the city was generally good.

1. Tenney Frank, *A History of Rome,* (1964 reprint), pp. 430-433.

> The police regulations of the city were strict and well executed. An attack was made on the exactions of publicans, and on the excessive power of freedmen. Law was growing in exactness owing to the influence of the Jurists, and was justly administered except where the Emperor's personal wishes intervened.[2]

3. *Population.* Located mainly on the left bank of the River Tiber, about fifteen miles from the Mediterranean Sea, the city of Rome was a teeming metropolis. The population of the city during the first century A.D. was formerly estimated as being between 1,200,000 and 2,000,000 inhabitants. In 1941, however, an inscription was discovered at Ostia with statistics indicating that in A.D. 14, the year of the death of Augustus, the city of Rome had a population of 4,100,000 inhabitants.[3]

This prodigious aggregation of human beings presented all the contrasts that are seen in any large city, only in an exaggerated form. Luxury and squalor, wealth and want existed side by side. The institution of slavery cast its baneful influence over the whole. Physical toil was despised and deemed fit only for slaves. Manufacturing and trade were considered the business of the slave and the foreigner. Only somewhat over half of the population were free citizens. Of these a comparatively small number were wealthy, while the vast majority were poor and lived on public or private charity. These pauper citizens were proud of their Roman citizenship and disdained the degradation of manual labor. "They cared for nothing beyond bread for the day, the games of the Circus, and the savage delight of gladiatorial shows."[4]

In the city might be found elements of almost every nationality, and each group brought its train of vices with it. One foreign element that left its impression on the life of the city was the Jewish population. This Jewish community had had its beginnings with the captives brought to Rome by Pompey after the taking of Jerusalem in 63 B.C. A number of these captive Jews were sold as slaves, but due to their obstinate adherence to their national customs they proved

2. William Sanday and Arthur C. Headlam, "A Critical and Exegetical Commentary on the Epistle to the Romans," *International Critical Commentary,* (1902), p. xvi.
3. Jack Finegan, *Light From the Ancient Past,* (Revised Ed., 1959), p. 368.
4. W. J. Conybeare and J. S. Howson, *The Life and Epistles of St. Paul,* (1949 reprint), p. 677. For a full description of Roman life and activities, see T. G. Tucker, *Life in the Roman World of Nero and St. Paul,* (1910); also see Jerome Carcopino, *Daily Life in Ancient Rome,* (1940).

troublesome to their masters and most of them were soon manumitted.

Because of the generally favorable attitude of the early emperors, the Jews became numerous in the city. When a deputation of fifty Jews from Judea arrived to complain of the misrule of Archelaus, no less than eight thousand Jews living in Rome attached themselves to the deputation to support its request.[5]

Because of continued disturbances among the Jews in the city, they were expelled from Rome by the edict of Claudius (Acts 18:2). Under Nero they returned in great numbers. They became sufficiently numerous in the city to have a number of synagogues.[6] Among the Roman Jews were a few aristocratic, influential men who had gained considerable wealth, but the majority of them were of the poorer type who haunted the markets with their baskets and wares.

4. *Religions.* The polytheistic heathen religion of Rome had fallen into the contempt of both the cultured and the uncultured classes of the city. This left the masses open to the ready penetration of various foreign religions being imported into the capital. There was in Rome a temple devoted to the worship of the Egyptian deities Isis and Serapis. Monuments of the worship of Mithras are known from the time of Tiberius. Nero himself reverenced the Syrian goddess Astarte.

The decay of Roman polytheism gave a ready entrance to the ethical monotheism proclaimed by the Jews. While the Jews with their strict observance of the Sabbath and rigid self-exclusion from the life of the masses aroused the hatred and contempt of their heathen neighbors, their religious creed attracted many who were in search of something better than that which the corrupt polytheistic religions had to offer them. "The inclination to Monotheism was very general; and the number of those who had gone over to Judaism was very great."[7] Around the various synagogues of the Jews there gradually grew up a considerable following of Gentiles more or less in active sympathy with their religion. Here as elsewhere in the Empire these "God-fearers" furnished fertile ground for the spread of Christianity.

5. Flavius Josephus, *Antiquities of the Jews,* XVII. xi. 1.
6. Alfred Wikenhauser, *New Testament Introduction,* (1963), says, "Thirteen are still known by name," p. 399, note, with source references.
7. Heinrich August Wilhelm Meyer, *Critical and Exegetical Hand-Book to the Epistle to the Romans,* (1884), p. 18.

THE CHURCH IN ROME

1. *Date of origin.* It is impossible to determine when Christianity was first introduced at Rome. When Paul wrote his epistle to the Roman congregation, it must have already been in existence for a number of years, for Paul informs them that "these many years" he has had a desire to visit them (15:23). He felt that the church there was sufficiently strong to assist him in carrying out his plans for missionary work in Spain (15:24). Zahn holds that in Romans "Paul nowhere says anything which implies that he is dealing with recent converts."[8] Paul does not regard the group as being inadequately instructed but definitely assures them that he is confident that they are "filled with all knowledge, able to admonish one another" (15:14). From what Paul says in chapter 12 it would appear that these Roman Christians constituted an organized church. But how far back its history extended is not known.

2. *Membership.* The generally accepted view is that when Paul wrote this epistle there was a church of considerable size at Rome. From the last chapter it appears that they met for worship in several different houses. Whether this was due to their lack of an adequate place for united assembly, or due to their scattered location in that great city, cannot be determined. Lenski, indeed, takes the singular position that the church at Rome was not large and that the list of names to whom greetings are sent in 16:3-16 in reality gives us "the whole congregation" at Rome.[9]

The contents of the epistle make it evident that the membership of the Roman church was composed of both Jewish and Gentile Christians, like most churches at that time. Evidences for the Jewish element in the church are found in the use of certain expressions in the epistle. In 4:1 Paul speaks of Abraham as "our forefather," and in 9:10 he speaks of "our father Isaac." In 7:1-6 a contrast is drawn between an earlier state under the law and the later state of freedom which suggests a Jewish background. It is often asserted that the character of the argumentation in the epistle likewise implies Jewish readers.

But the epistle gives fuller evidence of a Gentile element in the Roman church. In 1:5 Paul, who considered himself the Apostle of

8. Theodor Zahn, *Introduction to the New Testament,* (1909), Vol. I, p. 428.
9. R. C. H. Lenski, *The Interpretation of St. Paul's Epistle to the Romans,* (1936), pp. 20-22.

the Gentiles, addresses the church at Rome as included in his apostleship "among all the nations." In 1:13 Paul says that he desires to visit them in order that he may have some fruit in them "even as in the rest of the Gentiles." In 11:13 he addresses the Roman church by saying, "I speak to you that are Gentiles." And in 15:14-16 he courteously excuses himself for the earnestness with which he has written by an appeal to his commission to act as the priest who lays upon the altar the church of the Gentiles as his offering.

The question as to which of these two elements predominated in the Roman church has received directly opposite answers.[10] The issue was raised in all its sharpness by Baur, the head of the Tübingen school, who imported the Judaizing controversy into the Roman church and accordingly saw the church as largely Jewish. While it cannot be said with absolute certainty which element was predominant, it seems most likely that the majority of the members were from the Gentiles, but a minority were of Jewish origin. Because of the strong inclination to monotheism in Rome, it is evident that many Gentiles, already dissatisfied with their pagan religions, would be attracted to Christianity. Perhaps many of them had been among the "God-fearers" attending the Jewish synagogues formerly. While evidently there was a strong Jewish element in the Roman church, it does not necessarily follow, as Lange has pointed out, that they were anti-Pauline in their sympathies.[11] Many of Paul's staunchest supporters were Jewish Christians.

3. *Origin.* The question of the origin of the church at Rome is cloaked in historical obscurity. Three views have been advanced.

The Roman Catholic view has been that the church was founded by the apostle Peter. But historical evidence does not support this position. The claim that Peter went to Rome in A.D. 42, after his escape from prison under Herod Agrippa I (Acts 12), and remained there for twenty-five years is impossible in view of the evidence in the New Testament. This claim is now given up even by Roman Catholic scholars.[12] From Acts it is impossible to believe that Peter

10. For the different views and advocates, see Donald Guthrie, *New Testament Introduction,* (Revised Ed., 1970), pp. 395-396.
11. John Peter Lange, "The Epistle of Paul to the Romans," Lange's *Commentary,* (1950 reprint), p. 34.
12. J. J. Castelot, "Peter, Apostle, St.," *New Catholic Encyclopedia,* (1967), Vol. XI, p. 204, says: "An old tradition that he spent 25 years in Rome is quite unacceptable. All that can be said with certainty is that he went to Rome and was martyred there." Alfred Wikenhauser, *New Testament Introduction,* (1963), p. 399,

was in Rome for twenty-five years. Peter was still in Jerusalem during the Jerusalem Conference (Acts 15). There is no evidence in the New Testament earlier than our 1 Peter that Peter ever went to Rome, and that only on the uncertain assumption that "Babylon" really means Rome (1 Peter 5:13). If Peter had been in Rome when Paul wrote to the Romans he could not have failed to mention him. If Peter founded the church at Rome, for Paul to have written to them as he did would have been to violate his principle not to build upon another man's foundation (Rom. 15:20). Near the end of his two years' imprisonment in Rome, when writing to the Philippians, Paul gives no indication that Peter had yet seen the Roman capital. In view of Paul's announced principle not to transgress upon the field of labor of the other apostles, it is impossible to believe that, when Paul wrote Romans, the Roman church had as yet been the scene of any apostolic labors.

Another view has been that the church at Rome had its origin through the efforts of Roman Jews converted at Pentecost. Acts 2:10 informs us that there were Jews from Rome present at Jerusalem during the first Pentecost. Surely some of these must have been among the number saved. These, it is held, returned to Rome with their new faith, and through their influence the church there was started. In objection to this view it may be said that there is no other instance on record where any of these Pentecostal converts returned to their native land to establish a Christian church. These Pentecostal converts seem rather to have been foreign-born Jews who had taken up permanent residence in Jerusalem to end their days there.[13] If some of these Pentecostal converts did return to Rome, as is probable, their influence would have been exerted in the Jewish synagogues in Rome. And if they did succeed in winning a following in Rome, the result would have been definitely a Jewish-Christian church. Yet the church at Rome seems to be predominantly Gentile, at least definitely sympathetic toward the Pauline presentation of the Gospel. Yet how could such a church have been begun in Rome when as yet the Gospel had not even been opened up to the Gentiles in Palestine? We may say with Stifler, "It would be a much better guess to say that

asserts: "The Apostle Peter cannot have founded the community, for his arrival in Rome probably took place in the fifties at the earliest." But see John E. Steinmueller, *A Companion to Scripture Studies, Volume III,* (1969), p. 264.

13. R. C. H. Lenski, *The Interpretation of the Acts of the Apostles,* (1934), p. 62.

some from the household of Cornelius (Acts 10) carried to Rome the news of a Saviour for the Gentiles."[14]

The most likely view is that the church at Rome was begun when several small groups, or families of Christians, from Pauline churches in the East settled in Rome and, finding each other, got together for worship. The church seems to have been independent of the Jewish synagogues in Rome. From Acts 28 it appears that when Paul arrived in Rome there had as yet been no serious conflict between the Jewish synagogues and the Christians there. This suggests that the church was founded independently by converts from Pauline churches in the East who had gone to Rome for various reasons. The cities in which Gentile Christianity was firmly established in the eastern provinces—Antioch, Ephesus, Corinth—were in constant communication with Rome. Romans 16 shows that a number of Paul's acquaintances had moved to Rome and would be active in the Gospel there. It is safe to say that the self-propagating nature of Christianity carried it to Rome, not on one occasion only, but on different occasions and under varied circumstances. Thus apparently the church at Rome owed its origin to the migration to Rome of Christians from the eastern part of the Empire who had been converted as they came into contact with the Gospel as presented by Paul. Some of these would be Jews and others Gentiles.

4. *Status.* The epistle gives no direct information as to the inner condition of the Roman church. There is no refutation of any error into which the church has fallen. Neither does the epistle contain any statement concerning any church organization. (This stands in striking contrast to later ecclesiastical developments in Rome.) This does not, however, mean that the church was unorganized. The presence of a number of Paul's friends leaves it improbable that they were unorganized. All Jewish Christians, as well as Gentiles who had frequented the Jewish synagogues, would know how to organize such a group, namely, after the pattern of the synagogue. Paul recognized that they had different gifts and were using them in the church, (12:6-8) and felt that they were well able to "admonish one another" (15:14).

Paul says that this church was universally famous (1:8). This was no doubt due to the fact that all roads led to and from Rome. In the

14. James M. Stifler, *The Epistle to the Romans,* (1897), p. xi.

various cities where Paul worked in the East he would come into contact with people from Rome who knew about the Christians there.

From the last chapter of Romans it appears that the Christians in Rome met in several different places. Perhaps because they were widely scattered over that large city, they naturally met in local centers for worship. But since the epistle is addressed to all these groups, they doubtless had constant contacts with each other. This list of names in Romans 16 also suggests that the church was composed of freedmen as well as slaves. Those in the household of Aristobulus and Narcissus would belong to the latter group (16:10-11).

Some six years after the writing of this epistle, subsequent to Paul's two years at Rome, the Roman church was a very large group. At the outbreak of the Neronian persecutions in A.D. 64, the historian Tacitus speaks of the Christians in Rome as "an immense multitude."

### THE UNITY OF ROMANS

As with Second Corinthians, the critical problem of Romans centers around the unity rather than the authenticity of the epistle. The Pauline authorship of the epistle is beyond any doubt. It is one of the basic epistles of Paul accepted by all schools of criticism. Attacks against the Pauline authorship did not arise until the close of the eighteenth century and the subsequent development of the higher criticism. These radical critics have failed to make out their case against the epistle. Says C. H. Dodd, "The authenticity of the Epistle to the Romans is a closed question."[15] But that cannot yet be said concerning the question of the unity of Romans.

1. *Textual phenomena.* Certain variations in the text and certain facts reported on tradition with regard to the last two chapters of Romans have brought the question of the unity of the epistle into sharp focus. These phenomena may be briefly indicated, beginning with the traditional evidence.

It seems certain that Marcion did not have the last two chapters in his canon. It is known that his text did not contain the doxology. There is also evidence that the early Latin Version ended the epistle with chapter 14 and the doxology of 16:25-27. In a system of early Latin chapter-headings for the Pauline epistles our 15:1—16:24 is not

15. C. H. Dodd, "The Epistle of Paul to the Romans," *Moffatt Commentary,* (1932), p. xiii.

represented. However, there is no extant Greek manuscript which omits these two chapters.

There is, however, considerable variation in existing manuscripts concerning the place of the final doxology (16:25-27). In most of the very oldest manuscripts the doxology stands at the end of chapter 16 and there only.[16] Papyrus 46 stands alone in placing the doxology after 15:33. Codex L and Psi, a number of late cursives, Byzantine lectionaries, and a few Church Fathers place it at the end of chapter 14 and there only. Codex A and P and a few cursives have the doxology at the end of both chapter 14 and chapter 16. Codex F (Greek text) and G (which leaves a space after ch. 14) omit it entirely.

2. *Critical theories.* Aided by these textual phenomena as well as the contents of chapter 16, two different theories have been advanced attacking the unity of the epistle. The first of these holds that the last two chapters are not part of the original Epistle to the Romans. The second theory, advanced on subjective grounds, holds that the last chapter is not a part of the original epistle. Both positions may concede the Pauline authorship of the portion being excised but deny that it is a part of the Epistle to the Romans.

On the basis of the existing textual phenomena the view has been advanced that the last two chapters are not part of the epistle. But to hold that the epistle ended with chapter 14 is to leave it weak and the argument incomplete. Chapter 15:1-13 is the natural sequel to chapter 14. It seems incredible that Paul should have closed the epistle with chapter 14. That Paul wrote chapter 15 is now commonly admitted. But if it was not written in connection with chapter 14, how are we to account for the existence of an independent passage so eminently fitted to be joined to the epistle?

As an attempt to explain the existing phenomena in connection with these last two chapters, it has been postulated that Paul issued Romans in two editions, a longer and a shorter form. But it seems highly improbable that the Apostle would thus mutilate his own work. Much more probable is the view that Paul wrote the epistle in its long form and that it was later cut down by others. Some have thought that this was the work of Marcion, the noted heretic of the

16. For the textual variants see United Bible Societies, *The Greek New Testament,* (1966); for a discussion, William Sanday and Arthur C. Headlam, "A Critical and Exegetical Commentary on the Epistle to the Romans," *International Critical Commentary,* (1902), pp. lxxxix-xcviii; Werner Georg Kümmel, *Introduction to the New Testament,* (1966), pp. 222-224.

second century, whose theological anti-Semitism caused him to deal drastically with the Canon of the New Testament. It is quite possible that he disliked the references to the Jews and to the Old Testament in chapter 15 and therefore cut out these last two chapters. Tertullian accused Marcion of "cutting off" these last two chapters.

On the other hand, it is not impossible that the mutilation was done by orthodox editors or copyists in an effort to give the epistle a more universal tone. In seeking to adapt the epistle for use in other churches, these last two chapters, being largely of local and temporary interest, might be omitted. An apparent illustration of this universalizing tendency may be seen in Codex G which omits the words "in Rome" in 1:7 and 15 of the epistle.

Whatever the origin of the existing phenomena in regard to the last two chapters, it is admitted on all sides today that chapter 15 is an inherent part of the original epistle.

The second attack on the unity of Romans, which maintains that the last chapter only is not part of the original epistle, has proceeded entirely on internal grounds. Until the discovery of the Chester Beatty Papyrus, $P^{46}$, which places the doxology at the close of chapter 15, there had been no textual evidence to support this view. This discovery has been hailed as offering "striking support" to the view, first advanced on purely internal grounds, that the last chapter is really an independent letter and not part of the Epistle to the Romans.[17] It is held that this chapter is a separate letter, usually said to have been written to Ephesus. It is claimed that the long list of names in this chapter point to Ephesus rather than to Rome. "It is improbable," it is said, "that St. Paul knew so many people at Rome. . . . On the other hand St. Paul knew many in Ephesus, where he had laboured for two years."[18] Had Paul's friends migrated to Rome in a body even before he got there? Epaenetus, "the firstfruits of Asia unto Christ" (16:5), would most naturally be found in Asia. Aquila and Prisca were last heard of at Ephesus (1 Cor. 16:19). Moreover, in 2 Timothy 4:19 they are still seen at Ephesus while Paul was in Rome. In support of this view it is further pointed out that the sharp warning against heretics and schismatics in 16:17-20 does not agree with the earlier part of Romans but does suit Ephesus where such troubles did exist.

17. Edgar J. Goodspeed, *An Introduction to the New Testament*, (1937), p. 75.
18. W. H. Bennett and Walter F. Adeney, *A Biblical Introduction*, (1919), p. 380.

According to this view Romans 16 originated as a letter of introduction for Phoebe who was going to Ephesus on some business. And Paul took the occasion to send his greetings to his numerous friends at Ephesus and to issue a warning against the intrigues and divisions which were rife in Ephesus (Acts 20:19, 29-30).[19]

There is considerable to be said for this Ephesian hypothesis; it has received widespread support. But this view presents some definite difficulties.

To hold that chapter 16, which consists very largely of personal greetings, is an independent letter is to create a very odd letter indeed. It has been aptly remarked that such a letter, consisting almost entirely of greetings, would be a monstrosity for any other age than our modern penny picture-postcard age. The ancients would not have thought of writing such a letter.

The contention that Paul could not have known so many people at Rome is quite unfounded. Most of the people mentioned come from the very centers of Paul's labors that had had the most frequent intercourse with Rome. It was not at all unusual for people from the eastern part of the Empire to go to Rome and reside there. Zahn feels rather that this very list of names in this chapter is especially appropriate in an epistle to the Romans; Paul deliberately adds all these names to make the church at Rome feel that after all he is not such a stranger to them as may at first appear. Zahn contends that Paul "must have concluded his letter with a passage at least closely resembling 15:13—16:24."[20]

Further, to send individual greetings to a church where he knew all the members would be quite contrary to Paul's practice in his other epistles. No personal greetings are found in the letters to Thessalonica, Philippi, Corinth, or Galatia. The only epistle to a church which contains greetings to individuals is the one to the Colossians, to whom he was a stranger. Thus in writing to the church at Rome, where he has not yet been, it is but natural that he should send his greetings to the Christians there whom he knew.

Dodd points out that the unusual expression in 16:16, "All the churches of Christ salute you," finds its most natural explanation if it occurs in a letter to Rome written from Corinth at a time when Paul

19. James Moffatt, *An Introduction to the Literature of the New Testament,* (3rd Ed., 1939 reprint), pp. 134-139.
20. Theodor Zahn, *Introduction to the New Testament,* (1909), Vol. I, p. 389.

was in touch with the delegates from his various Gentile churches having a share in the collection. If these greetings were addressed to Ephesus the expression remains unexplained.[21]

The contention that the tone of the warning in 16:17-20 does not agree with the earlier part of the epistle does present a problem. The warning is added simply as a postscript and need not necessarily be in keeping with the theme of the epistle as a whole. It is very probable that Paul should personally have added such a note at the end because he well knew the dangers from the Judaizing party, having just recently battled with them in the Corinthian church.

The claim that our epistle cannot be a unit because it has four endings cannot be substantiated (cf. 15:33; 16:20; 16:24, A.V.; 16:25-27). The formula in 15:33 is nowhere else used by Paul to conclude an epistle but finds illustration in the body of his writings (cf. Rom. 15:5; 9:5). In 16:20 we do have one of Paul's formal conclusions (cf. 1 Thess. 5:28; 2 Thess. 3:18; Phil. 4:23; Philem. 25). It stands at the close of the formal part of the letter, but by way of postscript the Apostle adds some greetings from his companions. The ending in 16:24 in the King James Version, following the *Textus Receptus,* is not supported by manuscript evidence and is rightly omitted in the critical text. Following the greetings from his companions, the Apostle adds a final doxology in which he sums up the main thought of the epistle (16:25-27) and thus concludes on a lofty spiritual note.

3. *Conclusion.* We unhesitatingly conclude that Paul would not have terminated the epistle with chapter 14. The textual phenomena are best explained as due to later tampering with the text.

The balance of evidence seems definitely in favor of Romans 16 as part of the original letter. It is remarkable that Papyrus 46 has the doxology at the end of chapter 15, but this fact is no more conclusive proof that chapter 16 is an independent letter than the presence of the doxology at the end of 14 proves that the last two chapters do not belong to the original. Papyrus 46 has some curious readings which cannot be accepted as authentic. We reject the view that the chapter is a separate letter to the Ephesians as unjustified.

The recent conjecture of Knox that chapter 16 is "a pseudonymous addition to the letter to the Romans designed to bind the apostle

21. C. H. Dodd, "The Epistle of Paul to the Romans," *Moffatt Commentary,* (1932), pp. xx, 240.

more closely to Rome and to strengthen the hands of that church in its battle with the Gnostics in the second century,"[22] is without supporting evidence. We reject the hypothesis because it further stamps this closing chapter of Romans as spurious.

THE PLACE AND DATE OF ROMANS

1. *Place.* Viewed in the light of the Acts and the Corinthian epistles, the content of Romans clearly indicates that it was written from Corinth on the third missionary journey. As Paul writes the epistle he has not yet visited Rome, but he has high hopes of soon being able to fulfill that long-entertained desire (1:10; 15:22-23). A collection has been raised in the churches of Macedonia and Achaia for the saints in Judea, and he is now going to Jerusalem to deliver it (15:25-26). Considerable is said about this collection in the Corinthian epistles (1 Cor. 16:1-4; 2 Cor. 8 and 9). The incidental reference to this offering by Paul in his speech before Felix (Acts 24:17) makes it certain that it was raised on the third missionary journey. As he writes he is staying with Gaius (16:23). This Gaius seems to be the same man mentioned in 1 Corinthians 1:14 as one of the members of the church at Corinth. Erastus, the treasurer of the city, sends greetings (16:23), and this implies a capital, or at least a large city. Phoebe, a member of the church at Cenchreae, is on her way to Rome, and he mentions Cenchreae as though it were near at hand (16:1-2). He mentions that he has preached the Gospel "even unto Illyricum" (15:19), a statement which he could not have made until he got to Achaia on his third missionary journey. All of this points to the time of Paul's stay at Corinth for three months on the third journey (Acts 20:2-3).

2. *Date.* This epistle was written during Paul's stay of three months at Corinth, but certain factors seem further to limit the time for its composition. The tranquil atmosphere of the epistle suggests that it was written some time after Paul's arrival in Corinth, after all the harassing troubles in Corinth had been settled. The plans of Phoebe to go to Rome indicate a season when navigation was beginning to open up again. All navigation on the Mediterranean Sea ceased after November 11 and was not resumed again until March 10. Corinth would be very conscious of this resumption of its commercial ac-

22. John Knox and Gerald R. Cragg, "The Epistle to the Romans," *The Interpreter's Bible,* (1954), Vol. IX, p. 654. For his discussion see pp. 365-368; 653-658.

tivities. Paul's statement in Romans, "but now . . . I go to Jerusalem" (15:25), implies that he planned to sail for Palestine directly from Corinth, and Corinth would offer ample opportunities for the trip. But from Acts 20:3 we learn that because of a plot by the Jews against him he changed his plans and went by way of Macedonia. The epistle, therefore, seems to have been written before the discovery of this plot which necessitated the change in plans. Paul left for Jerusalem from Philippi immediately after the Easter season (Acts 20:6). These factors indicate a date for the epistle in the early months of the year A.D. 58, perhaps during the month of February.

3. *Bearer.* Nothing is directly said concerning the bearer of the epistle. It is generally supposed that the bearer was Phoebe—"a supposition which there is nothing to contradict."[23]

### THE OCCASION FOR ROMANS

The occasion for the writing of Romans is clear from its contents. It was not due to any internal conditions in the Roman church but rather to the development of Paul's own plans. He has finished his missionary labors in the eastern provinces (15:23) and now feels free to inaugurate in the West the labors he has anticipated for some time (Acts 19:21). As soon as he has taken the collection to Jerusalem, he plans to stop at Rome to visit the church there on his way to Spain (15:24). Doubtless the contents of the epistle had for some time been formulating themselves in his mind. When he learned of the impending visit of Phoebe to Rome he determined to avail himself of the opportunity to communicate with the Roman church and to inform them of his coming and his plans. The letter was dictated to a Christian scribe named Tertius, who is given liberty to add a greeting in his own name (16:22).

### THE PURPOSE OF ROMANS

Although the immediate occasion for the writing of Romans is obvious, the attempt of the scholars to determine the reason why Paul wrote the kind of letter that he did has produced a diversity of answers. Varied statements as to the purpose of Romans have been

23. Heinrich August Wilhelm Meyer, *Critical and Exegetical Hand-Book to the Epistle to the Romans,* (1884), p. 565.

given. Almost all of these statements strike one as containing definite truth. Denney has rightly pointed out that

> A writing of such comprehensive scope and such infinite variety of application—a writing at once so personal and historical, and so universal and eternal, is not easily reduced to a formula which leaves nothing to be desired.[24]

It seems obvious that when a man of Paul's ability sat down to write an epistle such as this one, several purposes would be in his mind. Several considerations entered into the actual production of the epistle.

1. *Missionary plans.* Paul wrote to enlist the cooperation and assistance of the church at Rome for the inauguration of his missionary campaign in the West. In planning for missionary work in the western part of the Empire, Paul had come to realize the importance of Rome. He clearly saw that it must become his base of operation for the western work, as Antioch had been for the work in the eastern provinces. In launching this new undertaking he needed the help of the Roman church. He clearly suggests that he expects assistance from his readers in the endeavor to carry the Gospel to Spain (15:24). But much more important than the financial assistance which they would be able to give him was the need for their moral support in the propagation of the Gospel.

2. *Center for Pauline Gospel.* Another purpose of the Apostle in writing was to win the church of Rome as the basis for his universal Gospel. His controversies with the Judaizers have fully established the fact of a free Gospel for the Gentiles. This victory, however, has brought into sharp relief the question of the relation between the Jew and the Gentile in the Gospel. The problem of this relation is now pressing upon the Apostle. He is seeking to bring about the union of Jew and Gentile in one universal Christian Church. His going to Jerusalem with the offering from his Gentile churches for the Judean saints is prompted by his desire to bring these two groups into effective union in the Gospel. As he looks toward the West he is anxious to have a strong basis for the spread of this universal Gospel. Accordingly, he unfolds before the Roman Christians the religious and moral strength of his Gospel and shows that it is fully

24. James Denney, "St. Paul's Epistle to the Romans," *Expositor's Greek Testament* (n.d.), Vol. II, p. 568.

adapted to save Jew and Gentile alike, uniting them both in one Body. He fully presents the doctrine of salvation through faith in the first eight chapters, and then in chapters 9-11 he deals with the problem of the relation of the Jews, the Chosen People, to this great salvation. In the remainder of the epistle he shows that this Gospel must have practical application in the lives of its followers (12:1–13:14) and that it is capable of solving the problem of the relationship between the Jew and Gentile (14:1–15:13). Of this epistle Barmby says,

> It is, in its ultimate drift, a setting forth of what we may call the philosophy of the gospel, showing how it meets human needs, and satisfies human yearnings, and is the true solution of the problems of existence, and the remedy for the present mystery of sin. And so it is meant for philosophers as well as for simple souls; and it is sent, therefore, in the first place, to Rome, in the hope that it may reach even the most cultured there, and through them commend itself to earnest thinkers generally.[25]

This presentation of his universal Gospel the Apostle feels will strengthen the faith of the Roman saints and prepare them to enter fully into the propagation of the Gospel in the West.

3. *Prayer support.* In writing to the Romans Paul also sought to enlist their prayers for his present venture at Jerusalem (15:30-33). He had serious misgivings as to the outcome of that journey. He could be certain that he would encounter the implacable hatred of the unbelieving Jews and was not too sure of the reaction to his presence among the Jewish Christians in Jerusalem. "He evidently looked forward to serious difficulties, and even dangers, in Jerusalem, and this might therefore easily be his last Epistle."[26] This aspect of the historical situation has caused some writers to see a *testamentary* purpose in the epistle. Miller states it thus,

> He bequeaths to them in the form of this Epistle the Gospel that he would preach to them, should he be permitted to reach there, and if not, they have his letter to read and refer to again and again.[27]

4. *Prophylactic intent.* A lesser purpose in writing the epistle seems

25. J. Barmby, "The Epistle of Paul to the Romans," *Pulpit Commentary,* (1950 reprint), p. x.
26. W. H. Griffith Thomas, "St. Paul's Epistles to the Romans," *Devotional Commentary,* (1946 reprint), p. 19.
27. Adam W. Miller, *An Introduction to the New Testament,* (1946), p. 209.

to have been to safeguard the Roman church against the errors and practices which had caused him so much trouble in the churches of Galatia and in Corinth. A church fully committed to the truths set forth in this epistle would not be readily swayed by the appeals of the Judaizers. This purpose is implied, although rather incidentally, in the warning in 16:17-20. This has been referred to as the *prophylactic* purpose of the epistle. This must not, however, be overstressed. As Lenski has said, "In its very nature truth is prophylactic and arms in advance against error; beyond that Romans shows no trace of prophylaxis."[28]

5. *Theological formulation.* While giving full recognition to all these historical indications as to the purpose of the epistle, it is evident that the Apostle is being divinely led to give to the Church of Christ this clear and comprehensive presentation of the doctrine of salvation by faith for all subsequent generations. Here is the touchstone by which all that claims to be Christian must be tested. It gives the heart of the Gospel without which there can be no salvation. And as such it has proved to be one of the major bulwarks of evangelical Christianity.

### THE CHARACTERISTICS OF ROMANS

1. *Character and style.* The Epistle to the Romans is the most formal of Paul's writings. If the distinction between a letter and an epistle were to be sharply drawn, this would be an epistle. Yet it is unnecessary to press the distinction in regard to the writings of Paul. "No writing in the New Testament is less causal; none is more catholic and eternal."[29] It thus stands in remarkable contrast to Galatians, which is so obviously causal in its nature and contents.

Although written to inhabitants of Rome, the epistle was composed in the Greek langauge. This is no matter of surprise, since Greek was in general use in Rome among large sections of its inhabitants, if not in the city as a whole. While Latin was the native language of Rome, there are evidences in the classics which point to the universal adoption of Greek habits and language at Rome.

The outstanding characteristic of Romans is its universalism. It

28. R. C. H. Lenski, *The Interpretation of St. Paul's Epistle to the Romans,* (1936), p. 19.
29. James Denney, "St. Paul's Epistle to the Romans," *Expositor's Greek Testament,* (n.d.), Vol. II, p. 574.

shows that in all times and nations men are sinners. This universal sinfulness of man is traced back to mankind's ultimate oneness in Adam. In the Gospel there is offered a full salvation that is available to all alike, whether Jew or Gentile, on the principle of faith. And this free salvation is treated "not in its relation to a single soul or even a single church, but in its relation to the creation itself and to every nation in it."[30] The resultant duties of the believer which arise out of this salvation are likewise comprehensively viewed in the epistle.

The epistle is characterized by the systematic and logical arrangement of its contents. It is one of the finest pieces of logic ever penned. It is full of originality of thought and is forceful in its presentation. Not infrequently its contents rise into grand eloquence. Says Stifler,

> Other epistles have eloquent passages, like I Corinthians xiii. and xv. or Ephesians iii. 8-21; but in this epistle there are such passages in almost every chapter (i. 16-23; ii. 4-11; iii. 21-26, etc.), but notably the conclusions of both chapter viii and chapter xi. The whole epistle is marked by a sustained elevation of thought and sentiment.[31]

The language of the epistle is marked by great energy, yet without vehemence. Sanday and Headlam say that the language is "rapid, terse, incisive; the argument is conducted by a quick cut and thrust of dialectic."[32]

2. *Contents.* The Epistle to the Romans is profoundly doctrinal. Yet it is an exaggeration of its contents to say that "in the Epistle to the Romans is contained, as it were, a system of Pauline doctrine."[33] It is not a systematic theology, nor was it intended to be. Several important aspects of Christian truth, expounded elsewhere by the Apostle, are not elaborated in Romans. The doctrine of the person of Christ is not developed as in the "Prison Epistles." The resurrection is assumed rather than argued as in 1 Corinthians 15. Eschatology, prominent in the Thessalonian epistles, has a comparatively minor place here. The epistle is rather a comprehensive statement of the doctrine of salvation by faith. In the first eight chapters the doctrine is presented; in chapters 9-11 the vital question of the relation of the

30. James M. Stifler, *The Epistle to the Romans,* (1897), p. xvii.
31. *Ibid.*
32. William Sanday and Arthur C. Headlam, "A Critical and Exegetical Commentary on the Epistle to the Romans," *International Critical Commentary,* (1902) p. lv.
33. Herman Olshausen, *Biblical Commentary on the New Testament, The Epistle to the Romans,* (1849), p. 52.

Jew to this salvation is considered; beginning with chapter 12 the Apostle shows the practical application of the doctrine in different areas.

There are more quotations from the Old Testament in this epistle than in all the other epistles together. Moule counts at least sixty-one direct quotations, and adds, "The allusions to Old Testament history, type, and doctrine extend, of course, far beyond even these verbal references."[34] The quotations are taken from at least fourteen different books of the Old Testament. The two books most frequently quoted are Isaiah and Psalms.

3. *Influence.* The Epistle to the Romans has exerted a profound influence upon the course of Christian theology and history. It has been said that the influence of this epistle was connected with every great spiritual revival in the history of the Church. Together with Galatians it lay at the basis of the Protestant Reformation. Luther found in this epistle the heart of the Gospel and used it as one of his keenest weapons in his fight with the Papacy. This epistle lay at the basis of the revivals in the eighteenth and the nineteenth centuries. Evangelical Christianity has always treasured the epistle as the touchstone of the Gospel. David Brown has pointed out the predominant influence of Romans in the following words,

> While all Scripture has stamped its impress indelibly on the Christian world, perhaps it is scarcely too much to say, that—apart from the Gospels—for all the *precision* and the *strength* which it possesses, and much of the *spirituality* and the *fire* which characterize it, the faith of Christendom in its best periods has been more indebted to this Epistle than to any other portion of the living oracles.[35]

### THE TRIBUTES TO ROMANS

The very grandeur of the Epistle to the Romans has called forth numerous eloquent tributes to it. It is rightly considered the masterpiece of the apostle Paul. The keenest theological minds of subsequent ages have confessed that it contains depths which they are unable to fathom. It is a treasure whose loss would immeasurably

34. H. C. G. Moule, "The Epistle of Paul the Apostle to the Romans," *Cambridge Bible for Schools,* (1881), p. 31.
35. David Brown, "The Epistle to the Romans," *Handbooks for Bible Classes,* (7th impression, 1950), p. xviii. Italics in original.

impoverish the Christian world. The following are worthy representatives of the tributes that have been bestowed upon the epistle.

In his famous "Preface to the Epistle to the Romans" (1522) Luther said,

> This Epistle is really the chief part of the New Testament and the very purest Gospel, and is worthy not only that every Christian should know it word for word, by heart, but occupy himself with it every day, as the daily bread of the soul. It can never be read or pondered too much, and the more it is dealt with the more precious it becomes, and the better it tastes.[36]

S. T. Coleridge, in his *Table-Talk* (June 15, 1833), felt constrained to say, "I think St. Paul's Epistle to the Romans the most profound book in existence."

Philip Schaff in his monumental *History of the Christian Church* says of this epistle,

> It is the most remarkable production of the most remarkable man. It is his heart. It contains his theology, theoretical and practical, for which he lived and died. It gives the clearest and fullest exposition of the doctrines of sin and grace and the best possible solution of the universal dominion of sin and death in the universal redemption by the second Adam.[37]

And a recent expositor states of the epistle,

> Romans, among the epistles of the New Testament, stands out like an imposing Cathedral. Its symmetry of form, its logically developed structure, its evidence of plan and design, its wide sweep of thought, its sublimity and grandeur of revelation, all combine to make it one of the loveliest edifices of truth in existence.[38]

## An Outline of Romans

### THE INTRODUCTION (1:1-17)

1. The salutation (1-7)
   a. The writer (1-6)
      1) His position (1)

36. Martin Luther, *Works of Martin Luther*, (1932), Vol. VI, p. 447.
37. Philip Schaff, *History of the Christian Church*, (1910), Vol. I, p. 766.
38. William G. Coltman, *The Cathedral of Christian Truth—Studies in Romans*, (1943), opposite table of contents.

2) His message (2-4)
   a) The Scriptural promise (2)
   b) The exalted theme (3-4)
3) His apostleship (5-6)
   a) The nature of his apostleship (5)
   b) The inclusion of the Romans in the apostleship (6)

b. The readers (7a)
c. The greeting (7b)

2. The fraternal relations to the Romans (8-16a)
   a. The thanksgiving for them (8)
   b. The prayer in relation to them (9-10)
   c. The desire to visit them (11-16a)
      1) The statement of the desire (11a)
      2) The purpose in the desire (11b-12)
      3) The hindrance to its fulfillment (13a)
      4) The explanation for the desire (13b)
      5) The motivation behind the desire (14-16a)
         a) His sense of obligation to all Gentiles (14)
         b) His personal readiness to preach at Rome also (15)
         c) His confidence in the Gospel (16a)
3. The Theme: The Gospel as God's Power Revealing the Righteousness of God (16b-17)

Part I: Doctrinal (1:8–8:39)

## THE RIGHTEOUSNESS OF GOD REVEALED IN THE GOSPEL

### I. THE NEED FOR RIGHTEOUSNESS BECAUSE OF UNIVERSAL SIN (1:18–3:20)

1. The condemnation of the Gentile world (1:18-32)
   a. The fact of the wrath of God against sin (18)
   b. The reasons for the wrath of God (19-23)
      1) Their knowledge of God leaves them without excuse (19-20)
      2) Their corruption of the knowledge of God shows them guilty (21-23)
   c. The revelation of the wrath of God (24-32)
      1) They were given up to uncleanness (24-25)

2) They were given up to vile passions (26-27)
3) They were given up to a reprobate mind (28-32)
a) The consequence of their deliberate choice (28a)
b) The description of their condition of mind (28b-32)
(i) The general description of the condition (28c)
(ii) The specific examples of their condition (29-31)
(iii) The deliberate approval of evil (32)

2. The condemnation of the Jew (2:1–3:8)
a. The principles of divine judgment (2:1-16)
1) The judgment of God according to truth (1-5)
a) The guilt of the one judging others (1)
b) The statement of the principle of judgment (2)
c) The appeal to the guilty one (3-5)
(i) His illogical conclusion about himself (3)
(ii) His perversion of God's grace brings judgment (4-5)
2) The judgment of God according to works (6-10)
a) The statement of the principle of judgment (6)
b) The two classes in the judgment (7-8)
c) The priority of the Jew in judgment (9-10)
3) The judgment of God without respect of persons (11-15)
a) The statement of the principle of judgment (11)
b) The explanation of the standard of judgment (12)
c) The obedience to the light as the test in the judgment (13-15)
4) The judgment in accord with Paul's Gospel (16)
b. The demonstration of the Jew's moral failure (2:17-29)
1) The claims of the Jew and their refutation (17-24)
a) The enumeration of the claims of the Jew (17-20)
(i) The sense of Jewish distinctiveness (17a)
(ii) The claims of Jewish personal privileges (17b-18)
(iii) The claims of Jewish superiority (19-20)
b) The refutation of the claims of the Jew (21-24)
(i) The questions refuting his superiority (21-22)
(ii) The assertion refuting personal privileges (23)
(iii) The charge of his adverse influence on the Gentiles (24)

2) The failure of the Jew to live up to covenant responsibilities (25-29)
a) The failure to fulfill the meaning of circumcision (25)
b) The value of obedience before God (26-27)
c) The false and true view of a Jew (28-29)
c. The anticipation of the Jew's objections (3:1-8)
1) The question raised by the Jew and its answer (1-4)
a) The statement of the question (1)
b) The answer to the question (2-4)
2) The objection raised by the Jew and its denial (5-8)
a) The indication of the objection (5)
b) The denial of the objection (6-8)
3. The condemnation of the whole world (3:9-20)
a. The charge that all are under sin (9)
b. The proof of universal corruption from Scripture (10-18)
1) The state of sin in character (10-12)
2) The practice of sin in conduct (13-17)
a) The sinful practice in speech (13-14)
b) The sinful practice in deed (15-17)
3) The source of the sinfulness (18)
c. The application to the Jew who has the law (19-20)

II. THE RIGHTEOUSNESS OF GOD IN JUSTIFICATION (3:21–5:21)
1. The nature of justification by faith (3:21-26)
a. The manifestation of the righteousness of God (21a)
b. The description of justification by faith (21b-26)
1) Its relation to the Old Testament (21b)
2) Its availability through faith (22-23)
3) Its basis of operation in Christ's redemption (24-25a)
4) Its aim the demonstration of God's justice (25b-26)
2. The corollaries of the doctrine of justification (3:27-31)
a. The exclusion of all personal merit (27-28)
b. The presentation of God in His true character (29-30)
c. The establishment of the principle of law (31)
3. The proof of justification by faith from Scripture (4:1-25)
a. The means of Abraham's justification (1-12)
1) The justification by faith, apart from law (1-8)

a) The question as to Abraham's experience (1)
b) The consideration of the means of his justification (2-3)
c) The comparison of the two ways of justification (4-5)
d) The confirmation from David's testimony (6-8)

2) The justification by faith, apart from circumcision (9-12)
a) The question as to circumcision in faith-righteousness (9-10a)
b) The answers from Abraham's condition as uncircumcised (10b)
c) The nature of Abraham's circumcision (11a)
d) The purpose of Abraham's circumcision (11b-12)

b. The promise of world inheritance achieved through faith (13-17a)
1) The means of attaining the inheritance (13)
2) The reason for the faith method (14-16a)
3) The recipients of the fulfilled promise (16b)
4) The harmony with Scripture (17a)

c. The exemplification of the path of faith by Abraham (17b-25)
1) The consideration of Abraham's faith (17b-22)
a) The object of his faith (17b)
b) The nature of his faith (18-21)
c) The reward of his faith (22)

2) The significance of Abraham's faith for us (23-25)

4. The permanency of justification (5:1-11)
a. The present results of justification inspiring hope (1-2)
b. The inability of tribulation to destroy this hope (3-5)
1) The observed effect of tribulation (3-4)
2) The subjective experience of God's love (5)

c. The love of God in Christ confirming this hope (6-11)
1) The objective facts of God's love (6-10)
a) The demonstration of His love for the lost (6-8)
b) The assurance of safety for the reconciled (9-10)

2) The subjective experience of the reconciliation (11)

5. The foundation of righteousness in Christ's headship (5:12-21)
a. The two representative men as federal heads (12-14)
1) The universal result of Adam's one act (12-14a)

2) The headship of Adam as a type of Christ (14b)
b. The differences between Adam's and Christ's headship (15-17)
1) The difference in quality (15)
2) The difference in operation (16)
3) The difference in consequences (17)
c. The similarities of Adam and Christ as federal heads (18-21)
1) The similarity as to their scope (18)
2) The similarity as to their operation (19)
3) The similarity as to their measure (20-21)

III. THE RIGHTEOUSNESS OF GOD IN SANCTIFICATION (6:1–8:39)

1. The believer's relationship to sin (6:1-23)
a. The believer's death to the principle of sin (1-14)
1) The question of remaining in the realm of sin (1)
2) The rejection of the suggestion (2)
3) The exposition of our position under the figure of baptism (3-11)
a) The question as to their ignorance concerning baptism (3)
b) The statement of the significance of baptism (4)
c) The application of the figure to believers (5-10)
(i) The two phases in the picture of baptism (5)
(ii) The significance of his death with Christ (6-7)
(iii) The significance of his resurrection with Christ (8-10)
d) The call to the believer to accept this position (11)
4) The exhortation to realize this position in experience (12-13)
5) The assurance of Christian victory (14)
b. The believer's death to the practice of sin (15-23)
1) The question of continued sin because of our position (15a)
2) The rejection of the suggestion (15b)
3) The answer from the illustration of slavery (16-23)
a) The question concerning the alternative services (16)
b) The believer's experience with both services (17-18)

c) The appeal to act out this new position (19)
d) The contrast between the two services (20-22)
e) The outcome of the two services (23)
2. The believer's relationship to law (7:1-25)
a. The believer's position as dead to law but alive to God (1-6)
1) The principle of the domination of law (1)
2) The illustration from the law of marriage (2-3)
a) The duration of the law of the husband (2)
b) The termination of the law of the husband (3)
3) The application of the principle to the (Jewish) believer (4-6)
a) The application to his relationship to law (4)
b) The contrast between the two positions (5-6)
b. The inability of the law to deliver from sin (7-25)
1) The relation of the law to sin (7-13)
a) The nature of the law as not sinful (7a)
b) The function of the law in relation to sin (7b-13)
(i) The revelation of sin through the law (7b)
(ii) The work of sin through the law (8-11)
(aa) The manner of sin's work (8)
(bb) The result of sin's work (9)
(cc) The use of the law by sin for its work (10)
(dd) The deceitfulness of sin's work (11)
(iii) The law's revelation of the sinfulness of sin (12-13)
2) The experience of the law's inability to give victory over sin (14-25)
a) The first confession of defeat by sin (14-17)
b) The second confession of indwelling sin (18-20)
c) The third confession and the way of victory (21-25)
3. The believer's victory effected by the indwelling Spirit (8:1-39)
a. The deliverance from the power of the flesh by the Spirit (1-11)
1) The believer's freedom from condemnation (1-2)
2) The believer's deliverance through the Spirit (3-10)
a) The basis for the deliverance (3)
b) The purpose in the deliverance (4)
c) The method of the deliverance (5-10)

(i) The two classes of men (5)
(ii) The two minds (dispositions) (6-7)
(iii) The two spheres of being (8-10)
3) The assured triumph over physical death (11)
b. The realization of a life of sonship through the Spirit (12-17)
1) The obligation to live after the Spirit (12-13)
2) The evidence of the life by the Spirit (14-17)
a) The leading of the Spirit (14)
b) The nature of the Spirit received (15)
c) The witness of the Spirit (16)
d) The heirship of the believer (17)
c. The assurance of glorification amid present suffering (18-30)
1) The evaluation of present suffering (18)
2) The assurances of the hope of glorification (19-30)
a) The assurance from the appeal of creation (19-22)
(i) The content of creation's expectation (19)
(ii) The reason for creation's expectation (20-21)
(iii) The present unsatisfied condition of creation (22)
b) The assurance from the believer's present hope (23-25)
(i) The content of the believer's hope (23)
(ii) The unrealized state of the hope (24-25)
c) The assurance from the action of the Spirit (26-27)
d) The assurance from God's working and purpose (28-30)
(i) The working of God on our behalf for good (28a)
(ii) The working of God in accord with His purpose (28b-30)
d. The exultant assurance of the believer's ultimate victory (31-39)
1) The believer's relation to God (31b-33)
2) The believer's relation to Christ (34)
3) The believer's relation to circumstances of evil (35-39)
a) The inability of evils of this world to separate from Christ (35-37)

b) The inability of evils from the invisible world to separate from Christ (38-39)

Part II: Dispensational (9:1—11:36)

## THE RIGHTEOUSNESS OF GOD HARMONIZED WITH HIS DEALINGS WITH ISRAEL AND MANKIND

I. THE SORROW OF THE APOSTLE AT ISRAEL'S REJECTION (9:1-5)
 1. The sincerity of his feeling (1)
 2. The intensity of his feeling (2-3a)
 3. The basis for his feeling (3b-5)

II. THE REJECTION OF ISRAEL AND GOD'S SOVEREIGNTY (9:6-29)
 1. The rejection of Israel and God's promise (6-13)
  a. The denial of the failure of God's Word (6a)
  b. The proof that the promise is not based on physical descent (6b-13)
   1) The proof from the family of Abraham (6b-9)
   2) The proof from the family of Isaac (10-13)
 2. The rejection of Israel and God's justice (14-29)
  a. The justice of God in the manifestation of His will (14-18)
   1) The question as to God's justice (14)
   2) The manifestation of God's will (15-17)
    a) His mercy is revealed according to His will (15-16)
    b) His judgment is exercised according to His will (17)
   3) The principle of God's action according to His will (18)
  b. The justice of God in the use of His sovereign power (19-29)
   1) The objecting question and the rebuke (19-20a)
   2) The right of God to act as He does (20b-21)
   3) The actual exercise of God's power (22-24)
    a) His endurance with the wicked (22)
    b) His revelation of glory to vessels of mercy (23-24)
   4) The Scriptural anticipation of the call of Jew and Gentile (25-29)

a) The anticipation of the call of the Gentile (25-26)
b) The announcement concerning the fate of Israel (27-29)

## III. THE REJECTION OF ISRAEL AND HUMAN RESPONSIBILITY (9:30–10:21)

1. The failure of Israel to achieve righteousness (9:30-33)
   a. The striking fact of Israel's failure (30-31)
   b. The reason for Israel's failure (32a)
   c. The explanation of Israel's failure (32b)
   d. The Scriptural confirmation of the results (33)
2. The refusal by Israel to accept God's righteousness (10:1–11)
   a. The cause for Israel's rejection of God's righteousness (1-4)
      1) The Apostle's desire and prayer for them (1)
      2) The paradox in Israel's failure (2)
      3) The nature of Israel's error (3)
      4) The termination of law for righteousness in Christ (4)
   b. The nature of faith-righteousness (5-11)
      1) The comparison of the two methods for righteousness (5-8)
         a) The righteousness through law-keeping (5)
         b) The righteousness through faith (6-8)
      2) The realization of faith-righteousness (9-10)
      3) The Scriptural assurance of righteousness by faith (11)
3. The neglect by Israel of the universal Gospel (12-21)
   a. The fact of a universal Gospel (12-13)
   b. The proclamation of the universal Gospel (14-15)
   c. The reaction of Israel to this universal Gospel (16-21)
      1) The Gospel was largely disregarded (16-17)
      2) The Gospel was scornfully rejected (18-21)
         a) The first plea and the answer (18)
         b) The second plea and the answer (19-21)

## IV. THE REJECTION OF ISRAEL AND GOD'S PURPOSE FOR THEIR FUTURE (11:1-32)

1. The rejection of Israel has left a present remnant (1-10)
   a. The denial that God has cast off His people (1-2a)

- b. The proof of a remaining remnant (2b-6)
  - 1) The proof from Scripture (2b-4)
  - 2) The proof from its present existence (5-6)
- c. The contrast of the remnant with the nation (7-10)
  - 1) The present contrasting situation (7)
  - 2) The Scriptural confirmation (8-10)

2. The rejection of Israel is not permanent (11-32)
   - a. The Apostle's teaching concerning Israel's condition (11-16)
     - 1) The fall of Israel is not permanent (11a)
     - 2) The fall of Israel overruled for Gentile salvation (11b)
     - 3) The restoration of Israel will bring world blessing (12-15)
     - 4) The indication of Israel's future from her past (16)
   - b. The Apostle's warning to the Gentiles (17-24)
     - 1) The warning against boastfulness (17-18)
     - 2) The warning against pride (19-21)
     - 3) The warning against presumption (22-24)
       - a) The admonition against presumption (22ab)
       - b) The warning of the result of presumption (22c)
       - c) The argument from the restoration of Israel (23-24)
         - (i) The possibility of Israel's restoration (23)
         - (ii) The probability of Israel's restoration (24)
   - c. The Apostle's prophecy of Israel's future restoration (25-32)
     - 1) The revelation concerning Israel's restoration (25-26a)
     - 2) The vindication of Israel's restoration (26b-32)
       - a) The harmonization with prophecy (26b-27)
       - b) The harmonization with the divine call of Israel (28-29)
       - c) The harmonization with God's purpose of mercy to all (30-32)

## V. THE DOXOLOGY OF THE APOSTLE IN PRAISE OF GOD (11:33-36)

1. The exclamation concerning God (33)
2. The questions about God (34-35)
3. The assertion about God (36a)
4. The ascription of praise to God (36b)

## Part III: Practical (12:1–15:13)

## THE RIGHTEOUSNESS OF GOD APPLIED TO THE DAILY LIFE OF THE BELIEVER

I. THE BELIEVER IN RELATION TO GOD (12:1-2)
   1. The believer's act of self-presentation to God (1)
   2. The believer's continued experience of transformation (2)

II. THE BELIEVER IN RELATION TO SOCIETY (12:3-21)
   1. The exercise of spiritual gifts in the Church with humility (3-8)
      a. The need for humility as members of the Body (3)
      b. The relation of the members to each other in the Body (4-5)
      c. The expression of humility in service with the gifts (6-8)
         1) The diversity of the gifts given (6a)
         2) The enumeration of the ministering gifts (6b-8)
   2. The practice of brother-love to members in the Church (9-13)
      a. The nature of this brother-love (9a)
      b. The manifestations of brother-love (9b-13)
   3. The manifestation of love to mankind generally (14-21)
      a. The manifestation of love to our enemies (14)
      b. The manifestation of love toward the interests of others (15)
      c. The manifestation of love toward our associates (16)
      d. The manifestation of love toward a hostile world (17-21)
         1) The passive forbearance of evil (17-19)
         2) The active beneficence toward the evil (20-21)

III. THE BELIEVER IN RELATION TO THE STATE (13:1–14)
   1. The believer's duties to the state (1-7)
      a. The duty of obedience to the state (1a)
      b. The reason for obedience to the state (1b)
      c. The significance of the refusal of obedience to the state (2)
      d. The motives for obedience to the state (3-5)
         1) The motive from the function of the state (3-4)
         2) The motive from Christian conscience (5)
      e. The illustration of obedience to the state (6)
      f. The call for obedience to the state (7)
   2. The believer's duties to the citizens of the state (8-10)
      a. The obligation concerning the debt of love (8a)

b. The payment of the debt of love (8b-10)
   1) The significance of love to the neighbor (8b)
   2) The confirmation from the nature of love (9-10a)
   3) The conclusion concerning love (10b)
3. The believer's motivation in the hope of Christ's return (11-14)
   a. The appeal to alertness from the season (11a)
   b. The explanation arousing alertness (11b-12a)
   c. The exhortation to alertness (12b-13)
   d. The provision for alertness (14)

IV. THE BELIEVER IN RELATION TO THE WEAK BROTHER (14:1–15:13)

1. The prohibition against judging the brother (14:1-12)
   a. The attitude toward the weak brother (1)
   b. The indication of the areas of difficulty (2-5)
      1) The first problem and its adjustment (2-4)
      2) The second problem and its adjustment (5)
   c. The viewpoint in making the adjustment (6)
   d. The motivation in the lordship of Christ (7-9)
   e. The rebuke for judging the brother (10-12)
      1) The questions of rebuke (10a)
      2) The basis for the rebuke (10b-12)
2. The prohibition against the violation of the brother's conscience (14:13-23)
   a. The exhortation not to judge one another (13)
   b. The Apostle's conviction concerning foods (14)
   c. The application of this conviction to conduct (15-20)
      1) The misuse of this conviction (15-18)
      2) The proper use of this conviction (19-20a)
      3) The restatement of the conviction (20b)
   d. The guiding principle for the strong brother (21)
   e. The appeal to both groups (22-23)
3. The effort toward unity by following Christ's example (15:1-13)
   a. The obligation of the strong brother (1)
   b. The appeal for unity from Christ's example (2-4)
      1) The statement of the appeal (2)
      2) The arguments for the appeal (3-4)
         a) The example of Christ (3)

b) The purpose of the Scriptures (4)
c. The supplication of the Apostle (5-6)
d. The command to receive one another (7)
e. The illustration from Christ's relation to Jew and Gentile (8-12)
1) The ministry of Christ (8-9a)
2) The Scriptural proof (9b-12)
f. The Apostolic prayer (13)

THE CONCLUSION (15:14–16:27)
1. The presentation of personal matters (15:14-33)
a. His explanation for writing (14-21)
1) His attitude in writing (14-16)
a) His courteous recognition (14)
b) His courage in writing to them (15)
c) His statement of his commission (16)
2) His vindication for writing (17-21)
a) His personal boasting (17)
b) His humility in speaking of his work (18a)
c) His ministry as Apostle to the Gentiles (18b-19)
d) His aim in selecting a field of labor (20-21)
b. His personal plans at the time of writing (22-29)
1) His unrealized plans (22-24)
a) His plans to visit Rome (22-23)
b) His plans about going to Spain (24)
2) His immediate engagement (25-27)
a) The nature of the present engagement (25)
b) The significance of the present engagement (26-27)
3) His anticipations for the future (28-29)
c. His personal request for their prayers (30-33)
1) The statement of the prayer request (30-32)
2) The benediction (33)
2. The presentation of friendship matters (16:1-23)
a. The commendation of Phoebe (1-2)
b. The greetings to his friends at Rome (3-16)
1) The greetings to individuals at Rome (3-15)
2) The mutual greetings among believers at Rome (16a)
3) The greetings from the churches to the Roman believers (16b)

c. The warning to the believers at Rome (17-20)
   1) The contents of the warning (17)
   2) The description of the men warned against (18)
   3) The reason for his warning to them (19)
   4) The promise of divine victory shortly (20a)
   5) The benediction (20b)
d. The greetings from his companions (21-23)
(omit verse 24)

3. The concluding doxology (25-27)
   a. The recipient of the praise (25-27a)
      1) To the One able to establish them (25-26)
      2) To the only wise God, through Christ (27a)
   b. The ascription of praise (27b)
   Amen.

## A Book List on Romans

Barrett, Charles Kingsley, "A Commentary on the Epistle to the Romans." *Harper's New Testament Commentaries.* New York: Harper & Row (1957).

Uses the author's translation. An important exegetical treatment of Romans by an erudite British scholar manifesting keen precision of thought. Not thoroughly conservative.

Beet, Joseph Agar, *A Commentary on St. Paul's Epistle to the Romans.* London: Hodder and Stoughton (10th Ed., 1902).

An interpretation of Romans by a Wesleyan British scholar of the past century. Contains many helpful insights, but manifests some doctrinal weakness in handling the deity of Christ. The doctrinal summaries offer a distinctive feature.

Black, Matthew, "Romans." *New Century Bible.* London: Marshall, Morgan and Scott (1973).

Based on the Revised Standard Version. A concise, scholarly treatment by a noted British scholar. Especially valuable for its frequent reference to sources for further study.

Bruce, F. F., "The Epistle to the Romans." *The Tyndale New Testament Commentaries.* Grand Rapids: Wm. B. Eerdmans Pub. Co. (1963).

Uses the King James Version, but the treatment, based on the original, reflects the noted evangelical author's wide knowledge of the pertinent literature. The comments, verse by verse, are of uneven length; sometimes they are too brief to be helpful, at other times exceptionally full.

Brunner, Emil, *The Letter to the Romans, A Commentary.* London: Lutterworth Press (1959).

A paragraph-by-paragraph treatment by a noted German neo-orthodox scholar, reflecting the author's doctrinal stance.

Calvin, John, "The Epistle of Paul the Apostle to the Romans and to the Thessalonians." *Calvin's Commentaries.* Translated by Ross Mackenzie. Grand Rapids: Wm. B. Eerdmans Pub. Co. (1961).

A new translation of this classical work. On Romans the great Reformation expositor was at his best; still of value in spite of its age.

Denney, James, "St. Paul's Epistle to the Romans." *The Expositor's Greek Testament.* Vol. II. Grand Rapids: Wm. B. Eerdmans Pub. Co. (reprint, n.d.).

Greek Text. An outstanding work by a Scottish theologian of the past generation. Characterized by accurate scholarship and fine exegetical insights.

Dodd, C. H., "The Epistle of Paul to the Romans." *The Moffatt New Testament Commentary.* New York: Harper & Brothers (1932).

Prints the Moffatt translation. The work of an able liberal British theologian, using a psychological approach to Paul and his teaching. Dodd does not hesitate to disagree with Paul's views on occasion.

Gifford, E. H., *The Epistle of St. Paul to the Romans.* London: John Murray (1886).

Originally published in *The Speaker's Commentary, New Testament, Vol. III* (1881). A thorough exposition of outstanding merit in scholarly accuracy and theological presentation. Richly rewarding without being profuse. Amillennial.

Godet, F., *Commentary on the Epistle to the Romans.* Translated from the French by the Reverend A. Cusin, with translation revised with introduction and appendix by Talbot W. Chambers. Grand Rapids: Zondervan Publishing House (1956 reprint of 1883 edition).

An exhaustive, technical treatment of Romans by one of the outstanding French scholars of evangelical Switzerland in the last century. The author surveys and refutes various liberal theories of his day and ably presents his own views. Important for the advanced student.

Haldane, Robert, *Exposition of the Epistle to the Romans.* London: The Banner of Truth Trust (reprint, n.d.).

A Reformed commentary that has enjoyed wide usage for over a century. First appearing during 1835-39, the work was based on lectures given by the author, a Scottish evangelist, to students in Geneva; they awakened a genuine movement of the Spirit among the students who heard them.

Hamilton, Floyd E., *The Epistle to the Romans, An Exegetical and Devotional Commentary.* Grand Rapids: Baker Book House (1958).

A thorough and strongly conservative exposition in the Reformed tradition. Aims at combining "grammatico-historical" exegesis with doctrinal and devotional methods.

Hodge, Charles, *Commentary on the Epistle to the Romans.* Grand Rapids: Wm. B. Eerdmans Pub. Co. (1886; 1950 reprint).

A weighty and learned verse-by-verse analysis of the text with frequent reference to the Greek. Doctrinal summaries and remarks appear at the end of each major section. The work of a Calvinistic scholar of the past century who lectured on the Pauline Epistles for over fifty years.

Johnson, Alan F., *The Freedom Letter.* Chicago: Moody Press (1974).

A fresh analysis of the message of Romans in the light of our contemporary age, centering on the important doctrinal themes of the epistle. Treats chapters 1-11 as the doctrinal foundation for Christianity, with chapters 12-15 setting forth the Christian life. The work of a competent evangelical scholar accepting a moderate premillennial position.

Kelly, William, *Notes on the Epistle of Paul the Apostle to the Romans, with a New Translation.* London: G. Morrish (1873; reprint, n.d.).

The product of careful scholarship and prolonged and devout study. Reflects the evangelical, premillenial views of this voluminous Plymouth Brethren scholar of the past century.

Knox, John, and Cragg, Gerald R., "The Epistle to the Romans," *The Interpreter's Bible.* Vol. IX. New York: Abingdon-Cokesbury Press (1954).

Prints the King James and Revised Standard versions at the top of the page. The exegesis by Knox, a noted liberal New Testament scholar, with varying fullness unfolds the meaning of the text by brief paragraphs; the exposition by Cragg offers much homiletical and practical material.

Lange, John Peter, and Fay, F. R., "The Epistle of Paul to the Romans." *Commentary on the Holy Scriptures.* Translated from the

German by Philip Schaff and M. B. Riddle. Grand Rapids: Zondervan Publishing House (reprint, n.d.).

The material on Romans in this massive volume (over 400 double-column pages) falls into three parts: exegetical and critical; doctrinal and ethical; homiletical and practical. The additions by Schaff and Riddle add to its fullness and value. Still offers much help to those willing to dig in its closely printed pages.

Lenski, R. C. H., *The Interpretation of St. Paul's Epistle to the Romans.* Columbus, Ohio: Lutheran Book Concern (1936), 934 pp.

Prints author's own literal translation. A massive work by a conservative Lutheran scholar, based on careful exegesis of the Greek text. Amillennial.

Liddon, H. P., *Explanatory Analysis of St. Paul's Epistle to the Romans.* Grand Rapids: Zondervan Publishing House (1961 reprint of the 1892 edition).

An excellent analysis of Romans in the form of a detailed outline with notes. The treatment, assuming a knowledge of the Greek, is detailed and technical, valuable for tracing the grammatical and logical connections in the epistle.

Moule, Handley C. G., "The Epistle of St. Paul to the Romans." *The Expositor's Bible.* Vol. V. Grand Rapids: Wm. B. Eerdmans Pub. Co. (1943 reprint).

A superb, scholarly exposition by an evangelical Anglican bishop of the past generation. The work is characterized by careful exegesis, evangelical theology, devotional warmth, and practical truth.

Murray, John, "The Epistle to the Romans." *The New International Commentary on the New Testament.* Two vols. Grand Rapids: Wm. B. Eerdmans Pub. Co. (1959, 1965).

An outstanding recent treatment of Romans by a noted evangelical Presbyterian scholar. The interpretation is careful and detailed, with strong emphasis upon doctrine. Presents a post-millennial view of chapters 9-11.

Newell, William R., *Romans Verse by Verse.* Chicago: Moody Press (1948).

A pungent, conservative, warm treatment with a clear premillennial emphasis. Contains various usable illustrations and practical comments.

Nygren, Anders, *Commentary on Romans.* Translated by Carl C. Rassmussen. Philadelphia: Muhlenberg Press (1949).

A fresh, provocative treatment by a Lutheran scholar in the Lundensian school of theology, and reflecting that viewpoint. Stresses the main argument of Romans.

Phillips, John, *Exploring Romans, The Gospel According to Paul.* Chicago: Moody Press (1969).

An extensive, popular exposition by a contemporary Bible teacher, rich in illustrations and quotations. The presentation is organized around a detailed alliterative outline; various word studies help to bring out the meaning of the text. The work of a gifted teacher.

Sanday, William, and Headlam, Arthur C., "A Critical and Exegetical Commentary on the Epistle to the Romans." *The International Critical Commentary.* New York: Charles Scribner's Sons (1895; 1952 reprint).

Greek text. A detailed, phrase-by-phrase explanation by two noted British scholars of the past century. Generally conservative in its views; Arminian in theology. Long ranked as one of the best exegetical treatments of Romans.

Shedd, William G. T., *A Critical and Doctrinal Commentary on the Epistle of St. Paul to the Romans.* Grand Rapids: Zondervan Publishing House (1967 reprint of the 1879 edition).

Greek text. An exhaustive exegetical treatment by a conservative and Calvinistic teacher of the past century. Intended for the theological student and clergyman.

Stifler, James M., *The Epistle to the Romans.* Chicago: Moody Press (1960 reprint).

A lucid and informative exposition, the result of years of study and teaching by a conservative Baptist professor of the past century. The treatment is verse by verse. Premillennial.

Thomas, W. H. Griffith, *St. Paul's Epistle to the Romans. A Devotional Commentary.* Grand Rapids: Wm. B. Eerdmans Pub. Co. (1946 reprint).

An accurate and helpful interpretation, written in a devotional vein and rich in homiletical suggestiveness. Conservative in viewpoint and warmly spiritual.

Vine, W. E., *The Epistle to the Romans, Doctrine, Precept, Practice.* London: Oliphants (1948).

A phrase-by-phrase treatment by a noted British Plymouth Brethren scholar noted for his *Expository Dictionary of New Testament Words.* Concise, rewarding, warm and clearly evangelical in tone. Brings out much of the force of the Greek for the English student.

Wilson, Geoffrey B., *Romans, A Digest of Reformed Comment.* London: The Banner of Truth Trust (1969).

A concise verse-by-verse interpretation; skillfully culls and blends views drawn from many Reformed interpreters. This digest provides a valuable introduction to Reformed exposition of Romans.

# *Part 3*

# CHRISTOLOGICAL GROUP

## *The Prison Epistles*

Colossians
Philemon
Ephesians
Philippians

# 11

# AN INTRODUCTION TO THE PRISON EPISTLES

COLOSSIANS, Philemon, Ephesians, and Philippians form the third group in the Pauline epistles and are commonly designated as the "Prison Epistles." In these letters for the first time Paul writes as a prisoner. He calls himself "the prisoner of Christ Jesus" (Eph. 3:1). All four contain explicit references to his imprisonment (Col. 4:3, 18; Philem. 10, 13, 22, 23; Eph. 3:1; 4:1; 6:20; Phil. 1:7, 13). These repeated references to his imprisonment reveal the deep mark that it has left on his heart and thinking. These references further indicate that the imprisonment has already been of considerable duration, thus distinguishing it from the brief imprisonments which the Apostle has previously experienced (2 Cor. 11:23).

2 Timothy, although likewise written while Paul was in prison, is not included under the term "Prison Epistles." The indications of the severity of the Apostle's confinement in that epistle show that it was an imprisonment different from that during which these epistles were written.

Except for Philemon, which is a personal note and contains no direct doctrinal teaching, these epistles are marked by their special emphasis on the person of Christ and are aptly characterized as the Christological group.

Two problems have been raised in connection with the four epistles of this group which call for some consideration. There is the question of the place of their composition and the further question of the order of their composition.

THE PLACE OF THEIR COMPOSITION

The prevailing testimony of the Church has been that these epistles were written by Paul from Rome during his two years of imprisonment there as recorded in Acts 28:30-31. As to the exact dates for this period there is no unanimity at present among the scholars. Suggested dates for its commencement have varied from A.D. 56 to 61. We agree with Zahn and Lenski[1] in dating it from the spring of A.D. 61 to 63. The traditional Roman origin of these epistles is being seriously questioned, and Caesarea and Ephesus have been advanced in opposition to Rome.[2]

Unmistakably, all four of these epistles were composed while Paul was a prisoner. Colossians, Philemon, and Ephesians form one group, not only because of their contents but also by the fact that they were all dispatched at the same time (Col. 4:7-9; Philem. 10-12; Eph. 6:21-22). Philippians reveals no such intimate connections with the rest. It is therefore commonly assumed that Philippians was written some time either before or after the other three. Some who accept the view that Philippians was written from Rome hold that the other three were written from Caesarea. Others just reverse this position. More recently the view has been advanced that one or more of these epistles were written during an Ephesian imprisonment.

1. *Caesarea.* Some definite indications as to the place of composition are found in Philippians. There is the mention of the fact that Paul's bonds are becoming manifest "in the whole Praetorium" (1:13, A.S.V. marg.), the reference to saints in "Caesar's household" (4:22), and the Apostle's anticipation that his case will soon be settled, resulting in his release (2:23-24). These references have commonly been understood as pointing definitely to Rome. In opposition to this it has been asserted that the reference to the Praetorium would equally suit Caesarea. It is pointed out that in the Gospels and the Acts "the Praetorium" is the Roman governor's palace in Jerusalem and Caesarea (Mark 15:16; John 18:28; Acts 23:35). But Paul's words in Philippians, in their context, cannot well refer to Herod's

1. Theodor Zahn, *Introduction to the New Testament,* (1909), Vol. III, p. 483; R. C. H. Lenski, *The Interpretation of St. Paul's Epistles to the Galatians, to the Ephesians, and to the Philippians,* (1937), p. 699.
2. See T. Henshaw, *New Testament Literature,* (1957), pp. 273-279; Werner Georg Kümmel, *Introduction to the New Testament,* (1966), pp. 229-235; Donald Guthrie, *New Testament Introduction,* (Revised Ed. 1970), pp. 472-478; Ralph P. Martin, "Colossians and Philemon," *New Century Bible,* (1974), pp. 22-32.

palace, since the added words, "and to all the rest," cannot mean other buildings. Both terms signify persons, and the American Standard Version rightly translates it "the whole praetorian guard." The reference is to the imperial guard. At Rome Paul was continually guarded by a soldier from this famous guard. Because of the rotating of the guards, and the interest created through their contacts with Paul, the nature of Paul's imprisonment has become known to the whole guard and beyond that to the non-Christians in general. The expression implies a wider sphere than the official palace of the governor in Caesarea. This widespread knowledge concerning the nature of Paul's imprisonment could not have prevailed at Caesarea until after the time when Festus entertained Agrippa II with a court sermon from Paul (Acts 25:23–26:32). But by that time the case had already been taken out of the hands of Festus by the appeal of Paul to Caesar, and Paul could not hope for a verdict of release.

The reference to "Caesar's household" cannot without much straining of language and facts be made to suit Caesarea. Against the acceptance of Caesarea is the fact that the Acts knows nothing of such a preaching ministry in Caesarea as Paul indicates in Philippians 1:14-20. Caesarea was already a familiar center of apostolic labors, while Paul's words indicate new ground for evangelization, which Rome would amply afford. Again, Paul indicates that the outcome of the verdict may be either life or death (Phil. 1:20ff). This would not be the case at Caesarea where he could always appeal the case to Caesar, a thing which he actually did.

While holding that Philippians was written from Rome, Meyer[3] and others maintain that the three letters to the province of Asia were written from Caesarea. Meyer thought it it would be more natural and probable that the slave Onesimus would go to Caesarea than to Rome which was much farther away and would be costly to reach. But a fugitive slave like Onesimus would be most likely to go to a great city like Rome where he would have a much better chance to lose himself among the teeming multitudes, even as fugitives today seek refuge in our large cities. Caesarea would offer comparatively fewer chances of avoiding detection and apprehension by the slave-catchers. At Caesarea Paul was confined in Herod's palace, and it

3. Heinrich August Wilhelm Meyer, *Critical and Exegetical Hand-Book to the Epistle to the Ephesians,* (1892), pp. 300-301.

seems highly improbable that a runaway slave would be bold enough to come into contact with Paul there.

Again it is said that since Onesimus is not commended to the Ephesian church, Tychicus must already have left him at Colossae. This would mean that Tychicus came from Caesarea and so would reach Colossae before going on to Ephesus. If Tychicus with Onesimus came from Rome, their first stop would be at Ephesus, and then Paul would have said something about Onesimus to them. But that fails to understand the problem concerning Onesimus. As Lenski says,

> On arrival at Ephesus it was best to keep his whole story quiet. It would have been the height of tactlessness on the part of Paul to commend this slave to the church at Ephesus or to any other congregation before this slave's Christian master had acted in his case, and before the congregation directly concerned had also acted.[4]

Meyer argued that in Ephesians 6:21 Paul could not have written "ye also" unless Tychicus had first reported about Paul's affairs elsewhere before arriving at Ephesus. He felt this implied that Tychicus came from Caesarea and had already reported at Colossae. But the words require only that the Ephesians, like the Colossians, will be informed about Paul's circumstances by Tychicus. The main mission of Tychicus was to Colossae, taking Paul's letter to that church and returning Onesimus to his master. Coming from Rome, their first stop would be Ephesus where Tychicus would doubtless inform the Ephesians that his main mission was to Colossae.

Paul's request of Philemon for a lodging (Philem. 22) because he was hoping to be released does not fit Caesarea as Meyer thought. During Paul's two years at Caesarea under Felix there was no hope of being released unless Paul was willing to resort to bribery to secure his release (Acts 24:26), a means he refused to employ. During the last part of the Caesarean imprisonment, under Festus, there likewise was no hope of release since he had appealed to Caesar, thus taking the case out of the hands of Festus.

If Paul wrote from Caesarea, how can we account for his silence about Philip the Evangelist who had shortly before his arrest entertained him in his home in Caesarea (Acts 21:8)? How could he have

4. R. C. H. Lenski, *The Interpretation of St. Paul's Epistles to the Galatians, to the Ephesians, and to the Philippians,* (1937), p. 327.

avoided the mention of Philip among those of the circumcision (Col. 4:10-11) if he wrote from Caesarea? To fail to mention him would have implied that the veteran evangelist was hostile to him.

This view still has some advocates,[5] but we confidently conclude that none of the Prison Epistles belong to the Caesarean imprisonment.

2. *Ephesus.* The view has been advocated in more recent years that Paul was in prison at Ephesus when the epistles were written. This view was first advanced by H. Lisco of Berlin at the beginning of the present century, and the view has received the support of several English and Continental scholars.[6] Some would place only Philippians in Ephesus, others hold that the three Asian epistles were written from there, while some would assign all the Prison Epistles to Ephesus.

The point of origin for these hypotheses is Paul's statement in 2 Corinthians 11:23, written shortly after his ministry in Ephesus: "in prisons more abundantly." The Acts hints of no imprisonment at Ephesus; however, in view of the incompleteness of Luke's record, it is not impossible that Paul was shut up once or twice while there. But Acts 20:31 more naturally suggests an unbroken ministry amid opposition and difficulty.

Advocates of the Ephesian hypothesis point out that neither the mention of the "Praetorium" nor the allusion to "Caesar's household" in Philippians is incompatible with the view that Philippians was written from Ephesus. It is known that Praetorium was the customary Latin word for government house in the various provinces, and that "Caesar's household" was used to designate those attached to the personal service of the Emperor, whether in Rome or elsewhere. It may be readily admitted that in themselves these expressions do not forbid the Ephesian hypothesis; but unless other indications demand Ephesus, their ordinary usage would point rather to Rome. Paul's use of the term Praetorium seems to refer to people, not to a house.

If Philippians was written from Ephesus it must be placed either shortly before or after 1 Corinthians. But since the collection for the

5. Bo Reicke, "Caesarea, Rome, and the Captivity Epistles," *Apostolic History and the Gospel*, W. W. Gasque and R. P. Martin, editors, (1970), pp. 277-286.
6. James Moffatt, *An Introduction to the Literature of the New Testament*, (3rd Ed., 1949 reprint), p. 622.

Judean saints was the great project which Paul had on his mind at this time, his silence concerning this collection is inexplainable. Further, it is unlikely that the Philippians would send Paul a gift at Ephesus where he was surrounded by a large circle of friends. The argument for this early date for Philippians from the affinity of its contents with the epistles of the second group is not convincing. Further, Paul's fear that the outcome of his trial might mean death (1:20-24) refutes the Ephesian hypothesis concerning Philippians, since in that case he could avert the death sentence by an appeal to Caesar (cf. Acts 22:25-29; 25:10-12). The Ephesian hypothesis offers no compelling reasons for abandoning the common view that Philippians was written from Rome.

Proponents of the Ephesian hypothesis generally name Colossians, Philemon, and Ephesians as having been written at Ephesus. The case is often based largely on Philemon and, by association, carries Colossians and Ephesians with it. It is claimed that Onesimus would be more likely to flee to Ephesus than to Rome, which was eight hundred miles from Colossae. While Onesimus would be more likely to seek refuge in Ephesus than in Caesarea, he would be even more likely to find his way to Rome in the effort to avoid detection.

In Philemon 22 Paul promises Philemon a visit by asking him to prepare a lodging for him. Clearly he hoped soon to visit Colossae. Would Paul have written thus, it is asked, if he was in Rome, when we remember that according to Romans 15:28 his plans were to go on to Spain from there? But in answer it must be remembered that the plan to visit Spain was announced before Paul became a prisoner, and the five years that have passed since that time have shown him the desirability of revisiting his churches in the East before beginning the new work in the West.

A tradition dating back to the early part of the third century relates that Paul was thrown to a lion in the arena at Ephesus and that the lion licked his feet. This story sounds like a later apocryphal invention to give a literal meaning to 1 Corinthians 15:32, "I fought with beasts at Ephesus." Paul's Roman citizenship rules out a literal event. Of the tower in Ephesus known as Paul's prison, Ramsay says, "Though the tower was certainly in existence at the time of St. Paul's residence in the city, there is no reason to think that he was ever imprisoned in Ephesus."[7]

7. W. M. Ramsay, *The Letters to the Seven Churches of Asia,* (n.d.), p. 213.

Indications in the Prison Epistles imply that they were written during a protracted confinement. The ministry of less than three years at Ephesus allows for no such protracted imprisonment. The arguments for Ephesus bristle with difficulties and often raise more questions than they answer.

We hold that the evidence points to the common position that all four epistles were written by Paul during his first Roman imprisonment (Acts 28:30-31). This view best accounts for the measure of freedom which Paul enjoyed and the preaching ministry which he was able to carry forward (Col. 4:2-4; Eph. 6:18-20; Phil. 1:12-18). It gives a natural and unstrained significance to the mention of "Caesar's household" and the "praetorian guard" (Phil. 4:22; 1:13). It accounts for his silence about Philip the Evangelist and gives the story of Onesimus its most natural setting. It provides the indicated conditions for the work of Paul's co-laborers in preaching during his imprisonment and explains the implication as to the decisive nature of the issue of his trial (Phil. 1:14-17, 20).

### THE ORDER OF THEIR COMPOSITION

That Colossians, Philemon, and Ephesians were written at about the same time is evident from the fact that all were dispatched at the same time. The question as to the exact order of their composition has elicited differing answers. The attempt categorically to decide the issue seems hazardous. Effort to find a clue from the nonmention of Timothy in Ephesians is useless, since it can be used to argue for the priority of either; Ephesians may have been written before Timothy joined Paul, or after he again left Paul on some mission for the Apostle. The endeavor to find a solution to the problem from a study of the inner relationship between Ephesians and Colossians has likewise led to opposite conclusions. In the words of Shaw,

> The grounds on which priority is usually based are mainly of a subjective kind, according as individual writers think that a general or a special treatment is the more likely to have come first.[8]

Our own preference is for the view that Colossians was written before Ephesians. In Colossians the Apostle is struggling with great and perplexing spiritual difficulties, and the epistle is forged in the heat of active controversy. The Ephesian epistle again breathes the spirit of

8. R. D. Shaw, *The Pauline Epistles,* (4th Ed., 1924 reprint), p. 277.

rest that follows conflict. It seems to be the quiet, contemplative review of the field from the vantage point already gained in previous conflict.

The question as to whether Philippians or the three Asian epistles were written first has likewise produced opposite conclusions. Lightfoot, followed by many scholars, held strongly to the priority of Philippians.[9] His major positive reason for assigning priority to Philippians was similarity of subject matter in Romans and Philippians. His motive was to place Colossians and Ephesians with their new themes and peculiar expressions as long after Philippians as possible in order to allow sufficient time for the necessary development. However, since Lightfoot accepted the Roman origin for all of the Prison Epistles, some three years at the least intervened between the writing of Romans and Philippians, while not more than fifteen months at the very utmost can be allowed between Philippians and the Asian epistles. This fact seems definitely to weaken the argument for the priority of Philippians drawn from the idea of development.

It is asserted that if Philippians was written last it must have revealed traces of and been colored by the theological developments which occasioned the Letter to the Colossians. Farrar felt that it was "psychologically certain" that such traces would have appeared in Philippians if it was written last.[10] But Shaw counters this with the remark,

> Paul had sufficient faculty of intellectual detachment to write to Philippi exactly as the occasion required, and it would have been very unlike him at any stage, late or early, to write to his converts there on matters that were probably quite foreign to their religious experience.[11]

Lightfoot, on the ground of similarity of content, placed Galatians just before Romans. It is now widely held that Galatians is earlier than the Corinthian epistles. If the Corinthian epistles can be interpolated between Galatians and Romans, there is no reason why these three Asian epistles could not come between Romans and Philippians. The argument from the affinity of contents is not decisive.

That Philippians comes last and near the end of the Roman im-

9. J. B. Lightfoot, *Saint Paul's Epistle to the Philippians,* (1898), pp. 32-46.
10. F. W. Farrar, *The Life and Work of St. Paul,* (1889), p. 593.
11. R. D. Shaw, *The Pauline Epistles,* (4th Ed., 1924 reprint), p. 274.

prisonment seems evident from the following considerations. The Apostle's imprisonment seems already to have been of considerable duration. The true nature of his imprisonment as due to his relation to Christ rather than any personal offense against the State has become manifest "throughout the whole praetorian guard, and to all the rest" (1:13). His presence as a prisoner has stimulated much preaching of Christ throughout the city (1:14-17).

The late date of Philippians is further suggested by the fact that friends who were with him during the early part of the imprisonment have now left him (2:20). Luke and Aristarchus, both of whom accompanied Paul to Rome (Acts 27:2) and sent greetings to the Colossians and to Philemon, are not mentioned in Philippians. This must mean that they were not with Paul when Philippians was written, for it would be strange indeed if Luke should not send greetings to the Philippians where he was so well known and had labored for some years. Could Paul have said that he had "no man likeminded" (Phil. 2:20) if Luke was with him?

To place Philippians in the earlier part of the Roman imprisonment apparently does not allow sufficient time for the events which have taken place between Paul's arrival in the city and the writing of the letter. Several journeys between Rome and Philippi are implied. The news of Paul's arrival in Rome must reach Philippi; money is collected and sent to Rome by Epaphroditus, who falls seriously ill following his arrival; news of his illness must reach Philippi, and news of the concern of the Philippians must again reach Rome. To place the letter in the early part of the imprisonment does not allow sufficient time for these things to transpire.

The letter indicates that a crisis has been reached in the Apostle's case. The Imperial Court has begun a consideration of the appeal of Paul (2:23). He promises to send Timothy as soon as he knows the verdict (2:23), and he hopes that he himself will soon be able to come (2:24). While he expects to be set free (1:25; 2:24), he yet realizes that the nature of the verdict is uncertain. He is ready for death if that should be the issue and even desirous of it on his own account (1:23). Whatever the result, the outcome is to be known before long. This definitely points to the last part of the Roman imprisonment. We conclude that Philippians was the last of the Prison Epistles.

# 12

# COLOSSIANS

## An Introduction to Colossians

It is due not to any spectacular events in the secular history of the city of Colossae, but rather to the simple fact that the apostle Paul addressed a letter to the Christian assembly in that small town, that the name of Colossae is today a familiar word throughout Christendom. Paul's epistle to the Colossian believers has forever enshrined that name in the thinking of Christians everywhere.

### THE CITY OF COLOSSAE

1. *Location.* Colossae was a Phrygian city located near the upper end of the Lycus valley, in the eastern portion of the Roman province of Asia. The Lycus River, on whose southern bank the city was located,[1] takes it rise in a series of vast springs at the upper eastern end. It flows in a northwesterly direction and empties into the Maeander River somewhat more than a hundred miles east of Ephesus. The city of Colossae was situated approximately twenty-four miles east and some south of the confluence of the two rivers.[2]

The city stood on a strategic spot on the important highway from Ephesus to the East in that it occupied the pass that led through the Cadmus range to the east. At this point the Lycus valley becomes a narrow gorge about ten miles long and less than two miles wide, being walled in by great precipices. To the south of the city Mount Cadmus rises to the height of about eight thousand feet. From its lofty heights flow two streams that hemmed in the city on both the

1. "Colossae was situated on the south bank of the river, but the buildings extended to the north bank." W. M. Ramsay, *The Church in the Roman Empire,* (1919), p. 473.
2. See the detailed map of the Lycus valley in W. M. Ramsay, *Ibid.*, opposite p. 472.

eastern and the western side. To the north appear the long ridges of Mount Messogis. To the west a low rocky ridge about two miles in breadth divided this glen from the lower Lycus.[3]

2. *Neighboring cities.* Two other cities, mentioned in the Epistle to the Colossians (2:1; 4:13, 16), were located in the Lycus valley. About eleven or twelve miles from Colossae, down the Lycus valley, stood the city of Laodicea. Unlike Colossae, it stood some ways back from the Lycus, being situated on an undulating hill, or group of hills, to the south of the river. It was washed on each side by small tributaries of the Lycus which take their rise in the snowy heights of Mount Cadmus to the south. The city had important road connections. Not only did it stand on the highway that ran through Colossae, but it also formed the junction at which five large roads met.[4]

Laodicea was a populous and thriving center. It was the chief city of the district, being the capital of one of the departments or counties into which the Roman province of Asia was divided for administrative and taxing purposes. The department which it headed included some twenty-five other cities. People from various places thronged its streets. It was a city of great wealth (cf. Rev. 3:14-22) and was an important banking center. The former greatness of the city is attested by the extensive ruins that still mark the site.

About six miles north of Laodicea, across the Lycus, on the northern edge of the valley, was the city of Hierapolis. Johnson describes the site as follows:

> The town stood on a terrace a mile and a third long and several hundred yards wide, from which a precipitous cliff drops down toward the Lycus plain. In the sunlight the cliff, over which several streams flow, is blinding white, though streaked here and there with yellow and black, and its appearance is that of a frozen waterfall.[5]

Its hot mineral springs[6] made Hierapolis famous as a health resort.

3. W. M. Ramsay, *The Church in the Roman Empire,* (1919), p. 472.
4. A. Lukyn Williams, "The Epistles of Paul the Apostle to the Colossians and to Philemon," *Cambridge Greek Testament,* (1928 reprint), p. x.
5. Sherman E. Johnson, "Laodicea and Its Neighbors," *The Biblical Archaeologist,* Feb. 1950, p. 12.
6. "The temperature of the pool is 95 degrees F. . . . The flow has been estimated at 10,000 gallons per minute, and about 26 cubic yards of deposit is laid down daily. It is estimated that the lower courses of the buildings are covered to a depth of at least six feet with this deposit." Sherman E. Johnson, "Laodicea And Its Neighbors," *Biblical Archaeologist,* Feb. 1950, p. 12.

Its streets and baths were thronged by visitors in search of pleasure or of health. Behind it, to the north, appeared the ridges of Mount Messogis. The city lay on the road that ran directly from Laodicea to Philadelphia and Sardis.

All three cities were within easy reach of each other and were in constant communication with one another. All of them might easily have been visited in one day. The Apostle reveals his awareness of this close relation between these cities when in the Colossian letter he sends greetings for the saints in Laodicea and directs an exchange of letters between the two cities (4:15-16).

3. *Topography.* The entire region is mountainous and volcanic, and earthquakes have been frequent throughout its history. The city of Laodicea was struck by disastrous earthquakes no less than four times between 125 B.C. and A.D. 235, the third shock coming probably in A.D. 65, a few years after the writing of Colossians, and striking all three cities.[7] The numerous springs and streams which swell the waters of the Lycus are thickly impregnated with calcareous matter, and consequently they lay down immense incrustations in their course. The result is that "the country is sprinkled with glacier-like streams and cataracts of limestone."[8] Specially noteworthy are the formations at Hierapolis and Colossae.

The region was and is still very fertile. The neighboring uplands provided excellent pastures on which were raised great flocks of sheep. One of the chief sources of the riches of the region was the trade in its jet-black wool; this wool from the Lycus valley was preferred even to that of Miletus.[9] According to one account this wool was naturally dyed a glossy black by the minerals in the water of that region.[10] The chemicals in the waters of the Lycus were peculiarly favorable to the dyer's art, and the thriving trade in wool and dyed stuffs was a source of rich profit. Colossae, formerly the chief center of this industry, gave its name (colossimus) to a valued purple dye.[11]

4. *Population.* The population of Colossae and the surrounding

7. J. B. Lightfoot, *Saint Paul's Epistles to the Colossians and to Philemon,* (1900 reprint), p. 38, note 1.
8. H. C. G. Moule, "The Epistles of Paul the Apostle to the Colossians and to Philemon," *Cambridge Bible for Schools,* (1932 reprint), p. 12.
9. Theodor Zahn, *Introduction to the New Testament,* (1909), Vol. I, p. 448.
10. H. C. G. Moule, "The Epistles of Paul the Apostle to the Colossians and to Philemon," *Cambridge Bible for Schools,* (1932 reprint), p. 12.
11. G. G. Findlay, "The Epistle of Paul to the Colossians," *Pulpit Commentary,* (1950 reprint), pp. i-ii.

region was of a heterogeneous character. Ethnologically, the three cities of the Lycus valley were generally regarded as being Phrygian cities, Colossae always so.[12] The bulk of the population apparently consisted of native Phrygians, people "marked by that tendency to mystical illusion and orgiastic excitement which made Phrygia the home of the frantic worship of Dionysius and of Cybele."[13] But this Phrygian substratum had long ago received an admixture of Greeks, and the Greek language and Greek manners prevailed and leavened the life and culture of the region.

All three of these cities had a considerable Jewish element in their population. Antiochus the Great (223-187 B.C.) transplanted two thousand Jewish families from Mesopotamia and Babylon into the rebellious regions of Phrygia and Lydia, with promises of assistance and material advantages.[14] Doubtless many of these found their way into the Lycus valley. Following the establishment of Jewish settlements in these regions, the inviting traffic in dyed wools which characterized the cities of the Lycus would soon insure a constant stream of new recruits for these colonies. Under Roman rule Jews gathered in these cities in considerable numbers.[15] It will be remembered that Phrygia is mentioned as among those countries that were represented at Jerusalem on the day of Pentecost (Acts 2:10), and it is not unlikely that some were from the Lycus valley. Judging from the bitter complaint of a Talmudist, these Phrygian Jews seem to have compromised their orthodoxy to a considerable extent: "The wines and the baths of Phrygia have separated the ten tribes from Israel."[16] These circumstances are of interest in view of the heresy that plagued the churches of the Lycus.

5. *Status.* When the apostle Paul wrote his Epistle to the Colossians, Colossae had already lost most of its former greatness. Because of its commanding position in the Cadmus pass, Colossae had early assumed a position of great importance. But by this time it had been outranked by its more prosperous neighbors and had dwindled to a third-rate town. Says Lightfoot, "Without doubt Colossae was the

12. J. B. Lightfoot, *Saint Paul's Epistles to the Colossians and to Philemon,* (1900 reprint), pp. 17-18.
13. G. G. Findlay, "The Epistle of Paul to the Colossians," *Pulpit Commentary,* (1950 reprint), p. ii.
14. Flavius Josephus, *Antiquities of the Jews,* xii, 3, 4.
15. Theodor Zahn, *Introduction to the New Testament,* (1909), Vol. I, p. 449.
16. Quoted from J. B. Lightfoot, *Saint Paul's Epistles to the Colossians and to Philemon,* (1900 reprint), p. 22.

least important church to which any epistle of St. Paul is addressed."[17]

6. *Cultural contacts.* Like its neighbors, Colossae was in a position to be in intimate touch with the varied intellectual and religious movements of the day. Its position on the highway between Ephesus and the interior, as well as the impact of its brisk commercial contacts with the outside, put it into constant touch with the cultural and thought movements of the day. In the words of Williams,

> It was no out-of-the-way village or country town, to which news travelled late. It was in touch with all shades of opinion, and was exposed more than most places of its size to influences both from the coast and from the eastern mainland.[18]

### THE CHURCH IN COLOSSAE

1. *Origin.* Concerning the founding of the churches in the Lycus valley, nothing is directly recorded in Scripture beyond what may be learned from the Epistle to the Colossians. That Paul did not personally found these churches seems assured from the contents of the epistle.[19] In it he presents his knowledge of the conditions in Colossae as being derived from others (1:4, 6-7). He speaks of himself as having heard about their faith in the Gospel (1:4). While they were properly instructed in the Gospel (1:5-6, 23) and knew of his preaching (1:23), yet nowhere does he intimate that they had learned the good news of the Gospel from him. If he ever visited Colossae, it seems passing strange that no hint of that visit should have been given in this epistle. Further, the language of 1:7 and 2:1 seems to us positively to forbid the view that Paul personally founded these churches. In 1:6-7 he clearly states that the Colossians first heard the Gospel from Epaphras. And in 2:1 he definitely seems to include the believers in Laodicea and Colossae as among those who "have not seen my face in the flesh."[20]

The churches in the Lycus valley, however, seem definitely to have been an outcome of Paul's three years of labor at Ephesus during the

17. *Ibid.*, p. 16.
18. A. Lukyn Williams, "The Epistles of Paul the Apostle to the Colossians and to Philemon," *Cambridge Greek Testament*, (1928 reprint), pp. ix-x.
19. For a negative review of the arguments that Paul was the founder see John Eadie, *A Commentary on the Greek Text of the Epistle of Paul to the Colossians*, (1884), pp. xiii-xxii.
20. These words do not forbid the view that Paul passed through Colossae on his way to Ephesus on the third missionary journey but do show that he did not stop to evangelize there.

third missionary journey. From Colossians it is evident that he considered these churches as within his parish. During these three years at Ephesus the work of evangelization was widely extended through the province of Asia. Luke indicates the extent of this work when he writes, "All they that dwelt in Asia heard the word of the Lord, both Jews and Greeks" (Acts 19:10). As the metropolis of Asia, visitors from all parts of the province thronged Ephesus, coming for business, worship, or pleasure. While in Ephesus many of these came in contact with the Gospel, were saved, and voluntarily went back or were commissioned to go back to their homes with the new message of salvation. Some of Paul's helpers were doubtless also sent out into various sections of the province to spread the Gospel. That a number of churches were founded in the province during this time is certain from 1 Corinthians 16:19, where Paul, writing to the Corinthians, says, "The churches of Asia salute you."

Among the many from the various cities and towns of the province of Asia who were won to the Gospel through the missionary work centered at Ephesus must have been citizens from the cities of the Lycus valley. "The relations between these places and Ephesus appear to have been unusually intimate."[21] Among the natives of Colossae thus won to the Lord were Epaphras (Col. 4:12) and Philemon (Philem. 19, 23).

In Colossians 1:7 Paul names Epaphras as the one from whom the Colossians heard the Gospel and then describes him as "a faithful minister of Christ on our behalf." This reading indicates that it was as Paul's representative that Epaphras had ministered in Colossae, and this justifies the Apostle in claiming the Colossians as his own charges. The proximity of these Lycus cities to each other would suggest that he was the founder of all three churches. The intense intercessory labors of Epaphras for the believers in all three cities likewise points that way (Col. 4:12-13).

2. *Membership.* Nothing in the epistle definitely indicates the size of the Colossian church. From Philemon 2 it is seen that the house of Philemon was a center of assembly for the church. Zahn insists that the believers in Colossae must have had more than one place of meeting.[22] Erdman thinks that the church "must have been large and

21. J. B. Lightfoot, *Saint Paul's Epistles to the Colossians and to Philemon,* (1900 reprint), p. 31.
22. Theodor Zahn, *Introduction to the New Testament,* (1909), Vol. I, p. 455.

influential."[23] The membership of the church consisted principally of Gentiles (1:27; 2:13), although there doubtless were Jewish Christians among them. References in the epistle indicate that the readers were quite familiar with Jewish customs and teachings. Paul praises the church for its steadfastness in spite of the attacks of the false teaching (2:5). As yet the heretical teaching had made no actual conquests in the church.

3. *History.* With the Epistle to the Colossians, the church practically disappears from Christian history. While the two neighboring churches played quite a prominent role in Early Church history, the church at Colossae was of little importance in the larger sphere of the Christian Church.

### THE AUTHENTICITY OF COLOSSIANS

1. *Traditional view.* Down through the centuries the Christian Church has always accepted this epistle as Pauline. The external evidence for the Pauline authorship is all that can be desired. In the words of Meyer,

> The external attestation of our Epistle is so ancient, continuous, and general, that no well-founded doubt can from this quarter be raised.[24]

The internal evidence is likewise satisfactory. Claiming to be by the Apostle, the contents of the epistle bear all the earmarks of being Pauline. Its close relation to the Epistle to Philemon argues strongly for its authenticity. Philemon is accepted as Pauline, and the authenticity of Philemon is a weighty argument for the authenticity of Colossians.

2. *Critical attacks.* It was left to the literary acumen of the radical critics of the modern era to discover that this epistle was not a genuine product from the hand of Paul! Their assault on the authenticity of the epistle has been on purely internal grounds. The first to raise objections against it was Mayerhoff (1838) on the grounds of its vocabulary, style, and thought. He was followed by others in the radical school of criticism.

The attempts to discredit the epistle have proceeded along three

23. Charles R. Erdman, *The Epistles of Paul to the Colossians and to Philemon,* (1933), p. 13.
24. Heinrich August Wilhelm Meyer, *Critical and Exegetical Hand-Book to the Epistles to the Philippians and Colossians, and to Philemon,* (1885), p. 200. See the external evidence in William Hendriksen, "Exposition of Colossians and Philemon," *New Testament Commentary,* (1964), pp. 35-37.

lines. It has been argued that the large number of words in this epistle not found in Paul's other epistles (fifty-five in all) reveals that it was not written by Paul. To this contention Salmon has aptly replied,

> I cannot subscribe to the doctrine that a man writing a new composition must not, on pain of losing his identity, employ any word that he has not used in a former one.[25]

Salmon points out that by a similar process of argument it can be shown that most of the works of Xenophon must be rejected as non-Xenophontic. The vocabulary of Colossians is quite what one would expect under the circumstances. As Moffatt says,

> When account is taken of the fact that Paul is writing upon a new subject to a strange church, in which no objection has been taken to his apostolic authority or gospel, the proportion of *hapax heuremena* is not unnatural.[26]

Again, it is argued that the Christology of Colossians is too much like the Logos doctrine of John (Col. 1:13-23; John 1:1-18), hence the epistle betrays a post-Pauline date. But granting the similarity of the two views, it remains yet to be shown why two apostles could not have this same view of the person of Christ. Why should the concept of the Cosmic Christ be limited to John alone? If we accept the Epistle to the Philippians as Pauline, we already have a Christological statement as explicit and profound as anything that is found in Colossians (Phil. 2:5-11).

Further, it has been maintained that the heresy combatted in Colossians did not arise until after the time of Paul. This argument proceeds upon the assumption that the epistle presupposes the full-blown Gnostic systems of the second century. But that is to misunderstand the situation in the epistle. The most that can be proved is that the epistle confronts an incipient form of Gnosticism. And this is now known to be entirely possible. Moffatt points out that recent research has proved that "such a religious temper as that controverted in Colossians could have prevailed during the first century. . . . The germs of what was afterwards gnosticism can be de-

25. George Salmon, *An Historical Introduction to the Study of the Books of The New Testament,* (9th Ed., 1904), p. 384.
26. James Moffatt, *An Introduction to the Literature of the New Testament,* (3rd Ed., 1949 reprint), p. 154.

tected in various quarters during the earlier half of the first century."[27]

The varied hypotheses which profess to see in this epistle an admixture of Pauline and non-Pauline elements have been very ingenious and complicated. However, because of their subjective character and total lack of any historical foundation, few have been convinced by them. One may well say with Meyer, "The *fabrication* of such an epistle *as that to the Colossians* would be more marvelous than its originality."[28]

## THE OCCASION FOR COLOSSIANS

Two factors apparently entered into the writing of the Epistle to the Colossians, the one quite accidental, the other the primary cause. The first of these was the problem of the return of Onesimus to his master at Colossae, the other was the visit and report of Epaphras. The former must have been on Paul's mind for some time, as he awaited an opportunity to carry it out. The latter presented a challenge to the Apostle which determined him to dispatch one of his helpers to Colossae with this epistle and to use the occasion to return Onesimus to Philemon.

Some five or six years seem to have passed since the founding of the church in Colossae under the influence of Epaphras. Apparently he continued on as the shepherd of the flock. Recently an insidious error had begun to manifest itself in Colossae. It seems that Epaphras had felt himself unable to cope with this new heretical movement, so he had gone to Rome to consult Paul about it (Col. 1:7-8). In making his report to Paul he had given a favorable account of the general condition of the church; he had told of its stability and growth in grace and assured the Apostle of its loyal affection for him. But the report also contained information of conditions at Colossae which filled the mind of Paul with a deep anxiety for them (Col. 2:1-4), an anxiety which Epaphras shared with him concerning them (Col. 4:12-13). It was this situation which determined the Apostle to write this letter to the Colossians to refute the error that was arising. The sending of this letter would offer the opportunity to return Onesimus to his master.

27. *Ibid.*, pp. 153-154.
28. Heinrich August Wilhelm Meyer, *Critical and Exegetical Hand-Book to the Epistles to the Philippians and Colossians, and to Philemon,* (1885), p. 203. Italics in original.

THE PLACE AND DATE OF COLOSSIANS

1. *Place.* The traditional view has placed the writing of Colossians at Rome during Paul's first Roman imprisonment. That Paul was a prisoner at the time of its writing the epistle clearly asserts (Col. 4:3, 18). Since the Book of Acts records no protracted imprisonment during which it could have been written prior to his arrest in Jerusalem (Acts 21:27ff), the common view has been that we are left with the alternative choice of Caesarea or Rome. In recent years the view has been advanced that the place of writing was Ephesus. The preponderance of evidence points to Rome as the place of writing. (See the Introduction to the Prison Epistles).

2. *Date.* Accepting the place of composition as being Rome, the date of Colossians must be placed during the two years of Paul's imprisonment in Rome. The dates for this period are variously given, but we may accept A.D. 61 to 63. The question remains as to what time during this period this epistle was written. References in the epistles show that Colossians, Philemon, and Ephesians were all dispatched at the same time (Col. 4:7-9; Philem. 10-11; Eph. 6:21-22). Philemon 22 seems to indicate that Paul's appeal to Caesar has not yet been taken up. We would then place the epistle in the summer of A.D. 62. Such a dating allows sufficient time for the development of conditions in Colossae, the arrival of the report in Colossae of Paul's presence in Rome, and the journey of Epaphras to Rome to report to Paul.

3. *Bearer.* The bearer of the epistle was Tychicus, himself a native of the province of Asia (Acts 20:4). Paul describes him as "the beloved brother and faithful minister and fellow-servant in the Lord" (Col. 4:7). He was accompanied by Onesimus who was being returned to his master at Colossae. From Ephesians 6:21 it is seen that Tychicus also carried our Epistle to the Ephesians. Tychicus was one of Paul's intimate associates and trusted helpers. The question as to why Paul sent Tychicus rather than Epaphras with this lettter cannot be satisfactorily cleared up. Perhaps Epaphras had reasons for remaining longer in Rome. Since in Philemon 23 Paul speaks of Epaphras as "my fellow-prisoner," it has been conjectured that his relations with Paul in Rome had excited suspicion and had led to his temporary confinement. More probable is the view that the state-

ment merely indicates that he was voluntarily sharing the Apostle's captivity by living with him.

### THE PURPOSE OF COLOSSIANS

Three phases of the Apostle's purpose may be traced in his earnest endeavor to help the Colossian saints.

1. *Stabilization.* The Apostle wrote to strengthen and to confirm the Colossian Christians in their adherence to the Gospel which they had received. He expresses joy at the report of their stability and growth in grace, assures them of his continuous prayers for them, and urges them to abide in that which they have received (1:3-8; 2:5-7). He seeks to impress upon them that, although he has never seen their faces, he is yet deeply interested in them and the furtherance of the true Gospel among them. He informs them that he has a deep concern for their spiritual welfare (2:1-5) and reminds them that his personal concern for them is in accordance with the ministry entrusted to him by the Lord for the whole Church (1:24-29). These assurances of his personal concern for them, given out of a full heart, are intended to strengthen and to stabilize them in their faith.

2. *Refutation.* The obvious purpose of the epistle is to crush the heretical teaching which has lifted its threatening head in Colossae. He sharply warns them to be alert against the danger of being taken captive by this new teaching with its vaunted philosophy and show of wisdom (2:8). Since the denunciations throughout the epistle are in the *singular* number, rather than in the plural as in Galatians, it seems that this Colossian heresy rested on the authority of some single teacher rather than on an appeal to Scripture or tradition.

It is difficult to determine the exact nature and origin of this so-called "Colossian Heresy." All that is definitely known as to the nature of this teaching must be learned from the incidental statements of Paul concerning it in this epistle. Since we are given no systematic presentation of its contents but only passing references to phases of it, differences of view as to its exact nature and its origin have been advanced.

It is in the second chapter, where the Apostle turns his full artillery on this teaching to demolish it, that we get the clearest indications as to its nature. This teaching came with the pretensions of being a philosophical system of truth (2:8). The Apostle warns the Colossians against being taken captive by these philosophical pretensions and scornfully calls it "vain deceit," that is, empty pretense. This system was but vain speculation without a foundation in truth and was empty of moral power for practical life.

Several elements in this teaching are apparent. It was *ritualistic* in its teachings and demands. It insisted that the Colossian Christians should observe religious days and seasons—"a feast day or a new moon or a sabbath day" (2:16).

It also had an *ascetic* element. It criticized the Colossian believers about their diet—"judge you in meat, or in drink" (2:16); it inculcated rigid ascetic rules—"handle not, nor taste, nor touch" (2:21); it was inspired by an antipathy to the bodily life (2:20-23).

It also revealed a *mystical* or speculative element. It promulgated a cult of angel worship, insisted on self-abasement of some kind, and indulged in praise of visions which were supposed to have definite meanings only to be understood after prolonged thought (2:18).

The exact origin and classification of these diverse elements are difficult to determine. Some have thought that this Colossian heresy was an attempt to unite Christian truths and the doctrines of the Essenes. Doubtless Jewish elements are present in the teaching. Others have seen in it the beginnings of Gentile Gnosticism. Gnostic elements are evident in the teaching. It seems impossible positively to identify this teaching with any exact system known to have existed at the time. Apparently it was a syncretistic religious system, an amalgam of Jewish elements, Oriental theosophy, and incipient Gnostic speculations.[29]

Basic to this false teaching was the postulate that God is holy and matter is evil, and that between spirit and matter there was a great gulf. Then speculation set to work seeking to bridge the gulf that had thus been created. This gave rise to the "doctrine of Aeons," or intermediate beings, between God and the world. According to this view, since matter is evil, God can have nothing to do with this world directly. Accordingly, He created another being somewhat inferior to Himself but worthy of having come from Him. This lower being, or emanation, produced another in a similar manner until a whole series of them, on a descending scale, came into existence. The lowest

29. For recent discussion of the "Colossian heresy" see Eduard Lohse, "Colossians and Philemon," *Hermenia,* (1971), pp. 127-131; Ralph P. Martin, "Colossians and Philemon," *New Century Bible,* (1974), pp. 9-19, and the literature cited.

was close enough to the world to create the world of evil matter. Then this host of intermediary beings, or angels, became the objects of worship rather than God Himself, since He was too holy to be approached directly. The problem of where to place Christ in this system at once raised Christological questions. The attempts to fit Him into this system of emanations at once degraded His person and undermined the sufficiency of His redemption.

Paul's method of refuting the error is instructive. He does not consume a lot of time denouncing the false teacher or expounding the heretical views. He plainly shows that the root of the error lies in an inadequate and erroneous view of the person and work of Christ. He accordingly "sets forth, as the great burden of his message, the nature and mission of the Son of God, His place in the universe, His relation to the Church, and His complete sufficiency for all human needs."[30] It is this fact that gives the epistle its abiding value. It offers the antidote for all heresy. "A true Christology is the final answer to every heresy that ever has been, or ever will be."[31]

3. *Instruction.* The Apostle uses the latter part of the epistle to instruct the Colossians in a well-rounded Christian life based on a true apprehension of and vital union with Christ the Head (3:5–4:6). The tendency of the Gnostic teaching was to lead its followers either into gross immortality or into asceticism. The Apostle's design is to show the proper relationship between the believer's union with Christ and a moral life. Christ is the antidote not only for theological error but for moral error as well. A true apprehension of the person and work of Christ manifests itself in ethical living. The Apostle pictures the life of the believer from the individual (3:5-17) as well as the social standpoint (3:18–4:6).

### THE CHARACTERISTICS OF COLOSSIANS

1. *Contents.* The outstanding characteristic of this epistle is its Christology. Its specific burden is the elaboration of the person and work of Christ as the answer to all error. The marvelous passage in 1:15-23, which presents Christ in His threefold relation to God, creation, and the Church, is the distinctive glory of this epistle among the Pauline writings. Concerning this passage Findlay says,

30. Charles R. Erdman, *The Epistles of Paul to the Colossians and to Philemon,* (1933), p. 19.
31. W. Graham Scroggie, *Know Your Bible, A Brief Introduction to the Scriptures, Volume II, The New Testament,* (n.d.), p. 190.

> This passage occupies a place in the Christology of St. Paul corresponding to that which belongs to Rom. iii. 19-26 in regard to his Soteriology. Here he treats directly and expressly of the sovereignty of Christ and the nature of his Person—subjects which elsewhere in his writings are for the most part matter of assumption or mere incidental reference. . . . It sets forth *who he is and what place he fills in the universe.*[32]

It presents Paul's picture of the Cosmic Christ. The Christology of the epistle is the one central and unifying theme of the whole. Every part of the letter directly or indirectly contributes to this exalted theme and acknowledges Him as "all and in all."

Since apparently this heresy at Colossae did not claim authorization from Old Testament Scripture, no reference to the Old Testament is made in the epistle.

2. *Language and style.* "In both language and style," says Alford, "the Epistle to the Colossians is peculiar. But the peculiarities are not greater than might well arise from the fact that the subject on which the Apostle was mainly writing was one requiring new thoughts and words."[33] The richness of the language is seen in the fact that there are fifty-five words in it which do not occur in any other Pauline epistle, and thirty-four of these occur nowhere else in the New Testament.

The tone of the epistle is definitely controversial. In it the mind of the Apostle is seen as anxious and perturbed, struggling with great spiritual difficulties of a profound and perplexing character. Fittingly the language is lofty and the thought movement intense.

The style of the epistle lacks something of the glow and vehemence of the controversial epistles of the second group. Peake says,

> The style of Colossians is slow and laboured, without the swift and rushing movement of the earlier polemical Epistles, differing from them also in its form of argument and its choice of logical particles. Synonyms are accumulated and clauses built up by curious combinations of words. There is a fondness for long compound words, many of which occur nowhere else in Paul, many but seldom. A large proportion is to be found in the second chapter, where the peculiarities

32. G. G. Findlay, "The Epistle of Paul to the Colossians," *Pulpit Commentary,* (1950 reprint), p. 7. Italics in original.
33. Henry Alford, *The Greek Testament,* (1958), Vol. III, pp. 39-40 Proleg.

of the subject matter largely account for the peculiarity of the diction.[34]

Findlay observes that the style of Colossians reveals that the writer is "such a one as Paul the aged" (Philem. 9) and goes to confirm the view that this epistle belongs "to the mellow afternoon rather than to the heyday of the apostle's vigour."[35]

"THE EPISTLE FROM LAODICEA"

In Colossians 4:16 Paul instructs the Colossians that they are to cause this epistle to be read in the Laodicean church and that they are also to "read the epistle from Laodicea." What was this "epistle from Laodicea"? This question has called forth an abundance of hypotheses in inverse proportion to the meagerness of the authentic information. The language clearly implies that it was a letter from the Apostle himself and so brushes aside all views that it means a letter *from* the Laodiceans. The two letters were apparently companion letters of some kind, and Paul felt that both churches would profit by the reading of both letters. This directive from the Apostle may throw some light on the question of the circulation of apostolic letters from the very beginning.

But can we identify this letter "from Laodicea"? Several different answers have been given. One view is that it was a separate and distinct letter written by the Apostle to the Laodiceans and that it has been lost. There is nothing improbable in itself in the view of a lost apostolic letter. We do know that the Apostle wrote some other letters which have not been preserved for us.

An imposing array of scholars hold that the letter referred to was our Epistle to the Ephesians. This answer proceeds on the view that our Epistle to the Ephesians is really a circular letter intended for the various churches in the province of Asia. They maintain that it is unnecessary to postulate the writing of a fourth letter at the same time, as would be if this has reference to a lost letter, since the Ephesian epistle is the logical complement to Colossians. If the encyclical theory concerning Ephesians is accepted, this identification is possible.

34. Arthur S. Peake, *A Critical Introduction to the New Testament,* (1919), pp. 50-51.
35. G. G. Findlay, "The Epistle of Paul to the Colossians," *Pulpit Commentary,* (1950 reprint), p. xi.

For a number of centuries many in the churches made a wholly different identification. In many sections of the Church, especially in the West, it was identified with the spurious "Epistle to the Laodiceans," a short letter of twenty verses, obviously forged to supply the missing letter mentioned in Colossians 4:16. This epistle is extant only in the Latin[36], but Lightfoot has given good reasons for believing that it was originally composed in the Greek. This Latin epistle is found among the Pauline epistles in manuscripts dating from the sixth to the fifteenth centuries. "For more than nine centuries this forged epistle hovered about the doors of the sacred Canon, without either finding admission or being peremptorily excluded."[37]

The epistle, as translated from the Latin by Moule, reads as follows:

> Paul an Apostle, not of men, nor through man, but through Jesus Christ, to the brethren who are at Laodicea. Grace unto you and peace from God the Father and the Lord Jesus Christ.
>
> I give thanks to God in every prayer of mine, that ye are abiding in Him, and persevering in His works, looking for the promise unto the day of judgment. And let not the vain speech of certain men beguile you, who teach in order that they may turn you away from the Gospel which is preached by me. And now God shall bring it about that those who proceed from me prove serviceable for the furtherance of the truth of the Gospel and doers of the goodness of the works which belong to the salvation of life eternal.
>
> And now are manifest my bonds, which I suffer in Christ; wherein I exult and rejoice. And this is to me for perpetual salvation; which also is done by your prayers and by the administration of the Holy Spirit, whether through life or through death. For to me to live is Christ and to die is joy. And His mercy shall do in you this very thing, that you should have the same love and be of the same mind.
>
> Therefore, dearly beloved, as you hearkened in my presence, so hold fast and do in the fear of God, and you shall have life forevermore; for it is God who worketh in you. And do without disputing whatsoever ye do.
>
> And for what remaineth, dearly beloved, rejoice in Christ; and beware of them who are defiled with gain. Let all your requests be manifest before God; and be ye stedfast in the mind of Christ. And

36. "Forty-seven MSS of it are now known to exist." James Moffatt, *An Introduction to the Literature of the New Testament,* (3rd Ed., 1949 reprint), p. 161.
37. J. B. Lightfoot, *Saint Paul's Epistles to the Colossians and to Philemon,* (1900 reprint), p. 297.

the things which are whole, and true, and grave, and just, and lovely, do. And the things which ye have heard and received in the heart, hold fast; and ye shall have peace.

The saints salute you.

The grace of our Lord Jesus Christ (be) with your spirit.

And see that (this) be read to the Colossians, and (that which is) of the Colossians to you.[38]

A mere reading of this epistle makes it obvious that it is simply a patchwork of Pauline phrases strung together without any definite purpose or connection. The larger part of the epistle comes from the Book of Philippians, but there are a few phrases that have been borrowed from other epistles, especially Galatians.

Erasmus contemptuously dismissed it as spurious, saying, "No argument against a Pauline authorship can be stronger than the Epistle itself."[39] Lightfoot aptly says of it,

> Unlike most forgeries, it had no ulterior aim. It was not framed to advance any particular opinions, whether heterodox or orthodox. It has no doctrinal peculiarities. Thus it is quite harmless, so far as falsity and stupidity combined can ever be regarded as harmless.[40]

Knox has revived the theory that "the epistle from Laodicea" is our letter to Philemon.[41] The theory is unconvincing and faces serious difficulties.[42] The latest conjecture is that it was a letter written by Epaphras to the Laodicean church.[43]

## An Outline of Colossians

### THE SALUTATION (1-2)

1. The writers (1)
2. The readers (2a)
3. The greetings (2b)

38. Quoted from H. C. G. Moule, "The Epistles of Paul the Apostle to the Colossians and to Philemon," *Cambridge Bible for Schools,* (1932 reprint), pp. 45-46.
39. Quoted in H. C. G. Moule, *Ibid.*, p. 46.
40. J. B. Lightfoot, *Saint Paul's Epistles to the Colossians and to Philemon,* (1900 reprint), pp. 279-280.
41. John Knox, *Philemon Among the Letters of Paul,* (Revised Ed., 1959), p. 45. J. B. Lightfoot, *Saint Paul's Epistle to the Colossians and to Philemon* (1927 reprint), pp. 278-279, mentions Wieseler as advocating the view in the middle of the past century.
42. See Donald Guthrie, *New Testament Introduction,* (Revised Ed., 1970), p. 438.
43. Charles P. Anderson, "Who Wrote 'The Epistle from Laodicea'?" *Journal of Biblical Literature,* Dec. 1966, pp. 436-440.

## I. PERSONAL: THANKSGIVING AND PRAYER (1:3-14)

1. The thanksgiving (3-8)
   a. The thanksgiving for the Colossians (3-5a)
      1) The continued prayer for them (3)
      2) The news about them (4-5a)
         a) The report of their faith and love (4)
         b) The inspiration of the heavenly hope (5a)
   b. The characterization of the Gospel (5b-6)
   c. The ministry of Epaphras (7-8)
2. The prayer (9-14)
   a. The account of the prayer for them (9a)
   b. The contents of the prayer for them (9b-12a)
      1) The statement of the request (9b)
      2) The purpose of the request (10a)
      3) The results of the answered request (10b-12a)
         a) Bearing fruit in every good work (10b)
         b) Increasing in the knowledge of God (10c)
         c) Being spiritually strengthened (11)
         d) Giving thanks unto the Father (12a)
   c. The reasons for thanksgiving (12b-14)
      1) We were made fit for the heavenly inheritance (12b)
      2) We experienced a change of allegiance (13)
      3) We have redemption in Christ (14)

## II. DOCTRINAL: THE PRE-EMINENCE OF CHRIST (1:15-23)

1. His divine person (15-18)
   a. His relationship to the Father (15a)
   b. His relationship to creation (15b-17)
      1) In relation to its origin (15b-16)
      2) In relation to its continuity (17)
   c. His relationship to the Church (18)
2. His redemptive work (19-23)
   a. The redemption which He wrought (19-20)
      1) The character of the Redeemer (19)
      2) The description of the redemption (20)
   b. The redemption applied to the Colossians (21-23)
      1) The past condition (21)
      2) The present position (22a)

3) The future presentation (22b-23)
a) The divine purpose (22b)
b) The human condition (23a)
c) The apostolic encouragement (23b)

III. MINISTERIAL: THE APOSTLESHIP OF PAUL (1:24–2:7)

1. The ministry of Paul to the whole Church (1:24-29)
   a. The nature of his ministry (24)
   b. The circumstances of his ministry (25)
   c. The message of his ministry (26-27)
      1) It is the mystery of God (26-27a)
      2) It is Christ Himself (27b)
   d. The methods of his ministry (28a)
   e. The object of his ministry (28b)
   f. The accompaniments of his ministry (29)
2. The solicitude of Paul for the Colossians (2:1-7)
   a. His striving for them (1-3)
      1) The magnitude of the striving (1a)
      2) The persons for whom he strives (1b)
      3) The purpose of the striving (2-3)
   b. His warning to them (4)
   c. His praise of them (5)
   d. His appeal to them (6-7)
      1) Their reception of Christ (6a)
      2) Their continued walk in Christ (6b-7)

IV. POLEMICAL: THE FALSE PHILOSOPHY AND THE TRUE FAITH (2:8–3:4)

1. The warning against the false philosophy (2:8)
2. The elaboration of the sufficiency in Christ (2:9-15)
   a. The fullness available in Christ (9-10)
   b. The nature of the union with Christ (11-12)
      1) The inner reality of spiritual circumcision (11)
      2) The burial and resurrection with Him in baptism (12)
   c. The results of the union with Christ (13-15)
      1) The experience of a spiritual resurrection (13)
      2) The cancellation of the bond of the law (14)
      3) The triumph over the powers of evil (15)

3. The warnings against spiritual dangers (2:16-19)
   a. The warning against asceticism (16-17)
      1) The elements of this asceticism (16)
      2) The true view of these things (17)
   b. The warning against dethroning Christ (18-19)
      1) The warning against being robbed of their prize (18a)
      2) The description of the robbers (18b-19a)
      3) The nature of Christ the true Head (19b)
4. The resultant exhortations (2:20—3:4)
   a. The call to realize the meaning of their death with Christ (2:20-23)
      1) The position of the believer (20a)
      2) The protest against a false submission (20b-21)
      3) The reasons for the rejection of such submission (22-23)
         a) They assign a false value to temporal things (22a)
         b) They are but the doctrines of men (22b)
         c) They fail of their objective (23)
   b. The exhortation to realize their resurrection with Christ (3:1-4)
      1) The position of the believer (1a)
      2) The consequent duties of the believer (1b-2)
         a) To seek the things above (1b)
         b) To have the mind on these things (2)
      3) The grounds for this exhortation (3-4)

V. PRACTICAL: THE CHRISTIAN LIFE (3:5—4:6)

1. The believer's individual life (3:5-17)
   a. Negative—The putting off of the old (5-11)
      1) The contents of the exhortations (5-9a)
         a) The exhortation to slay the old members (5-7)
            (i) The description of the old members (5)
            (ii) The consequence of their practice (6)
            (iii) The reminder of their past life (7)
         b) The exhortation to strip off the old sins (8-9a)
            (i) The present contrast to the former life (8a)
            (ii) The list of the old sins (8b-9a)
      2) The basis for the exhortations (9b-11)
         a) The nature of the transaction experienced (9b-10)

b) The result of the transaction experienced (11)
b. Positive—The putting on of the new (12-17)
1) The attire of the new man (12-14)
a) The characterization of the believer (12a)
b) The wardrobe of the soul (12b-14)
(i) The personal virtues (12b)
(ii) The social reactions (13)
(iii) The bond of love (14)
2) The principles for the new life (15-17)
a) Be ruled by the peace of Christ (15)
b) Be indwelt by the Word of Christ (16)
c) Do all in the name of Christ (17)
2. The believer in social relations (3:18—4:6)
a. The duties in household relations (3:18—4:1)
1) The duties of wives and husbands (3:18-19)
2) The duties of children and parents (3:20-21)
3) The duties of servants and masters (3:22—4:1)
a) The obedience of the servants (22-25)
(i) The call for obedience (22a)
(ii) The nature of the obedience (22b)
(iii) The motive for obedience (23)
(iv) The encouragement in obedience (24)
(v) The warning against wrongdoing (25)
b) The directive to the masters (4:1)
b. The duties in Gospel relations (4:2-6)
1) The duties concerning prayer and intercession (2-4)
a) The exhortation to steadfastness in prayer (2)
b) The request for intercession for the preachers (3-4)
2) The duties of life in relation to the unsaved (5-6)
a) The duty as to their walk (5)
b) The duty as to their speech (6)

VI. PERSONAL: THE FRIENDS OF PAUL (4:7-17)

1. The bearers of the letter (7-9)
a. The statement concerning Tychicus (7-8)
1) The information to be given by Tychicus (7a)
2) The commendation given Tychicus (7b)
3) The purpose in sending Tychicus (8)

b. The statement concerning Onesimus (9a)
c. The joint report concerning his affairs (9b)
2. The greetings from his companions (10-14)
 a. The greetings from those of the circumcision (10-11)
  1) The designation of the friends (10-11a)
  2) The description of these friends (11b)
 b. The greetings from those of the Gentiles (12-14)
  1) The greeting from Epaphras (12-13)
   a) The description of Epaphras (12a)
   b) The prayer-labors of Epaphras for them (12b)
   c) The testimony given to Epaphras (13)
  2) The greeting from Luke and Demas (14)
3. The concluding messages (15-17)
 a. The personal greetings to be conveyed (15)
 b. The instructions concerning the exchange of epistles (16)
 c. The exhortation to be given to Archippus (17)

THE CONCLUSION (4:18)

1. The salutation with his own hand
2. The request to remember his bonds
3. The benediction

## A Book List on Colossians

Abbott, T. K., "A Critical and Exegetical Commentary on the Epistles to the Ephesians, and to the Colossians." *The International Critical Commentary*. Edinburgh: T. & T. Clark (n.d.).

Greek text. Primarily philological; rich in word studies and linguistic exegesis. Valuable for the Greek student. Reverent if not always thoroughly evangelical.

Beare, Francis W., and MacLeod, G. Preston, "The Epistle to the Colossians," *The Interpreter's Bible*. Vol XI. New York: Abingdon Press (1955).

Prints the King James and Revised Standard versions at the top of the page. Introduction and exegesis by Beare, exposition by MacLeod. The work of two Canadian liberal scholars. Beare maintains that the authorship of Colossians remains an open question and refuses to use Paul's career or personality to interpret its contents.

Carson, Herbert M., "The Epistles of Paul to the Colossians and Philemon." *The Tyndale New Testament Commentaries.* Grand Rapids: Wm. B. Eerdmans Pub. Co. (1960).

A concise, exegetical, verse-by-verse treatment of these epistles from a conservative viewpoint. The brief analytical outlines of the epistles are used in the text to organize the material for the reader. Designed for the lay person; technical matters are kept to a minimum.

Cragg, Herbert W., *The Sole Sufficiency of Jesus Christ. Studies in the Epistle to the Colossians.* London: Marshall, Morgan and Scott (1961).

A devotional exposition based upon Bible readings given at the Keswick Convention in 1960.

Eadie, John, *A Commentary on the Greek Text of the Epistle of Paul to the Colossians.* Grand Rapids: Zondervan Publishing House (1957 reprint).

First published in 1855, this is a full and rich exegetical treatment of Colossians by a conservative Scottish Presbyterian scholar of the last century. Although innocent of the later theological developments, it still has value for the Greek student for its exegetical insights.

Harrison, Everett F., "Colossians, Christ All-Sufficient." *Everyman's Bible Commentary.* Chicago: Moody Press (1971).

A handy, well-outlined interpretation by a contemporary evangelical theologian. A valuable addition to any library at its modest price.

Hendriksen, William, "Exposition of Colossians and Philemon." *New Testament Commentary.* Grand Rapids: Baker Book House (1964).

Uses the author's own translation. Following an informative introduction espousing the traditional Roman origin, the verse-by-verse treatment blends scholarly insight with simplicity of expression; more technical matters are dealt with in the footnotes. Each major section is concluded with a doctrinal summary. The work of a voluminous scholar in the Reformed tradition.

Kelly, William, *Lectures on the Epistles of Paul the Apostle to the Colossians, with a New Translation.* London: G. Morrish (reprint, n.d.).

A series of expository lectures by a voluminous Plymouth Brethren scholar of the past century.

Lenski, R. C. H., *The Interpretation of St. Paul's Epistles to the Co-*

*lossians, to the Thessalonians, to Timothy, to Titus and to Philemon.* Columbus, Ohio: Lutheran Book Concern (1937).

Lightfoot, J. B., *Saint Paul's Epistle to the Colossians and to Philemon.* London: Macmillan and Co. (1927 reprint).

Greek text. A definitive commentary by a noted conservative British scholar of the past century. Much valuable material in the lengthy introductions and the appended dissertation on the Essenes which now needs updating.

Lohse, Eduard, "Colossians and Philemon, A Commentary on the Epistles to the Colossians and to Philemon." *Hermenia–A Critical and Historical Commentary on the Bible.* Translated by William R. Poehlmann and Robert J. Karris. Edited by Helmut Koester. Philadelphia: Fortress Press (1971).

Greek text. A veritable mine of scholarly information for the advanced student. The exposition is supported by extensive footnotes. Interspersed throughout the text are excurses covering various themes related to Colossians. Offers a wealth of references to words, usages, and concepts, as well as a nearly exhaustive bibliography of commentaries and articles, with full indexes. Not always thoroughly evangelical.

Maclaren, Alexander, "The Epistles of St. Paul to the Colossians and to Philemon," *The Expositor's Bible.* Vol. VI. Grand Rapids: Wm. B. Eerdmans Pub. Co. (1943 reprint).

One of the richest expositions in this famous series. Maclaren is here at his best; rich exposition with valuable application.

Martin, Ralph P., "Colossians and Philemon." *New Century Bible Based on the Revised Standard Version.* London: Oliphants (1974).

An exegetical treatment of the text with numerous references to further sources for study. Both letters are assigned to an Ephesian imprisonment during the time of Acts 19-20. The work of an erudite evangelical scholar.

———, *Colossians: The Church's Lord and the Christian's Liberty.* Grand Rapids: Zondervan Publishing House (1973).

An up-to-date scholarly commentary aiming first at a full investigation of the text and then indicating the letter's current relevance. Accepts an Ephesian origin for Colossians. Important for the latest on "the Colossian errorists."

Moule, C. F. D., "The Epistles of Paul the Apostle to the Colossians and to Philemon." *Cambridge Greek Testament Commentary.* Cambridge: University Press (1957).

Greek text. Part of a new edition of the Cambridge Greek Testament. Valuable introduction. An exegetical commentary based on a linguistic and theological interpretation of the original text.

Moule, H. C. G., "The Epistle of Paul the Apostle to the Colossians and to Philemon." *Cambridge Bible for Schools and Colleges.* Cambridge: University Press (1893; 1932 reprint).

A concise, lucid treatment of these epistles by a conservative Anglican scholar of the past generation. Includes several valuable appendixes.

Radford, Lewis B., "The Epistle to the Colossians and the Epistle to Philemon." *Westminster Commentaries.* London: Methuen & Co. (1931).

A lengthy introduction (142 pages) dealing with various problems in the interpretation of Colossians. A full exegetical commentary aiming at presenting the meaning of the epistle in the light of modern knowledge for the English student. The phrase-by-phrase treatment is supplemented by various additional notes. The work of an Anglican bishop of Australia.

Robertson, A. T., *Paul and the Intellectuals: The Epistle to the Colossians.* Revised and edited by W. C. Strickland. Nashville: Broadman Press (1959).

A series of expository lectures, originally published in 1928, which unite accurate scholarship with spiritual edification by a master of the Greek. Abounds in flashes of light from the Greek for the common reader.

Simpson, E. K., and Bruce, F. F., "Commentary on the Epistles to the Ephesians and the Colossians." *The New International Commentary on the New Testament.* Grand Rapids: Wm. B. Eerdmans Pub. Co. (1957).

The commentary on Colossians by Bruce reflects the noted author's broad scholarship while presenting the interpretation in a warm and readable manner. Details concerning the Greek and references to further sources are relegated to the footnotes. The work of Simpson on Ephesians is highly scholarly and expressed in erudite language.

Thomas, W. H. Griffith, *Studies in Colossians and Philemon.* Edited by Winifred G. T. Gillespie, his daughter. Grand Rapids: Baker Book House (1973).

The material on Colossians is a revision of an older work entitled *Christ Pre-eminent,* and expanded on a basis of a later analysis by the author and supplemented by material from his other books. The material on Philemon was compiled by Thomas' daughter on the basis of unpublished notes. Characterized by the evangelical warmth and insights of the noted author.

Vaughan, Curtis, *Colossians. A Study Guide.* Grand Rapids: Zondervan Publishing House (1973).

A concise, well-outlined treatment of Colossians by a conservative Southern Baptist professor. On problem passages presents the varied views. Frequently quotes from modern translations to illustrate shades of meaning.

Vine, W. E., *Epistles to the Philippians and Colossians.* London: Oliphants (1955).

A phrase-by-phrase interpretation of these epistles by a late British Plymouth Brethren scholar. Combines scholarly insight with simplicity of diction. Conveys much of the force of the original for the English student. Has index of Greek words treated.

White, R. E. O., *In His the Fulness. Homiletic Studies in Paul's Epistle to the Colossians.* Old Tappan, N.J.: Fleming H. Revell (1973).

A series of twenty-six expository meditations by an evangelical British preacher. Focuses upon the centrality of Christ for Christian faith and experience. Good model of expository preaching.

Wuest, Kenneth S., *Ephesians and Colossians in the Greek New Testament for the English Reader.* Grand Rapids: Wm. B. Eerdmans Pub. Co. (1953).

A simplified commentary on the Greek for the benefit of the English reader; an expanded translation with exegetical comments and word studies.

# 13

# PHILEMON

## An Introduction to Philemon

The brief Letter to Philemon is unique among the correspondence of Paul that has come down to us. While not strictly a private letter, it yet is concerned with a personal problem and gives us a remarkable glimpse of the Apostle in his dealings with such personal affairs as they touched the lives of his converts. In its artless revelation of Paul's devoted love to individual souls we may discover one of the secrets of his success as a missionary. It was because of his affectional personal interest in men wherever he went that the Apostle was able to exercise such a powerful grip upon the hearts of his friends. This little letter gives us a striking illustration of this characteristic of the Apostle.

### THE HOME OF PHILEMON

The Epistle to Philemon is the only book in the New Testament which gives us a glimpse into a Christian household of that time. The members are named in the salutation of the letter (vv. 1-2). Philemon, a native or at least a resident of Colossae,[1] was a convert of the apostle Paul, as appears from verse 19. He seems to have been among those who were converted through their contacts with Paul during his Ephesian ministry. Apparently he was a well-to-do householder in Colossae. This appears, not from the fact that he was the owner of a slave, for he might have owned only one or two, but from the facts that his house was commodious enough to serve as an assembly place for believers in Colossae and that he was in a position

1. Col. 4:9 identifies Onesimus with Colossae. Cf. Theodor Zahn, *Introduction to the New Testament,* (1909) Vol I, p. 446.

to show his benevolence to an extended circle of fellow Christians (vv. 2, 7).

Philemon apparently was a lay member of the Colossian church. Paul's title for him as a "fellow-worker" (v. 1), although not an official designation, was yet a noble testimony to his evangelistic interests. His interest apparently manifested itself in his generous demonstrations of practical love "toward all the saints" (v. 5). All who came into contact with him spoke appreciatively of his hospitality. Although we know nothing about Philemon beyond what is indicated in this brief letter, it yet gives us an appealing picture of the man. Hackett summarized the picture as follows:

> His character, as shadowed forth in this Epistle, is one of the noblest which the sacred record makes known to us. He was full of faith and good works, was confiding, obedient, sympathizing, benevolent, and a man who, on a question of simple justice, needed only a hint of his duty to prompt him to go even beyond it.[2]

It is generally assumed that Apphia was the wife of Philemon and Archippus his son. Both likewise were Christians, although no hint is given as to the means of their conversion. Archippus apparently held some office in the church. Paul calls him "our fellow-soldier" (v. 2), an expression which indicates active and self-denying service for the Lord. Just where he had been a companion with the Apostle in spiritual warfare is not known. It seems that Archippus had been entrusted with pastoral responsibilities in the Colossian church when Epaphras went to Rome. In Colossians 4:17 Paul concludes with an admonition to Archippus:

> And say to Archippus, Take heed to the ministry which thou hast received in the Lord, that thou fulfill it.

This need not imply any censure of Archippus, as is often thought, but may be merely a message of stimulation and encouragement to him in view of the duties that had devolved upon him because of the absence of Epaphras. Lightfoot thought that this "ministry" was that of an "evangelist" (cf. Eph 4:11) and that the admonition connected him with Laodicea.[3] But Zahn, rightly we think, insists that a proper

2. In additions by Horatio B. Hackett in J. J. Van Oosterzee, "The Epistle of Paul to Philemon," Lange's *Commentary*, (1950 reprint), p. 5.
3. J. B. Lightfoot, *Saint Paul's Epistles to the Colossians and to Philemon,* (1900 reprint), p. 307.

understanding of Colossians 4:15-17 connects Archippus with the Colossian church only.[4]

To this Christian household Onesimus belonged as a slave. He probably was only one of a number of slaves in this household. That a Christian such as Philemon should own slaves may seem strange to us today, but slavery was a commonly accepted feature of the society of that day. Angus says, "The Greek and the Roman saw no more wrong in having slaves than we see in having domestic servants."[5] Not infrequently both master and slave were Christians (1 Tim. 6:1-2). Because of this situation Paul included instructions for Christian slaves as well as masters in writing to the Colossians and the Ephesians (Col. 3:22–4:1; Eph. 6:5-9).

THE AUTHENTICITY OF PHILEMON

Only during two periods in Church history has the authenticity of Philemon been even called into question. There were a few in the fourth century who, absorbed in their theological disputations, held that it was unworthy of Paul because it contained no doctrinal teaching. The epistle was successfully vindicated by Jerome, Chrysostom, and Theodore of Mopseustia.[6]

In the modern era a few radical critics, inspired by purely subjective motives and without adequate reason, have laid rough hands on this beautiful letter. The real reason that these critics have denied its authenticity is the fact that it gives strong support to the authenticity of Colossians. Shaw aptly remarks,

> Philemon is so closely linked with Colossians, and gives that difficult Epistle such invincible support, that it is felt to be quite impossible to admit it. It must go simply because Colossians must. As Sabatier says, We have here the wolf's argument against the lamb: "If it was not you, it was your brother."[7]

And Zahn curtly dismisses the efforts of these destructive critics with one sentence:

> The fact that this letter has been declared spurious notwithstanding its wealth of original material, and in spite of the lack of all support

4. Theodor Zahn, *Introduction to the New Testament,* (1909), Vol. I, p. 446.
5. S. Angus, *The Environment of Early Christianity,* (1932), p. 38.
6. J. B. Lightfoot, *Saint Paul's Epistles to the Colossians and to Philemon,* (1900 reprint), pp. 314-315.
7. R. D. Shaw, *The Pauline Epistles,* (4th Ed., 1924 reprint), p. 298.

> from tradition and the impossibility of discovering any sufficient motive for its forgery, deserves only to be mentioned.[8]

All the attacks of the critics have utterly failed to dislodge the epistle. In 1919 Peake concluded, "It is now amply recognized on all hands."[9]

## THE OCCASION FOR PHILEMON

The occasion for this brief yet impressive note to Philemon is obvious from its contents. Onesimus, a slave of Philemon, had wronged, and possibly robbed his master of money, and had fled. He had found his way to Rome, apparently hoping to lose himself in that seething mass of humanity, thus eluding the slave-catchers who would doubtless be on the lookout for the fugitive. But in some way quite unknown to us, at Rome Onesimus had come into touch with the apostle Paul.[10] Perhaps one of Paul's co-workers came across him in the city and brought him to Paul. As a result of his contacts with the Apostle he was led to Christ (v. 10). As a new creature in Christ, Onesimus, whose name meant "profitable" (v. 11), began to live up to the connotation of his name and for some short time rendered highly appreciated service to the Apostle in his imprisonment (v. 13). Closer acquaintance with this new convert revealed that there was much worthy of love in this man who had sinned and repented. A strong attachment sprang up between Paul and Onesimus (v. 12). But Paul felt that something more was necessary. "Onesimus had repented, but he had not made restitution."[11] Paul felt that Onesimus must return to his master in accordance with the demands of the law. That Onesimus agreed to this proves the reality of his conversion. He well knew what the possible consequences for him might be.[12]

Circumstances soon demanded that Tychicus be dispatched to Colossae with the epistle to that church, and there was the opportunity to return Onesimus to his master. But in sending Onesimus back, Paul felt it expedient to write a letter to Philemon explaining

8. Theodor Zahn, *Introduction to the New Testament,* (1909), Vol. I, p. 455.
9. Arthur S. Peake, *A Critical Introduction to the New Testament,* (1919), p. 47.
10. For some interesting conjectures as to how this happened, see F. W. Farrar, *The Life and Work of St. Paul,* (1889), p. 624.
11. J. B. Lightfoot, *Saint Paul's Epistles to the Colossians and to Philemon,* (1900 reprint), p. 311.
12. "Roman law . . . practically imposed no limits to the power of the master over his slave. . . . Slaves were constantly crucified for far lighter offences than his. A thief and a runaway, he had no claim to forgiveness." J. B. Lightfoot, *Saint Paul's Epistles to the Colossians and to Philemon,* (1900 reprint), p. 312.

the situation and entering a plea for Onesimus. Such was the occasion for this beautiful little letter.

### THE PLACE AND DATE OF PHILEMON

1. *Place.* The letter was composed while Paul was in prison (vv. 9, 10, 13). Tradition has identified that imprisonment with Paul's two-year imprisonment at Rome (Acts 28:30-31). Its intimate connection with Colossians determines that it was written at the same time as that epistle. The preponderance of evidence points to Rome as the place of composition for these epistles, although some have advocated Caesarea, and lately Ephesus. (See the Introduction to the Prison Epistles).

2. *Date.* The date of Philemon is the same as that for Colossians, since they were dispatched together (Col. 4:7-9; Philem. 12). We accordingly date this letter during the summer of A.D. 62.

3. *Bearer.* From Colossians 4:7-9 it is seen that Onesimus accompanied Tychicus on his trip to Colossae with Paul's epistle to that church. His going to Colossae offered the desired opportunity to return Onesimus to his master. Paul had realized that it would not be safe to send Onesimus back alone, for the slave-catchers would be very apt to apprehend him, especially as he neared Colossae. Under this arrangement, Onesimus was placed in the care of Tychicus and so would be safe. Upon arrival in Colossae Tychicus would not only speak for Onesimus but would also present Philemon with this letter from the hand of Paul beseeching him for his spiritual son (v. 10).

### THE PURPOSE OF PHILEMON

The design of the Apostle in writing this little note was to assure Philemon of the writer's high regard for both the master and the slave and to persuade Philemon to receive, forgive, and reinstate Onesimus. This was to be done because a new relation now existed between them; Onesimus is "no longer a mere slave but something more than a slave—a beloved brother" (v. 16, Moffatt). The granting of the request is to be done as though done to Paul himself (v. 17). As his spiritual father, Paul obligates himself to Philemon for the debt of Onesimus (v. 19). Paul closes his appeal with the confident assertion that Philemon will do even beyond that which he is asking (v. 21). This has frequently been taken to mean that Paul is hinting at emancipation for Onesimus. Others see in it merely a general compliment to Philemon's character, an expressed assurance that Philemon will do all that is right. Thus Clogg holds that

> Philemon is not bidden to release Onesimus, but to love him—a far harder thing. Thus the sting of slavery was withdrawn, and the principle laid down which in the end led to the abolition of slavery.[13]

Although Philemon will be the sole legal arbiter in the case, Paul by his reference to the other members of his house and the church that assembles in his home reminds Philemon that he will act as a member of a spiritual society and that all alike, because of the distinctly spiritual nature of the action, will be interested in the outcome.

An entirely different reconstruction of the background and purpose of this letter has been advanced. It is held that the owner of the slave is not Philemon but Archippus and that the primary purpose of Paul is to induce Archippus to free Onesimus and return him to Paul for the service of the Gospel. The freed Onesimus, it is postulated, later became the bishop of the church at Ephesus and was the agent who collected Paul's letters.[14] But this ingenious theory has not commended itself to most modern students.[15]

### THE CHARACTERISTICS OF PHILEMON

1. *Charm.* The beauty and charm of this letter have been universally recognized. Its loving spirit and masterly skill in dealing with a lowly yet delicate task, a task once thought below the dignity of the Apostle, have elicited many eulogies of it. To cite two or three will suffice. Lightfoot said of it,

> As an expression of simple dignity, or refined courtesy, of large sym-

13. Frank Bertram Clogg, *An Introduction to the New Testament,* (3rd Ed., 1949), p. 91.
14. John Knox, *Philemon Among the Letters of Paul,* (Revised Ed., 1959); Knox, "The Epistle to Philemon," *The Interpreter's Bible,* Vol. XI, *Introduction and Exegesis,* (1955); Edgar J. Goodspeed, *New Solutions of New Testament Problems,* (1927); *The Meaning of Ephesians,* (1933); *The Key to Ephesians,* (1956).
15. See C. F. D. Moule, "The Epistles of Paul the Apostle to the Colossians and to Philemon," *Cambridge Greek Testament Commentary,* (1957), pp. 14-21; William Hendricksen, "Exposition of Colossians and Philemon," *New Testament Commentary,* (1964), pp. 23-27; Donald Guthrie, *New Testament Introduction,* (1970), pp. 635-638.

> pathy, and of warm personal affection, the Epistle to Philemon stands unrivalled.[16]

Luther, in his 1522 preface to the epistle, wrote,

> This Epistle gives us a masterly and tender illustration of Christian love; for here we see how St. Paul takes the part of poor Onesimus and advocates his cause with the master all that he can, and acts no differently than if he were himself Onesimus, who had done wrong. And yet he does this, not with force or compulsion, as was his right, but he lays aside his rights and thus compels Philemon, also, to waive his rights. What Christ has done for us with God the Father, that St. Paul does for Onesimus with Philemon. . . . For we are all his Onesimi, if we believe.[17]

The epistle caused Alexander Maclaren to comment,

> That must have been a great intellect, and closely conversant with the Fountain of all light and beauty, which could shape the profound and far-reaching teachings of the Epistle to the Colossians, and pass from them to the graceful simplicity and sweet kindliness of this exquisite letter.[18]

In this letter the Apostle reveals himself a master of Christian courtesy. The task confronting him was one of peculiar difficulty. He must write a letter that will win the favor and desired response of Philemon, while yet truthfully presenting the case of guilty Onesimus without offending him. The successful execution of such a task reveals Paul as a master in the art of dealing with men.

It has often occurred to scholars to compare this letter by Paul to a letter written by Pliny the Younger, asking his friend Sabinian to forgive an offending freedman. The letter of Pliny is the twenty-first in the ninth book of his epistles and translated reads as follows:

> C. Plinius to his friend Sabinianus, Greeting.
>
> Your freedman, with whom you had told me you were vexed, came to me and, throwing himself down before me, clung to my feet, as if they had been yours. He was profuse in his tears and his entreaties; he was profuse also in his silence. In short, he convinced me of his penitence. I believe that he is, indeed, a reformed char-

16. J. B. Lightfoot, *Saint Paul's Epistles to the Colossians and to Philemon,* (1900 reprint), p. 317.
17. Martin Luther, *Works of Martin Luther,* (1932), Vol. VI, p. 473.
18. Alexander Maclaren, "The Epistles of St. Paul to the Colossians and to Philemon," *The Expositor's Bible,* (1903), p. 419.

acter, because he feels that he has done wrong. You are angry, I know; and you have reason to be angry, this also I know; but mercy wins the highest praise just when there is the most righteous cause for anger. You loved the man, and I hope you will continue to love him; meanwhile, it is enough that you should allow yourself to yield to his prayers. You may be angry again, if he deserves it; and in this you will be more readily pardoned if you yield now. Concede something to his youth, something to his tears, something to your own indulgent disposition. Do not torture him, lest you torture yourself at the same time. For it is torture to you when one of your gentle temper is angry. I am afraid lest I should appear not to ask, but to compel, if I should add my prayers to his. Yet I will add them the more fully and unreservedly, because I scolded the man myself with sharpness and severity; for I threatened him straitly that I would never ask you again. This I said to him, for it was necessary to alarm him; but I do not use the same language to you. For, perchance, I shall ask again and shall be successful again; only let my request be such as it becomes me to prefer, and you to grant. Farewell.

Pliny's appeal is a graceful and kindly letter, written by a cultured gentleman of the age. But while it is deservedly admired as a classic letter full of skill and kindness, the letter to Philemon by comparison is admittedly much superior to this polished appeal by Pliny. It is superior not only in its spirit of moving Christian love, of which Pliny was ignorant, but also in the loftiness of its thought, its pathos, and its persuasive tact and delicacy.[19]

2. *Contents.* The personal character and object of this brief letter afforded no occasion for doctrinal instruction. But the letter in itself is a practical commentary upon the precepts concerning the mutual relations of slaves and masters given in the contemporary epistles.

Notwithstanding its briefness, it contains no less than eight words which occur nowhere else in Paul's epistles, and five of these do not occur elsewhere in the New Testament.

In this short letter no fewer than eleven persons are mentioned, five in the salutation (vv. 1-2), five in the greetings at the close (vv. 23-24), and Onesimus the central figure.

Twice in the letter the Apostle makes a word-play on the name of Onesimus, which means "profitable." In verse 11 he plays upon the

19. For an instructive comparison and contrast between the two letters see F. W. Farrar, *The Life and Work of St. Paul,* (1889), pp. 627-628.

meaning of this name when he says, "who once was unprofitable [*achrēston*] to thee, but now is profitable [*euchrēston*] to thee and to me." And again in verse 20 he says, "Brother, let me gain something from you because of your union with the Lord" (*The Twentieth Century New Testament*).

3. *Value.* This brief letter, the only one of its kind from the pen of Paul that has survived the ravages of time, is valuable out of all proportion to its length. How much we would have missed if it had not been preserved! Scroggie has succinctly summarized its value in the following paragraph:

> Its Personal value consists in the light which it throws upon the character of Paul. Its Ethical value consists in its balanced sensitiveness to what is right. Its Providential value consists in its underlying suggestion that God is behind and above all events. Its Practical value consists in its application of the highest principles to the commonest affairs. Its Evangelical value consists in the encouragement it supplies to seek and to save the lowest. Its Social value consists in its presentation of the relation of Christianity to slavery and all unchristian institutions. And its Spiritual value consists in the analogy between it and the Gospel Story.[20]

4. *Social impact.* This epistle has exerted a profound impact upon the movement for the amelioration of social conditions. Dealing with a problem arising out of the institution of slavery, it has figured prominently in the controversy about slavery. It has been confidently appealed to both by those who sanctioned slavery as well as those who advocated its abolition. While it is true that the words of the Apostle here cannot be construed to advocate the abolition of slavery, yet the spirit of the epistle has definitely supported that position. The manner in which Paul treats the problem of Onesimus indicates the way in which Christianity grappled with the evils of human society. To have directly antagonized the institution of human slavery, inwrought as it was in the very warp and woof of the Roman Empire, would have precipitated an immediate conflict between Rome and Christianity, would have stigmatized Christianity as being anti-social, and would have turned all the powers of the Empire against it in an effort to crush such teachings. Instead of making a

20. W. Graham Scroggie, *Know Your Bible, A Brief Introduction to the Scriptures, Volume II, The New Testament,* (n.d.), p. 201.

frontal attack upon the institution of slavery, Christianity inculcated a spirit of love and consideration which ultimately meant the death-knell of that institution.[21]

## An Outline of Philemon

### I. THE SALUTATION (1-3)

1. The writers (1a)
2. The readers (1b-2)
   a. The addressee (1b)
   b. The associates (2)
3. The greeting (3)

### II. THE THANKSGIVING (4-7)

1. The nature of the thanksgiving (4)
2. The cause for the thanksgiving (5)
3. The contents of the prayer (6)
4. The basis for the thanksgiving (7)

### III. THE APPEAL (8-21)

1. The preparation for making the appeal (8-16)
   a. The one making the request (8-9)
      1) His attitude (8-9a)
      2) His position (9b)
   b. The one for whom the appeal is being made (10-11)
      1) His relation to Paul (10)
      2) His transformed personality (11)
   c. The action of Paul in the case (12-14)
      1) The action stated (12a)
      2) The action interpreted (12b-14)
         a) The action from Paul's viewpoint (12b-13)
         b) The action from Philemon's viewpoint (14)
   d. The suggestion of God's overruling hand in the case (15-16)
      1) The temporary departure bringing permanent fellowship (15)
      2) The spiritual gain out of the temporal loss (16)
2. The formulation of the request (17-21)

21. For Paul's approach to slavery see further D. Edmond Hiebert, *Personalities Around Paul,* (1973), pp. 193-195.

a. The statement of the request (17)
b. The promise of Paul to Philemon (18-19)
   1) The assumption of the debt of Onesimus (18)
   2) The authentication of the offer (19a)
   3) The basis for the offer (19b)
c. The appeal to Philemon (20)
d. The confidence of Paul (21)

IV. THE CONCLUSION (22-25)

1. The personal request (22)
2. The greetings from Paul's associates (23-24)
3. The benediction (25)

### A Book List on Philemon

Carson, Herbert M., "The Epistle of Paul to the Colossians and Philemon." *The Tyndale New Testament Commentaries.* Grand Rapids: Wm. B. Eerdmans Pub. Co. (1960).

Drysdale, A. H., "The Epistle of St. Paul to Philemon." *Devotional Commentaries.* London: The Religious Tract Society (1870; 1925 reprint).

Rich in devotional value, yet a work of scholarly exposition. Full, lucid, and abounding in practical applications.

Ernst, Karl J., *The Art of Pastoral Counselling. A Study of the Epistle to Philemon.* Grand Rapids: Zondervan Publishing House (1941).

Philemon viewed as a case in pastoral counseling. Interesting and stimulating analysis of the epistle.

Gaebelein, Frank E., *Philemon the Gospel of Emancipation.* Wheaton: Van Kampen Press (1939).

A brief exposition based on careful study of the text, with applications to daily life.

Hendriksen, William, "Exposition of Colossians and Philemon." *New Testament Commentary.* Grand Rapids: Baker Book House (1964).

Hiebert, D. Edmond, "Titus and Philemon." *Everyman's Bible Commentary.* Chicago: Moody Press (1968).

An exegetical treatment of both epistles in the light of the original as the basis for an interpretation of the text.

Johnson, Philip C., "The Epistles To Titus and Philemon." *Shield Bible Study* Series. Grand Rapids: Baker Book House (1966).

A concise, well-outlined interpretation intended as a study guide to these epistles.

Kelly, William, *An Exposition of the Epistle of Paul to Titus and of that to Philemon, With Translation of an Amended Text.* Denver: Wilson Foundation (1968 reprint).

A careful exposition by a voluminous Plymouth Brethren scholar of the past century.

Knox, John, and Buttrick, George A., "The Epistle to Philemon," *The Interpreter's Bible.* Vol. XI. New York: Abingdon Press (1955).

Introduction and exegesis by Knox; exposition by Buttrick. Knox propounds the novel view that the real owner of Onesimus was Archippus and that the purpose of the letter was to secure the return of Onesimus to Paul for his own service.

Lenski, R. C. H., *The Interpretation of St. Paul's Epistles to the Colossians, to the Thessalonians, to Timothy, to Titus and to Philemon.* Columbus, Ohio: Lutheran Book Concern (1937).

Lightfoot, J. B., *Saint Paul's Epistle to the Colossians and to Philemon.* London: Macmillan and Co. (1927 reprint).

Lohse, Eduard, "Colossians and Philemon, A Commentary on the Epistles to the Colossians and to Philemon." *Hermenia—A Critical and Historical Commentary on the Bible.* Translated by William R. Poehlmann and Robert J. Karris. Edited by Helmut Koester. Philadelphia: Fortress Press (1971).

Maclaren, Alexander, "The Epistles of St. Paul to the Colossians and to Philemon," *The Expositor's Bible.* Grand Rapids: Wm. B. Eerdmans Pub. Co. (1943 reprint).

Martin, Ralph P., "Colossians and Philemon." *New Century Bible Based on the Revised Standard Version.* London: Oliphants (1974).

Müller, Jac. J., "The Epistles of Paul to the Philippians and to Philemon." *The New International Commentary on the New Testament.* Grand Rapids: Wm. B. Eerdmans Pub. Co. (1955).

A concise interpretation by a conservative professor of South Africa. Seeks to maintain a balance between exact scholarship and the practical import of the letters. Technical matters are confined to the footnotes.

Moule, C. F. D., "The Epistles of Paul the Apostle to the Colossians and to Philemon." *Cambridge Greek Testament Commentary.* Cambridge: University Press (1957).

Moule, H. C. G., "The Epistle of Paul the Apostle to the Colossians and to Philemon." *Cambridge Bible for Schools and Colleges.* Cambridge: University Press (1893; 1932 reprint).

Radford, Lewis B., "The Epistle to the Colossians and the Epistle to Philemon." *Westminster Commentaries.* London: Methuen & Co. (1931).

Scroggie, W. Graham, *A Note to a Friend, Paul to Philemon.* London: The Hulbert Publishing Co. (n.d.).

An in-depth study of this brief letter, based upon a detailed outline, with warm practical lessons. Richly rewarding.

Thomas, W. H. Griffith, *Studies in Colossians and Philemon.* Edited by Winifred G. T. Gillespie, his daughter. Grand Rapids: Baker Book House (1973).

Vincent, Marvin R., "A Critical and Exegetical Commentary on the Epistles to the Philippians and to Philemon." Edinburgh: T. & T. Clark (1897; 1950 reprint).

Greek text. A scholarly, generally conservative interpretation with valuable introductions and word studies and exegetical comments.

# 14

# EPHESIANS

## An Introduction to Ephesians

Ephesians is the most impersonal of all the Pauline epistles. Because of the lofty nature of its contents it has well been called a "heavenly epistle." In it the believer is truly made to dwell "in heavenly *places* in Christ Jesus."

### THE CITY OF EPHESUS

1. *Location.* Ephesus was located on the western shores of Asia Minor, in a plain at the mouth of the River Cayster. It was some three hundred miles due east from Corinth. The Cayster, on whose southern bank Ephesus was located, is the central and shortest of three rivers in western Asia Minor which empty their waters into the Aegean Sea. In ancient times Ephesus was a seacoast town, but the heavy silting of the Cayster had gradually filled up the gulf until, in the time of Paul, the city was about three miles from the sea.[1] Its port, a landlocked basin, was connected with the sea by a broad channel. Although the river was still navigable to the city, the port was becoming increasingly difficult for large ships to reach. Constant dredging was needed.

2. *Commerce.* When Paul labored in Ephesus it was the great commercial center of western Asia Minor, ranking with Antioch and Alexandria as the three greatest trading centers in the eastern Mediterranean. Her prosperity was to a large extent due to her geographical location. At her extensive docks might be found ships from every maritime nation of that day. As the western terminus of the great

1. See W. M. Ramsay, *The Letters to the Seven Churches of Asia,* (n.d.), for a conjectural map of the changing shoreline at Ephesus, p. 212, and pp. 214-215 for a discussion of the changes.

overland route to the Euphrates, she was likewise assured of an abundance of trade. The gorgeous description of the merchandise of "Babylon" in Revelation 18:12-13 in all probability was inspired by John's personal experience with Ephesus.

3. *Status.* Ephesus prided herself on being the commercial and religious metropolis of the Roman province of Asia. Although it is often said that Ephesus was the capital of the province of Asia, it appears rather that Pergamum, the old capital of the kings, continued to be the "official capital and titular seat of Roman authority."[2] But because of its location and influence, Ephesus was recognized as the first city of the province. It was the natural gate by which the Roman governors and visitors from the West entered the province. Under the Romans Ephesus enjoyed the status of a free city. It had an assembly and council of its own and a governor (Acts 19:38). The "townclerk," keeper of the city records, was an official of great influence and responsibility (Acts 19:35).

4. *Buildings.* The chief glory of Ephesus and its top attraction was its magnificent temple, dedicated to its patron goddess. By the Greeks she was called Artemis, by the Romans, Diana.[3] This temple was reckoned as one of the seven wonders of the ancient world. Built of shining marble, it stood outside the city walls. The temple, facing the east, was erected on a platform about 425 feet by 240 feet and was reached by a flight of fourteen steps. The temple measured 343 feet by 164 feet and had more than a hundred columns about sixty feet high, thirty-six of which were beautifully carved. In the inner shrine was the image of the goddess, claimed to have fallen from Heaven (Acts 19:35). It was a mummy-like figure with many breasts, the symbol of fertility. Behind the sacred shrine was the "treasury"; it served as the bank of Asia. Nowhere could money be more safely bestowed than here. Ephesus prided herself on being the "temple-keeper" of the great Artemis (Acts 19:35). As seen in the case of Demetrius (Acts 19:24-28), the worship of Artemis was intimately related to business. However, when in A.D. 262 the temple was destroyed by the Goths, its influence had so far deteriorated that it was never rebuilt.

2. W. M. Ramsay, *The Letters to the Seven Churches of Asia* (n.d.), p. 290; see also p. 227.
3. Although in Acts Luke always uses the name Artemis, the K.J.V. and the A.S.V. uniformly use Diana as the translation. The R.S.V., N.A.S.B., and other recent versions properly use Artemis.

Another architectural wonder, figuring in the Biblical account of Ephesus, was the great theater, located on the west side of Mount Coressus. It was the largest Greek theater in Asia Minor and is reputed to have accommodated fifty thousand spectators. Northeast of the theater was the stadium where races were run and wild beast fights were staged.

5. *Magic.* The practice of magic was intimately related to the worship of Artemis. On the statue of the goddess were inscribed certain mystic formulae to which a magic efficacy was ascribed. This led to the manufacture of the famous "Ephesian letters," mystical monograms, which were used as charms. As implied in Luke's record of the Ephesian ministry (Acts 19:13-19), Ephesus was "preeminently the city of astrology, sorcery, incantations, amulets, exorcisms, and every form of magical imposture."[4]

### THE CHURCH IN EPHESUS

1. *Origin.* It is not clear when and by whom the Gospel was first brought to Ephesus. Although there were Jews from Asia present at Jerusalem during Pentecost (Acts 2:9), there is no indication that they brought the message back to Ephesus. During his second missionary journey Paul made a weekend visit to the synagogue in Ephesus and left his helpers, Aquila and Priscilla, there in anticipation of his return to that city for an extended ministry (Acts 18:18-21). Before Paul's return, Apollos came to Ephesus with his imperfect knowledge concerning Christianity and was fully instructed by Priscilla and Aquila (Acts 18:24-26). When Apollos decided to go to Achaia, the "brethren" at Ephesus gave him a letter of recommendation to the disciples (Acts 18:27). Thus it appears that there was a group of Christians in Ephesus before Paul began his ministry there. The church, however, seems to have received its definite organizational beginnings with the ministry of Paul in Ephesus (Acts 19:9).

2. *Paul's work.* Following his arrival in Ephesus during his third missionary journey, Paul, in accordance with his usual practice, began his ministry in the Jewish synagogue. When fierce opposition arose, he separated the disciples, organized the believers as a separate and distinct group, and began a two-year ministry centered in the lecture hall of Tyrannus (Acts 19:8-10). The Gospel ministry

4. F. W. Farrar, *The Life and Work of St. Paul,* (1889), p. 359.

in Ephesus made a profound impression on the city and reached out into various parts of the province (Acts 19:10). Devastating inroads on the worship of Artemis were registered (Acts 19:26), and the magical arts practiced in Ephesus suffered a great reverse (Acts 19: 18-19). Tumultuous opposition finally caused the Apostle to leave the city after nearly three years of ministry there (Acts 20:31). He did not again set foot in the city until after his release from the first Roman imprisonment (1 Tim. 1:3).

3. *History.* The church at Ephesus was composed mainly of Gentile converts, although there doubtless were numbers of Jewish Christians in its membership. Upon Paul's departure the church was left to carry on under the leadership of its own elders (Acts 20:17). Following his release from the imprisonment at Rome, Paul made another visit to Ephesus, dealt with the difficulties that had arisen in the church, and left Timothy in charge of the supervision of the work (1 Tim. 1:18-20; 1:3). The testimony of the early Church Fathers says that the apostle John in his later years took up residence at Ephesus and spent the remaining years of his life supervising the work of the Gospel in Asia.[5] In the seven letters from the risen Lord in Revelation 2 and 3, the Ephesian church was the first to be addressed (2:1-7).

The Ephesian church was a kind of mother church to the others in the province and long retained its position of leadership among them. It played a leading role in early ecclesiastical history. However, with the decay of the city of Ephesus the church also declined. Ultimately the "candlestick" was removed out of its place (Rev. 2:5), and spiritual darkness settled over the place of former enlightenment.

### THE AUTHENTICITY OF EPHESIANS

1. *Traditional view.* The unanimous position of the ancient Church was to receive this epistle as from the hand of the apostle Paul. Even Marcion, though he differed as to the destination of the epistle, admitted its Pauline origin. The external evidence for the epistle is strong, and the differences do not prove authorship by another writer. As Barker observes, "The external attestation for the knowledge and use of the book as a genuine Pauline writing in the ancient Church

5. For a discussion of John's connection with Ephesus see A. Plummer, "The Epistles of S. John," *Cambridge Bible for Schools,* (1938 reprint), pp. 9-27.

is wholly positive."[6] The contents of the epistle likewise are of such a nature as to leave the ordinary, unbiased reader with the firm conviction that Paul wrote it.

2. *Critical attacks.* As in the case of Colossians, the companion epistle, it remained for the radical critics of the modern era to raise questions concerning the authenticity of Ephesians. And here again, disregarding the external evidence, the attacks have been launched solely on internal grounds. The attacks resemble those used against Colossians.

The style of Ephesians has been used as an argument against its authenticity. Admittedly the style is slower and more cumbersome than in the epistles of the second group. The epistle does reveal "a tendency to accumulation of epithets, a fondness for synonyms, and a drawing out of subordinate clauses, which contrast with the general vivacity and forcible brevity of Paul's earlier manner."[7] These features occur mainly in those sections characterized by an atmosphere of praise and prayer. Colossians reveals similar stylistic features. They also occur to some degree in the unquestioned letters. Cadbury aptly asks,

> Which is more likely—that an imitator of Paul in the first century composed a writing ninety or ninety-five per cent in accordance with Paul's style or that Paul himself wrote a letter diverging five or ten per cent from his usual style?[8]

An evaluation of these differences in relation to authorship is a subjective matter. The differences do not *prove* differences in authorship. In view of the external evidence, they may be accounted for by the differences in the subject matter, the circumstances, and the author's temperament.

The vocabulary of the epistle has been objected to. It contains forty-two words found nowhere else in the New Testament, and over eighty which occur in none of the other Pauline epistles. Hence, say the critics, Paul cannot have written it. Yet practically the same phenomena occur in the accepted Pauline epistles. Paul Ewald answers with the remark,

6. G. W. Barker, "Ephesians, Letter of Paul to the," *The Zondervan Pictorial Encyclopedia of the Bible,* (1975), Vol. II, p. 317a.
7. R. D. Shaw, *The Pauline Epistles,* (4th Ed., 1924 reprint), p. 346.
8. H. J. Cadbury, "The Dilemma of Ephesians," *New Testament Studies,* Jan. 1959, Vol. V, No. 2, p. 101.

> One may roll the lexicon or rather the concordance around as one will, there appear almost with comical precision almost always the identical percentages in the disputed as in the acknowledged letters.[9]

Barker's own investigation leads him to conclude, "Every study of non-Pauline vocabulary supports the Pauline authorship of Ephesians."[10]

The attack on the authenticity of Ephesians from the point of its language is carried still further when it is asserted that the writer of this epistle uses synonyms instead of Paul's usual words. For example, it is pointed out that this writer uses *diabolos* (Devil) while Paul, it is claimed, uses only *Satanas* (Satan). But *diabolos* is used in all three Pastoral Epistles. But why should Paul not be permitted to use a synonymous word without the threat of losing his identity? Again, it is said that several words like *mystery, stewardship,* and *possession,* are used in a new sense which is not Pauline. This is doubtful. But must a man always use a word with the same meaning in every context?

It is asserted that the theology of the epistle is different from the unquestioned Pauline epistles and shows a later development. Thus, the view of the Church as one in this epistle is claimed to reveal a later period. The view of the Church in this epistle is indeed the highest found in the Pauline writings, but this view has its foundations in earlier epistles (cf. I Cor. 12:28; 15:9; Gal. 1:13). Such a view of the Church is but to be expected when viewed in its relation to the Cosmic Christ. The view is that of a spiritual unity rather than an organizational unity and need not reflect a time after the death of Paul. The charge, formerly made, that the epistle reflects post-Pauline traces of Gnosticism is now known to be groundless.

It is argued that the reference to "the holy apostles and prophets" (3:5) shows that the writer's consciousness distinguished himself from the apostles. Paul would not thus speak of himself as holy. But "holy" is a standard term applied to all believers (1:1), and "holy prophets" is a common designation for the men through whom God communicated His revelations. It is not his personal holiness but God's hallowing that is in view and extends to all God's people. The

9. Quoted from R. C. H. Lenski, *The Interpretation of St. Paul's Epistles to the Galatians, to the Ephesians, and to the Philippians,* (1937), p. 341.
10. G. W. Barker, "Ephesians, Letter of Paul to the," *The Zondervan Pictorial Encyclopedia of the Bible,* (1975), Vol. II, pp. 317-318.

author's description of himself as "less than the least of all saints" (3:8) is fully in accord with Paul's attitude toward himself.

Influenced by the objections raised against Pauline authorship, some critics have espoused the compromise view that Ephesians is the work of some apt pupil of Paul's who had thoroughly imbibed the spirit of Paul and wrote it in his name. Tychicus, Timothy, and Luke have been given this honor. But if the epistle was not written by Paul, the one who wrote it must have been the equal of Paul to produce such a writing. But where among the companions of Paul is such an imitator or counterfeiter to be found? From the very nature of the epistle Farrar concludes that such an imitation would be "a psychological impossibility."[11]

Goodspeed has theorized that Onesimus wrote Ephesians near the end of the first century as a covering letter for the Pauline epistles when he published them as a group, after they had been lying largely unused for a generation since their original composition.[12] This novel theory must assume that Ephesians stood at the head of the Pauline corpus, but there is no evidence that it ever stood in this position. Further, Goodspeed's assumption, that the Christian Church had forgotten all about Paul's letters since his death and that Onesimus in publishing them as a group rescued them from oblivion, is unfounded speculation.

3. *Conclusion.* While admittedly the characteristics of this epistle are such as to lend some color to the arguments of the critics, the case for the spuriousness of Ephesians has not been made out. We hold that there are no unsurmountable obstacles to the traditional view of the Pauline authorship of this epistle. We fully agree with Davies when he says,

> Those who cannot read the Epistle to the Ephesians without being awed by the peculiar loftiness, by the grandeur of conception, by the profound insight, by the eucharistic inspiration, which they recognize in it, will require strong evidence to persuade them that it was written by some other man who wishes it to pass as St. Paul's. . . . In the lifetime of St. Paul the pious fraud would not have been attempted. Within a few years after his death, the difficulty of deceiving his friends and the Church in such a matter must have been

11. F. W. Farrar, *The Life and Work of St. Paul,* (1889), pp. 633-634.
12. Edgar J. Goodspeed, *An Introduction to the New Testament,* (1937), ch. XIV; *The Meaning of Ephesians,* (1933); *The Key to Ephesians,* (1956).

> very great. At a later time, the estimation in which St. Paul's writings were held would have ensured the careful scrutiny of any previously unknown work put forward in his name. And there are no signs that the genuineness of the Epistle to the Ephesians was ever doubted in the Church.[13]

A few critics have pronounced this epistle a verbose and insipid production or a tedious and unskilled compilation. Yet such a verdict only reveals the subtle effect that unbelief has upon the literary insights of the critics when the theme is spiritual.

### THE DESTINATION OF EPHESIANS

1. *Traditional designation.* This epistle has always borne the title "To the Ephesians" as far back as we have any knowledge. While admittedly the titles of the New Testament writings cannot be regarded as parts of the original documents, they yet carry the traditional views of the Church. The only objection of any kind to this title for the epistle that has come down to us is that of Marcion (A.D. 140); in his canon he entitled it "To the Laodiceans." Yet Marcion's action shows the great antiquity of the received title, since Tertullian charged him with *changing* the title. The tradition for the received title thus reaches back to about seventy years or so of the actual time of its composition. Added to this is the fact that all known manuscripts, except five, have the words *en Ephesō* in 1:1. Further, all the ancient versions produce this phrase in their translations.

2. *Contrary phenomena.* But the problem is not as simple as would at first appear. Because of doubts as to the textual genuineness of *en Ephesō* in Ephesians 1:1, as well as apparent support from internal evidence, serious questioning has arisen as to the correctness of the traditional designation. In an effort to harmonize the existing phenomena, an encyclical destination is commonly asserted for the epistle. The problem of its destination is admittedly beset with real difficulties.

The confusion begins in connection with the question concerning the true reading of the *text* in verse one. The question is whether or not the reading *en Ephesō* can be accepted as the original text. If agreement could be reached here the problem would be practically settled. These two words are not found in the originals of the two

13. J. Llewelyn Davies, *The Epistles of St. Paul to the Ephesians, the Colossians, and Philemon,* (1884), pp. 9-10.

great Uncials, Aleph and B, both dating from the fourth century, and Codex 1739 from the tenth century; a corrector, who followed an old text, deleted them from Codex 424, dating from the eleventh century. Manuscript evidence for the omission was pushed back more than a century with the discovery of the Chester Beatty Papyrus, $P^{46}$, dated at around A.D. 200.

The testimony of the *Fathers* is likewise interesting. Tertullian writing against Marcion about the year A.D. 208 accused Marcion of changing the *title* in contradiction to the true testimony of the Church; but since he does not accuse Marcion of falsifying the text, but with supplying a new title, it would appear that he cannot have known the reading *en Ephesō* in his text, because a simple appeal to the words of the text would have refuted Marcion.[14] Origen (A.D. 185-254) must not have had the words in his text since he seeks to interpret the words "who are" (*tois ousin*) in an absolute or transcendental sense as meaning "the saints who are." Basil (A.D. 330-379) likewise must not have had the reading in his text since he agrees with Origen's metaphysical interpretation and says that it was confirmed by the oldest manuscripts that he had examined.

Did Paul then write the opening verse of the epistle without the words *en Ephesō,* or were they later dropped out? Both views have their ardent advocates. The former view is supported by those who hold that the epistle had a catholic or encyclical destination.

It is scarcely fair to say that the Greek of Ephesains 1:1 is absolutely incapable of a rational explanation without the words *en Ephesō,* yet it cannot be denied that there is definite question as to its interpretation without them. It must be admitted that in parallel passages the expression is always used with a place designation (Rom 1:7; 1 Cor. 1:2; 2 Cor. 1:1; Phil. 1:1). To omit all place designation really makes it a *catholic* epistle addressed to Gentile Christians in general; but such a view is inconsistent with its contents, since 1:15ff and 6:22 show that Paul had a definite group in mind when he wrote the epistle.

How are the phenomena in connection with this opening verse to be accounted for? Zahn, in supporting the omission of the words *en*

14. Alford holds that Tertullian may have used the word *titulum* in a wide sense to include the title and the corresponding portion in the text. Henry Alford, *The Greek Testament,* (1958), Vol. III, p. 17 Proleg. So also G. Stoeckhardt, *Commentary on St. Paul's Letter to the Ephesians,* (1952), pp. 14-17.

*Ephesō,* suggests that the words were added to the original text because of the title which had been assigned to this epistle when Paul's letters were first collected and thinks that the inappropriate title must be attributed to the ecclesiastical prominence of the Ephesian church as the leading church in the province.[15] On the other hand, Meyer, a convinced proponent of the Ephesian destination, holds that the words *en Ephesō* are "decidedly genuine" and believes that their omission must be explained by the operation of "ancient historical criticism" which inferred from the epistle that the readers were unknown to the Apostle, hence could not be the Ephesians.[16] And so the doctors disagree on the problem.

While some of the Fathers apparently did not have the words *en Ephesō* in their text, they all accepted the traditional title of the epistle. In the light of the solid tradition for the Ephesian destination, may not the absence of the words be best accounted for by the assumption that they were early omitted? May not this have been done in order to adapt the epistle for use in neighboring churches? We have an example in Codex G (ninth century) which omits "in Rome" (Rom. 1:7, 15). Two cursives (1739 and 1908) of the tenth and eleventh centuries mark the deletion in the margin at verse 7 but not at verse 15. Ephesians would readily lend itself to such generalization.

Those who oppose the local destination of this epistle point to the impersonal tone and contents of this epistle as offering confirmation of their view. The conspicuous absence of the personal element in the epistle cannot escape the attentive reader. Findlay has summarized this feature of the epistle as follows:

> There is *an official distance and formality* in the writer's attitude, such as we find in no other epistle, and very different from Paul's manner toward his friends and disciples. Not once does he address his readers as "brethren" or "beloved"; "my brethren" in Eph. vi. 10 is an insertion of the copyists. There is not a single word of familiarity or endearment in the whole letter. The benediction at the end (ch. vi. 23, 24) is given in the third person, not in the second as everywhere else: "Peace to *the brethren!* . . . Grace be with *all that love our Lord Jesus Christ*"; not "Grace be *with you.*" Nowhere do

15. Theodor Zahn, *Introduction to the New Testament,* (1909), Vol. I, pp. 486-487.
16. Heinrich August Wilhelm Meyer, *Critical and Exegetical Hand-Book to the Epistle to the Ephesians,* (1892), pp. 291-293.

> we see less of *this* or *that* church, and more of *the* Church; nowhere less of the man, and more of the apostle in St. Paul.[17]

It is asserted that the Apostle could not have written thus if this epistle had been addressed to the Ephesians with whom he was so intimately acquainted (Acts 20:17-38). It is held to be inconceivable that in writing to the Ephesians no personal greetings should have been included. But a consideration of the actual facts in the Pauline epistles shows that this argument is not conclusive. Personal greetings are found in greatest abundance in Romans, written to a church which Paul had not yet visited. Colossians contains personal greetings although he was personally unknown to that church. On the other hand, in writing to those churches where he knew the whole group, no personal greetings are added, as to the Corinthians, Galatians, Philippians, and Thessalonians. A review of the actual phenomena as to the greetings leads Alford to conclude:

> The general salutations found in several of these cases, the total omission of all salutation in others, seem to follow no rule but the fervour of his own mind, and the free play of his feeling as he writes. The more general and solemn the subject, the less he seems to give to these individual notices: the better he knows those to whom he is writing, as a whole, the less he seems disposed to select particular persons for his affectionate remembrance.[18]

In view of the lofty nature of this epistle, these personal notices might well be left to be conveyed by Tychicus, the bearer of the letter (6:21). If Paul wrote Ephesians as a circular letter, why did he not so indicate in the salutation, as he did in Galatians?

Of more weight for the encyclical view is the language of Ephesians 1:15-16. Viewed in comparison with Colossians 1:4 and taken in their natural sense, Paul's words seem to signify that he had in mind readers of whose conversion he only knew by report. The language in Colossians and Ephesians is almost identical. Paul had never been in Colossae (Col 2:1) and so had only heard about their faith. Would not that imply that the readers of this epistle were personally unknown to him? But in both epistles the words point rather to the report of their continued abounding in Christian graces, and not to

17. George G. Findlay, *The Epistles of Paul the Apostle,* (4th Ed., n.d.), pp. 177-178. Italics in original.
18. Henry Alford, *The Greek Testament,* (1958), Vol. III, p. 13 Proleg.

their initial conversion. Since Paul had been absent from the province of Asia then for about five years, he would rejoice to *hear* that report. Why should not Paul be permitted to say that he had *heard* of their faith and love after that length of time? These words then do not rigidly exclude the Ephesians as the readers; yet other readers, personally unknown to the Apostle, may have been in the writer's mind as he wrote.

3. *Conclusion.* Three views as to the destination of Ephesians exist: (1) That the epistle was addressed to Gentile Christians as such. (2) That it was a circular letter sent to the churches of Asia, of which Ephesus was chief.[19] (3) That it was written for and sent directly to Ephesus.[20] The choice must lie between the last two. The view that it is a catholc epistle addressed to Gentile Christians as such is opposed to all traditions as to its destination as well as the contents of the epistle itself.

The encyclical theory, popularized by Archbishop Ussher (1581-1656), holds that our epistle was really a circular letter sent to the various churches of Proconsular Asia of which Ephesus was the chief. This view seeks to harmonize the contents of the epistle with its destination. One form of this theory holds that in the original Paul left a blank space after the words "that are" in 1:1 which was to be filled in with the name of the church to which it was delivered. According to this theory Marcion was acquainted with a copy sent to Laodicea, the traditional text goes back to a copy sent to Ephesus, and Aleph, B, and Chester Beatty Papyrus to a copy in which the blank for the address had never been filled in at all. This theory seems rather unduly influenced by modern "carbon copy" methods. In antiquity when each copy had to be produced by hand such a multiplicity of copies would not have been thought of. The reference in Colossians 4:16 suggests rather the direct circulation of the original apostolic letter. Others think that the original contained no place designation but that this was to be supplied by Tychicus as he read the letter in the various churches.

19. As advocates of this view may be named Usher, Eichhorn, Hug, Horne, Schott, Neander, Luenemann, Olshausen, Bloomfield, Macknight, Steir, Farrar, Conybeare and Howson, David Smith, Shaw, Schaff, Williams, Erdman, and others.
20. As advocates of this view may be named Calvin, Bucer, Wolf, Estius, Chandler, Whitby, Lardner, Davidson, Stuart, Alexander, Alford, Meyer, Newland, Eadie, Wordsworth, Braune, Lenski, Stoeckhardt, and others.

While this circular theory has become very popular and seems to account for the facts and clear up the difficulties, some of the arguments used to support it are without much weight. The traditional view that it was sent to Ephesus offers no serious difficulties. Perhaps the most probable solution to the problem is the position that the epistle was written to the Ephesians and addressed to them, but that the Apostle intentionally cast it into a form which would make it suitable to the Christians in the neighboring churches and intended that it should be communicated to them.

### THE OCCASION FOR EPHESIANS

Unlike the other Pauline epistles, the contents of Ephesians offer no indication as to the occasion for its composition. It does not appear to have been written to meet any particular crisis. In striking contrast to Colossians, it makes no mention of any false teachers nor hints at any attack on his apostolic authority. Its admonitions arise out of general experience and are in accordance with the theme of the epistle.

Judging from its close relation to Colossians, it appears that the conflict which caused the writing of Colossians likewise called forth this epistle. The Colossian conflict revealed to Paul the need for a fuller statement of God's program for the universe as it centers in Christ in His relationship to the Church. The trip of Tychicus to Asia offered the immediate occasion for the fulfillment of such a need.

### THE PLACE AND DATE OF EPHESIANS

1. *Place.* The epistle clearly states that Paul was a prisoner when it was written (3:1; 4:1; 6:20). That it was composed about the same time as Colossians is seen from the fact that Tychicus is the common bearer of both (Col. 4:7-8; Eph. 6:21-22) as well as from the contents of the two epistles. We conclude that Ephesians was written during Paul's first imprisonment at Rome as recorded in Acts 28:30-31. (See introduction to the Prison Epistles.)

2. *Date.* Its close affinity to Colossians and Philemon suggests a date contemporaneous with those two epistles. We therefore date Ephesians as written during the summer of A.D. 62.

THE PURPOSE OF EPHESIANS

The purpose of the Apostle in writing Ephesians is nowhere indicated in the epistle but must be gathered from its occasion and contents. That its purpose was not polemical is evident from the fact that it contains no definitely controversial elements. This epistle seems rather to be the aftereffect of the conflict that had occupied the Apostle's mind in Colossians. It would seem that while the theme of Colossians was still fresh on his mind, Paul decided to write this epistle in which he would set forth the positive significance of the truths which possessed him. Eadie says,

> In Colossians, theosophic error is pointedly and firmly refuted; but in Ephesians, principles are laid down which might prove a barrier to its introduction. . . . The epistle before us may therefore be regarded as prophylactic more than corrective in its nature.[21]

The Christians gripped with the truths of this epistle would not be swayed by the philosophical speculations troubling the Colossian church. In it the Apostle sets forth God's purpose of summing up "all things in Christ, the things in the heavens, and the things upon the earth" (Eph. 1:10), and gives emphasis to the place that the Church as the Body of Christ holds in this universal program (3:10-11). Farrar feels that as Paul began to dictate this epistle

> The one overwhelming thought in the mind of the Apostle was the ideal splendour and perfectness of the Church of Christ, and the consequent duty of holiness which was incumbent on all its members. The thought of Humanity regenerated in Christ by an eternal process, and the consequent duty of all to live in accordance with this divine enlightenment—these are the double wings which keep him in one line throughout the rapturous flight. Hence the Epistle naturally falls into two great divisions, doctrinal and practical; . . . the glorious unity of the Church in Christ its living head, and the moral exhortations which sprang with irresistible force of appeal from this divine mystery.[22]

THE CHARACTERISTICS OF EPHESIANS

1. *Language and style.* The richness of the thought of Ephesians

21. John Eadie, *A Commentary on the Greek Text of the Epistle of Paul to the Ephesians,* (3rd Ed., 1883), pp. l-li.
22. F. W. Farrar, *The Life and Work of St. Paul,* (1889), p. 635.

is reflected in the richness of its vocabulary. It contains forty-two words that occur nowhere else in the New Testament and thirty-nine that occur nowhere else in the Pauline epistles. It also abounds in new word combinations. "The language," says Williams, "is rich, in harmony with the sublime thoughts which clamor for expression by the apostle's pen."[23] Alford states that the elevation and sublimity of the thoughts and language are so marked that in this respect the epistle takes "a place of its own among the writings of Paul."[24] Farrar thus graphically describes the style of the epistle:

> The style of St. Paul may be compared to a great tide ever advancing irresistibly towards the destined shore, but broken and rippled over every wave of its broad expanse, and liable at any moment to mighty refluences as it foams and swells about opposing sandbank or rocky cape. With even more exactness we might compare it to a river whose pure waters, at every interspace of calm, reflect as in a mirror the hues of heaven, but which is liable to the rushing influx of mountain torrents, and whose reflected images are only dimly discernible in ten thousand fragments of quivering colour, when its surface is swept by ruffling winds.[25]

2. *Contents.* It is generally conceded that Ephesians is the deepest book in the New Testament. Its vision of the purpose of God stretches from eternity to eternity. And it is also "by far the most difficult of all the writings of Paul."[26] The difficulties are not so much on the surface, where at first all seems quite smooth. The difficulties are encountered in seeking to penetrate into the inner depths of the thought of the Apostle.

The epistle is characterized by the absence of personal and historical references. Only two personal facts appear in all the epistle, the fact of the Apostle's imprisonment (3:1; 4:1; 6:20) and the sending of Tychicus with oral communications for the readers (6:21-22). It contains no personal greetings. Even the benediction is in the third person (6:23-24); this is unlike any other New Testament epistle. On the other hand this epistle is distinguished by its universalism. No

23. Charles B. Williams, *An Introduction to New Testament Literature,* (1929), p. 191.
24. Henry Alford, *The Greek Testament,* (1958), Vol. III, p. 24 Proleg.
25. F. W. Farrar, *The Life and Work of St. Paul,* (1889), p. 633.
26. Henry Alford, *The Greek Testament,* (1958), Vol. III, p. 24 Proleg.

local church is mentioned, but its theme is rather the Church universal, the Church as the Body of Christ. In this connection the word *body* occurs eight times. From this vital union with Christ flow the duties incumbent upon the believer. This living union between Christ and the believer is made prominent by the repeated use of the little word *in* which occurs no less than one hundred and twenty times (Greek) in the epistle. "It is the biggest word in the book."[27] Of note is the frequent use of such expressions as *in him, in whom,* and *in the beloved.* Every vital truth in the epistle is thus directly related to Christ.

Concerning the contents of this epistle, Schaff says,

> It certainly is the most spiritual and devout, composed in an exalted and transcendent state of mind, where theology rises into worship, and meditation into oration. It is the Epistle of the Heavenlies, a solemn liturgy, an ode to Christ and his spotless bride, the Song of Songs in the New Testament. The aged apostle soared high above all earthly things to the invisible and eternal realities in heaven. From his gloomy confinement he ascended for a season to the mount of transfiguration. The prisoner of Christ, chained to a heathen soldier, was transformed into a conqueror, clad in the panoply of God, and singing a paean of victory.[28]

While the entire contents of the epistle are noteworthy, certain passages are especially striking. One of the most amazing passages is the "Hymn of Grace" in 1:3-14, a three-stanza hymn celebrating the salvation wrought by our triune God. Schaff says that this one profound sentence rises "like a thick cloud of incense higher and higher to the very throne of God."[29] A number of other passages might be cited, such as the two prayers of the Apostle (1:15-23; 3:14-21), or the passage on the mystery (3:2-12); but the passage that has most profoundly impressed itself upon the thinking of the common Christian is the description of the Christian's armor in chapter 6 (11-17).

3. *Relation to Colossians.* There are striking likenesses as well as striking differences between Ephesians and Colossians. The likenesses are readily apparent. The presentation of the writer's circum-

27. Norman B. Harrison, *His Very Own, Paul's Epistle to the Ephesians,* (1930), p. 14.
28. Philip Schaff, *History of the Christian Church,* (1910), Vol. I, p. 780.
29. *Ibid.*

stances (Eph. 3:1; 4:1; Col. 4:3) and the commission to Tychicus are essentially the same (Eph. 6:21-22; Col. 4:7-8). Both contain a number of passages that are identical or nearly identical in language. "It is calculated, indeed, that in some seventy-eight out of 155 verses we have much the same phraseology."[30] Again, the relationship between Christ and His Church is the dominant theme in both, and the ethical teachings in both epistles are very much alike.

But the differences are as notable as the similarities. The tone of the two stands in marked contrast. In Colossians there are the ringing sounds of spiritual conflict with present antagonists; in Ephesians there is the tranquil and meditative peace of deep reflection. In Colossians everything is definite and local; in Ephesians the presentation is impersonal and lofty in tone. While both deal with the theme of Christ and His Church, each uses a different approach. In Ephesians the major emphasis is on the Church as the Body of Christ, who is the Head, while in Colossians the emphasis is on the person of Christ as the Head of the Church, which is His Body. "Ephesians shows us our position in Christ as His Body. Colossians bids us realize our completeness in Christ as our Head."[31] Findlay summarizes the contrasted natures of Colossians and Ephesians as follows:

> The first is like the mountain stream cleaving its way with swift passage, by deep ravines and sudden, broken turnings, through some barrier thrown across its path; the second is the far-spreading lake in which its chafed waters find rest, mirroring in their clear depths the eternal heavens above.[32]

4. *Relevance.* The ecumenical concerns of the twentieth-century churches have underlined the abiding relevance of the message of Ephesians. Its glorious picture of the true nature of the Church is God's message for a day marked by deep concern about the disunity of Christendom. Its message of the spiritual oneness of the Church as the Body of Christ is vital for the thought and movements within the contemporary Christian community.

30. S. D. F. Salmond, "The Epistle of Paul to the Ephesians," *Expositor's Greek Testament,* (n.d.), Vol. III, p. 215. On pp. 215-216 Salmond lists a large number of these parallel passages.
31. Norman B. Harrison, *His Very Own, Paul's Epistle to the Ephesians,* (1930), p. 13.
32. George G. Findlay, *The Epistles of Paul the Apostle,* (4th Ed., n.d.), p. 181.

## An Outline of Ephesians

THE SALUTATION (1:1-2)

1. The writer (1a)
2. The readers (1b)
3. The greeting (2)

I. DOCTRINAL: THE STANDING OF BELIEVERS IN THE HEAVENLIES (1:3–3:21)

1. The thanksgiving for our redemption (1:3-14)
   a. The statement of the theme (3)
   b. The elaboration of the theme (4-14)
      1) The Father's part in our redemption (4-6)
         a) His choice of us (4)
         b) His foreordination of us (5-6a)
         c) His bestowal of His grace on us (6b)
      2) The Son's part in our redemption (7-12)
         a) The redemption in His blood (7)
         b) The gracious revelation of His administration (8-10)
            (i) The basis in the abounding grace (8)
            (ii) The revelation of His will (9a)
            (iii) The motivation in His good pleasure (9b)
            (iv) The purpose to sum up all things in Christ (10)
         c) The divine heritage in the saints (11-12)
            (i) The saints as a heritage in Christ (11a)
            (ii) The basis in the executed purpose (11b)
            (iii) The statement of the divine intention (12)
      3) The Spirit's part in our redemption (13-14)
         a) The sealing of the believers with the Spirit (13)
         b) The significance of the sealing with the Spirit (14a)
         c) The purpose of God (14b)
2. The prayer for their spiritual illumination (1:15-23)
   a. The basis for the prayer (15)
   b. The nature of his prayers (16)
   c. The God addressed in the prayer (17a)
   d. The gift requested in his prayer (17b-18a)
      1) The nature of the gift (17b)
      2) The result of the gift (18a)

e. The aim of the prayer (18b-23)
  1) That they may realize the hope of His calling (18b)
  2) That they may realize the riches of His inheritance (18c)
  3) That they may know His surpassing power (19-23)
    a) The nature of His power (19)
    b) The manifestation of His power in Christ (20-23)
      (i) In His resurrection and exaltation (20)
      (ii) In His present position of authority (21-23)
        (aa) His supremacy over all orders of existence (21)
        (bb) His enthronement over all things (22a)
        (cc) His headship over the Church (22b-23)

3. The power of God manifested in our salvation (2:1-10)
  a. The condition of the lost (1-3)
    1) The description of the condition (1)
    2) The manifestations of the condition (2-3a)
    3) The character of the lost (3b)
  b. The contrasted position in Christ (4-10)
    1) The source of the position in God's love (4)
    2) The present results of our position in Christ (5-6)
      a) The result as to our condition (5)
      b) The result as to our position (6)
    3) The future purpose of the position (7)
    4) The cause of our salvation (8-9)
    5) The outcome of our position in Christ (10)

4. The union of Jew and Gentile in one Body in Christ (2:11-22)
  a. The Gentiles before the Gospel came to them (11-12)
    1) The position of the Gentiles (11)
    2) The condition of the Gentiles (12)
  b. The union of Gentile and Jew in Christ (13-18)
    1) The Gentiles were "made nigh" in Christ (13)
    2) The two were made "one new man" in Christ (14-17)
      a) The character of Christ as our peace (14a)
      b) The work of Christ in making peace (14b-16)
        (i) The things He did (14b-15a)
        (ii) The purposes He had (15b-16a)
        (iii) The effect He achieved (16b)
      c) The proclamation of peace by Christ (17)

3) The proof of the union in the common access to God (18)
c. The results for the Gentiles of this union (19-22)
1) They are citizens (19a)
2) They are members of God's household (19b)
3) They are built into God's temple (20-22)
a) The foundation of the building (20)
b) The rearing of the structure (21)
c) The building as a habitation for the Spirit (22)

5. The Apostle as a messenger of this mystery (3:1-13)
a. His relation to this mystery (1-5)
1) His position as prisoner on behalf of the Gentiles (1)
2) His stewardship of God's grace toward the Gentiles (2)
3) His knowledge of this mystery (3-5)
a) The reception of it by revelation (3a)
b) The previous reference to it (3b-4)
c) The description of the revelation of it (5)
b. His statement of this mystery (6)
c. His ministry in connection with this mystery (7-12)
1) The source of this ministry (7)
2) The attitude of the one given this ministry (8a)
3) The contents of the ministry (8b-9)
4) The purpose of the ministry (10-11)
5) The blessings realized in present experience (12)
d. His request concerning their attitude to his sufferings (13)

6. The prayer for their experiential realization of these blessings (3:14-19)
a. The introduction of the prayer (14-15)
b. The statement of the request (16-17a)
1) The measure for the answer (16a)
2) The elements of the request (16b-17a)
c. The results of the answered requests (17b-19)
1) The persons in whom the results are attained (17b)
2) The enumeration of the results attained (18-19)

7. The concluding doxology (3:20-21)
a. The ability of the one addressed (20)
b. The ascription of praise (21)

## II. PRACTICAL: THE LIFE OF BELIEVERS HERE ON EARTH (4:1–6:20)

1. The walk of believers as God's saints (4:1–5:21)
   a. The exhortation to walk worthily, in inward realization of Christian unity (4:1-16)
      1) The appeal for a walk worthy of their calling (1)
      2) The duty of keeping the unity of the Spirit (2-3)
      3) The description of this unity (4-6)
      4) The achievement of spiritual unity (7-16)
         a) The gifts of Christ to His Church (7-11)
            (i) The diversity of the gifts to the members (7)
            (ii) The gifts as the outcome of Christ's victory (8-10)
               (aa) The quotation of Scripture (8)
               (bb) The inferences from the Scripture (9-10)
            (iii) The enumeration of the gifts to the Church (11)
         b) The achievement of unity as the purpose of the gifts (12-13)
            (i) The purpose in reference to the individual saint (12)
            (ii) The purpose in reference to the whole Church (13)
         c) The results of the unity achieved (14-16)
            (i) Negative—The results avoided (14)
            (ii) Positive—The results achieved (15-16)
               (aa) The result for the individual (15)
               (bb) The result for the whole Body (16)
   b. The exhortation to walk differently, in outward manifestation of our changed position (4:17-32)
      1) The contrast between the old and the new life (17-24)
         a) The old life of the unregenerate man (17-19)
            (i) The prohibition against continuing the old life (17ab)
            (ii) The description of the old life (17c-19)
               (aa) The condition in the old life (17c-18a)
               (bb) The cause for the condition (18b)
               (cc) The outcome of the condition (19)

b) The new life in Christ (20-24)
(i) The nature of the experience with Christ (20-21)
(ii) The result of the experience with Christ (22-24)
(aa) The putting off of the old man (22)
(bb) The renewal of the new man (23-24)

2) The duties of a changed relation to the neighbor (25-32)
a) The areas for the manifestation of the change (25-30)
(i) The change as to the truth being spoken (25)
(ii) The change as to sinful anger (26-27)
(iii) The change as to the means of acquisition (28)
(iv) The change in the character of their speech (29-30)
(aa) The commands as to the change in language (29)
(bb) The prohibition against grieving the Spirit (30)

b) The summary of the changed relation to the neighbor (31-32)
(i) The prohibition against manifestations of evil (31)
(ii) The exhortation to a kindly attitude (32)

c. The exhortation to walk lovingly, in upward imitation of our Father (5:1-17)
1) The walk as children of love (1-7)
a) The call to imitate God as beloved children (1)
b) The call to a Christ-like walk in love (2)
c) The exclusion of sensual practices from such a walk (3-7)
(i) The enumeration of these sins (3-4)
(aa) The sensual sins of deed (3)
(bb) The sensual sins of speech (4)
(ii) The consequences of these sins (5-6)
(aa) The exclusion from the Kingdom of God (5)
(bb) The coming of the wrath of God (6)
iii) The prohibition against partaking with such sinners (7)

2) The walk as children of light (8-14)
  a) The basis for the walk (8a)
  b) The command to walk as children of light (8b)
  c) The fruit of the walk in light (9)
  d) The attitude in a walk as children of light (10-12)
    (i) The approval of what is pleasing to God (10)
    (ii) The reaction against the works of darkness (11-12)
      (aa) The statement of the attitude (11)
      (bb) The justification for the attitude (12)
  e) The effect of the walk in light (3-14)
    (i) The light manifests the character of sin (13)
    (ii) The light is a call to spiritual life (14)
3) The walk as children of wisdom (15-17)
  a) The command to walk carefully (15)
  b) The activity of the walk in wisdom (16-17)

d. The secret and summary of the Christian life (5:18-21)
  1) The prohibition against drunkenness with wine (18a)
  2) The command to live the Spirit-filled life (18b-21)
    a) The command to be filled with the Spirit (18b)
    b) The results of being filled with the Spirit (19-21)
      (i) A life of joy and singing (19)
      (ii) A life of thanksgiving (20)
      (iii) A life of submission (21)

2. The duties of believers as God's family (5:22–6:9)
  a. The duties of wives and husbands (5:22-33)
    1) The subjection of the wives to their own husbands (22-24)
      a) The duty of her subjection to her husband (22a)
      b) The manner of her subjection (22b)
      c) The reason for her subjection (23)
      d) The description of her subjection (24)
    2) The love of the husbands for their wives (25-30)
      a) The duty of loving their wives (25a)
      b) The manner of their love (25b-27)
        (i) The comparison to Christ's love for the Church (25b)
        (ii) The description of Christ's love for the Church (25c-27)

(aa) In love He gave Himself up for it (25c)
(bb) In love He sanctified and cleansed it (26)
(cc) In love He will present it perfect to Himself (27)
c) The reasons for loving one's wife (28-30)
(i) Because she is his body (28)
(ii) Because he must regard his body as Christ regards the Church (29-30)
3) The implications from Christian marriage (31-33)
a) Marriage is an intimate union of two lives (31)
b) Marriage pictures the relation between Christ and the Church (32)
c) Marriage carries the duty of mutual love and reverence (33)
b. The duties of children and parents (6:1-4)
1) The obedience of the children to their parents (1-3)
a) The duty of obedience to their parents (1)
b) The confirmation from the Scripture (2-3)
2) The duties of parents to their children (4)
c. The duties of servants and masters (6:5-9)
1) The duty of servants to obey their masters (5-8)
a) The designation of the masters they serve (5a)
b) The attitude of the servants (5b)
c) The manner of their service (6-7)
d) The motive for such service (8)
2) The duty of the masters toward their servants (9)
3. The warfare of believers as God's soldiers (6:10-20)
a. The call to arms (10-11)
1) The call to be strong (10)
2) The call to be armored (11)
b. The foe to be faced (12)
c. The armor provided (13-17)
1) The appropriation of the armor (13a)
2) The purpose of the armor (13b)
3) The description of the armor (14-17)
a) The girdle of truth (14a)
b) The breastplate of righteousness (14b)
c) The shoes of the Gospel of peace (15)

d) The shield of faith (16)
e) The helmet of salvation (17a)
f) The sword of the Spirit (17b)
d. The supply line of prayer (18-20)
1) The manner of the praying (18)
2) The scope of the prayer (18c-19)
a) For all the saints (18c)
b) For the writer and his ministry (19-20)

## THE CONCLUSION (6:21-24)

1. The personal matters (21-22)
a. The commissioning of Tychicus as his messenger (21)
b. The purpose in sending Tychicus to them (22)
2. The benediction (23-24)
a. The wish to the brethren (23)
b. The benediction upon all those loving Christ (24)

### A Book List on Ephesians

Abbott, T. K., "A Critical and Exegetical Commentary on the Epistles to the Ephesians, and to the Colossians." *The International Critical Commentary*. Edinburgh: T. & T. Clark (n.d.).

Barth, Marcus, "Ephesians." *The Anchor Bible*. Two vols. Garden City, N.Y.: Doubleday & Co. (1974).

Uses the author's own translation; its printed form reflects the form-critical assumption of the use of hymns, fragments of hymns, or confessional formulae in Ephesians. The extended introduction holds Pauline authorship as most probable, and Rome A.D. 62 as the best guess of origin. The commentary material divides into two parts: phrase-by-phrase *Notes* relate to the explanation of the text itself; extended *Comments* relate to various matters connected with the thought of the passage. The 800-page work provides full bibliographies and indexes.

Bruce, F. F., *The Epistle to the Ephesians. A Verse-by-Verse Exposition*. Westwood, N.J.: Fleming H. Revell (1961).

A clear and non-technical exposition of Ephesians by a leading conservative British scholar. Intended as a popular treatment of the letter for the general Christian reader interested in serious Bible study.

Carver, William Owen, *The Glory of God in the Christian Calling. A Study of the Ephesian Epistle.* Nashville: Broadman Press (1949).

The fruit of more than a half century of interest in Ephesians by a noted Southern Baptist teacher of the past generation. Contains a detailed outline, a careful verse-by-verse exegesis, and the author's own translation. Four lengthy theological discussions (75 pages) precede the exegesis of the text.

Chafer, Lewis Sperry, *The Ephesian Letter Doctrinally Considered.* New York: Loizeaux Brothers (1935).

Divides the epistle into fifteen sections and treats them from a doctrinal standpoint. The work of a late pre-millennial, dispensational theologian.

Eadie, John, *Commentary on the Epistle to the Ephesians.* Grand Rapids: Zondervan Publishing House (1883; reprint, n.d.).

Greek text. A very full unfolding of the theological truths of the epistle by a conservative Scottish New Testament scholar of the past century. Presents a full exhibition of the various views of commentators up to the author's own times.

Findlay, G. G., "The Epistle to the Ephesians," *The Expositor's Bible.* Vol. VI. Grand Rapids: Wm. B. Eerdmans Pub. Co. (1943 reprint).

A valuable exposition by a conservative British Methodist Biblical scholar of the past generation.

Foulkes, Francis, "The Epistle of Paul to the Ephesians." *The Tyndale New Testament Commentaries.* Grand Rapids: Wm. B. Eerdmans Pub. Co. (1963).

A perceptive interpretation for the pastor or lay student, effectively combining sound scholarship with a clear presentation of the message of Ephesians. The work of a conservative New Zealand scholar.

Good, Kenneth H., *"Chosen in Him" Studies in Ephesians.* Elyria, Ohio: The Fellowship of Baptists for Home Missions (1967).

An analytical study of Ephesians by a contemporary conservative scholar, combining careful exegesis, strong emphasis upon basic doctrines, and homiletical suggestiveness. Elaborate discussions on election, the church in Ephesians, and sanctification are inserted. Intended as a basic textbook for use in the Candidate School of the Fellowship of Baptists for Home Missions.

Harrison, Norman B., *His Very Own, Paul's Epistle to the Ephesians.* Chicago: Moody Press (1930).

A rich devotional unfolding of the contents of Ephesians by means of an outline, a chart, notes, and comments on the text. The work of a conservative Bible teacher of the past generation.

Hendriksen, William, "Exposition of Ephesians." *New Testament Commentary*. Grand Rapids: Baker Book House (1967).

Uses author's translation. The informative introduction offers a comparison of Ephesians with Colossians in parallel columns. The commentary, the work of an evangelical scholar in the Reformed tradition, combines accurate scholarship and practical presentation. Brief summaries conclude each chapter. The outline developed for Ephesians is rather fanciful.

Hodge, Charles, *A Commentary on the Epistle to the Ephesians.* Grand Rapids: Wm. B. Eerdmans Pub. Co. (1950 reprint).

A full doctrinal and practical treatment by a conservative Presbyterian professor of the past century.

Lenski, R. C. H., *The Interpretation of St. Paul's Epistles to the Galatians, to the Ephesians, and to the Philippians.* Columbus, Ohio: Lutheran Book Concern (1937).

Lock, Walter, "The Epistle to the Ephesians." *Westminster Commentaries.* London: Methuen & Co. (1929).

Prints the English Revised Version at the top of the page. A concise verse-by-verse exposition with some additional longer notes. Lock accepts the Roman origin of the letter and holds it "far more probable" that the author is Paul himself than a disciple steeped in his teaching.

MacDonald, William, *Ephesians, The Mystery of the Church.* Wheaton: Harold Shaw Publishers (1968).

A verse-by-verse treatment using the author's unique Bible-text outline. Combines a clear exposition of the biblical text with practical applications. Rich in homiletical suggestiveness.

Miller, H. S., *The Book of Ephesians, with Outlines and Notes.* Houghton, N.Y.: The Word-Bearer Press (1931).

An evangelical verse-by-verse commentary that is expository, doctrinal, and practical. The explanations are virtually word studies plus a clear and simple interpretation of the text.

Moody, Dale, *Christ and the Church.* Grand Rapids: Wm. B. Eerdmans Pub. Co. (1963).

A paragraph-by-paragraph exposition of Ephesians by a Southern Baptist theologian, with special application to some contemporary Church issues.

Moule, H. C. G., "The Epistle of Paul the Apostle to the Ephesians." *Cambridge Bible for Schools and Colleges.* Cambridge: University Press (1886; 1935 reprint).

Provides an informative introduction and a paraphrastic presentation of the argument of Ephesians. A rewarding phrase-by-phrase interpretation by a conservative Anglican scholar of the past century.

Robinson, J. Armitage, *St. Paul's Epistle to the Ephesians. A Revised Text and Translation with Exposition and Notes.* London: Macmillan and Co. (1903).

The treatment of Ephesians is in two distinct parts. Following the introduction, Part I provides a translation and exposition for the English reader; Part II is a valuable exegetical treatment of the Greek text with emphasis on the philological, followed by additional studies of important terms in Ephesians. In 1929 the expository portion was published without the philological section. An important volume for the serious student.

Simpson, E. K., and Bruce, F. F., "Commentary on the Epistles to the Ephesians and the Colossians." *The New International Commentary on the New Testament.* Grand Rapids: Wm. B. Eerdmans Pub. Co. (1957).

Stoeckhardt, G., *Commentary on St. Paul's Letter to the Ephesians.* Translated by Martin S. Sommer. St. Louis: Concordia Publishing House (1952).

A straightforward, penetrating commentary by a conservative Lutheran professor of the past generation. Most helpful for those who know Greek.

Summers, Ray, *Ephesians: Pattern for Christian Living.* Nashville: Broadman Press (1960).

A devotional verse-by-verse treatment of Ephesians which stresses that its teachings provide a pattern for Christian living. The work of an evangelical Southern Baptist professor.

Vaughan, W. Curtis, *The Letter to the Ephesians.* Nashville: Convention Press (1963).

A simple, well-outlined interpretation; originally prepared as a study course guide for Southern Baptist Church groups. Well suited for a beginning study of Ephesians.

Welch, Charles H., *In Heavenly Places. An Exposition of the Epistle to the Ephesians.* London: The Berean Publishing Trust (n.d.), 430 pp.

An elaborate discussion of Ephesians by a British hyperdispensational Bible teacher. The author's characteristic introversion outline approach is prominent in his unfolding of the structure of the epistle. Contains important word studies.

Westcott, Brooke Foss, *Saint Paul's Epistle to the Ephesians.* Grand Rapids: Wm. B. Eerdmans Pub. Co. (1906; 1950 reprint).

Greek text. The contents were edited by J. M. Schulhof from material left by Westcott. Appendixes list the doctrinal heads in Ephesians as well as various additional notes. Most valuable for the Greek student.

Wuest, Kenneth S., *Ephesians and Colossians in the Greek New Testament for the English Reader.* Grand Rapids: Wm. B. Eerdmans Pub. Co. (1953).

# 15

# PHILIPPIANS

## An Introduction to Philippians

Paul's Letter to the Philippians is like an open window into the Apostle's very heart. In it we have the artless outpouring of his unrestrained love for and his unalloyed joy in his devoted and loyal Philippian friends. It is the most intimate and spontaneous of his writings.

### THE CITY OF PHILIPPI

1. *Location.* The city of Philippi, first visited by Paul on his second missionary journey, was a fortified city of Macedonia near the Thracian border. It was an inland town and was situated about eleven miles north of the seaport of Neapolis. Located thirty-three miles east of Amphipolis, it stood astraddle the famous Roman highway the Via Egnatia which ran from Dyrrachium on the Adriatic Sea to the Hellespont. A spur of this highway connected Philippi with its seaport town Neapolis. According to Lewin, the Egnatian Way ran through the city and divided it into two parts, the Upper and the Lower Town.[1] The Upper Town, containing the ancient citadel, was located on the rocky slopes of a steep hill overlooking the fertile plain of Drama, watered by the Gangites, or Angites, River. The Lower Town, south of the Egnatian Way, was a later addition and extended some distance into the spacious plain. This was the most important section of the city. Here were located the forum and the market place, the centers of the city's life. The geographic position of Philippi early gave its importance. It stood guard at the place where the mountain barrier of the Balkans sinks into a pass through which ran the Egnatian Way.

1. Thomas Lewin, *The Life and Epistles of St. Paul,* (1878), Vol. I, pp. 210-211.

2. *History.* The ancient name of the place was Crenides, "The Little Fountains," so called because of the numerous springs in the region. Philip II of Macedonia, the father of Alexander the Great, recognized the strategic importance of the place and seized the territory in order to protect Macedonia from the Thracians. In 356 B.C. the place was enlarged, fortified, and renamed Philippi by him. He energetically worked the gold mines in the region, said to have produced one thousand talents a year. This gold enabled him not only to enlarge the Macedonian army and to give Macedonia a gold currency, but also to practice the fine art of bribery. This is evidenced by the statement attributed to him that "no fortress was impregnable to whose walls an ass laden with gold could be driven."

By the time of the Roman conquest of the territory, two centuries later, the old mines had already been exhausted. Following the battle of Pydna (168 B.C.), Philippi as a part of Macedonia passed under the control of the Romans. The Romans divided Macedonia into four districts politically, Philippi being in the first; but in 146 B.C. the entire territory was formed into the Roman province of Macedonia. In 42 B.C. Philippi witnessed the death-struggle of the Roman Republic and the birth of the Roman Empire in the defeat of the Republican armies of Brutus and Cassius by the forces of Octavian (afterward Augustus) and Mark Anthony. Octavian, proud of the victory that had been won at Philippi, elevated the city to a colony under the name of "Colonia Julia Philippensis." Eleven years later, following the victory of Octavian over Mark Anthony in the battle of Actium (31 B.C.), the city was reinforced by the settlement of many of the followers of Mark Anthony who had been dispossessed in Italy to make room for the veterans of Octavian. To commemorate this event the name of the city was changed to "Colonia Julia (Victrix) Philippensium."[2]

3. *Status.* Luke describes Philippi as "a city of Macedonia, the first of the district, a *Roman* colony" (Acts 16:12). The meaning of the expression, "the first of the district," has been debated. Lewin held that it designated Philippi as the capital of that section of Macedonia, hence the first politically.[3] But it is known that Amphipolis was the capital of the first district. Lightfoot held that it meant that it was

2. M. N. Tod, "Philippi," *The International Standard Bible Encyclopaedia,* (1939), Vol. IV, p. 2369b.
3. Thomas Lewin, *The Life and Epistles of St. Paul,* (1878), Vol. I, p. 202.

geographically the first city which met the traveler as he entered the region of Macedonia.[4] Adams interprets the expression "as referring primarily to the strategic position of Philippi as a border town in Roman defenses, and its recognized status as a Roman colony, rather than any claimed headship as a political and administrative center."[5]

As a Roman colony its primary business was to ward off attacks from barbarian hordes and to preserve the Roman peace on the edges of the Empire. As a colony Philippi was granted the coveted *Jus Italicum* which put it on a level with Roman colonies in Italy. Its citizens were Roman citizens, their names were enrolled in the annals of Rome. It enjoyed the privilege of exemption from the oversight of the provincial governor, immunity from poll and property taxes, and the right to hold land in full ownership under the laws of Rome. As a Roman colony, it was in ideal a miniature reproduction of the city of Rome. The spirit and practices of Rome prevailed. The official language was Latin, but a knowledge of the Greek was a necessity for all its residents. Inscriptions in both languages have been found at the place, the Latin being somewhat more numerous than the Greek.

At the head of the city were two officials, the praetors or *duumviri*, who combined civil and military authority in their persons. Lictors attended the praetors, bearing the official bundles of rods or fasces with a mace protruding from the center, symbols of power and authority. The Roman spirit and atmosphere in Philippi are quite evident in the narrative of Luke. This was appealed to by the owners of the slave girl in stimulating opposition to Paul and Silas. This likewise was the power that obtained the redress for the mistreated prisoners and forced an apology from the unwilling praetors.

4. *Population*. The population of the city was mixed, consisting of three main elements. The Roman colonists constituted the dominant and ruling class; the old Macedonian stock was numerically the strongest section; the third element consisted of a considerable admixture of Orientals. Being situated on the famous Egnatian Way, Philippi was daily visited by strangers from many lands. It was truly a meeting-place of East and West. Because Philippi was a military and agricultural rather than a commercial city, few Jews had been attracted to the city. There were not enough Jews in the city to have

4. J. B. Lightfoot, *Saint Paul's Epistle to the Philippians*, (1898 reprint), p. 50, note.
5. J. McKee Adams, *Biblical Backgrounds*, (7th Ed., 1943), p. 456.

a regular synagogue, but they did maintain their religious practices at a "place of prayer" situated outside the city by the riverside.

## THE CHURCH IN PHILIPPI

1. *Origin.* The church in Philippi was established as the direct result of the labors of Paul and his co-workers there during the second missionary journey. Since it is based on Luke's personal observations, the story of the Philippian mission is told in minute detail and with dramatic vividness.[6] By means of a series of negative leadings Paul had been brought down to Troas (Acts 16:6-8). At Troas, where Luke apparently joined the missionary party, Paul received his "Macedonian Call," and the missionary party at once set sail for Macedonia (16:9-10). Their journey was speeded by favorable winds, and after two days they arrived at Neapolis, the seaport of Philippi. They proceeded at once to Philippi which was eleven miles inland. Having settled in Philippi and gotten their bearings of the field, the work of evangelism was begun on the Sabbath day with the few Jews of the city. They went to the place of prayer outside the city and spoke to the women that had assembled there. The first convert in Philippi was a proselyte to Judaism, Lydia, a business woman from Thyatira (16:12-14). Her own conversion led to the conversion of her whole household, the first instance of such a household conversion recorded in Acts. The opening of her home to the missionaries provided a base of operation for the work and a place of assembly for the young church (16:15). The work continued favorably for some time, and converts were won.[7]

A crisis arose when Paul cast out the spirit of divination from the slave girl who had for many days been following the missionaries with her cries (16:16-18). Realizing that with that act "the hope of their gain was gone" (16:19), the masters of the girl seized Paul and Silas and dragged them into the market place before the magistrates. They accused the missionaries of teaching a religion which was illegal for them as Romans to receive. Because the mob threatened violence, the magistrates acted without stopping to investigate. The accused were beaten with rods and ordered jailed. Because of the orders given him to keep them safe, the jailer thrust them into the

6. Luke's presence is confidently assumed from the fact that the mission at Philippi is included in the first "we section" of Acts (16:10-40).
7. Perhaps Euodia and Syntyche were among these (Phil. 4:2). They may, however, have been converts and fellow workers of a later visit.

inner jail and put their feet in the stocks. That night the imprisoned missionaries gave the first Christian concert in that pagan city, and God honored it by sending an earthquake that opened all the prison doors and loosed everyone's bands. The attempt of the jailer to commit suicide, because he thought that the prisoners had escaped, was halted by Paul's cry. Instead he received the message of salvation, and he and his whole house became Christians. When day had come, the praetors, doubtless alarmed by the report of what had happened at the jail that night, sent the lictors with the message to the jailer, "Let those men go" (16:35). When the jailer brought the report to Paul, Paul resolutely refused to go and demanded that the praetors themselves come and conduct them out (16:36-39).

Paul's firm refusal to be spirited away without a public recognition of their rights was more than a desire for personal justice. It was prompted rather by a desire to safeguard the young church. The rights of Paul and Silas as Roman citizens had been seriously violated. Roman law exempted Roman citizens from all degrading forms of punishment, such as beating with rods, scourging, or crucifixion. The praetors by their hasty action had made themselves liable to severe punishment. By securing the vindication of the missionaries, Paul removed any possibility of later reflection on the Philippian church. The praetors were made to understand that Roman citizens were behind the preaching of the Gospel and that it was no illegal or clandestine movement. The security of the church was thus assured. The crisis, however, made necessary the departure of the missionaries. Luke apparently remained behind in Philippi to guide the affairs of the church.

2. *Characteristics.* The Philippian church reveals several interesting characteristics. The prominence of women in the church is noteworthy. This is in accordance with the general status of the women in the province of Macedonia. The first convert in Philippi was the business woman Lydia. Her own fervor and spirit of liberality seem to have diffused themselves throughout the church. In the letter to the Philippians two women, Euodia and Syntyche, are mentioned as having been co-workers together with Paul (4:2).

The membership of the church was unquestionably Gentile in its background. It apparently contained but few Jewish converts. "If there were any Jewish-Christians in the Church, they had not made themselves obnoxious by laying special emphasis on the characteristic tenets of their party."[8] If the constituent elements in the population of the city were fairly represented in the church, the membership must have been cosmopolitan in character. The first three recorded converts at Philippi have been regarded as typical of the different nationalities and social levels represented in the church.[9] It was upon the basis of this view that Schaff remarked,

> Lydia, the purple dealer of Thyatira and a half proselyte to Judaism, a native slave-girl with a divining spirit, which was used by her masters as a means of gain among the superstitious heathen, and a Roman jailer, were the first converts, and fitly represent the three nationalities (Jew, Greek, and Roman) and the classes of society which were especially benefitted by Christianity.[10]

The Philippians were among the Macedonian Christians whose liberality Paul held up as an example to the Corinthians (2 Cor. 8:1-15). Their liberality is confirmed by the unique monetary record that they attained in their relations to Paul (Phil. 4:15-16).

3. *Relations to Paul.* Born out of the labor and travail of the Apostle, the Philippian church maintained its intimate relations with their founder. His warm words of affection for them in his letter show that they were very near his heart. The Philippians reciprocated that feeling. Shortly after Paul left their midst they sent a financial contribution "once and again" to him while he was laboring at Thessalonica (Phil. 4:16). A further contribution was sent him while he was at Corinth (Phil. 4:15; Acts 18:5; 2 Cor. 11:9). In this matter the Philippians had a distinctive record, as Paul himself reminds them in his letter (4:15). From them he received the support that he refused to receive from the Corinthians (2 Cor. 11:7-10). That fact reveals his feeling toward the Philippians. As Shaw says,

> Only from friends who lay deep in his love and confidence would Paul have received gifts of money. We can measure his tenderness for them by the strength of the principle which absolutely forbade him to take such help from any others. He not only knew that by them he would never be misunderstood, but he could not find it in his heart to refuse aught they offered.[11]

8. H. A. A. Kennedy, "The Epistle of Paul to the Philippians," *Expositor's Greek Testament,* (n.d.), Vol. III, p. 402.
9. While it is not directly stated that the slave-girl became a Christian, it may safely be assumed that such was the case.
10. Philip Schaff, *History of the Christian Church,* (1910), Vol. I, p. 789.
11. R. D. Shaw, *The Pauline Epistles,* (4th Ed., 1924 reprint), p. 408.

During the third missionary journey, after an absence of about five years, Paul again visited the church at Philippi. It was at a time when he was under a great strain because of the trying conditions at Corinth (2 Cor. 2:12-13; 7:5-6). Perhaps he was with his Philippian friends when he wrote 2 Corinthians. In the spring of the following year he again returned to Philippi and kept the Passover season with them (Acts 20:6).

His contacts with the Philippians were not confined to these occasional visits. He doubtless kept in touch with them through messengers sent to them (cf. Acts 19:22). Doubtless the Philippians also on their part continued to communicate with him. That they established communications with Paul while he was a prisoner in Rome is evident from the letter to them. If, as we believe, the Pastoral Epistles relate to a period subsequent to the imprisonment in Acts, Paul visited Macedonia at least once more (1 Tim. 1:3).

4. *Subsequent history.* With the letter to the Philippians that church fades from the Biblical records. Its last prominent mention in Church history is in connection with the visit of the Christian martyr Ignatius, early in the second century, on his way to Rome under military guard. The Philippian believers were not ashamed of his chains but kindly entertained him and escorted him some distance on his way. Their action caused Polycarp, a friend of Ignatius, to write to them, commending them for their kindness. Following this event, save for the fact that its bishops are rarely mentioned in connection with councils in the fourth and fifth centuries, the church sinks into historical oblivion. Even the site of the city of Philippi is today in ruins. This history caused Lightfoot to remark, "Born into the world with the brightest promise, the Church of Philippi has lived without a history and perished without a memorial."[12] Yet what finer or more enduring memorial could any church desire than the letter which the apostle Paul wrote to that church, a letter which has forever enshrined the name of that church in the hearts of God's people everywhere!

## THE AUTHENTICITY AND UNITY OF PHILIPPIANS

1. *Authenticity.* No trace of doubt concerning the authenticity of Philippians was ever raised until modern times. The external evi-

12. J. B. Lightfoot, *Saint Paul's Epistle to the Philippians,* (1898), p. 65.

dence in its favor is remarkably strong and full. To all but the most ultraskeptical the internal evidence is likewise conclusive. Relative to the internal evidence for the epistle, Lightfoot says,

> This evidence is of two kinds, positive and negative. On the one hand the epistle completely reflects St. Paul's mind and character, even in their finest shades. On the other, it offers no motive which could have led to a forgery. . . . A forger would not have produced a work so aimless (for aimless in his case it must have been), and could not have produced one so inartificial.[13]

However ingenious they may be, the objections raised against Philippians by a few hypercritics really originate in *a priori* views. The attack, launched by Evanson, was pursued by Baur in his famous work on Paul. But the objections of Baur were pronounced futile even by scholars whose views represent extreme critical positions.[14] It is commonly accepted today that the authenticity of Philippians cannot reasonably be questioned.

2. *Unity.* The debate today concerns the unity of Philippians. Efforts to sever its unity find no support from its textual history but are launched by the abrupt change of tone and content at 3:1. The change is so harsh, it is asserted, that its traditional unity cannot be accepted; the sudden warning against opponents can only be understood as due to an interpolation from another letter. But "it is psychologically more credible that Paul in writing an informal letter would make such a sudden transition, than that a later editor would fuse two separate writings at such an improbable junction."[15] The critics cannot agree where the interpolation ends.[16] If different letters were actually thus fused, would not the "seams" be more obvious? Vincent concludes, "If the partition theory is admitted, the attempt to fix the dividing lines must be regarded as hopeless in the face of the differences of the critics.'[17] We accept the unity of Philip-

13. *Ibid.*, p. 74.
14. For a full statement and reply to these attacks on Philippians see James Moffatt, *An Introduction to the Literature of the New Testament,* (3rd Ed., 1949 reprint), pp. 170-172.
15. D. E. Hiebert, "Philippians, Letter to the," *The Zondervan Pictorial Encyclopedia of the Bible,* (1975), Vol. IV, p. 763.
16. For the varied proposals see Frank Stagg, "Philippians," *The Broadman Bible Commentary,* (1971), Vol. 11, p. 180, note 3.
17. Marvin R. Vincent, "A Critical and Exegetical Commentary on the Epistles to the Philippians and to Philemon," *The International Critical Commentary,* (1950 reprint), p. xxxii.

pians and hold that it is best to try to understand the letter as we have it, apart from such dubious reconstructions.[18]

### THE OCCASION FOR PHILIPPIANS

The immediate occasion for the writing of Philippians was the return of Epaphroditus to Philippi following his serious illness in Rome (2:25-30). The occasion cannot have been the information concerning the disagreement between two women in the church (4:2), since the matter is quite minor, and Paul does not censure the church for internal factions. Even the gift from the Philippians was not the *immediate* occasion for the letter. The gift, brought by Epaphroditus as the official representative of the church (4:18), had been received some time ago. This is evident from the fact that already enough time had elapsed to allow Epaphroditus to recover from his serious illness since coming to Rome (2:27-30). Now that he had sufficiently recovered to undertake the return journey, he was anxious to return. The knowledge that the Philippians were deeply concerned about him added to the yearning of Epaphroditus to return home (2:26). If we may assume, as does Lenski,[19] that some other members from the Philippian church accompanied Epaphroditus to Rome, then Paul would send back his thanks for the gift with them. Perhaps they also carried back the report of the illness of Epaphroditus. The view that Paul had already expressed his thanks for the gift agrees with the fact that the gift is not mentioned until the end of the letter. If, however, we hold that Epaphroditus came alone, then sufficient time must be allowed for the report of his illness to reach Philippi some other way and the report of their concern for him to get back to Rome. At any rate, some time had elapsed since the gift was received, and Paul now uses the opportunity offered by the return of Epaphroditus to write to his beloved friends at Philippi. It was truly a friendship letter.

### THE PLACE AND DATE OF PHILIPPIANS

1. *Place.* It is commonly agreed that the indications in the letter point to the conclusion that Paul was a prisoner in Rome when it was

18. See further in Werner Georg Kümmel, *Introduction to the New Testament,* (1966), pp. 235-237; Frank Stagg, "Philippians," *The Broadman Bible Commentary,* (1971), Vol 11, pp. 179-181; Donald Guthrie, *New Testament Introduction,* (1970), pp. 536-539.
19. R. C. H. Lenski, *The Interpretation of St. Paul's Epistles to the Galatians, to the Ephesians, and to the Philippians,* (1937), p. 696.

written. The letter makes clear that he is a prisoner and that his presence has caused considerable interest in the Gospel (1:7, 13-20). Further, it is evident that he has been in that situation for some time, since it has become known "throughout the whole praetorian guard, and to all the rest" that his imprisonment is solely due to his relation to the Gospel and not for any offenses against public order (1:13). His presence and circumstances have given most of the brethren in the city more confidence and boldness to preach Christ (1:14). But some have also been stirred up to preach Christ "even of envy and strife" (1:15), thinking thereby to add to his afflictions (1:17). Circumstances as a whole have resulted rather in the furtherance of the Gospel (1:12), and there are saints even in "Caesar's household" (4:22). These indications point strongly to Rome as the place of imprisonment. A few writers have advocated Caesarea, and more lately even Ephesus, as the place of composition, but the known conditions of the Apostle's confinement agree best with the Roman imprisonment.[20]

2. *Date.* The indications in the epistle of the lapse of considerable time, as well as the Apostle's hope of a speedy release, forbid the view that it was written during the early part of Paul's Roman imprisonment. The contacts between Paul and the Philippians revealed in the letter cannot well be compressed into a few months. News of Paul's arrival in Rome must have time to reach Philippi; money was collected and sent to Rome by Epaphroditus, who fell violently ill after he reached Rome; news of his sickness again reached Philippi, and the report of their concern for Epaphroditus again reached Rome. All this supposes that considerable time has elapsed and places the time in the latter half of the imprisonment. The decisive factor as to the date is the indication in Philippians 2:23 that the Imperial Court has begun to consider Paul's case and that he expects a verdict soon which will enable him to visit Philippi before long (2:24). This places the epistle in the closing months of the imprisonment. Zahn has shown quite conclusively that this hope of a speedy release makes a date during the early part of the imprisonment quite impossible.[21] Those who hold that Philippians is the earliest of the Prison Epistles do so primarily because of its affinities

20. See further D. E. Hiebert, "Philippians, Letter to the," *The Zondervan Pictorial Encyclopedia of the Bible,* (1975), Vol. IV, pp. 764-765.
21. Theodor Zahn, *Introduction to the New Testament,* (1909), Vol. I, pp. 539-550.

to Romans and Galatians. Yet the actual interval between Philippians and these epistles, on the one hand, and the other Prison Epistles on the other, makes the argument from the natural development of their contents very precarious. We conclude that Philippians was written near the close of Paul's first Roman imprisonment and date it in the early part of A.D. 63.

3. *Bearer.* The bearer of the letter is Epaphroditus. He is not mentioned elsewhere beyond this epistle and must not be confused with Epaphras, the founder of the Colossian church (Col. 1:7-8; 4:12-13). Paul describes Epaphroditus as "my brother and fellow-worker and fellow-soldier, and your messenger and minister to my need" (2:25). The first three terms indicate his relations to Paul. "The first designates him as a partner of Paul's faith, the second as his partner in office or labor, the third as sharer of his conflicts and dangers."[22] The last two terms describe him in relation to the Philippians. The first of these designates him as the messenger of the Philippians to Paul, the second designates him as the servant of the Philippians who carried out their ministration. "Your . . . minister to my need" (2:25) suggests that Epaphroditus had been commissioned not only to take the money but also to stay and assist Paul on their behalf. That he was one of their bishops (1:1) is not obvious, although often assumed. In sending back their zealous and trusted representative, Paul desired that he be given all due honor (2:29-30).

### THE PURPOSE OF PHILIPPIANS

There are those who profess to see evidence in the letter that Paul is writing in answer to a letter from the Philippians. Such intimations are supposedly seen in 1:12, 19, 25-26; 3:2 and 4:10-15. It is even assumed that the Philippians have written to him apologizing for not having sent a gift earlier or expressing fear that the Apostle was not satisfied with the gift that had been sent. Further, it is thought that the warning in 3:2-16 is in answer to an inquiry about this teaching which has assaulted them. We cannot help but feel that this is reading more between the lines than is there. Meyer concludes that "there is neither direct occasion nor any other sufficient reason for going beyond the oral communications of Epaphroditus in order to

22. Karl Braune, "The Epistle of Paul to the Philippians," Lange's *Commentary,* (1950 reprint), p. 47.

account for the apostle's acquaintance with the circumstances of the Philippians."[23]

The letter was not occasioned by any special crisis such as caused Paul, for example, to write Galatians or 2 Corinthians. It is rather a letter of love, inspired by friendship motives.

1. *Information.* The letter was written to provide the Philippian church with official information about his circumstances. The Philippians naturally were anxious to get the latest information concerning developments in Paul's case. He informs them of the generally satisfactory results of his imprisonment (1:12-20) and imparts the important news that the Imperial Court has actually begun to dispose of his appeal to Caesar (2:23). He promises to dispatch Timothy to them as soon as the verdict is known (2:19-23). The verdict is yet to be given. He is hopeful that it will be favorable (2:24), yet the possibility remains that it may be otherwise. This shadow hangs over him and he writes accordingly (1:21-26). Yet on the whole, he is definitely hopeful and confident.

2. *Affection.* The letter is marked by a spontaneous outpouring of his personal regard and affection for the Philippians. The thought of them fills him with thanksgiving and gratitude and inspires yearning and prayer for them (1:3-11). Terms of endearment are indicative of his deep love for them. Notice the epithets in 4:1. He thanks them for the gift they have sent him (4:10-19).

3. *Warning.* His love and concern for the Philippians causes him to warn them against two dangers which he senses. He strikes a note of solemn warning against the Judaizers on the one hand (3:2-16) and Antinomianism on the other (3:17–4:1). There is no evidence that either of these teachings had made any serious inroads on the Philippian church. Perhaps because of something that Epaphroditus had mentioned, and mindful of the fierce conflicts he has had with such teachers, he deems it desirable to warn them to be on guard against them. With a true instinct, he recognizes the first appearance of these noxious weeds and hastens to pluck them up forthwith.

4. *Exhortation.* His fatherly concern for them finds expression in exhortation and counsel. He exhorts the cultivation of three graces

23. Heinrich August Wilhelm Meyer, *Critical and Exegetical Hand-Book to the Epistles to the Philippians and Colossians, and to Philemon,* (1885), p. 3.

in particular. He exhorts them to unity. They are urged to cultivate unity in aim and work (1:27-29), to endeavor to foster that which will promote the common good (2:2-4), and to avoid any personal disagreements that have arisen (4:2-3). He also urges upon them the cultivation of humble-mindedness (2:3), a virtue commended by the example of our Lord Himself (2:5-11). He further desires that they foster the spirit of joy and thanksgiving (3:1; 4:4-9). He is rejoicing in his prison; they are also to rejoice.

### THE CHARACTERISTICS OF PHILIPPIANS

1. *Personal nature.* The attentive reader of Philippians cannot fail to be impressed with its intensely personal nature. It has all the marks of a free and spontaneous letter to beloved friends. In it he freely opens his heart and affections to them. In it he mentions himself more often than in any of his other epistles.[24] It has the free, personal flow of a letter to intimate friends. It accordingly lacks the rigid outline of a formal treatise. In the words of Hayes,

> It rambles along just as any real letter would with personal news and personal feelings and outbursts of personal affection between tried friends. It is the most spontaneous and unaffected of the Pauline Epistles.[25]

No other epistle is so warm in its expressions of personal affection as Philippians. Six times he addresses the readers as "brethren" (1:12; 3:1, 13, 17; 4:1, 8) and thrice he uses the term "beloved" (2:12; 4:1 twice). In the last reference he seems hardly able to find words to pour out the fullness of his love for his readers. And his love for them is not tempered by mixed feelings, as in some of his other epistles. In 2 Corinthians his love is mingled with grief and indignation, due to the attitude of the Corinthians; not so in Philippians. In Galatians his love is straitened by the doctrinal instability of the readers; the Philippians have proved loyal to him and the Gospel. The warnings in chapter three are rather safety measures for those whom he loves.

2. *Joyfulness.* The note of joy is predominant in Philippians. It is so prominent that it has even crept into the titles of expositions of

24. The first person singular pronoun, either alone or in the Greek verb, occurs no less than 120 times in Philippians.
25. Doremus Almy Hayes, "Philippians, The Epistle to," *The International Standard Bible Encyclopaedia,* (1939), Vol. IV, p. 2373b.

the epistle.[26] The words *joy* or *rejoice* occur sixteen times in the letter (Greek).[27] Bengel summarized the contents of the epistle thus: "Summa epistolae; Gaudeo, gaudete: The sum of the Epistle is: I rejoice, rejoice ye." But lest any should think that this state of heart is due to fortunate circumstances, let it be remembered that it was written while the Apostle was in prison, chained day and night to a soldier, with few friends to cheer him, and not a few enemies seeking to add to his affliction (2:20-21; 1:15-16). "Christian joy is more and better than happiness, because it does not depend on what happens."[28] The joyousness of this epistle is an eloquent testimony to the triumph of the Christian faith over all adversity and affliction.

3. *Theological importance.* Philippians, like the other Prison Epistles, contains a profound Christological passage (2:5-11). It has well been called "the crowning revelation concerning Jesus in the Pauline Epistles."[29] It tersely presents the pre-existence, incarnation, and exaltation of Jesus Christ. But its high Christology is implicit rather than explicit.

This profound passage was written with an ethical rather than a doctrinal purpose. It was intended to enforce the practical Christian virtue of humility in the interest of ecclesiastical unity. It is a clear illustration of Paul's practice of reinforcing the common, everyday duties of the Christian life by undergirding them with the most profound doctrinal truths.

This passage has been the subject of much recent scholarly discussion.[30] It is commonly regarded as a hymn quoted by Paul, either of pre-Pauline origin, or composed before Paul wrote Philippians. Arguments advocating a non-Pauline origin Harrison regards as "less than decisive."[31] It cannot reasonably be denied that Paul was capable of writing such an exalted poetic passage. Others think that it was written by a contemporary of Paul who was influenced by his teaching. There is no scholarly agreement concerning the poetic

26. As A. T. Robertson's *Paul's Joy in Christ,* or Norman B. Harrison's *His in Joyous Experience.*
27. Found in 1:4, 18, 25; 2:2, 17, 18, 28, 29; 3:1; 4:1, 4, 10.
28. W. Graham Scroggie, *Know Your Bible, A Brief Introduction to the Scriptures, Volume II, The New Testament,* (n.d.), p. 224.
29. Doremus Almy Hayes, "Philippians, The Epistle to," *The International Standard Bible Encyclopaedia,* (1939), Vol. IV, p. 2374a.
30. For the most comprehensive recent study, see R. P. Martin, *Carmen Christi,* (1967). He regards the hymn as pre-Pauline. In an earlier work, *An Early Christian Confession* (1960), he accepted its Pauline origin.
31. Everett F. Harrison, *Introduction to the New Testament,* (1971), p. 343.

form of the passage.[32] Stagg well thinks it "strange that scholars are so sure of the hymnic nature of the passage and so unsure of its poetic structure."[33] That the passage is part of the epistle as Paul wrote it is certain. Its poetic structure may be accounted for by the inspiration of the lofty thoughts as well as to Paul's repeated careful thought as to its most effective formulation in his preaching and teaching.

### An Outline of Philippians

THE SALUTATION (1:1-2)

1. The writers (1a)
2. The readers (1b)
3. The greetings (2)

I. PAUL'S RELATIONS TO THE PHILIPPIANS (1:3-11)

1. His thanksgiving for them (3-5)
   a. The stimulus for the thanksgiving (3)
   b. The expression of the thanksgiving (4)
   c. The cause for the thanksgiving (5)
2. His confidence in them (6-7)
   a. The nature of the confidence (6)
   b. The justification for the confidence (7)
3. His longing for them (8)
4. His prayer for them (9-11)
   a. The contents of the prayer (9)
   b. The purpose of the prayer (10a)
   c. The results of the answered prayer (10b-11)

II. PAUL'S ACCOUNT OF HIS CIRCUMSTANCES (1:12-26)

1. His rejoicing at the furtherance of the Gospel (12-20)
   a. His imprisonment has furthered the Gospel (12-14)
      1) The assertion about the effect of his circumstances (12)
      2) The manner of their furthering the Gospel (13-14)
         a) In interpreting his position (13)
         b) In arousing others to preach Christ (14)
   b. His indication of the motives of the preachers (15-17)

32. See Frank Stagg, "Philippians," *The Broadman Bible Commentary,* (1971), Vol. 11, p. 194.
33. *Ibid.*

1) The nature of their motives (15)
2) The purposes behind their preaching (16-17)
c. His reasons for rejoicing in all preaching of Christ (18-20)
1) Because it spreads the message of Christ (18)
2) Because it will work out to his salvation (19)
3) Because it will magnify Christ (20)
2. His contemplation of the prospects of life and death (21-26)
a. His view of life and death (21)
b. His dilemma between the two alternatives (22-26)
1) The attractiveness of life in the flesh (22)
2) The competing desires leave him undecided (23-24)
3) The assurance of a longer life (25-26)

III. PAUL'S PRACTICAL APPEALS TO THE PHILIPPIANS (1:27–2:18)

1. The appeal for steadfastness (1:27-30)
a. The appeal to live a worthy citizen life (27a)
b. The task of united steadfastness (27b)
c. The attitude in the contest (28)
d. The basis for their steadfastness (29)
e. The encouragement from his own experience (30)
2. The appeal for unity (2:1-4)
a. The basis for the appeal (1)
b. The contents of the appeal (2)
c. The implications of the appeal (3-4)
3. The appeal for humility (2:5-11)
a. The example of Christ Jesus urged (5)
b. The self-humbling of Christ (6-8)
1) The nature of His humiliation (6-7a)
2) The manner of His humiliation (7b)
3) The extent of His humiliation (8)
c. The Father's exaltation of Christ (9-11)
1) The nature of the exaltation (9)
2) The purpose of the exaltation (10-11)
4. The appeal to realize God's salvation (2:12-18)
a. The power of inner realization (12-13)
1) Negative—Not based on his presence with them (12a)
2) Positive—The twofold power for the realization (12b-13)

- b. The exhortation to outward manifestation (14-16a)
  - 1) The hindering attitude prohibited (14)
  - 2) The results of the personal realization (15-16a)
- c. The significance to him of their victory (16b-18)
  - 1) His future boasting in them (16b)
  - 2) His present sacrifice for their faith (17-18)

## IV. PAUL'S PLANS FOR HIS COMPANIONS (2:19-30)

1. His plans for Timothy (19-24)
   - a. The statement of the plan (19a)
   - b. The motive he has for the plan (19b)
   - c. The reasons for the choice of Timothy (20-21)
   - d. The relation of Timothy to himself (22)
   - e. The time of Timothy's sending (23)
   - f. The hope for a speedy personal visit (24)
2. His plans for Epaphroditus (25-30)
   - a. The statement of the plan (25a)
   - b. The testimony to Epaphroditus (25b)
   - c. The reason for sending Epaphroditus (26-27)
   - d. The welcome to be given Epaphroditus (28-30)
     - 1) The motive he has in sending him (28)
     - 2) The reception to be given him (29-30)

## V. PAUL'S WARNING AGAINST ERRORS (3:1—4:1)

1. The warning against legalism (3:1-16)
   - a. The joy in the Lord as the antidote to error (1-3)
     - 1) The admonition to rejoice (1)
     - 2) The admonition to watch the Judaizers (2)
     - 3) The identification of the true Israelites (3)
   - b. The confirmation from his own experience (4-11)
     - 1) His former Jewish privileges (4-6)
       - a) His possession of grounds for legalistic pride (4)
       - b) His enumeration of grounds for legalistic pride (5-6)
     - 2) His complete change of values (7-11)
       - a) The nature of the change (7)
       - b) The present evaluation of all things (8a)
       - c) The reasons for the change (8b)
       - d) The motives for the change (8c-11)

(i) To gain Christ (8c)
(ii) To be found in Christ (9)
(iii) To get knowledge of Christ Himself (10)
(iv) To attain unto the resurrection from the dead (11)

c. The Christian life viewed as one of progress (12-16)
1) His attitude as to his own perfection (12)
2) His efforts to reach the goal (13-14)
a) Negative—Counts himself not as having laid hold (13a)
b) Positive—Puts forth unrelenting effort (13b-14)
3) His exhortation to the mature (15-16)

2. The warning against false brethren (Antinomianism) (3:17—4:1)
a. The safety in imitating him (3:17)
b. The warning against the false brethren (18-19)
1) Their character (18b)
2) Their fate (19a)
3) Their motives (19b)
c. The motives of the true believer (20-21)
1) Our present position (20a)
2) Our continuing expectation (20b)
3) Our glorious transformation (21)
d. The admonition to steadfastness (4:1)

VI. PAUL'S EXHORTATIONS TO THE PHILIPPIANS (4:2-9)

1. The exhortation to unity (2-3)
a. The appeal for unity between two women (2)
b. The appeal to his yokefellow to help these women (3)

2. The exhortation to holy living (4-7)
a. The call to rejoicing (4)
b. The duty of gentleness (5)
c. The practice of prayerfulness (6-7)
1) The prohibition against worry (6a)
2) The precept to prayer (6b)
3) The promise of peace (7)

3. The exhortation to holy meditation and action (8-9)
a. The things they are to think on (8)
b. The things they are to do (9)

VII. PAUL'S THANKSGIVING TO THE PHILIPPIANS (4:10-21)

1. His rejoicing at their gift (10)
2. His revelation of his condition (11-13)
    a. His independence of material need (11a)
    b. His explanation of his secret (11b-12)
    c. His source of strength (13)
3. His thanksgiving for their gift (14-18)
    a. His appreciation of the gift (14)
    b. His reminder of their past record (15-16)
    c. His attitude toward their gift (17)
    d. His receipt for the gift (18)
4. His counterpromise to them (19-20)

THE CONCLUSION (4:21-23)

1. The salutations (21-22)
2. The benediction (23)

### A Book List on Philippians

Barth, Karl, *The Epistle to the Philippians.* Translated by James W. Leitch. Richmond: John Knox Press (1962).

A brief exegetical commentary written primarily for the non-theologian but reflecting the views of the noted neoorthodox scholar.

Beare, F. W., "A Commentary on the Epistle to the Philippians." *Harper's New Testament Commentaries.* New York: Harper & Brothers (1959).

Prints author's translation. The introduction advocates the author's view that Philippians is a compilation of three different letters of Paul which probably originated in Rome. Holds that Philippians 2:5-11 is a hymn of non-Pauline origin, adding "nothing to our knowledge of Jesus" (p. 32). Gives a phrase-by-phrase critical interpretation of the text.

Boice, James Montgomery, *Philippians, An Expositional Commentary.* Grand Rapids: Zondervan Publishing House (1971).

A series of forty-five expository messages by a conservative radio preacher and pastor. Expository preaching at its best.

Eadie, John, *A Commentary on the Greek Text of the Epistle of Paul to the Philippians.* Grand Rapids: Zondervan Publishing House (1859; reprint).

A full exegetical commentary by a conservative Scottish scholar of the past century; presents the various views up to the time of the author. Contains excellent definitions of Greek words, also homiletical truths.

Erdman, Charles R., *The Epistle of Paul to the Philippians.* Philadelphia: The Westminster Press (1932).

A paragraph-by-paragraph devotional exposition based on a careful analysis of the text. Well adapted to the lay Bible student.

Harrell, Pat Edwin, "The Letter of Paul to the Philippians." *The Living Word Commentary.* Austin, Tex.: R. B. Sweet Co. (1969).

Uses the Revised Standard Version. A verse-by-verse exegetical commentary by a modern conservative scholar. Stresses suggestions in the letter of Paul's concern for the Philippian church.

Harrison, Norman B., *His in Joyous Experience. Paul's Epistle to the Philippians.* Minneapalis: The Harrison Service (1926).

A non-technical, devotional unfolding of the epistle by means of an outline, chart, notes, and comments on the text. Characterized by devotional warmth and practical applications.

Hendriksen, William, "Exposition of Philippians." *New Testament Commentary.* Grand Rapids: Baker Book House (1962).

Prints author's own translation. A full introduction defends the Pauline authorship and unity of Philippians. A verse-by-verse treatment which combines accurate exegesis with practical application. Technical matters are relegated to footnotes.

Herklots, H. G. G., *The Epistle of St. Paul to the Philippians. A Devotional Commentary.* London: Lutterworth Press (1946).

A devotional verse-by-verse interpretation by a conservative Anglican minister. Abounds in interesting sentence quotations from a wide range of literature.

Johnstone, Robert, *Lectures Exegetical and Practical on the Epistle of Paul to the Philippians.* Grand Rapids: Baker Book House (1875; 1955 reprint).

A thorough conservative exposition abounding in apt illustrations and practical applications. The revised translation and notes on the Greek text following the lectures add to the importance of the volume.

Jones, Maurice, "The Epistle to the Philippians." *Westminster Commentaries.* London: Methuen & Co. (1918).

A very full introduction to the epistle is followed by a paraphrase and brief judicious verse-by-verse comments on the text. Significant discussion of the Christology of Philippians; supports Christ's full deity.

Jowett, John Henry. *The High Calling: Meditations on St. Paul's Letter to the Philippians.* London: Andrew Melrose (1909).

A series of thirty-nine expository meditations aimed at inspiring devotion and joy in the believer's daily life. The work of a noted English Congregational minister, author of many devotional books.

Kelly, William, *Lectures on the Epistle of Paul the Apostle to the Philippians, with a New Translation.* London: G. Morrish (reprint, n.d.).

A series of expository lectures by a voluminous Plymouth Brethren scholar of the past century.

King, Guy H., *Joy Way. An Expositional Application of the Epistle to the Philippians.* London: Marshall, Morgan and Scott (1952).

A devotional exposition of real merit in a rich homiletical style.

Lenski, R. C. H., *The Interpretation of St. Paul's Epistles to the Galatians, to the Ephesians, and to the Philippians.* Columbus, Ohio: Lutheran Book Concern (1937).

Lightfoot, J. B., *Saint Paul's Epistle to the Philippians.* London: Macmillan and Co. (1868; 1927 reprint).

Greek text. A standard commentary; deals thoroughly with grammatical and interpretative problems of the epistle. Contains an elaborate introduction and two lengthy dissertations (half of the volume) on "The Christian Ministry" and "Saint Paul and Seneca."

Martin, Ralph P., "The Epistle of Paul to the Philippians." *The Tyndale New Testament Commentaries.* Grand Rapids: Wm. B. Eerdmans Pub. Co. (1959).

The introduction deals with various critical problems concerning the epistle and presents a conservative view. The verse-by-verse exposition provides a full and clear unfolding of the message of the letter.

Michael, J. Hugh, "The Epistle of Paul to the Philippians." *The Moffatt New Testament Commentary.* London: Hodder and Stoughton (1929).

Prints the Moffatt translation, but offers a thorough study of the epistle on the basis of the original. Accepts Pauline authorship but denies the unity of the letter and posits an Ephesian origin of its contents. A provocative treatment by a liberal scholar.

Moule, Handley C. G., "The Epistle of Paul the Apostle to the Philippians." *Cambridge Bible for Schools and Colleges.* Cambridge: University Press (1889; 1934 reprint).

Verse-by-verse comments by a noted Church of England conservative scholar. Compact, clear, and informative.

Müller, Jac. J., "The Epistles of Paul to the Philippians and to Philemon." *The New International Commentary on the New Testament.* Grand Rapids: Wm. B. Eerdmans Pub. Co. (1955).

Robertson, A. T., *Paul's Joy in Christ: Studies in Philippians.* Revised and edited by W. C. Strickland. Nashville: Broadman Press (1959).

A popular exposition by a master of the Greek; technical matters are relegated to the footnotes. The work of a noted conservative New Testament teacher of the past generation.

Scott, Ernest F., and Wicks, Robert R., "The Epistle to the Philippians," *The Interpreter's Bible.* Vol. XI. New York: Abingdon Press (1955).

Prints King James and Revised Standard Versions at the top of the page. Introduction and exegesis by Scott; exposition by Wicks. Holds to the Pauline authorship and unity of Philippians. Liberal in its theological stance.

Vincent, Marvin R., "A Critical and Exegetical Commentary on the Epistles to the Philippians and to Philemon." *The International Critical Commentary.* Edinburgh: T. & T. Clark (1897; 1950 reprint).

Vine, W. E., *Epistles to the Philippians and Colossians.* London: Oliphants (1955).

Vos, Howard, *Philippians.* Grand Rapids: Zondervan Publishing House (1975).

A refreshingly full study guide on Philippians by a conservative scholar. Holds that the central theme of Philippians is an appeal for Christian unity and outlines the epistle on the basis of this approach. Excellent for individual or group study.

Wuest, Kenneth S., *Philippians in the Greek New Testament for the English Reader.* Grand Rapids: Wm. B. Eerdmans Pub. Co. (1942).

A simplified commentary on the Greek for the benefit of the English reader; seeks to convey the meaning of the original by means of an expanded translation with exegetical comments and word studies.

# *Part 4*

# ECCLESIOLOGICAL GROUP

*The Pastoral Epistles*

1 Timothy

Titus

2 Timothy

# 16

# AN INTRODUCTION TO THE PASTORAL EPISTLES

THE THREE LETTERS addressed to Timothy and Titus constitute the fourth and last group among the Pauline epistles. They were written in the closing years of Paul's life. They form a unit in that all of them give prominent consideration to matters of Church order and discipline. Hence they are properly described as the Ecclesiological group. They were addressed to two of Paul's trusted associates who at the time of writing stood in places of important ecclesiastical responsibility. Although they were directed to individuals and contain much that related directly to their specific task, the nature and importance of their contents gives them an abiding value for the Church as a whole. "It is scarcely likely their author anticipated that their mission would end in their private reception."[1] But it must not be supposed that they are general manuals of Church organization, Church discipline, or Church methods.

These three letters are now commonly designated as the Pastoral Epistles. The term was first used by D. N. Berdot (1703), and in 1726 P. Anton used it in the title of his commentary; it soon became a recognized designation in Germany, and has since attained universal currency. Although the term is convenient, it is not altogether appropriate.[2] It suits 1 Timothy and Titus quite well if the term is not used to misinterpret the position of these men. It is much less suitable to 2 Timothy, which is quite largely personal. The epistles contain more than is implied in the term.

Because they are addressed to individuals, these epistles were at

1. R. D. Shaw, *The Pauline Epistles,* (4th Ed., 1924 reprint), p. 425.
2. The terms "pastor," "shepherd," "flock," and "sheep" do not occur.

first separated from those written to churches and were grouped with Philemon as personal letters to Paul's friends. But with the recognition that these epistles had a definite bearing on Church life and practice, they were soon distinguished from Philemon, which deals with a personal matter. Philemon is not included in the term the Pastoral Epistles.

Before turning to a consideration of the individual epistles, it is necessary to consider briefly some problems relating to them as a group.

### THE AUTHORSHIP OF THE PASTORAL EPISTLES

Since the beginning of the nineteenth century the Pastoral Epistles have been a fierce battleground, being more severely attacked than any other Pauline writings. Schmidt in 1804 first suspected and Schleiermacher in 1807 positively denied the genuineness of 1 Timothy. But because of the close relation of the three epistles, it was inevitable that the arguments of Schleiermacher against the one would soon be applied to all three. Eichhorn and others followed by denying the genuineness of all. The battle has continued to rage, until today the scholars are divided into three camps. The conservative scholars refuse to surrender the fortress of the Pauline authorship of the epistles and continue to hold that they were written during the last years of Paul's life.[3] On the other hand the radical camp denies the Pauline authorship entirely, usually placing the epistles well within the second century.[4] Then there is the mediating group which seeks to strike a compromise between these two positions. While denying that the epistles are entirely by Paul, they yet admit that they contain fragments of genuine Pauline writings. They think that the epistles in their present form are the work of a later Paulinist who skillfully worked them up in the name of Paul.[5]

1. *Conservative position.* The conservative position has in its favor all the weight of the external evidence. Although these epistles were

3. See Donald Guthrie, *New Testament Introduction,* (1970), pp. 584-622; William Hendriksen, "Exposition of the Pastoral Epistles," *New Testament Commentary,* (1957), pp. 4-32.
4. See Edgar J. Goodspeed, *An Introduction to the New Testament,* (1937), pp. 327-344; Martin Dibelius and Hans Colzelmann, "The Pastoral Epistles," *Hermeneia,* (1972), pp. 1-10.
5. See Ernest Findlay Scott, *The Literature of the New Testament,* (1948 reprint), pp. 191-197; C. K. Barrett, "The Pastoral Epistles," *New Clarendon Bible,* (1963), pp. 4-12.

rejected by a few heretics like Marcion and Tatian,[6] the Church as a whole received them as from Paul and revered them for their authority and intrinsic value. The external evidence is so strong that Findlay can say,

> There is not a shred of historical evidence against the letters. The witness of the early Church to their place in the New Testament Canon and their Pauline authorship is as clear, full, and unhesitating as that given to the other epistles.[7]

Conservatives hold that the contents of these epistles agree with their asserted Pauline authorship. The writer's characterization of himself is distinctly Pauline. Who but Paul would have called himself an insolent person (1 Tim. 1:13) or the "chief" of sinners (1 Tim. 1:15)? He has the Pauline sense of the divine call and appointment (1 Tim. 1:12; 2:7; 2 Tim. 1:11). The doctrinal teaching is in harmony with Paul's doctrine. "He has the same conception of grace, redemption through the death of Christ, the purpose of the law, the Scriptures, the need of practical godliness, the universality of Christ's provision against sin, etc., as we find in the well-recognized Epistles of Paul."[8] The stress upon proper Church organization and discipline are in accord with the demands of the time; the rising tide of heretical teachings convinced Paul of the necessity of having the churches properly ordered and equipped if they were to be able to resist the ravages of these forces of evil.

The large number of personal names introduced into these epistles is very striking and offers a strong argument in favor of their genuineness. And they are not introduced as mere empty names but often represent already known figures. A forger would have taken refuge in generalities and would have put the desired teachings into the Apostle's mouth without running the risk of self-exposure by inventing such apparent historical details in the life of Paul or his companions.[9] If it is claimed that these notes were added to give the epistles the appearance of genuine letters, it must be replied that other writers who forged apostolic epistles did not feel that was a necessity. Known

6. Tatian is supposed to have rejected those to Timothy, but accepted Titus.
7. George G. Findlay, *The Epistles of Paul the Apostle,* (n.d.), p. 211.
8. Henry Clarence Thiessen, *Introduction to the New Testament,* (1943), p. 256.
9. For example, what forger would have dreamed of inserting the verse about Paul's cloak and the books and parchments left at Troas (2 Tim. 4:13)? Or, the suggestion to Timothy that he should be "no longer a drinker of water, but use a little wine" (1 Tim. 5:23)?

forgeries do not reveal such a liberal use of names.[10] The majority of the names used, while quite lifelike, do not appear in the rest of the New Testament. And the names that might have been drawn from known Pauline writings are often mentioned in connections such as a forger would little have guessed from their previous mention.[11]

In each epistle the writer calls himself Paul (1 Tim. 1:1; 2 Tim. 1:1; Tit. 1:1). If they are not from the pen of Paul, as they claim to be, then they are artful forgeries, written for the deliberate purpose of deception. Yet the very nature of these epistles is the greatest objection to such a supposition. In the words of Hervey,

> Is it possible to suppose that writings so grave, so sober, so simple and yet so powerful; breathing such a noble spirit of love and goodness, of high courage and holy resolves; replete with such great wisdom and such exalted piety; having no apparent object but the well-being of the Christian societies to which they refer; and so well calculated to promote that well-being; were written with a pen steeped in lies and falsehood? It is impossible to suppose it.[12]

Down through the centuries the Christian Church has always regarded the contents of these epistles as being in harmony with the Pauline authorship. Such peculiarities as they contain, it was felt, could be accounted for by the fact that they belonged to the closing years of Paul's life. Only since the beginning of the nineteenth century has the internal evidence been thought to be such as to discredit the Pauline authorship.[13] This uniform acceptance by the Church of the contents of these epistles as Pauline "can only be dismissed on the lofty presumption that until this late age they were never studied with any real insight or intelligence."[14]

If they were forgeries, where could a forger be found capable of producing them? There is nothing in the sub-apostolic writings

10. Cf. Theodor Zahn, *Introduction to the New Testament,* (1909), Vol. II, p. 123.
11. A forger, for example, might have taken the name of Demas from Col. 4:14 and Philem. 24; but after being listed with Luke as one of Paul's co-workers, what could have induced him to invent the sharp and unfavorable contrast between him and Luke in 2 Tim. 4:10-11? And what led him to associate him with Thessalonica?
12. A. C. Hervey, "I Timothy," *Pulpit Commentary,* (1950 reprint), p. ii.
13. The rejection of these epistles by Marcion and Tatian was based not on critical grounds but on the basis of their dislike for the doctrines that they contained.
14. R. D. Shaw, *The Pauline Epistles,* (4th Ed., 1924 reprint), p. 433.

comparable to them. Godet with rhetorical flourish thus states this fact:

> When one has had enough of the pious amplifications of Clement of Rome, of the ridiculous inanities of Barnabas, of the genial oddities of Ignatius, of the well-meant commonplaces of Polycarp, of the intolerable verbiage of Hermas, and of the nameless platitudes of the *Didache*,—and after this promenade in the first decade of the second century, reverts to our Pastoral Epistles, one will measure the distance that separates the least striking products of the apostolic literature from what has been preserved to us as most eminent in the ancient patristic literature.[15]

2. *Critical objections.* All criticism of the traditional view is based entirely on objections derived from the internal evidence. The attack in general proceeds along several lines.

(a). *Chronological.* The objection is made that these epistles cannot be fitted into any period of the Apostle's life known to us. The objectors assert that Paul was imprisoned but once in Rome, and since these epistles cannot be fitted into the Acts narrative it follows that they cannot be genuine. Some unsuccessful attempts have been made to find a place for them in the Acts period, but such attempts are now generally held to be futile. Knowling thinks that defenders of the epistles "would act wisely in giving up all attempts to fit them into any scheme of Paul's life which is covered by the Acts and the Apostle's acknowledged Epistles."[16] The objection, then, resolves itself into a question as to whether Paul was released from the imprisonment of Acts 28.

The burden of proof that Paul was not released from that imprisonment lies upon those who assert it. The epistles of the third group do imply his release. It was Paul's hope when he wrote to Philemon (v. 22) and his confident expectation when he wrote to the Philippians (1:25-26; 2:24). The Pastoral Epistles themselves bear strong witness to the release. Even though their Pauline authorship be denied, their very contents are witness to the early belief of the Church that he was released. The abrupt ending of Acts cannot be made to prove either the acceptance or rejection of his release. It is a gratuitous assumption that Paul was put to death at the close of the

15. F. Godet, "Introduction," p. 600, quoted in R. D. Shaw, *The Pauline Epistles*, (4th Ed., 1924 reprint), p. 441.
16. R. J. Knowling, *The Testimony of St. Paul to Christ*, (1905), p. 134.

two-year imprisonment mentioned in Acts. It would be contrary to Luke's references to the favorable attitude of the Roman governors to Paul. Christianity had not yet been declared a *religio illicita,* and according to Roman law there was no just reason for a sentence of death against him.

Tradition affirms the release of Paul. Such writers as Cyril of Jerusalem, Chrysostom, Theodoret, and Jerome all speak of Paul's trip to Spain, a thing impossible unless he was released. The Muratorian Canon (c. A.D. 170) speaks of Paul's going to Spain. Clement of Rome, writing about A.D. 96, says of Paul:

> After preaching both in the east and west, he gained the illustrious reputation due to his faith, having taught righteousness to the whole world, and came to the extreme limit of the west, and suffered martyrdom under the prefects.[17]

Some have sought to interpret the expression "the extreme limit of the west" to mean Rome itself. But Clement was in Rome, the center of the Empire, when he wrote, and it is highly improbable that he would speak of Rome as "the extreme limit of the west."[18]

There is no contrary tradition, nor is it easy to see what could have been gained by this one if it were not true. The references to Paul's movements in the Pastoral Epistles, as well as the tradition of the Church Fathers, find a ready solution if we accept the view that Paul was released.

(b). *Ecclesiastical.* It is asserted that the Pastoral Epistles reveal a stage of Church organization too far advanced for Paul's time. Obviously these epistles pay more attention to Church officers than any of Paul's previous epistles. But the references in them to bishops, elders, and deacons do not imply a monarchical episcopacy such as was advocated by Ignatius early in the second century. On the first missionary journey Paul had already ordained "elders in every church" (Acts 14:23); and in Philippians he addressed the church, "with the bishops and deacons" (1:1). The terms "bishop" and "elder" are used interchangeably (Titus 1:5-7). Thus the epistles speak of only two orders, not three, as in the second century. Further, "the pre-Christian Dead Sea Scrolls describe an officer in the Qumran

17. "The First Epistle of Clement to the Corinthians," ch. 5, in *The Ante-Nicene Fathers,* (1950 reprint), Vol. I, p. 6.
18. See William Hendriksen, "Exposition of the Pastoral Epistles," *New Testament Commentary* (1957), p. 27 and note 14.

community who bears remarkable similarity to the bishops who appear in the Pastorals. Instructions for the appointment of elders by Timothy and Titus (1 Timothy 5:22; Titus 1:5) are not due to advanced hierarchical Church government, but to the starting of new churches under missionary conditions."[19] The position which Timothy and Titus occupied as Paul's representatives was temporary and did not affect the organization of the local churches.

(c). *Doctrinal.* It used to be said that the heresies combated in the Pastoral Epistles belonged to the second century, but later research has shown that this position is untenable. It is asserted that such fundamental truths of Paul's Gospel as the believer's union with Christ, the power and witness of the Spirit, or reconciliation, are entirely lacking and could not have been omitted by Paul in three successive letters. But these doctrines are not entirely forgotten. (See 2 Tim. 1:9-11; 2:11ff; Titus 3:4-7; 1 Tim. 4:1; 2 Tim. 1:14; Titus 3:5; 1 Tim. 1:15; 2:6.) There was no need to dwell on these doctrines when writing to these trusted workers who were well acquainted with his teaching. Such an objection could be used to discredit large portions of the genuine epistles.

The attention to details of organization, it is held, is inconsistent with Paul's belief in the imminence of the Advent. In these epistles, it is said, Paul's conception of the work of the Church "as a short, intensive campaign in preparation for the Lord's return" gives way to "a longer perspective" which requires that "the churches must be definitely organized with responsible officers" so they will be able effectively to gird themselves for the long, long conflict that lies ahead.[20] But the writer of these epistles does believe in the nearness of the return; this is seen in his charge to Timothy to keep the commandment without reproach "until the appearing of our Lord Jesus Christ" (1 Tim. 6:14). And Paul's hope of the Lord's return did not make him so impractical as to be indifferent to the need for proper organization and discipline; witness his dealing with the Corinthian disorders.

It is asserted that Paul's characteristic use of the word *faith* to denote the believer's personal faith is replaced in these epistles by the objective use of the word to denote "the faith," almost in the sense of a creed. But this objective connotation of the word *faith* is not

19. Robert H. Gundry, *A Survey of the New Testament,* (1970), p. 324.
20. Edgar J. Goodspeed, *An Introduction to the New Testament,* (1937), p. 327.

wanting from the earlier epistles. Thus he speaks of preaching "*the faith* of which he once made havoc" (Gal. 1:23). See also Galatians 3:23; 6:10; Philippians 1:25, 27. And the subjective connotation of the word is not absent from these epistles (cf. 1 Tim. 1:14; 2:15; 3:13; 2 Tim. 1:13; 3:15). As in the earlier epistles, both senses of the word occur. Since in these epistles the stress is on the preservation of the truth that has been revealed, it is but natural that emphasis upon *the faith* should be prominent (1 Tim. 4:1; 5:8, 12; 6:10, 21; 2 Tim. 3:8; 4:7; Titus 1:13; 2:2; 3:15).

(d). *Linguistic.* The linguistic peculiarities of the Pastoral Epistles are considered one of the strongest arguments against their genuineness. It is said that the "significant absence of many characteristically Pauline terms" definitely points that way.[21] But Aherne, after examining this supposed list of Paul's favorite words absent in these epistles, concludes that their similar absence from some of the genuine epistles would equally discredit them. He asserts, "By a similar process, with the aid of a concordance, it could be proved that every Epistle of St. Paul has an appearance of spuriousness."[22]

Moffatt contends that "the difference in the use of the particles is one of the most decisive proofs of the difference between Paul and this Paulinist."[23] But a study of the other epistles shows that Paul's use of particles was not uniform. "Particles were required in the argumentative portions of St. Paul's Epistles, but they are used very sparingly in the practical parts, which resemble the Pastorals."[24]

Much is made by the critics of the fact than an exceptionally large number of words are found in these epistles which occur nowhere else in the Pauline writings. Due to variant readings, the scholars differ somewhat as to the exact number.[25] Workman found 168, and on calculating the average number per page, he discovered that 2 Timothy showed 11 and Titus and 1 Timothy showed 13.[26] This is about

21. James Moffatt, *An Introduction to the Literature of the New Testament,* (3rd Ed., 1949 reprint), p. 406. See the list in Moffatt.
22. C. Aherne, "Timothy and Titus, Epistles to," *The Catholic Encyclopedia,* (1940), Vol. XIV, pp. 727b-728a.
23. James Moffatt, *An Introduction to the Literature of the New Testament* (3rd. Ed., 1949 reprint), p. 407.
24. C. Aherne, "Timothy and Titus, Epistles to," *The Catholic Encyclopedia,* (1940), Vol. XIV, p. 728b.
25. Van Oosterzee, (*Lange Commentary, Pastorals,* p. 3), said 188; Findlay, (*Epistles of Paul,* p. 212), said 171; and Hervey, (*Pulpit Commentary, Pastoral Epistles,* pp. xx-xxii) lists 165; Thayer, (*Lexicon,* p. 706f.), 168.
26. Quoted by C. Aherne, pp. 728b-729a.

twice the average per page found in any other of Paul's epistles. But Aherne points out that these *hapax legomena* (words occurring only once) "are not evenly distributed over the Epistles; they occur in groups. Thus, more than half of those in Colossians are found in the second chapter, where a new subject is dealt with. This is as high a proportion as in any chapter of the Pastorals."[27]

This phenomenon of the occurrence of new words is common in literature. The use of unusual words is a variable quantity in any author. Workman has shown that the number of new words per page in Shakespeare varies all the way from 3.4 in *Julius Caesar* to 10.4 in *Hamlet*. Even greater divergencies in the occurrence of *hapax legomena* are found in the poetical works of Milton or Shelley.[28] Vocabulary is greatly influenced by the material being dealt with. New ideas require new words. As an educated man Paul had a large vocabulary at his command. And a study of the different groups reveals that he had a tendency to use an increasing number of new expressions as time went on. Workman found this same tendency in the writings of Carlyle.

One is reminded of the comment of Thayer in reference to his lists of words peculiar to individual New Testament writers:

> The monumental misjudgments committed by some who have made questions of authorship turn on vocabulary alone will deter students, it is to be hoped, from misusing the lists exhibiting the peculiarities of the several books.[29]

The style of the Pastorals is held to be un-Pauline. Moffatt asserts, "The comparative absence of rugged fervour, the smoother flow of words, and the heaping up of epithets, all point to another sign-manual than that of Paul."[30] The linguistic peculiarities of these epistles is admittedly one of the strongest arguments against Pauline authorship. Several suggestions have been advanced to explain them: 1) they are due to Paul's old age; 2) they can be explained by Paul's new environment during his Roman imprisonment; 3) he used a different amanuensis who was given considerable freedom in their

27. *Ibid.*, p. 729a.
28. See R. D. Shaw, *The Pauline Epistles*, (4th Ed., 1924 reprint), pp. 438f.
29. Joseph Henry Thayer, *A Greek-English Lexicon of the New Testament*, (1889), p. 689.
30. James Moffatt, *An Introduction to the Literature of the New Testament*, (3rd Ed., 1949 reprint), p. 407.

composition.[31] These suggestions contribute toward an explanation of the peculiarities but do not fully explain them. Hinson has recently advanced the view that a stronger case for Pauline authorship can be made by recognizing that "the Pastorals contain a large number of quotations and near quotations, some indicated by introductory formulas, taken from earlier sources."[32] This source criticism approach would ease the difficulty since Paul's style cannot be judged by these quoted materials. But there is the problem of identifying the quoted materials more fully.

White calls attention to the fact that early Greek Christian critics, who commented on "the un-Pauline style of Hebrews, and the un-Johannine style of the Apocalypse," yet never spoke of the "un-Pauline style of the Pastorals."[33]

3. *Integrity.* The mediating camp holds that "the Epistles cannot have come from Paul's hand in their present form, yet that they contain not a little Pauline material."[34] It is a compromise position necessitated by the unmistakable Pauline elements in the epistles. It is postulated that some brief notes from Paul, addressed most likely to Timothy and Titus, had fallen into the hands of a later admirer of Paul, and that using these fragments as a nucleus, he composed the present epistles and issued them in the name of Paul.[35] Who this remarkable person was we may never know, "since his pious aim was to sink himself in the greater personality of the apostle whose spirit he sought to reproduce."[36]

While accepting the presence of "genuine fragments" imbedded in these epistles, the critics are not agreed among themselves on their identity. The amount of Pauline material accepted varies with each writer.[37] 2 Timothy is held to contain the greatest amount.

It is evident that the conclusions of the critics are governed by their

31. George G. Findlay, *The Epistles of Paul the Apostle*, pp. 213-214; F. R. Montgomery Hitchcock, "The Latinity of the Pastorals," *Expository Times*, May 1928, pp. 347-352; J. N. D. Kelly, "A Commentary on the Pastoral Epistles," *Harper's New Testament Commentaries*, (1963), pp. 25-27.
32. E. Glenn Hinson, "1-2 Timothy and Titus," *The Broadman Bible Commentary*, (1971), Vol. 11, p. 300.
33. Newport J. D. White, "Introduction to the Pastoral Epistles," *Expositor's Greek Testament*, (n.d.), Vol. IV, p. 63.
34. Arthur S. Peake, *A Critical Introduction to the New Testament*, (1919), p. 71.
35. E. F. Scott, "The Pastoral Epistles," *Moffatt Commentary*, (1948 reprint), pp. xxii-xxiii.
36. James Moffatt, *An Introduction to the Literature of the New Testament*, (1949 reprint), p. 414.
37. Cf. James Moffatt, *Ibid.*, pp. 403-404 for the variations.

subjective standards of what is truly Pauline. Shaw tartly observes, "Each writer feels free to give the kaleidoscope a fresh turn, and then records with blissful confidence what are called the 'latest results.'"[38]

If these same subjective principles were to be applied to the writings of some modern authors, some strange and interesting results would be obtained. Shaw illustrates this as follows,

> Burns could never have written half the poems attributed to him; for there are "radical and inexplicable differences" in the very nature of the poet who wrote *Tam o' Shanter,* as compared with the other poet who wrote *To Mary in Heaven.* And not only so, some of the poems differ so wonderfully within themselves, that they cannot possibly be homogeneous or all from the same pen.

Shaw well concludes, "Surely it is time that such vagaries of criticism were laughed out of court."[39]

If these epistles are the result of the skillful combination and composition of a later follower of Paul and were published around the year A.D. 100, as Scott suggests,[40] would not the fact that at such a late date professedly genuine Pauline epistles were suddenly brought to light have raised suspicion and caused them to be carefully scrutinized as to their genuineness? But the universal favor with which they were regarded shows that they were received in all good faith as authentic. To believe that such a writer could have been able to palm off his productions on the Church without detection until modern times requires more credulity than to accept their Pauline authorship.

This hypothesis does not eliminate the moral issue in a forgery. It is frequently asserted that due to the literary standards of that day, "with quite a good conscience, a writer could issue as Paul's work these letters which contained only a few fragments of his actual composition."[41] Such a dictum is questionable. Even though such a thing may have been possible in later times when the Church became largely saturated with the vicious idea that the end justifies the means, it seems incredible that in Pauline circles with their high emphasis on truthfulness and honesty, such a thing should have been

38. R. D. Shaw, *The Pauline Epistles,* (4th Ed., 1924 reprint), p. 483.
39. *Ibid.,* p. 484.
40. Ernest Findlay Scott, *The Literature of the New Testament,* (1948 reprint), p. 194.
41. *Ibid.*

perpetrated. Paul's warning to the Thessalonians about forgeries in his name shows what he would have thought about it. (2 Thess. 2:2). Regardless of his pious intentions, such a pious fraud would have made the writer guilty of the vice, which he himself specially condemns, of "speaking lies in hypocrisy" (1 Tim. 4:2, A.V.).[42]

4. *Conclusion.* While admittedly the question of the authorship of the Pastoral Epistles presents perplexing difficulties, we conclude that to deny the Pauline authorship raises as serious difficulties as those which have been urged against the well-established tradition of their genuineness. Rutherfurd boldly concludes, "The Pastoral Epistles may be used with the utmost confidence, as having genuinely come from the hand of Paul."[43] That is the position here accepted.

### THE JOURNEYS OF PAUL IN THE PASTORAL EPISTLES

1. *Post-Acts.* A study of the references to Paul's travels found in the Pastorals compels the conclusion that they refer to a time following the close of the Book of Acts. They do not fit into the Acts narrative.

From 1 Timothy 1:3 we learn that Paul had gone from Ephesus into Macedonia and had left Timothy behind at Ephesus in charge of the work. In the epistle Paul requests him to remain there (1:3-4). The Acts and the previously written Pauline epistles offer no circumstances which can be made to fit these indications. Paul had been at Ephesus previously but under different circumstances. During the second journey he briefly touched Ephesus (Acts 18:19-21), but then he went to Syria and not into Macedonia. During the third journey he spent nearly three years at Ephesus (Acts 19:20-31). On leaving Ephesus Paul did go into Macedonia, but Timothy was not left behind at Ephesus with instructions to remain there. Timothy, whom Paul had previously sent into Macedonia, seems to have returned to Ephesus before Paul left there and was with Paul in Macedonia when Paul wrote 2 Corinthians (2 Cor. 1:1, 19). And Timothy appears to have remained in the company of Paul during the remainder of the trip to Jerusalem with the collection (Acts 20:4).

From 2 Timothy we learn that Paul had recently been at Troas,

42. For a discussion of the moral problem, see R. D. Shaw, *Ibid.*, pp. 477-482; Donald Guthrie, *New Testament Introduction,* (1970), pp. 671-684.
43. John Rutherfurd, "Pastoral Epistles, The," *International Standard Bible Encyclopaedia,* (1939), Vol. IV, p. 2262b.

Corinth, and Miletus (4:13, 20). When he wrote the epistle he was a prisoner in Rome (1:17), suffering imprisonment as a malefactor because of his relation to the Gospel (1:8; 2:9). We further learn that he had already made an appearance before the Imperial Court, and that, although he had escaped condemnation, he expected that his final condemnation and execution were not far off (4:6). He longed to see Timothy and hoped that he would be able to come to him before the end came (4:9, 21). This presents a situation quite different from that during the first imprisonment. Then he was treated with indulgence, being permitted to live "in his own hired dwelling" (Acts 28:30). Here he is imprisoned as "a malefactor" (2:9) and found by his friends only after diligent search (1:16-17). Then he confidently expected to be released (Phil. 1:25-26; 2:24); now he is anticipating death (4:6-8). The difference becomes intelligible on the assumption that it refers to a second imprisonment. The difference is due to the changed attitude of the Roman government.

From Titus we learn that Paul had recently been engaged in mission work on the island of Crete and had left Titus behind with instructions to complete the organization of the churches and to supervise the work there (1:5). Paul further informed Titus that he planned on spending the winter at Nicopolis and requested Titus to meet him there when a replacement worker arrived (3:12). The previous epistles hint of no work in Crete. The Acts knows of only one time when Paul touched the island of Crete—when on the way to Rome as a prisoner (Acts 27:8-13). But obviously that trip allowed no time for the work indicated in Titus, nor do we have any record that Titus was with Paul at that time. But the references are clear if they refer to a ministry subsequent to his first imprisonment in Rome.

We conclude that the references to Paul's journeys in the Pastorals refer to a time following his release from his imprisonment in Rome as recorded in Acts 28. It offers the best solution to the problem of the Pastoral Epistles.

2. *Tentative reconstruction.* The effort to reconstruct the journeys of Paul following his release from Rome is beset with great difficulty. We must agree with Farrar when he says, "We feel that our knowledge of his movements is plunged into the deepest uncertainty the

moment that we lose the guidance of St. Luke."[44] Efforts to reconstruct the course of Paul's travels have not produced agreement. The meagerness of the materials makes it impossible to reach unquestioned certainty on the arrangement of the data. Our reconstruction can at best only be probable.

Several problems present themselves in the attempt to outline Paul's journeys. Did Paul go to Spain from Rome before he revisited his churches in the East? Some scholars like Zahn,[45] think that he did. We think it more probable that he first revisited his churches in the East. The report of developments at Colossae would impress upon him the desirability of visiting them again before going to far-off Spain. His discovery of affairs at Ephesus doubtless confirmed the wisdom of this decision (1 Tim. 1:3-4, 19-20). Further, in view of the promise of a speedy visit to the church at Philippi (Phil. 2:24), as well as the promised visit to Colossae (Philem. 22), it seems improbable that Paul would postpone these visits until after the visit to distant Spain. Also, the work that Paul planned on doing in Spain would require considerable time. After having revisited the churches from which he had of necessity been separated for some years, he would be at liberty to extend his stay in Spain as necessary.

Did Paul revisit Ephesus itself? In Acts 20:25 we have the statement by Paul to the Ephesian elders that they would see his face no more. Advocates of the one-imprisonment theory have claimed that it made the theory of Paul's release untenable. Findlay, while accepting the view of Paul's release, felt that they made Paul's return to Ephesus itself impossible.[46] If Paul's words to the Ephesian elders were prophecy, uttered by divine revelation, any reconstruction that includes a visit to Ephesus would be impossible. But Paul's statement was not a prophetic utterance but simply his personal conclusion drawn from the Spirit's warnings that imprisonment awaited him in Jerusalem. Contrary to his natural expectations, Paul did return to Ephesus.

Where are these epistles to be placed in relation to the visit to Spain? The general practice is to place them as near the end of Paul's life as possible, hence all after the visit to Spain. This late date is

44. F. W. Farrar, *The Life and Work of St. Paul,* (1889), p. 650.
45. Theodor Zahn, *Introduction to the New Testament,* (1909), Vol. II, pp. 65-67. But cf. Vol. I, pp. 547-548.
46. George G. Findlay, *The Epistles of Paul the Apostle,* (n.d.), pp. 216-218.

generally thought to be demanded by the internal evidence. But that presents the highly complicated task of seeking to find a plausible combination of all the notices in the three epistles on this last journey to the East. Further, unlike 2 Timothy, 1 Timothy and Titus contain no hint that Christianity had yet been declared a *religio illicita.* The opposition encountered in these epistles bears no traces of being government inspired. This would suggest that 1 Timothy and Titus belong to the period before the beginning of the Neronian persecution, while 2 Timothy definitely belongs to that period. We, therefore, would place 1 Timothy and Titus before the visit to Spain and 2 Timothy after the return from Spain.

We would suggest the following tentative outline of events.

(1) The acquittal at Rome. This apparently occurred in the late spring of A.D. 63 and was in accordance with the hope expressed in the Prison Epistles (Philem. 22; Phil. 2:23-24).

(2) The sending of Timothy to Philippi. As soon as the outcome of the trial was announced, Paul dispatched Timothy to Philippi as he had promised (Phil. 2:19-23). Timothy probably took the land route, going along the Appian and the Egnatian ways to Philippi, stopping at Thessalonica with the news of Paul's release. He was apparently instructed to meet Paul at Ephesus.

(3) The journey to Asia. Probably Paul went directly to provincial Asia by sea. Arriving at Ephesus, Paul made a short visit there and then went on to Colossae, according to his promise to Philemon (Philem. 22), and to the neighboring churches in the Lycus valley.

(4) The return to Ephesus. At Ephesus Paul encountered some heretical teachers and found it necessary to attend to the expulsion of Hymenaeus and Alexander (1 Tim. 1:20). Timothy rejoined Paul at Ephesus. The situation in Asia apparently convinced Paul of the necessity of leaving Timothy there to repel the further development of the errors (1 Tim. 1:3-4).

(5) The journey into Macedonia. Leaving Timothy to supervise the work at Ephesus, Paul left for Macedonia (1 Tim. 1:3). He had hoped to return to Ephesus before long, but conditions might detain him for some time, so he wrote 1 Timothy from Macedonia (1 Tim. 3:14-15).

(6) The visit to Crete. Apparently Paul was able to return to Ephesus as he had planned. From Ephesus Paul went to Crete,

where apparently Titus was already at work. Because Paul could not stay there very long to continue with the work, he left Titus there to complete the organization of the churches and to repel the errorists in Crete.

(7) Journey to Corinth. From Crete Paul went on to visit the believers at Corinth. Here he came into touch with Zenas and Apollos who were planning a journey that would take them by Crete. Taking the opportunity thus afforded him, Paul wrote the Letter to Titus and sent it with them. In this letter he announced his plans to winter at Nicopolis and asked Titus to join him there when a replacement worker had been sent to Crete (3:12). The selection of Nicopolis reveals that Paul was planning a trip to the West in the spring.

(8) The journey to Spain. In the spring of A.D. 64 Paul left Nicopolis for work in Spain. He remained there perhaps two years. Thus Paul was away in Spain at the time of the burning of Rome (July 19-24, A.D. 64) and the beginning of the consequent persecution of the Christians, which Zahn thinks began in October of that year.[47]

(9) The return to the East. If Paul remained in Spain for two years, he would be returning to the East as soon as navigation opened up in the spring of A.D. 66. He would most likely avoid Rome and go directly to the East. Hints of some of the places visited on this journey are found in 2 Timothy. Mention is made of a visit at Troas with Carpus, with whom he left his cloak, and his books and parchments (4:13). He found it necessary to leave his companion Trophimus at Miletus because of sickness (4:20). He seems also to have been at Corinth where Erastus remained (4:20).

(10) The imprisonment in Rome. 2 Timothy reveals that Paul again became a prisoner. Where and when Paul was again taken into imprisonment is not revealed. Lewin contends that the fact that Paul left his books and parchments at Troas, materials vitally necessary for his missionary labors, shows that he was arrested at Troas.[48] Back East once more, his many enemies soon contrived to bring about Paul's arrest as a leader of the Christian sect, now officially branded as an illegal religion.

In 2 Timothy Paul is a prisoner in Rome for the sake of the Gospel (1:12, 17; 2:8-9). He is suffering imprisonment "as a malefactor"

47. Theodor Zahn, *Introduction to the New Testament,* (1909), Vol. II, p. 57.
48. Thomas Lewin, *The Life and Epistles of St. Paul,* (1878), Vol. II, pp. 369-370.

(2:9). The severity of the imprisonment must be ascribed to the changed attitude of the Roman government toward Christianity. Christianity had been declared a *religio illicita* and Christians were being regarded as enemies of the State. When writing 2 Timothy, Paul had already made one appearance before the Imperial Court but by his defense had escaped immediate condemnation. He had been remanded back to prison and did not anticipate a release (4:6-8, 16-17). His execution by beheading occurred before the end of the year, or soon after the beginning of A.D. 67.

### THE ORDER OF THE PASTORAL EPISTLES

Those who reject the Pauline authorship of the Pastoral Epistles hold that 2 Timothy is the earliest of the three. This is postulated on the basis of the fact that 2 Timothy is richest in personal allusions. These references are held to reflect the presence of genuine Pauline fragments, while the other two epistles are thought to be later, being more nearly free compositions after the manner of Paul. The greater definiteness in the description of the false teachers in 1 Timothy and Titus is also held to reflect a later period of development.

Accepting, as we do, the Pauline authorship of the Pastorals, 2 Timothy will naturally be placed last in the group. In it Paul is again in prison and not expecting release, while in 1 Timothy and Titus he is free to move about at will. On the question as to whether 1 Timothy or Titus comes first, there is little evidence on which to base a conclusion. That they were written not far apart is evident. It has been suggested that Titus as the shorter and simpler of the two is the earlier.[49] But that does not necessarily follow. The differences may be due simply to the differing circumstances on Crete and at Ephesus. Paul's statement in 1 Timothy 3:14 that he hoped to return to Ephesus "shortly" implies that it was written before Titus, since his return could not be "shortly" if he had already arranged "to winter" at Nicopolis (Titus 3:12). Our reconstruction of Paul's journeys also favors the common view that 1 Timothy was written first.

49. Walter Lock, "A Critical and Exegetical Commentary on The Pastoral Epistles," *International Critical Commentary,* (1924), p. xxxiv.

# 17

# FIRST TIMOTHY

## An Introduction to 1 Timothy

Because of his intimate and enduring friendship with Paul, the name of Timothy has been lastingly enshrined in the annals of the early Christian Church in connection with that illustrious Apostle. Timothy was one of Paul's most devoted and constant companions. His name is connected with all four groups among the Pauline epistles, the only companion so honored. No other name does Paul associate as often with his own in the salutations of his epistles as that of Timothy (1 and 2 Thess., 2 Cor., Col., Philem., and Phil.). And two of the three letters that compose the fourth group are addressed to him.

### THE ADDRESSEE OF 1 TIMOTHY

1. *Ancestry.* Timothy was a native, at least a resident, of Lystra, a Lyconian city in the Roman province of Galatia (Acts 16:1-3).[1] He was the son of a Greek father (Acts 16:1), apparently dead at the time of the story in Acts, and a Jewish mother, Eunice by name (2 Tim. 1:5). His name, which means "honoring God," or "honored by God," was apparently given him by his pious mother in the hope that he would exemplify it in later life. From a youth up he had received careful instruction in the Hebrew Scriptures from his loving mother and pious grandmother (2 Tim. 1:5; 3:15) and inherited their earnest faith. The marriage of Eunice to a Greek and the fact that Timothy was not circumcised as a child[2] apparently indicate an

1. That Timothy was a resident of Lystra, rather than Derbe, is evident from the fact that the brethren who commended him to Paul were from Lystra and Iconium, but no mention is made of Derbe. The same is implied in Acts 20:4, where Gaius is said to be of Derbe, but not Timothy.
2. The omission of circumcision may have been due to the objection of the father. See D. E. Hiebert, *Personalities Around Paul,* (1973), pp. 99-100.

absence of strict Jewish legalism, which, since it was not inconsistent with "unfeigned faith" (2 Tim. 1:5), must have made them openly receptive to the message of Paul.

2. *Conversion.* Timothy was apparently one of Paul's personal converts, won while Paul was at Lystra on the first missionary journey (Acts 14:8-20). That Paul considered Timothy his convert is evident from his language about him. In 1 Corinthians 4:17 Paul describes him as his "beloved and faithful child in the Lord." In 1 Timothy 1:2 he addresses him as "my true child in faith," and in 2 Timothy 1:2 as "my beloved child." Apparently Timothy's mother was also converted during that first visit to Lystra, for upon Paul's return to that city she is spoken of as "a Jewess that believed" (Acts 16:1)

3. *Call.* When Paul revisited Lystra on the second journey, Timothy was already an active Christian who had gained the approval and generous praise of the brethren in Lystra and Iconium (Acts 16:2). Paul was attracted to this earnest young worker and decided to take him along as his assistant on his journeys. Timothy and his mother acquiesced in Paul's desire. In order to remove any hindrances to Timothy's usefulness in the work of evangelization among the Jews, Paul took him and circumcised him as a matter of concession to Jewish prejudices (Acts 16:4). Before beginning the new life of traveling with Paul, Timothy was ordained to the ministry by the presbytery, Paul himself participating in it (1 Tim. 4:14; 2 Tim. 1:6).

4. *Work.* Timothy became one of the most constant companions of the Apostle. He was with Paul at Troas when the Macedonian Call was received and was in the group which began work at Philippi. It seems that he remained behind at Philippi on some mission for Paul and rejoined the Apostle at Beroea. He remained there with Silas when Paul was forced to flee (Acts 17:14). Upon Timothy's arrival in Athens Paul sent him back to Thessalonica to establish and comfort the believers there in their persecution (1 Thess. 3:1-2). He returned to Paul at Corinth (Acts 18:5) and was with him at the time that both of the letters to the Thessalonian church were written (1 Thess. 1:1; 2 Thess. 1:1). Following this we hear nothing more of him for about five years.[3]

We again hear of him as being with Paul at Ephesus during the third missionary journey. From Ephesus Paul sent him and another

3. Alfred Plummer, "The Pastoral Epistles," *Expositor's Bible,* (1903), p. 254.

assistant on a mission into Macedonia (Acts 19:22). From 1 Corinthians 4:17 and 16:10-12 it is apparent that Timothy was also to go on to Corinth. Scripture does not record his visit there. He apparently rejoined Paul at Ephesus before Paul left for Macedonia and was with him when he wrote 2 Corinthians in Macedonia (2 Cor. 1:1). Doubtless he accompanied Paul on his visit to Corinth. He was among the group of companions with Paul when he left for Jerusalem with the collection by way of Philippi (Acts 20:3-4).

We have no reference to Timothy during the two years that Paul was a prisoner in Caesarea. We again hear of him as being with the Apostle in Rome during his first imprisonment there. His name is joined with Paul's in the epistles to the Colossians and to Philemon. In the letter to the Philippians Paul promises to send him to Philippi as soon as he learns the outcome of his trial (2:19, 23). As soon as the verdict was announced, Timothy must have hurried on to Philippi, doubtless following the Appian Way to the Adriatic and then following the Egnatian Way across Macedonia to Philippi. Not long afterwards Paul must have left Rome on his way to revisit the churches in the East as he had promised (Philem. 22; Phil. 2:24). Timothy and Paul met again at Ephesus. When Paul left for Macedonia he left Timothy at Ephesus to supervise the work in his absence (1 Tim. 1:3).

In the Second Epistle to Timothy Paul summons him to Rome, hoping to see him once more before he dies (2 Tim. 4:9, 21). Nothing further is known about Timothy except the little note at the end of Hebrews, which reads, "Know ye that our brother Timothy hath been set at liberty; with whom, if he come shortly, I will see you" (13:23). Because of the uncertainty concerning the authorship and place of origin of Hebrews, the precise significance of that statement is problematical.

5. *Character.* The character of Timothy as set forth in the Scriptures is singularly attractive. He was of a tender and affectionate disposition and proved himself unswervingly faithful and loyal to Paul. He evidently was inclined to be somewhat timid and retiring, a feeling increased by his youthfulness (1 Cor. 16:10-11; 1 Tim. 4:12) as well as his lack of robust health (1 Tim. 5:23). He did not possess the bold aggressiveness that characterized Paul but was more reserved and reflective. Plummer suggests that the intimate friendship

between Paul and Timothy was due to the fact that in their differing natures each was a real complement of the other.[4] Paul leaned on Timothy while he guided and stimulated him. Timothy was specially close to him and seems to have caught the spirit and reflected the purposes of Paul in a remarkable way. Paul told the Corinthians that he had sent Timothy to them as the best means of putting them "in remembrance of my ways which are in Christ" (1 Cor. 4:17). That Timothy had the confidence of Paul is evident from the fact that he delegated to Timothy some very difficult and delicate tasks during the course of their prolonged association (1 Thess. 3:1-2; 1 Cor. 4:17; 1 Tim. 1:3). That Paul dearly loved Timothy is evident from the two epistles addressed to him. He was one of his most intimate friends, and when Paul's end drew near, it was Timothy that he yearned to have with him and for whom he specially sent (2 Tim. 4:9, 13).

From the directions and instructions given Timothy in his epistles, different failures and defects in Timothy's character have at times been inferred.[5] But these inferences may be wrong. The Scriptures do not specifically charge him with failure, and these assumptions seem rather unfair to him in view of his esteemed relation to Paul.

### THE OCCASION FOR 1 TIMOTHY

The occasion for 1 Timothy is evident from the epistle. Upon his return to Ephesus following his release at Rome, Paul had found that Ephesus was the storm center of false teaching, as he had predicted to the Ephesian elders (Acts 20:29-30). Paul had dealt with the leaders of the trouble (1:19-20), but, anticipating further trouble (6:3-5), had left Timothy in charge of the situation when he went into Macedonia (1:3). He had hoped to return soon, but it now appeared that he would be detained there longer than he had expected (3:14-15). Feeling that Timothy would need encouragement and authorization to proceed with the difficult task entrusted to him, Paul wrote this letter to him.

Timothy, like Titus on the island of Crete, was not the "pastor" of the church at Ephesus. The Ephesian church was under the lead-

4. Alfred Plummer, "The Pastoral Epistles," *Expositor's Bible*, (1903), pp. 19-20.
5. For example, from Paul's statement to Timothy to "stir up the gift of God" (2 Tim. 1:6), it has been inferred that Timothy was getting cold and needed reviving. But the tense of the original shows that Timothy is to keep stirring up the gift as he has been doing. It is not censure but admonition to continue as he has done in view of the difficult times ahead for him.

ership of its own elders (Acts 20:17). Neither was he the "bishop" with episcopal jurisdiction over a group of churches. That was a later ecclesiastical development. In the words of Zahn, "Timothy was acting as a temporary representative of Paul in his apostolic capacity at Ephesus, as he had done earlier in Corinth, and in Thessalonica and Philippi (1 Cor. 4:17; 1 Thess. 3:2f; Phil. 2:19-23)."[6] His was the task of supervising the organization, worship, and life of the various churches in Asia as the representative of Paul. His work did not affect the local organization of the churches.

### THE PLACE AND DATE OF 1 TIMOTHY

1. *Place.* This epistle was addressed to Timothy, stationed at Ephesus, sometime after Paul had left for Macedonia (1:3). He appears to be in Macedonia at the time of writing (perhaps at Philippi), but it is possible that he may have gone on to Greece when he wrote.

2. *Date.* The epistle must be dated after Paul's release from the imprisonment in Rome in the spring of A.D. 63. The exact date will depend upon the place assigned to it in the reconstruction of Paul's journeys following his release. If the letter was written, as many think, after Paul returned from Spain, the date would be near the end of his life. We think it more probable that it was written before the journey to Spain, hence within the first year after his release. We accordingly suggest the date as being in the early fall of the year A.D. 63.

### THE PURPOSE OF 1 TIMOTHY

The purpose of the epistle may be viewed from the standpoint of Timothy's personal position as well as from the standpoint of the churches in Asia generally.

1. *Personal.* Addressed to Timothy personally, the purpose of the epistle was, first of all, to aid Timothy in his difficult task. Paul seemingly felt that Timothy would need some explicit credential from himself, beyond that of a mere verbal commission, to enable him for a longer period to exercise the authority wherewith Paul had invested him as his personal representative. In his struggle with the heretical teachers, it was desirable that Timothy be able "to exhibit documentary proof of St. Paul's agreement with himself, and con-

6. Theodor Zahn, *Introduction to the New Testament,* (1909), Vol. II, pp. 34-35.

demnation of the opposing doctrines."[7] This the epistle would give him. Paul urges Timothy to devote himself to the task (4:15-16) and not to allow his youth to intimidate him (4:11-13). He holds before him a pattern for his personal life (4:6-16) and instructs him as to his attitude in his official work with various groups (5:1–6:5).

2. *Ecclesiastical.* In writing Paul also had the larger interests of the churches in mind. There was a negative task that Timothy had to perform. He had been left behind to check the evil influence exerted by certain would-be teachers there (1:3-7). Paul had already dealt with two of the leaders (1:18-20), but conditions had indicated that further trouble would be encountered (6:3-5). These false teachers seem to have been Gnostic Judaists.[8] They aspired to be "teachers of the law" (1:7), yet wholly misunderstood the real nature and function of the law (1:7-11). They wasted their energies on "fables and endless genealogies" (1:4) and revealed themselves as being "sick about questionings and disputes of words" (6:4, marg.). The teaching emphasized certain ascetic practices which Paul regarded as of very little practical value (4:8). And some of these teachers were tainted by covetousness and sought to turn their profession of Christianity into "a way of gain" (6:5). Because of the pernicious effects of this teaching (1:4; 6:4-5), the welfare of the Church necessitated that these teachers be refuted.

But Timothy was also to perform a constructive task in the churches. He was to engage in positive teaching (4:11, 16; 6:2b). He was exhorted to "pay close attention to the reading, to the exhortation, to the teaching" being carried on in the churches (4:13, Lenski). He was to give guidance concerning public worship (2:1-12) and instructions concerning proper qualifications for church leaders (3:1-13). The proper attitude to church leaders was to be inculcated (5:17-18), and he was to exercise care in selecting worthy leaders for the churches (5:19-25).

### THE CHARACTERISTICS OF 1 TIMOTHY

Although addressed to Timothy personally, this epistle is more than just a personal letter like Philemon. Because of the public posi-

7. W. J. Conybeare and J. S. Howson, *The Life and Epistles of Saint Paul,* (1949 reprint), p. 747.
8. Everett F. Harrison, *Introduction to the New Testament,* (1971), pp. 349-351; E. Glenn Hinson, "1-2 Timothy and Titus," *The Broadman Bible Commentary,* (1971), p. 302.

tion of Timothy, Paul doubtless felt that it would have a wider ministry. It is the most "pastoral" of the three epistles of this group. The personal matters which it contains are generally of such a nature as to allow an application to Christian workers elsewhere.

The contents of the epistle may be summarized under three chief topics: a pure Gospel, a worthy worship, and a faithful ministry. The epistle is not concerned so much with the elaboration of doctrine as with the practical application of sound doctrine to outward conduct.

The epistle contains several distinctive passages. In 2:1-4 we have a pivotal passage on the nature, scope, and effect of prayer as a definite part of the work of the Church. The unique statement in 3:16 gives a compact doctrinal summary of the work of Christ from His incarnation to His final glory. It is generally held that 3:16 and 6:15-16 are quotations from hymns sung in the Early Church (cf. Eph. 5:19). The statement concerning the "one mediator" in 2:5 is of profound doctrinal importance. The prophecy of the coming apostasy in 4:1-3 helpfully lays bare the source of false doctrine, a revelation widely neglected today.

The masterly passages concerning the Christian and his relations to material wealth (6:6-10, 17-19) have no parallel in the Pauline epistles. Dealing both with the rich and the would-be rich, they have a vital message for believers today.

The special peculiarity of this epistle, together with Titus, is its attention to the matter of church government. Chapter three gives the most detailed instructions concerning the qualifications of bishops and deacons found in Scripture. And the restriction upon the function of women in public worship (2:8-15) has left its definite mark on the history of the Church. And the instructions concerning the support of worthy widows (5:3-16) convey a timely impetus concerning the social obligations of contemporary churches.

## An Outline of 1 Timothy

### THE SALUTATION (1:1-2)

1. The writer (1)
2. The reader (2a)
3. The greeting (2b)

I. THE CHARGE TO TIMOTHY CONCERNING FALSE TEACHERS (1:3-20)

1. The charge to Timothy to preserve the purity of the Gospel (3-11)
   a. The nature of the charge (3-4)
      1) The impartation of the charge (3a)
      2) The contents of the charge (3b-4)
   b. The aim of the charge (5)
   c. The reason for the charge (6-11)
      1) The ignorance of the false teachers (6-7)
      2) The truth concerning the law (8-11)
         a) The nature of the law (8)
         b) The purpose of the law (9-10)
         c) The harmony of this with the Gospel (11)
2. The Apostle's thanksgiving for his relation to the Gospel (12-17)
   a. The thanksgiving for his call into God's service (12)
   b. The description of the one called (13a)
   c. The explanation for the appointment (13b-16)
      1) The appointment was due to God's grace (13b-14)
      2) The appointment was to make him an example of grace to others (15-16)
         a) The divine purpose in grace with mankind (15a)
         b) The divine purpose in grace through him (15b-16)
   d. The doxology of praise (17)
3. The renewal of the charge to Timothy (18-20)
   a. The committal of the charge (18a)
   b. The work of Timothy (18b-19a)
   c. The shipwreck of certain men (19b-20)

II. THE INSTRUCTIONS CONCERNING CHURCH ORDER (2:1–3:16)

1. The regulations concerning public worship (2:1-15)
   a. The duty of public prayer (1-7)
      1) The nature of public prayer (1a)
      2) The scope of public prayer (1b-2a)
      3) The result of public prayer (2b)

4) The basis for such prayer (3-7)
   a) It is good and acceptable to God (3)
   b) It is according to God's will (4)
   c) It is in accord with Christian doctrine (5-6)
   d) It is in accord with his ministry (7)

b. The manner of public prayer (8-10)
   1) The praying of the men (8)
   2) The adorning of the women (9-10)

c. The position of women in public worship (11-15)
   1) The command concerning the women (11)
   2) The restriction concerning women (12)
   3) The vindication of the restriction (13-15)
      a) The vindication from the order of creation (13)
      b) The vindication from the story of the fall (14-15)

2. The qualifications of Church officers (3:1-13)
   a. The qualifications of the bishop (1-7)
      1) The desirability of the office (1)
      2) The qualifications for the office (2-7)
         a) The first seven qualifications (2)
         b) The second seven qualifications (3-6)
            (i) In action toward others (3a)
            (ii) In personal disposition (3b)
            (iii) In home relations (4-5)
            (iv) In length of his Christian life (6)
         c) The qualification as to community standing (7)
   b. The qualifications for the deacons (8-12)
      1) The personal qualifications of the deacon (8-9)
      2) The testing of deacons (10)
      3) The qualifications of the women (deaconesses) (11)
      4) The domestic qualifications of the deacon (12)
   c. The reward for faithful service (13)

3. The personal word to Timothy in view of Christian truth (3:14-16)
   a. The purpose in writing to Timothy (14-15b)
   b. The nature of the Church (15c)
   c. The substance of Christian truth (16)

III. THE ADVICE TO TIMOTHY IN VIEW OF THE CHARGE (4:1–6:2)

1. His personal work in view of the apostasy (4:1-16)
   a. The objective warning against false teaching (1-5)
      1) The prediction of the coming apostasy (1a)
      2) The characterization of the apostates (1b-3a)
      3) The error of the apostates (3b-5)
         a) The divine creation of these things (3b)
         b) The true reaction to these things (4-5)
   b. The subjective fortification against error (6-16)
      1) The fortification through a faithful ministry (6-11)
         a) The characterization of the good minister (6)
         b) The activity of a good minister (7-9)
            (i) Negative—The refusal of myths (7a)
            (ii) Positive—The exercising of himself unto godliness (7b-9)
               (aa) The assertion of the superiority of godliness (8a)
               (bb) The ground for the superiority of godliness (8b)
               (cc) The seal of this superiority (9)
         c) The motivation of the good minister (10)
         d) The duty of the good minister (11)
      2) The fortification through becoming personal conduct (12-16)
         a) The personal duties of the minister (12-14)
            (i) To make his youth respected because of his example (12)
            (ii) To attend to the duties of the public ministry (13)
            (iii) To exercise and improve his gift (14)
         b) The exhortation diligently to fulfill these duties (15-16)
2. His official work with various groups (5:1–6:2)
   a. The attitude toward the different groups (5:1-2)
   b. The duty in regard to widows (5:3-16)
      1) The duty of supporting widows (3-8)
         a) The command to honor genuine widows (3)

b) The various classes of widows (4-6)
(i) The widow having children (4)
(ii) The widow who is a genuine widow (5)
(iii) The widow living in pleasure (6)
c) The instructions concerning parental support (7-8)
2) The instructions concerning the enrollment of widows (9-15)
a) The qualifications of those enrolled (9-10)
b) The rejection of the young widows (11-13)
(i) The command to reject young widows (11a)
(ii) The reasons for the rejection (11b-13)
c) The apostolic directive for young widows (14-15)
3) The duty of a believing woman (16)
c. The duty towards elders (5:17-25)
1) The directions concerning honor for the elders (17-18)
a) The statement concerning their honor (17)
b) The substantiation from Scripture (18)
2) The instructions concerning the trial of an elder (19-21)
a) The caution in receiving an accusation against him (19)
b) The judgment upon the sinning (20)
c) The impartiality in the judgment (21)
3) The advice concerning the ordination of elders (22)
4) The suggestion concerning Timothy's use of some wine (23)
5) The enunciation of principles for testing candidates (24-25)
d. The instructions concerning the slaves (6:1-2)
1) The duty of any man's slave (1)
2) The duty of the slave of a believer (2a)
3) The admonition to Timothy to teach these things (2b)

IV. THE CONCLUDING WARNING AND EXHORTATIONS TO TIMOTHY (6:3-21a)

1. The description of the false teachers (3-5)
a. The identification of the false teacher (3)
b. The verdict on the false teacher (4-5)
2. The relation of godliness and wealth (6-10)

a. The gain of true godliness (6-8)
   1) The abstract statement of the fact (6)
   2) The personal statement of the fact (7-8)
b. The danger to those seeking wealth (9-10)
   1) The nature of the danger (9)
   2) The reason for the danger (10a)
   3) The verification of the danger (10b)

3. The exhortation to an active life in view of Christ's return (11-16)
   a. The characterization of the person addressed (11a)
   b. The statement of the specific duties (11b-12)
   c. The restatement of the charge (13-16)
      1) The solemnity of the charge (13)
      2) The contents of the charge (14a)
      3) The termination of the charge (14b-16)
         a) The statement of the termination (14b)
         b) The explanation of the termination (15-16)
4. The charge concerning the rich (17-19)
   a. The persons to be charged (17a)
   b. The contents of the charge (17b-18)
      1) Negative—The dangers they are to avoid (17b)
      2) Positive—The duties they are to fulfill (18)
   c. The motive in carrying out the charge (19)
5. The final appeal to Timothy (20-21a)
   a. The positive appeal to guard the deposit (20a)
   b. The negative safeguard in rejecting the spurious (20b-21a)

THE BENEDICTION (6:21b)

## A Book List on the Pastoral Epistles

Barrett, C. K., "The Pastoral Epistles in the New English Bible." *New Clarendon Bible.* Oxford: Clarendon Press (1963).

Based on the New English Bible, but with constant critical reference to the underlying Greek text. Barrett maintains that these letters by an "unknown author" contain only genuine Pauline fragments, and that their primary value is their contribution to the theology of the Early Church.

Bernard, J. H., "The Pastoral Epistles." *Cambridge Greek Testament for Schools and Colleges.* Cambridge: University Press (1889; 1922 reprint).

Greek text. The introductions provide a satisfactory study of the problems connected with the Pastorals from a conservative viewpoint. The exegetical notes on the text of the epistles are thorough, thoughtful, and scholarly.

Brown, Ernest Faulkner, "The Pastoral Epistles." *Westminster Commentaries.* London: Methuen & Co. (1917).

A concise, conservative, phrase-by-phrase interpretation by a missionary in India who understands the positions of Timothy and Titus in the light of his own missionary experience.

Dibelius, Martin, and Conzelmann, Hans, "The Pastoral Epistles." *Hermenia–A Critical and Historical Commentary on the Bible.* Translated by Philip Buttolph and Adela Yarbro. Edited by Helmut Koester. Philadelphia: Fortress Press (1972).

Greek text. The work of two liberal German scholars which rests upon the assumption that the Pastorals are unauthentic and that form-critical "insights" are necessary for their exegesis. Contains a mine of technical information for the advanced student in the extensive footnotes and bibliographies. Of great value for the discerning student but barren for those seeking spiritual nurture from these epistles.

Fairbairn, Patrick, *Commentary on the Pastoral Epistles, I and II Timothy, Titus.* Grand Rapids: Zondervan Publishing House (1874; 1956 reprint).

Uses the Greek text of Tischendorf and the author's translation on facing pages. A voluminous (nearly 450 pages) exposition by a conservative Scottish theologian. Still worth consulting but devoid of the results of recent scholarship.

Gealy, Fred D., and Noyes, Morgan P., "The First and Second Epistles to Timothy and the Epistle to Titus," *The Interpreter's Bible.* Vol. XI. New York: Abingdon Press (1955).

Prints the King James and Revised Standard versions at the top of the page. Introduction and exegesis by Gealy, who proceeds on the assumption that the epistles are pseudonymous and to be dated A.D. 130-150. Holds that the primary purpose of the letters was to combat the heresies corrupting the Church, which must be viewed in a Marcionite-Gnostic context. More than the usual amount of space in this series is given to the exegesis of these epistles.

Guthrie, Donald, "The Pastoral Epistles." *The Tyndale New Testa-*

*ment Commentaries.* Grand Rapids: Wm. B. Eerdmans Pub. Co. (1957).

The noted evangelical British scholar maintains a happy balance between the extremes of being overly technical and frustratingly brief. Traces the thought of the Greek original through the King James for the ordinary Bible student.

Hendriksen, William, "Exposition of the Pastoral Epistles." *New Testament Commentary.* Grand Rapids: Baker Book House (1957).

Uses author's own translation. The introduction presents a competent treatment of the critical problems from a conservative viewpoint. A thorough, readable exposition, with a compact synthesis at the end of each chapter.

Hiebert, D. Edmond, "First Timothy." *Everyman's Bible Commentary.* Chicago: Moody Press (1957).

A non-technical, exegetical interpretation of 1 Timothy; a detailed outline included in the body of the volume aids the reader to keep in view the progression of the thought.

Humphreys, A. E., "The Epistles to Timothy and Titus." *Cambridge Bible for Schools and Colleges.* Cambridge: University Press (1895; 1925 reprint).

The introduction adequately treats the critical problems from a conservative position. Full and informative notes on the text; valuable appendixes.

Huther, Joh. Ed., "Critical and Exegetical Handbook to the Epistles of St. Paul to Timothy and Titus." H. A. W. Meyer's *Critical and Exegetical Commentary on the New Testament.* Translated from the fourth German edition by David Hunter. Edinburgh: T. & T. Clark (1893)

Greek text. A full exegetical treatment of these epistles by an evangelical German scholar of the past century. Scholarly and technical, providing references to scholarly views of the author's own times.

Kelly, J. N. D., "A Commentary on the Pastoral Epistles." *Harper's New Testament Commentaries.* New York: Harper & Row (1963).

Uses author's translation. An independent phrase-by-phrase interpretation by a distinguished British scholar. Favors Pauline authorship and dates the letters in the sixth decade of the first century. Shows how the letters throw much light on Paul's relations with his intimate co-workers and on the life of the first-century Church.

Kelly, William, *An Exposition of the Two Epistles to Timothy with a Translation of an Amended Text.* London: C. A. Hammond (1889; 1948 reprint).

A full, vigorous interpretation with a clear Plymouth Brethren emphasis.

Kent, Homer A., Jr., *The Pastoral Epistles, Studies in I and II Timothy and Titus.* Chicago: Moody Press (1958).

Good treatment of critical problems from a conservative viewpoint. The exegetical interpretation of the text avoids the technical while giving a full unfolding of the meaning of the original.

King, Guy H., *A Leader Led. A Devotional Study of I Timothy.* London: Marshall, Morgan and Scott (1951).

A fresh and vigorous devotional unfolding of the epistle with rich homiletical suggestiveness.

Lenski, R. C. H., *The Interpretation of St. Paul's Epistles to the Colossians, to the Thessalonians, to Timothy, to Titus, and to Philemon.* Columbus, Ohio: Lutheran Book Concern (1937).

Liddon, H. P., *Explanatory Analysis of St. Paul's First Epistle to Timothy.* London: Longmans, Green, and Co. (1897).

A careful grammatical analysis of the Greek text of 1 Timothy, consisting of an outline with notes and comments. Includes some good patristic references.

Lilley, J. P., "The Pastoral Epistles." *Handbooks for Bible Classes.* Edinburgh: T. & T. Clark (1901).

Uses author's own translation. A scholarly, conservative work giving a comprehensive discussion of the Pastorals as a group as well as the individual epistles. A verse-by-verse exposition characterized by spiritual warmth and practical appeal.

Lock, Walter, "A Critical and Exegetical Commentary on the Pastoral Epistles." *The International Critical Commentary.* Edinburgh: T. & T. Clark (1924).

Greek text. Lock leans to the conservative view but makes no pronouncements on the vexing critical problems. The notes on the Greek text are rather thin. Not up to the high standard of this series.

Oosterzee, J. J. Van, "The Pastoral Letters," J. P. Lange's *Commentary on the Holy Scriptures.* Translated from the German. Grand Rapids: Zondervan Publishing House (1863; reprint, n.d.).

The abundant material is in three sections: exegetical and critical; doctrinal and ethical; homiletical and practical. A full evangelical treatment by a Dutch Reformed minister and theologian of the past century.

Scott, E. F., "The Pastoral Epistles." *The Moffatt New Testament Commentary.* London: Hodder and Stoughton (1936; 1948 reprint).

Uses the Moffatt translation as the point of departure for the interpretation of the original. Scott concedes only scattered fragments of genuine Pauline material in the Pastorals, mostly in 2 Timothy. A readable commentary reflecting the author's advanced critical views.

Simpson, E. K., *The Pastoral Epistles.* Grand Rapids: Wm. B. Eerdmans Pub. Co. (1954).

Greek text. Presents a robust defense of Pauline authorship. The notes on the text are designed to give an adequate understanding of the original message, reinforced by a wealth of classical learning.

Spain, Carl, "The Letters of Paul to Timothy and Titus." *The Living Word Commentary.* Austin, Texas: R. B. Sweet Co. (1970).

Prints Revised Standard Version at the top of the page. A careful, phrase-by-phrase exegetical treatment by a conservative scholar. Suggests that Paul's use of Luke as his scribe may account for the linguistic features of these letters.

Vine, W. E., *The Epistles to Timothy and Titus: Faith and Conduct.* Grand Rapids: Zondervan Publishing House (1965).

Significant notes by a British Plymouth Brethren scholar of the past generation, developing the view that these letters were intended to give instruction concerning the character, testimony, and care of local churches.

Ward, Ronald A., *Commentary on 1 and 2 Timothy and Titus.* Waco: Word Books (1974).

Uses the Revised Standard Version, but refers to the Greek whenever felt necessary; the work of an evangelical Anglican preacher-scholar. The preacher and teacher are constantly kept in mind in the verse-by-verse interpretation of the meaning of the text.

Wuest, Kenneth S., *The Pastoral Epistles in the Greek New Testament for the English Reader.* Grand Rapids: Wm. B. Eerdmans Pub. Co. (1952).

Designed to put the reader of the English Bible into possession of some of the riches of the Greek through an expanded translation and Greek word studies. Does not deal with the critical problems of the Pastorals.

# 18

# TITUS

## An Introduction to Titus

Although one of Paul's intimate friends, Titus is never mentioned in the Acts. All that we know of him must be gathered from the references to him in the Pauline epistles. His name occurs only thirteen times in the New Testament, nine times in 2 Corinthians. Yet these scanty notices give us an attractive picture of the young man to whom Paul addressed the Epistle to Titus. He is seen to be one of Paul's devoted companions and a capable and trusted worker for the Lord.[1] It is a testimony to Paul's practical wisdom and foresight that he drew into association with himself such young men as Titus and Timothy in the work of the Gospel.

### THE ADDRESSEE OF TITUS

1. *Background.* By nationality Titus was a Greek (Gal. 2:3) and seems to have been converted to Christ directly out of heathenism. Since Paul addresses him as "my true child after a common faith" (Titus 1:4), it is evident that he was one of the Apostle's own converts. His home apparently was in Syrian Antioch. Humphreys conjectures that Titus as a lad was converted during that remarkable revival at Antioch under Barnabas and Saul mentioned in Acts 11:25-26.[2] At any rate, it is known that Paul took Titus along to the Jerusalem Conference as an example of his Gentile converts and used him as a test case at Jerusalem for the validity of his Gospel (Gal. 2:1-5). The fact that Titus was not compelled to be circumcised confirmed the position of Paul.

2. *Work.* We hear nothing about the work of Titus as Paul's asso-

1. D. E. Hiebert, *Personalities Around Paul,* (1973), pp. 114-122.
2. A. E. Humphreys, "The Epistles to Timothy and Titus," *Cambridge Bible for Schools,* (1925 reprint), p. 69.

ciate until on the third missionary journey. Apparently Titus remained at Syrian Antioch until Paul came through there at the beginning of the third journey (Acts 18:22). We may assume that Titus accompanied him on this journey from Antioch. It is at Ephesus that we first hear of him as one of Paul's assistants. It is in connection with his work at Corinth that he comes into the picture.

Apparently Paul sent Titus to Corinth on three different occasions. It seems that some time before the writing of 1 Corinthians Paul sent Titus to Corinth from Ephesus to initiate the project of the offering for the Judean saints (2 Cor. 8:6, 10). Following the writing of 1 Corinthians Paul again sent Titus to Corinth to learn the effects of that letter and to take a hand in straightening out the tangled affairs in that church. Titus had been instructed to meet Paul at Troas. When Titus failed to arrive at Troas as planned, Paul became deeply troubled about the possible turn of affairs at Corinth and left Troas for Macedonia, hoping thus the sooner to meet Titus (2 Cor. 2:12-13). In Macedonia Titus met Paul with the cheering news of the success of his difficult mission to Corinth (2 Cor. 7:5-7). Cheered by this welcome news, Paul wrote 2 Corinthians and dispatched it by the hand of Titus, accompanied by two other brethren (2 Cor. 8:16-24). Because the Corinthians had touched his heart, Titus readily accepted this return assignment. He was commissioned to complete the matter of the offering at Corinth (2 Cor. 8:6, 16-24). The success of Titus in dealing with this thorny Corinthian situation reveals his tact and ability.

Again there is a long blank in the history of Titus, for we hear no more of him until we come to the Pastoral Epistles. In the epistle addressed to Titus we learn that Paul had been engaged in mission work with him on the island of Crete. When Paul found it necessary to leave, he commissioned Titus to remain there as his representative to complete the organization of the Cretan churches and to repel the false teachers rampant on the island (Titus 1:5-16). When writing to him, Paul informs Titus of his plans to winter at Nicopolis and asks Titus to join him there as soon as someones arrives to take his place (3:12).

From 2 Timothy 4:10 we learn Titus was with Paul in Rome during his second imprisonment, but at the time of the writing of that letter he had gone to Dalmatia, evidently on an evangelistic errand for the Apostle.[3] With that passing reference Titus passes from the pages of Scripture.

3. *Character.* That Paul had a high esteem for Titus is seen from the fact that he speaks of Titus as his child, his brother, and his fellow-worker. Loving intimacy is reflected in Paul's address to Titus as "my true child after a common faith" (Titus 1:4). In speaking about his anxiety at Troas when Titus failed to arrive there as planned, Paul affectionately calls him "Titus my brother" (2 Cor. 2:13). In commissioning him to return to Corinth to complete the offering, Paul describes Titus as "my partner and *my* fellow-worker to you-ward" (2 Cor. 8:23). These expressions of love and esteem show that Titus was no ordinary man. From the difficulty of the tasks which Paul assigned to Titus it is evident that he "was not merely a good but a most capable man, tactful and resourceful and skillful in the handling of men and of affairs."[4] Titus must have been a man of strong affection, winsome personality, and devout enthusiasm. As a servant fully yielded to their common Lord, Paul loved and trusted Titus and used his abilities to great advantage.

### THE CHURCHES ON CRETE

1. *Location.* Titus, when Paul wrote to him, was working with the churches on Crete, an important island in the Mediterranean. Crete is one hundred and fifty-six miles long and about thirty miles at the broadest and lies due south of the Aegean Sea. The inhabitants of Crete had an evil reputation, a fact witnessed to not only by Paul (1:12-13), but also by Livy, Plutarch, Polybius, Strabo, and others.[5] Their falsehood was proverbial. The expression "to Cretize" was synonymous with "to lie," and "to play the Cretan with a Cretan" meant "to out-trick a trickster." Their morals were low. The wine of Crete was famous, and drunkenness prevailed. They were known as a turbulent people.[6] In such an environment were located the churches to which Titus ministered.

2. *Origin.* We have no record of how Christianity was first brought to Crete. There were many Jews of wealth and influence on Crete.

3. Cf. Theodor Zahn, *Introduction to the New Testament,* (1909), Vol. II, pp. 11-12.
4. John Rutherfurd, "Titus," *The International Standard Bible Encyclopaedia,* (1939), Vol. V, p. 2989b.
5. See Henry Alford, *The Greek Testament,* (1958), Vol. III, pp. 110-111 Proleg., for these testimonies in the original Greek.
6. David Smith, *The Life and Letters of St. Paul,* (n.d.), p. 614.

In Acts 2:11 we read of Cretans present in Jerusalem on the day of Pentecost. It is possible that some of these were converted and brought the Gospel back to Crete, but there is no record of that. It is evident that Paul had no opportunity to found any churches there when he briefly touched Crete on his journey to Rome (Acts 27:7-13). If there were Christians on the island at that time, he could have had little, if any, contact with them. Following his release at Rome, Paul was with Titus on Crete for some time. It would seem that Titus had already been at work there before Paul arrived. Paul remained there long enough to observe the distressing moral conditions and, no doubt, to make some converts. But it seems evident that he himself did not establish the churches. The letter to Titus contains not a single reference to what he had taught and preached on Crete. The churches seem already to have been in existence for some time, "but quite in their infancy of arrangement and formal constitution."[7] Titus was left behind to complete the organization of the churches (1:5).

3. *Conditions.* The emphasis upon worthy Christian conduct in the epistle implies that moral conditions in the churches were not what might be desired. The low standard of morality among the Cretans generally had doubtless had its adverse influence on the lives of the believers. Standards of morality consistent with the Christian faith needed to be stressed.

In their inadequately organized condition the Cretan churches were plagued with the presence of many false teachers. It appears that these were largely Jewish, "they of the circumcision" (1:10). They boasted of their special knowledge of God yet led a godless life (1:16). They brought forward their "Jewish fables, and commandments of men" (1:14), indulged in "foolish questions, and genealogies," and consumed their energies on points of controversy about the law (3:9, A.V.). Their work was causing divisions in the churches, drawing whole families into destruction (1:11).

### THE OCCASION FOR TITUS

The immediate occasion for the writing of Titus seems to have been the forthcoming visit of Apollos and Zenas to Crete (3:13). Paul took the opportunity thus afforded him to write to Titus. He was prompted to write because of his personal observation of condi-

7. Henry Alford, *The Greek Testament,* (1958), Vol. III, p. 109 Proleg.

tions on Crete and his realization that Titus would need the encouragement and authorization which the letter would give him.

Titus had been left in Crete as Paul's personal representative. Tradition has made Titus the first bishop and patron saint of Crete. But the position of Titus was not that of Bishop of Crete. His position was temporary, as seen from the fact that Paul was planning on sending another worker to replace him there (3:12). He was acting as the Apostle's representative, commissioned to carry on his apostolic office in the organization and supervision of the churches.[8]

### THE PLACE AND DATE OF TITUS

1. *Place.* The subscription to Titus in the King James Version reads, "It was written to Titus, ordained the first bishop of the church of the Cretans from Nicopolis of Macedonia." The statement as it stands is an accumulation of scribal additions and is not authoritative. It is based on the mistaken assumption that Paul was already at Nicopolis when he wrote. It is evident, however, that Paul had not yet reached Nicopolis at the time of writing but was planning on going there for the winter (3:12).

There is nothing in the epistle to prove where Paul was when it was written. The place assigned to it varies according to the conjectural course adopted of Paul's journeys after his release at Rome. Ephesus, Macedonia, and Corinth have been advocated. Our conjecture would be that it was written at Corinth, following his arrival there from Crete.

2. *Date.* The date, likewise, is bound up with the reconstruction accepted of Paul's journeys. Those who place it after the visit to Spain assign a date ranging from 65-67, usually only a short time before 2 Timothy. If it is placed on the journey East before going to Spain, it must be assigned to the first year after Paul's release. We would suggest that it was written from Corinth during the fall of A.D. 63 after his arrival there from Crete.

3. *Bearers.* That the letter was brought to Titus by Zenas and Apollos seems evident from the statement in 3:13. It is unlikely that they were working with Titus on the island before the letter arrived; then greetings to them would have been included. Nor could Paul have so entirely overlooked the work of a teacher so distinguished as

8. Theodor Zahn, *Introduction to the New Testament,* (1909), Vol. II, pp. 53, 89.

Apollos. The natural assumption is that they brought the letter to Titus and that the first stage of their journey brought them to Crete. From there, replenished and aided by Titus, they would resume their journey.[9]

#### THE PURPOSE OF TITUS

1. *Authorization.* One of the purposes of the epistle was to provide Titus with the needed written authorization for his work on Crete. Paul was aware that, having been left there as his representative, Titus would encounter opposition in carrying out the instructions given him. Some would despise him, as implied in the admonition, "Let no man despise thee" (2:15b). Others would openly reject him. This may be assumed from the explicit statement at the opening of the epistle that he had been left there to order the affairs of the churches (1:5), as well as from Paul's strong words about the false teachers: "whose mouths must be stopped" (1:11). The epistle, then, was intended to strengthen Titus personally and to arm him with apostolic authorization for his work "by placing in his hand written instructions to which he might be able to appeal, whenever the occasion should arise, in proof that he was not acting arbitrarily, but in accordance with positive Apostolic directions."[10]

2. *Instruction.* The epistle was further intended to provide Titus with specific instructions concerning his work in the churches. He is enjoined to appoint elders in the various churches who have the necessary moral and doctrinal qualifications (1:6-9), and this is urged as all the more important in view of the work of the false teachers there (1:10-16). He is also urged to insist on the need for sound teaching and a high type of moral living on the part of Christians (2:1-10; 3:1-3). This demand for consistent Christian living must be grounded in a personal faith in the basal truths of the Gospel (2:11-14; 3:4-8).

3. *Information.* The epistle also served to impart information to Titus personally. It served as Paul's message of commendation and instruction to him concerning Zenas and Apollos (3:13). It further informed Titus of Paul's decision to spend the winter at Nicopolis (3:12). Zahn lists nine cities by that name in various parts of the

9. Theodor Zahn, *Introduction to the New Testament,* (1909), Vol. II, p. 49.
10. J. J. Van Oosterzee, "The Epistle of Paul to Titus," Lange's *Commentary,* (1950 reprint), p. 2.

Roman world, commemorating some victory.[11] The Nicopolis Paul had reference to was located on the western shores of Greece, in the ancient Epirus. The city was founded by Augustus as a memorial of the victory over Mark Anthony at Actium. The letter also served to notify Titus that Paul was planning on sending either Artemas or Tychicus to replace him and that he wished for Titus to join him at Nicopolis.

### THE CHARACTERISTICS OF TITUS

While covering the same general ground as 1 Timothy, Titus is briefer and more compact. It is less personal than 1 Timothy and more official. The epistle contains less than seven hundred words in the Greek, yet, what words they are! Of it Luther said, "This is a short Epistle, but a model of Christian doctrine, in which is included, in masterly fashion, all that is necessary for a Christian to know and live by."[12]

In 1 Timothy the emphasis is more on sound doctrine, while in Titus the stress falls on worthy conduct. This is due to the different circumstances at Ephesus and Crete. Conditions in Crete caused Paul to stress godliness as befitting sound teaching and to insist that believers "adorn the doctrine of God our Saviour in all things" (2:10). Such godly behavior not only adorns the Gospel but safeguards it against being blasphemed (2:5). "This Epistle pre-eminently teaches us what effects the grace of God must show in our whole life."[13]

The epistle is characterized by classic summaries of Christian doctrine. The salutation of the epistle is loaded with doctrinal truth and for fullness is surpassed only by the opening sentence in Romans. The classic New Testament passage on the grace of God is found in 2:11-14. Its majestic sweep carries us from Christ's first advent to His final return in glory. It presents God's grace in its past, present, and future aspects. It pictures the Christian life both negatively and positively (v. 12). "Only the inspired wisdom of the greatest of the Apostles," says Farrar, "could have traced so divine a summary with so unfaltering a hand."[14] And in chapter three (4-7) we are given

11. Theodor Zahn, *Introduction to the New Testament,* (1909), Vol. II, pp. 53-54.
12. *Works of Martin Luther,* (1932), Vol. VI, p. 472.
13. Quoted in J. J. Van Oosterzee, "The Epistle of Paul to Titus," Lange's *Commentary,* (1950 reprint), p. 3.
14. F. W. Farrar, *The Life and Work of St. Paul,* (1889), p. 663.

"another concentrated summary of Pauline doctrine unparalleled for beauty and completeness."[15]

### An Outline of Titus

THE SALUTATION (1:1-4)

1. The writer (1-3)
   - a. The designation of his office (1a)
   - b. The nature of his office (1b)
   - c. The basis of his office (2-3a)
   - d. The function of his office (3b)
2. The reader (4a)
3. The greeting (4b)

I. CONCERNING ELDERS AND ERRORISTS IN CRETE (1:5-16)

1. The appointment of elders in the Cretan churches (5-9)
   - a. The duties of Titus in Crete (5)
   - b. The qualification of elders in the congregations (6-9)
     - 1) The general qualifications of the elder (6)
     - 2) The personal qualifications of the bishop (7-8)
       - a) The need for blamelessness as God's steward (7a)
       - b) The qualifications as God's steward (7b-8)
     - 3) The doctrinal qualification of the bishop (9)
2. The refutation of the false teachers in Crete (10-16)
   - a. The picture of the false teachers (10-13a)
     - 1) The character of the false teachers (10)
     - 2) The necessary refutation of the false teachers (11a)
     - 3) The effect of the seductive work of these teachers (11b)
     - 4) The justification for the severity (12-13a)
   - b. The exhortation to the churches concerning false teaching (13b-14)
   - c. The condemnation of the false teachers (15-16)
     - 1) The impurity of mind of the false teachers (15)
     - 2) The self-contradictory position of the false teachers (16)

II. CONCERNING THE NATURAL GROUPS IN THE CONGREGATIONS (2:1-15)

15. *Ibid.*

1. The instructions to the groups as to character and conduct (1-10)
   a. The duty of Titus properly to instruct the members (1)
   b. The instructions relative to various age groups (2-6)
      1) The instructions concerning the old men (2)
      2) The instructions concerning the old women (3)
      3) The instructions concerning the young women (4-5)
      4) The instructions concerning the younger men (6)
   c. The personal example of Titus (7-8)
      1) The duty to be an example of good works (7a)
      2) The directions concerning the nature of his teaching (7b-8a)
      3) The result of such an example (8b)
   d. The exhortation to the slaves (9-10)
      1) The attitude to be enjoined on slaves (9a)
      2) The conduct of the slaves (9b-10a)
      3) The motive for such conduct by slaves (10b)
2. The grace of God as the motive power for the Christian life (11-14)
   a. The manifestation of the grace of God (11)
   b. The instruction of the grace of God (12)
   c, The expectation of Christ's return (13)
   d. The summary of our redemption (14)
3. The restatement of the duty of Titus (15)

III. CONCERNING BELIEVERS AMONG MEN GENERALLY (3:1-11)

1. The obligations of believers as citizens (1-2)
   a. The obligation in relation to the government (1)
   b. The obligation in relation to citizens generally (2)
2. The motives for such a godly life (3-8a)
   a. The motive from our past life (3)
   b. The motive from our present salvation (4-7)
      1) The source of the salvation (4)
      2) The basis of the salvation (5a)
      3) The means of the salvation (5b-6)
         a) The washing of regeneration (5b)
         b) The renewing of the Holy Spirit (5c-6)
      4) The result of the salvation (7)

c. The motive from the connection between doctrine and conduct (8a)

3. The reaction of spiritual truth and error (8b-11)
   a. The evaluation of these things as profitable (8b)
   b. The attitude of Titus toward false teaching (9-11)
      1) His attitude toward false teaching (9)
      2) His attitude toward a factious man (10-11)

THE CONCLUSION (3:12-15)

1. The personal matters (12-14)
   a. The instructions concerning Titus himself (12)
   b. The instructions concerning Zenas and Apollos (13)
   c. The instructions concerning the Cretan Christians (14)
2. The salutations (15)
3. The benediction (16)

## A Book List on Titus

(See also the Book List under 1 Timothy.)

Hiebert, D. Edmond, "Titus and Philemon." *Everyman's Bible Commentary.* Chicago: Moody Press (1957).

Johnson, Philip C., "The Epistles To Titus and Philemon." *Shield Bible Study.* Grand Rapids: Baker Book House (1966).

Kelly, William, *An Exposition of the Epistle of Paul to Titus and of that to Philemon, With Translation of an Amended Text.* Denver: Wilson Foundation (1968 reprint).

Patterson, Paige, *Living in Hope of Eternal Life. An Exposition of the Book of Titus.* Grand Rapids: Zondervan Publishing House (1968).

Uses author's own translation. An exegetical verse-by-verse treatment from a conservative viewpoint by a young Southern Baptist minister. Breathes the practical insights of an effective witness for the Lord.

Taylor, Thomas, *An Exposition of Titus.* Grand Rapids: Christian Classics, (1658, reprint, n.d.), 325 pp.

A voluminous old Puritan phrase-by-phrase treatment, containing an abundance of material for those willing to persevere with the author in his elaborate development of doctrinal points and practical uses of the text.

# 19

# SECOND TIMOTHY

## An Introduction to 2 Timothy

Second Timothy has appropriately been called Paul's "swan song." In it we have the final, moving words of that mighty warrior of the cross as he faces death unafraid. It is the dying appeal of the Apostle to his young associate, exhorting him to steadfastness in the ministry in the face of appalling difficulties. It is the most personal of the Pastoral Epistles. It is rich in personal details and gives us a fitting closing picture of the dauntless messenger of Christ, tender and sympathetic, heroic and grand to the very end.

### THE HISTORICAL SITUATION IN 2 TIMOTHY

When 2 Timothy was written Paul again was a prisoner. He refers to himself as the Lord's prisoner (1:8), mentions the fact that he is chained (1:16), and says that he is suffering "hardship unto bonds, as a malefactor" (2:9). He is again in Rome. This is evident from Paul's statement that Onesiphorus had visited him "when he was in Rome" (1:17).

The references to his circumstances in the epistle make it evident that it cannot belong to the imprisonment mentioned in Acts 28. The circumstances of this imprisonment are quite different from conditions during the Acts imprisonment. At that time he was treated with considerable indulgence by the Roman government, being permitted to live "in his own hired dwelling" (Acts 28:30); now he is kept in close confinement and regarded as a "malefactor" (1:16; 2:9). Then he was accessible to all who wished to see him (Acts 28:30); now even Onesiphorus could find him only after diligent search and at personal risk (1:16-17). In his first imprisonment he was surrounded by a considerable circle of co-workers and friends (Acts 28:17-31; Col. 4:10-14; Phil. 1:13-14); in this imprisonment he is almost alone (4:11), and former friends are turning away from him (1:15). During the Acts imprisonment he confidently expected to be released (Phil. 1:25-26; 2:24); now he is looking forward, not to release, but to death (4:6-8). Thus the situation reflected in this epistle is seen to be vastly different from that during the first Roman imprisonment. It can only be explained on the assumption that Paul was released and later again apprehended and imprisoned in Rome. Second Timothy clearly belongs to the time following Nero's edict making Christianity a *religio illicita.* This changed attitude toward Christianity came about while Paul was away in Spain.

On July 19, A.D. 64, a great fire burst forth in Rome and raged incessantly for six days and seven nights. Further destructive fires followed a few days later. Half of the city's fourteen wards were razed to the ground, and only four wholly escaped the damages of the mighty conflagration.[1] Nero was at Antium when the fire broke out, but he hastened back to Rome and enjoyed the sight from a turret of his palace, singing "The Burning of Troy" to his guitar. Apparently well-founded rumors circulated freely that Nero had ordered the conflagration. Such was the testimony of some wretches who were caught deliberately spreading the fire. When various efforts of the Emperor failed to remove the odium of suspicion from him, Nero propagated the calumny that the Christians were the criminals and issued an edict that they should be arrested and punished.[2] Thus Christianity became a *religio illicita,* and in the savage persecutions that followed many Christians perished. Zahn thinks that this persecution began not before October of A.D. 64.[3] The reaction to Christianity soon spread to the provinces. When Paul returned to the East in the Spring of A.D. 66, his enemies, taking advantage of the turn of events against Christianity, soon contrived to bring about his arrest and imprisonment.

Because it had become a dangerous thing openly to espouse the cause of Christianity or to befriend its outstanding leader, many of Paul's former friends had evaded all contact with him. This shines out in Paul's statement that "all that are in Asia turned away from me"

1. Thomas Lewin, *The Life and Epistles of St. Paul,* (1878), Vol. II, p. 359.
2. Charles Merivale, *St. Paul at Rome,* (n.d.), pp. 147-148.
3. Theodor Zahn, *Introduction to the New Testament,* (1909), Vol. II, p. 57.

(1:15). Following his arrest, upon being charged with a capital crime, Paul had appealed to notable Christians in Asia, men familiar with his work and character, to come to Rome and testify in his behalf. But because of the apparent hopelessness of his case and the danger to themselves that it would incur, they all turned away from him, not daring to identify themselves with Paul. Thus, at his first trial before the Imperial Court, no one had dared to plead his cause (4:16). Men like Luke or Timothy could not have acted in this capacity, since they were Paul's assistants and had aided and abetted him in the alleged crime. Having no one to plead his cause, Paul took up his own defense, boldly confronted his adversaries, and repelled every accusation. The defense was successful; his testimony prevented a verdict of guilty. Paul was remanded to Prison and the case adjourned for further study by the court (4:17). Under these conditions he wrote 2 Timothy.

### THE OCCASION FOR 2 TIMOTHY

The occasion that called forth the writing of 2 Timothy may be viewed from the standpoint of Timothy as well as Paul.

1. *Timothy's need.* The epistle was largely prompted by the Apostle's fatherly concern for young Timothy. It was a dark day indeed for Timothy. He was painfully aware that his beloved teacher had been arrested and was facing certain death. The hostile attitude of the government to Christianity was terrifying indeed. Humanly speaking, the Church was trembling on the brink of annihilation. Only a man of unclouded faith in its divine destiny could foresee any other fate. Knowing his natural timidity, Paul had reason to be concerned lest the situation and the threatening prospects should overwhelm Timothy. "Timothy stood awfully lonely, yet awfully exposed, in face of a world of thronging sorrows. Well might he have been shaken to the root of his faith."[4] Thus Paul wrote to Timothy, knowing well that Timothy would need all the encouragement he could offer him to rally his courage and to keep him steadfast in that dark hour.

2. *Paul's yearning.* Viewed from Paul's own standpoint, the letter was prompted by his deep sense of loneliness. His heart craved for human sympathy and understanding love as he anticipated the hour

4. H. C. G. Moule, "The Second Epistle to Timothy," *Devotional Commentary,* (1905), p. 14.

of his martyrdom. He yearned to see Timothy once more and so wrote to ask him to come to him as soon as possible (4:9, 21). He also felt his need for the ministries of John Mark and requested that he be brought along (4:11). The prospects of the coming winter in a cold, damp dungeon made him think of his cloak which he had left at Troas. And the long, lonely hours of his imprisonment caused him to long to have with him the books and parchments he had left with Carpus (4:13). Thus Timothy's coming could also supply these personal needs.

### THE DESTINATION OF 2 TIMOTHY

Unlike the other Pastorals, 2 Timothy does not contain any clear indication as to Timothy's place of residence at the time. The contents of the epistle, however, point to the conclusion that Timothy was at Ephesus or somewhere in the vicinity. His presence in Ephesus is inferred from the fact that he is directed to salute the house of Onesiphorus (4:19). From 1:18 it appears that Onesiphorus was a resident of Ephesus. In 2:17 Hymenaeus is stigmatized as a teacher of false doctrine. He seems to be the same person whom Paul dealt with at Ephesus in 1 Timothy 1:19-20. The request that Timothy bring back Paul's cloak and the books and parchments left at Troas (4:13) reveals that he was at a place where his route to Rome would lead through Troas. In starting for Rome from Ephesus, Timothy would, by the quickest route, pass through Troas, to Philippi, and through Macedonia along the Egnatian Way. Further, in 4:11 Timothy is told to pick up Mark and bring him along to Rome. Our last notice of Mark was in the letter to the Colossians where Paul commended him to that church (Col. 4:10); Paul's statement to them may imply that Mark was to be a resident laborer in the Gospel among them. If Mark was at Colossae, he could easily be summoned from Ephesus to accompany Timothy to Rome. Timothy is also asked to salute Prisca and Aquila (4:19). When we last heard of them they were in Rome (Rom. 16:3), but with the burning of Rome and the resultant persecution there, it is quite natural to assume that they would again return to Ephesus. Since Timothy is urged to "do the work of an evangelist" (4:5), a term equivalent to itinerant missionary, it may be assumed that Timothy was engaged in this work in the province of Asia, having his headquarters at Ephesus. Since no other place seems better suited to meet these indications, we conclude that Timothy was stationed at Ephesus when 2 Timothy was written.

### THE PLACE AND DATE OF 2 TIMOTHY

1. *Place.* As already indicated, Paul was in prison in Rome when he wrote 2 Timothy. Paul's statement about the visit he had received from Onesiphorus "when he was in Rome" (1:17) identifies the place of writing.

2. *Date.* The epistle must be dated only a few months before Paul's death. If Paul returned from Spain in the early spring of A.D. 66, his arrest took place somewhere in the East, perhaps at Troas, during the summer of that year. In the letter Paul summons Timothy to Rome and urges him to come before the winter closes down all navigation on the Mediterranean. We would therefore date 2 Timothy in the early autumn of A.D. 66.

3. *Bearer.* It appears that Tychicus was the bearer of this letter. Although there is some ambiguity about the precise significance of the statement, this seems implied from Paul's words, "Tychicus I sent to Ephesus" (4:12). If the aorist is an epistolary aorist, as seems probable, it means "Tychicus I am sending to Ephesus." Then Tychicus not only would deliver the epistle to Timothy but was being commissioned to fill the position of Timothy during his absence.

### THE PURPOSE OF 2 TIMOTHY

1. *Encouragement.* Paul's primary object in writing this epistle was to encourage, strengthen, and instruct Timothy in his ministry. He urges him to suffer hardship "as a good soldier of Christ Jesus" (2:3). Three times in the epistle this note of suffering hardship is mentioned (1:8; 2:3; 4:5). He appeals to him to give himself to his ministry without fear or shrinking (1:7-8). Fear of personal danger is not to make him ashamed of the Gospel ministry; Paul is not ashamed to suffer for Christ, neither must he be ashamed (1:8-12). He must be bold to preach the Gospel in its fullness (4:1-2). This boldness is particularly necessary in view of the growing number of false teachers who, by their persuasive appeals to the itching ears of the people, will make his stand for the truth even harder (4:3-5). Paul is asking Timothy to come to Rome, but he is not sure that he will get there before his end comes. Therefore he sets forth these things in this

epistle. "The letter therefore is calculated in some measure to supply what his own mouth would, if he were permitted to speak to him face to face, still more fervently urge on him."[5]

2. *Summons.* Paul's further purpose is to summon Timothy to Rome as soon as possible (4:9, 21a). As the result of his first appearance before the court he has been remanded to prison for an indefinite time, yet he has no hopes of a release (4:17; 4:6-8). Ever yearning for the presence of his beloved Timothy in the loneliness of his imprisonment (1:4), he asks him to come to Rome with haste. Otherwise he may be too late. In coming he is to bring Mark along (4:11) and also bring the needed cloak and the books and parchments which he had left at Troas (4:13).

3. *Testimony.* But the epistle also offered Paul an opportunity to record his own valedictory. Having years ago been brought into right relation with God the Father through Jesus Christ as his Saviour and Lord, now, with a full life of service behind him, he can look death in the face unafraid. He can bear ringing testimony to the believer's triumph over life and death in Christ. There are no more beautiful words of Christian victory than those which the Apostle utters in view of his impending martyrdom:

> For I am already being offered, and the time of my departure is come. I have fought the good fight, I have finished the course, I have kept the faith: henceforth there is laid up for me the crown of righteousness, which the Lord, the righteous judge, shall give to me at that day; and not to me only, but also to all them that have loved his appearing (4:6-8).

### THE CHARACTERISTICS OF 2 TIMOTHY

1. *Last words.* 2 Timothy has that peculiar appeal that belongs to the last words of a great man. The epistle records his dying testimony and advice. As Timothy read these words, not knowing whether he would ever see his beloved teacher alive again, his heart must have been deeply stirred with the realization that this was the Apostle's dying legacy to him. The effect that the epistle must have produced on Timothy can hardly be adequately imagined. Its earnest and passionate appeals must have been irresistible. What comfort, strength, and new resolves must have come to Timothy as he read

5. Henry Alford, *The Greek Testament,* (1958), Vol. III, p. 104 Proleg.

the promises, warning, and affectionate admonitions of the epistle! And down through the centuries this priceless epistle has continued its ministry of giving strength and encouragement to discouraged and troubled workers, needed consolation to isolated missionaries yearning for human sympathy and Christian fellowship, and new inspiration to weary messengers of God confronted with seemingly insuperable obstacles and relentless antagonisms.

2. *General contents.* In many respects 2 Timothy is most unlike the First Epistle. There is hardly an allusion here to the question of church organization, a matter prominent in the First Epistle. In fact, the only reference to it is contained in the instructions, "And the things which thou hast heard from me among many witnesses, the same commit thou to faithful men, who shall be able to teach others also" (2:2).

The First Epistle was quite largely pastoral; this one is definitely personal. It is a personal appeal to Timothy himself in view of the appalling conditions confronting him. While making a strong entreaty for boldness, courage, and steadfastness, the Apostle does not picture the future in rosy and unrealistic colors. Paul faces life as it really is, yet he shows that Christ can give victory over every difficulty that may arise.

The epistle is rich in personal references. No fewer than twenty-three people are mentioned in this epistle, at least twelve of whom are never mentioned elsewhere. Four Christians are named as sending greetings to Timothy, one of whom is Claudia. Some expositors believe that she was a British princess.[6] A study of these various personal references shows that the epistle indeed constitutes a judgment seat. A number of them, like Onesiphorus (1:16-17), are mentioned with approbation, some, like Demas (4:10), with sorrow, and still others, like Alexander the coppersmith (4:14), with condemnation.

3. *Prophecies.* The epistle contains two definite prophetic utterances concerning the coming apostasy (3:1-6; 4:3-4). The fact of this apostasy lies in the background of the epistle. In this closing epistle Paul is given to see what will take place in the history of the Church. He foresaw that "grievous times" would come (3:1) when there would be a deliberate refusal to hear and accept the truth, but a ready acceptance of teachings to their liking (4:3-4). The result

6. See the full discussion on Claudia in Thomas Lewin, *The Life and Epistles of St. Paul,* (1878), Vol. II, pp. 392-397.

would be a professing church "holding a form of godliness, but having denied the power thereof" (3:5). The Apostle already saw the evidences of that apostasy in the growing number of false teachers in the churches (2:16-18; 3:6-7).

4. *Important passages.* Besides the two important doctrinal passages about the coming apostasy, the epistle contains some further statements of doctrinal importance. There is the vital statement concerning the inspiration and function of the Scriptures: "Every scripture is inspired by God and is useful for teaching, for reproof, for correction, and for instruction in right doing; so that the man of God may be complete, perfectly equipped for every good work" (3:16-17, Weymouth). There is, further, the admonition rightly to divide the word of truth (2:15, A.V.); also the passage about the firm foundation of God with its twofold seal (2:19). Of abiding interest is the sevenfold picture of the believer found in chapter two: a child (1), a soldier (3, 4), an athlete (5), a husbandman–farmer (6), a workman (15), a vessel (20, 21), and a servant (24). Of note also is the reference to different "lovers" in 3:2-4: "self-lovers," "money-lovers," "no-lovers-of-good," "pleasure-lovers," and "God-lovers."

The epistle further contains some very interesting personal references. Of great interest is the reference to Timothy's godly upbringing (1:5; 3:14-15). Paul's recognition of the courageous action of Onesiphorus is touching (1:16-18). Of unparalleled interest and importance is Paul's personal testimony to his assurance and hope in the face of imminent death (4:6-8). In these stirring words he reviews his whole life, present (6), past (7), and future (8). It will ever remain the classic expression concerning the triumphant death of the Christian. Although the Apostle is in very distressing circumstances, there is not a word of fear, complaint, or murmuring, but rather the confident shout of victory.

Of deep pathetic interest is Paul's request to have his cloak, and his books and parchments brought to him (4:13). Although this verse has been criticized as beneath the dignity of inspiration, its insertion gives us a glimpse of the Apostle's character we would otherwise have missed. He felt the need for his cloak, a sort of "overall" made of heavy material, to protect him against the cold and damp of the approaching winter.[7] But he is not only interested in his physical com-

7. See F. W. Farrar, *The Life and Work of St. Paul,* (1889), p. 682.

fort. He longs also for his books, especially the parchments, doubtless copies of the Old Testament Scriptures. At the end of life he has not lost interest in life; in the face of death he is still eager to read and to study. His busy life has not afforded him much time for such activity, but in his present confinement he longs to improve the long hours which hang heavily on his hands. It gives us a glimpse of the Apostle as a student and lover of books.

The request of the Apostle for his cloak and his books brings to mind a similar request made many years later by another eminent prisoner of the Lord, William Tyndale, written during the last winter of his life (1535-36). The letter, written by Tyndale from the damp cell of his prison at Vilvoorde, reveals that the great Bible translator's enthusiasm for his work remained unimpaired to the end, in spite of the rigor of a harsh and unjust imprisonment. His letter, addressed to someone in authority, possibly the Marquis of Bergen, reads as follows:

> I believe, right worshipful, that you are not unaware of what may have been determined concerning me. Wherefore I beg your lordship, and that by the Lord Jesus, that if I am to remain here through the winter, you will request the commissary to have the kindness to send me, from the goods of mine which he has, a warmer cap, for I suffer greatly from cold in the head, and am afflicted by a perpetual catarrh, which is much increased in this cell; a warmer coat also, for this which I have is very thin; a piece of cloth, too, to patch my leggings. My overcoat is worn out; my shirts also are worn out. He has a woollen shirt, if he will be good enough to send it. I have also with him leggings of thicker cloth to put on above; he has also warmer night-caps. And I ask to be allowed to have a lamp in the evening; it is indeed wearisome sitting alone in the dark. But most of all I beg and beseech your clemency to be urgent to the commissary, that he will kindly permit me to have the Hebrew Bible, Hebrew grammar and Hebrew dictionary, that I may pass the time in that study. In return may you obtain what you most desire, so only that it be for the salvation of your soul. But if any other decision has been taken concerning me, to be carried out before winter, I will be patient, abiding the will of God, to the glory of the grace of my Lord Jesus Christ; whose Spirit (I pray) may ever direct your heart. Amen.
>
> W. Tindalus.[8]

8. Quoted in F. F. Bruce, *The Books and the Parchments,* (1950), p. 9.

## An Outline of 2 Timothy

THE INTRODUCTION (1:1-5)

1. The salutation (1-2)
   a. The writer (1)
   b. The reader (2a)
   c. The greeting (2b)
2. The thanksgiving (3-5)
   a. The fact of his gratitude to God (3a)
   b. The reasons for his gratitude to God (3b-5)
      1) His memories concerning Timothy (3b)
      2) His longing for Timothy (4)
      3) His reminder of Timothy's faith (5)

I. THE EXHORTATIONS TO STEADFASTNESS IN THE MINISTRY (1:6–2:13)

1. The essential qualities of the steadfast minister (1:6-18)
   a. The zeal of the minister (6-7)
      1) The appeal for zeal (6)
      2) The incentive to zeal (7)
   b. The courage of the minister (8-12)
      1) The appeal for courage (8)
      2) The incentive to courage (9-12)
         a) The truths of the Gospel (9-10)
            (i) The saving act of God (9a)
            (ii) The gift of grace in Christ (9b-10a)
            (iii) The redeeming work of Christ (10b)
         b) The position and attitude of the Apostle (11-12)
            (i) His position in relation to the Gospel (11)
            (ii) His attitude in suffering for the Gospel (12)
   c. The steadfastness of the minister (13-18)
      1) The appeal for steadfastness (13-14)
         a) The exhortation to hold the pattern of sound words (13)
         b) The exhortation to guard the good deposit (14)
      2) The incentive to steadfastness (15-18)
         a) The desertion of those in Asia (15)
         b) The courageous example of Onesiphorus (16-18)
            (i) The prayer for the house of Onesiphorus (16a)

(ii) The ministry of Onesiphorus at Rome (16b-17)
(iii) The prayer for Onesiphorus (18a)
(iv) The ministry of Onesiphorus at Ephesus (18b)

2. The duties of the steadfast minister (2:1-13)
   a. The duty of personal strengthening (1)
   b. The duty of transmitting the truth (2)
   c. The duty of suffering steadfastly for the Gospel (3-13)
      1) The demands of the Christian life (3-7)
         a) The call to suffer hardship as a soldier (3)
         b) The pictures of the Christian life (4-6)
            (i) The picture of the soldier (4)
            (ii) The picture of the athlete (5)
            (iii) The picture of the farmer (6)
         c) The duty of understanding the pictures (7)
      2) The motivation for a life of suffering (8-13)
         a) The constant remembrance of Christ (8)
         b) The suffering of the Apostle for the Gospel (9-10)
            (i) The nature of his suffering for the Gospel (9a)
            (ii) The liberty of the Gospel (9b)
            (iii) The reason for his suffering for the Gospel (10)
         c) The certainty of the future reward (11-13)
            (i) The positive statement of the reward (11-12a)
            (ii) The negative warning as to the reward (12b-13)

II. THE EXHORTATIONS TO DOCTRINAL SOUNDNESS (2:14–4:8)

1. The minister's reaction to doctrinal error (2:14-26)
   a. The urgent activity amid doctrinal error (14-19)
      1) The nature of his activity amid doctrinal error (14-16a)
         a) His warnings against doctrinal error (14)
         b) His example as a master-workman (15)
         c) His shunning of profane babblings (16a)
      2) The reasons for his activity amid doctrinal error (16b-19)
         a) Because of the destructive effect of error (16b-18)
            (i) The effect on the errorists (16b-17a)
            (ii) The example of the working of error (17b-18a)
            (iii) The destructive effect of their error (18b)
         b) Because of the security of divine truth (19)

- b. The needed holiness of life amid doctrinal error (20-26)
  - 1) The picture of the mixed condition in the "great house" (20-21)
    - a) The two types of utensils in the great house (20)
    - b) The need for separation for a position of honor (21)
  - 2) The application to the minister's work (22-26)
    - a) The exhortation to personal purity of life (22)
    - b) The command to disdain foolish and ignorant questions (23)
    - c) The directions for dealing with those in error (24-26)
      - (i) The manner of his dealings with them (24-25a)
      - (ii) The purpose in his dealings with them (25b-26a)
      - (iii) The outcome of his dealings with them (26b)

2. The minister and the coming apostasy (3:1-17)
   - a. The prophecy concerning the apostasy (1-9)
     - 1) The announcement of the coming grievous times (1)
     - 2) The description of the coming apostates (2-5)
       - a) The description of their character (2-4)
       - b) The description of their religion (5a)
       - c) The believer's separation from such apostates (5b)
     - 3) The work of such apostates (6-9)
       - a) The description of the work of the apostates (6a)
       - b) The victims of the work of the apostates (6b-7)
       - c) The attitude and character of the apostates (8)
       - d) The limitation on the success of the apostates (9)
   - b. The power to meet the coming apostasy (10-17)
     - 1) The past association with Paul in his sufferings for Christ (10-13)
       - a) The reminder of the past sufferings (10-11)
       - b) The explanation for such sufferings (12-13)
     - 2) The stand in the power of the Scriptures for the future (14-17)
       - a) The experience of Timothy with the Scriptures (14-15)
       - b) The nature and function of the Scriptures (16-17)
3. The final charge to Timothy (4:1-8)
   - a. The charge to preach the Word (1-4)

1) The solemnity in making the charge (1)
2) The statement of the charge (2)
3) The reason for the charge (3-4)
 a) The coming of an apostate season (3)
 b) The character of the apostate season (4)

b. The charge to a sober fulfillment of his ministry (5-8)
1) The contents of the charge to Timothy (5)
2) The basis of the charge in Paul's impending death (6-8)
 a) The Apostle's present circumstances (6)
 b) The Apostle's retrospect of the past (7)
 c) The Apostle's prospect for the future (8)

THE CONCLUSION (4:9-22)

1. The Apostle's personal requests and reflections (9-18)
 a. His loneliness and need for assistance (9-12)
  1) The request for Timothy to come quickly (9)
  2) The explanation concerning his companions (10-11a)
  3) The instructions concerning Mark (11b)
  4) The statement about the sending of Tychicus to Ephesus (12)
 b. His directions concerning his cloak and books (13)
 c. His warning concerning Alexander the coppersmith (14-15)
 d. His experience at his first trial (16-18)
  1) The absence of patron friends at the trial (16)
  2) The strengthening presence of the Lord at the trial (17)
  3) The assurance concerning the future (18)
2. The salutations (19-21)
 a. The greetings to be delivered to his friends (19)
 b. The information about two of his companions (20)
 c. The request for Timothy to come before winter (21a)
 d. The greetings from friends at Rome (21b)
3. The benediction (22)

## A Book List on 2 Timothy

(See also the Book List under 2 Timothy.)

Berry, Harold J., *Gems From the Original, Vol. II, Studies in II Timothy*. Lincoln, Nebr.: Back to the Bible Broadcast (1975).

A verse-by-verse treatment seeking to share the riches of the Greek with the English reader. Greek terms are transliterated, and a knowledge of the original is not required.

Hiebert, D. Edmond, "Second Timothy." *Everyman's Bible Commentary.* Chicago: Moody Press (1958).

King, Guy H., *To My Son. An Expositional Study of II Timothy.* London: Marshall, Morgan and Scott (1944).

Moule, H. C. G., "The Second Epistle to Timothy." *Devotional Commentaries.* London: The Religious Tract Society (1905).

Marked by careful scholarship, spiritual insight, and reverent faith. One of the outstanding volumes of the series. Appended is a long poem by the author on the martyrdom of Paul.

Stott, John R. W., "Guard the Gospel." *The Bible Speaks Today.* Downers Grove, Ill.: Inter-Varsity Press (1973).

A fresh treatment by a conservative Anglican preacher-scholar. The volume has an announced threefold aim: to expound the text with accuracy, to relate it to contemporary life, and to be readable.

Woychuk, N. A., *An Exposition of Second Timothy, Inspirational and Practical.* Old Tappan, N.J.: Fleming H. Revell (1973).

A phrase-by-phrase conservative exposition by the founder and executive director of the Bible Memory Association. Rich in careful interpretation, historical references, and apt quotations from a wide variety of sources.

# BIBLIOGRAPHY

Note: The volumes listed in the various Book Lists are not included here, except as they are cited or referred to in the body of the text.

## I. BIBLICAL TEXT

### The Greek Text


Aland, Kurt; Black, Matthew; Metzger, Bruce M.; and Wikgren, Allen, *The Greek New Testament.* London: United Bible Societies (1966).

Nestle, Erwin, and Aland, Kurt, *Novum Testamentum Graece.* New York: American Bible Society (24th Ed.).

Westcott, Brooke Foss, and Hort, Fenton John Anthony, *The New Testament in the Original Greek.* New York: The Macmillan Co. (1935 reprint).


### English Versions


*American Standard—The Holy Bible Containing the Old and New Testaments.* New York: Thomas Nelson & Sons (1901).

Darby, J. N., *The 'Holy Scriptures,' A New Translation from the Original Languages.* Kingston-on-Thames, England: Stow Hill Bible and Tract Depot (1949 reprint).

King James—*The Holy Bible Containing The Old and New Testaments.* Cambridge: Cambridge Univeristy Press (n.d.).

Moffatt, James, *The New Testament, A New Translation.* New York: George H. Doran Co. (Revised Ed., n.d.).

Montgomery, Helen Barrett, *Centenary Translation, The New Testament in Modern English.* Philadelphia: The Judson Press (1924; 1964 reprint).

*New American Standard Bible.* Chicago: Moody Press (1973).

*New Berkeley Version—The Modern Language Bible.* Grand Rapids: Zondervan Publishing House (1969).

*New International Version—The Holy Bible, The New Testament.* Grand Rapids: Zondervan Publishing House (1973).

*Revised Standard—The New Covenant Commonly Called The New Testament of Our Lord and Saviour Jesus Christ.* New York: Thomas Nelson & Sons (1952).

Scofield, C. I., and others, eds., *The New Scofield Reference Bible.* New York: Oxford University Press (1967).

*The Twentieth Century New Testament, A Translation into Modern English.* Chicago: Moody Press (reprint, n.d.).

Weymouth, Richard Francis, *The New Testament in Modern Speech.* Newly revised by James Alexander Robertson. New York: Harper & Brothers (5th Ed., 1929).

Williams, Charles B., *The New Testament. A Private Translation in the Language of the People.* Chicago: Moody Press (1949 reprint).

## II. NEW TESTAMENT INTRODUCTION

Allen, Willoughby C., and Grensted, L. W., *Introduction to the Books of the New Testament.* Edinburgh: T. & T. Clark (3rd Ed., 1936 reprint).

Bennett, W. H., and Adeney, Walter F., *A Biblical Introduction.* London: Methuen and Co. (7th Ed., 1919).

Cambier, Jules, "The Second Epistle to the Corinthians," in A. Robert and A. Feuillet, *Introduction to the New Testament.* New York: Desclee Co. (1965).

Cartledge, Samuel A., *A Conservative Introduction to the New Testament.* Grand Rapids: Zondervan Publishing House (1938).

Cerfaux, Lucien, "The Epistle to the Galatians," in A. Robert and A. Feuillet, *Introduction to the New Testament.* New York: Desclee Co. (1965).

Clogg, Frank Bertram, *An Introduction to the New Testament.* London: University of London Press (3rd Ed., 1949).

Findlay, George G., *The Epistles of Paul the Apostle.* London: Robert Culley (4th Ed., n.d.).

Goodspeed, Edgar J., *An Introduction to the New Testament.* Chicago: University of Chicago Press (1937; 1945 reprint).

Gundry, Robert H., *A Survey of the New Testament.* Grand Rapids: Zondervan Publishing House (1970).

Guthrie, Donald, *New Testament Introduction.* Downers Grove, Ill.: Inter-Varsity Press (Revised Ed., 1970).

Harrison, Everett F., *Introduction to the New Testament.* Grand Rapids: Wm. B. Eerdmans Pub. Co (Revised Ed., 1971) .

Henshaw, T., *New Testament Literature in the Light of Modern Scholarship.* London: George Allen and Unwin (1952; 1957 reprint).

Heward, Percy W., *God's Letters to His Church.* London: The Bible Training College (1904).

Kerr, John H., *An Introduction to the Study of the Books of the New Testament.* New York: Fleming H. Revell Co. (13th Ed., 1931).

Knox, John, *Philemon Among the Letters of Paul.* Nashville: Abingdon Press (Revised Ed., 1959).

Kümmel, Werner Georg, *Introduction to the New Testament.* Translated by A. J. Mattill, Jr. Nashville: Abingdon Press (1966).

Lake, Kirsopp, and Lake, Silva, *An Introduction to the New Testament.* London: Christophers (1938).

Miller, Adam W., *An Introduction to the New Testament.* Anderson, Ind.: The Warner Press (2d Ed., 1946).

Moffatt, James, *An Introduction to the Literature of the New Testament.* Edinburgh: T. & T. Clark (3rd Ed., 1949).

Peake, Arthur S., *A Critical Introduction to the New Testament.* New York: Charles Scribner's Sons (1919).

Robert, A., and Feuillet, A., *Introduction to the New Testament.* New York: Descelle Company (1965).

Round, Douglas, *The Date of St. Paul's Epistle to the Galatians.* Cambridge: Cambridge University Press (1906).

Salmon, George, *An Historical Introduction to the Study of the Books of The New Testament.* London: John Murray (9th Ed., 1904).

Scott, Ernest Findlay, *The Literature of the New Testament.* New York: Columbia University Press (1932; 1948 reprint).

Scroggie, W. Graham, *Know Your Bible, A Brief Introduction to the Scriptures, Volume II, The New Testament.* London: Pickering & Inglis (n.d.).

Shaw, R. D., *The Pauline Epistles. Introductory and Expository Studies.* Edinburgh: T. & T. Clark (4th Ed., 1924 reprint).

Steinmueller, John E., *A Companion to Scripture Studies. Volume III. Special Introduction to the New Testament.* Houston: Lumen Cristi Press. (Revised Ed., 1969).

Tenney, Merrill C., *New Testament Survey.* Grand Rapids: Wm. B. Eerdmans Pub. Co. (Revised Ed., 1961).

Thiessen, Henry Clarence, *Introduction to the New Testament.* Grand Rapids: Wm. B. Eerdmans Pub. Co. (1943).

Weigle, Luther A., and others, *An Introduction to the Revised Standard Version of the New Testament.* No publisher given (1946).

Wikenhauser, Alfred, *New Testament Introduction.* New York: Herder and Herder (1963).

Williams, Charles B., *An Introduction to New Testament Literature.* Kansas City, Mo.: The Western Baptist Pub. Co. (1929).

Zahn, Theodor, *Introduction to the New Testament.* Vols. 1-3. Translated from the third German edition by J. M. Trout, W. A. Mather, L. Hodous, E. S. Worchester, W. H. Worrell, and R. B. Dodge under the direction and supervision of M. W. Jacobs, assisted by C. S. Thayer. Edinburgh: T. & T. Clark (1909).

III. NEW TESTAMENT COMMENTARIES

Alford, Henry, *The Greek Testament.* Vols. II, III. Chicago: Moody Press (1958).

Barmby, J., and others, "The Epistle of Paul to the Romans," *The Pulpit Commentary.* Grand Rapids: Wm. B. Eerdmans Pub. Co. (1950 reprint).

Barrett, C. K., "A Commentary on the First Epistle to the Corinthians," *Harper's New Testament Commentaries.* New York: Harper & Row (1968).

———, "The Pastoral Epistles in the New English Bible," *The New Clarendon Bible.* Oxford: The Clarendon Press (1963).

Beet, Joseph Agar, *A Commentary on St. Paul's Epistles to the Corinthians.* London: Hodder and Stoughton (1882).

———, *A Commentary on St. Paul's Epistle to the Galatians.* London: Hodder and Stoughton (1885; 5th Ed.).

Bernard, J. H., "The Second Epistle of Paul to the Corinthians," *The Expositor's Greek Testament.* Vol. III. Grand Rapids: Wm. B. Eerdmans Pub. Co. (reprint, n.d.).

Blunt, A. W. F., "The Epistle of Paul to the Galatians," *The Clarendon Bible.* Oxford: The Clarendon Press (1950 reprint).

Braune, Karl, "The Epistle of Paul to the Philippians," J. P. Lange's *Commentary on the Holy Scriptures.* Grand Rapids: Zondervan Publishing House (reprint, n.d.).

Brown, David, "The Epistle to the Romans," *Handbooks for Bible Classes.* Edinburgh: T. & T. Clark (1950 reprint).

Bruce, F. F., *The Acts of the Apostles.* London: The Tyndale Press (1951).

———, "Commentary on the Book of the Acts," *The New International Commentary on the New Testament.* Grand Rapids: Wm. B. Eerdmans Pub. Co. (1954).

Burton, Ernest DeWitt, "A Critical and Exegetical Commentary on the Epistle to the Galatians," *The International Critical Commentary.* Edinburgh: T. & T. Clark (1950 reprint).

Coltman, William G., *The Cathedral of Christian Truth—Studies in Romans.* Findlay, Ohio: Fundamental Truth Publishers (1943).

Davies, J. Llewelyn, *The Epistles of St. Paul to the Ephesians, the Colossians, and Philemon.* London: Macmillan and Co. (1884).

Denney, James, "St., Paul's Epistle to the Romans," *The Expositor's Greek Testament.* Vol. II. Grand Rapids: Wm. B. Eerdmans Pub. Co. (reprint, n.d.).

———, "The Second Epistle to the Corinthians," *The Expositor's Bible.* Vol. II. New York: A. C. Armstrong and Son (1903).

Dibelius, Martin, and Conzelmann, Hans, "The Pastoral Epistles," *Hermeneia—A Critical and Historical Commentary on the Bible.* Translated by Philip Buttolph and Adela Yarbro. Philadelphia: Fortress Press (1972).

Dodd, C. H., "The Epistle of Paul to the Romans," *The Moffatt New Testament Commentary.* New York: Ray Long and Richard R. Smith (1932).

Duncan, George S., "The Epistle of Paul to the Galatians," *The Moffatt New Testament Commentary.* London: Hodder and Stoughton (1948 reprint).

Eadie, John, *A Commentary on the Greek Text of the Epistle of Paul to the Colossians.* Edinburgh: T. & T. Clark (2d Ed., 1884).

———, *A Commentary on the Greek Text of the Epistle of Paul to the Ephesians.* Edinburgh: T. & T. Clark (1883).

Erdman, Charles R., *The Epistles of Paul to the Colossians and to Philemon.* Philadelphia: The Westminster Press (1933).

———, *The Epistles of Paul to the Thessalonians.* Philadelphia: The Westminster Press (1935).

Filson, Floyd V., and Reid, James, "The Second Epistle to the Corinthians," *The Interpreter's Bible.* Vol. X. New York: Abingdon Press (1953).

Findlay, G. G., and others, "The Epistle of Paul to the Colossians," *The Pulpit Commentary.* Grand Rapids: Wm. B. Eerdmans Pub. Co. (1950 reprint).

Findlay, G. G., "The Epistle to the Galatians," *The Expositor's Bible.* New York: A. C. Armstrong and Sons (1903).

———, "The First Epistle of Paul to the Corinthians," *The Expositor's Greek Testament.* Vol. II. Grand Rapids: Wm. B. Eerdmans Pub. Co. (reprint, n.d.).

Gloag, P. J., "The First Epistle of Paul to the Thessalonians," *The Pulpit Commentary.* Grand Rapids: Wm. B. Eerdmans Pub. Co. (1950 reprint).

———, "The Second Epistle of Paul to the Thessalonians," *The Pulpit Commentary.* Grand Rapids: Wm. B. Eerdmans Pub. Co. (1950 reprint).

Grant, F. W., *The Numerical Bible, Acts to 2 Corinthians.* New York: Loizeaux Brothers (1901; reprint, n.d.).

Harrison, Norman B., *His in Joyous Experience, Paul's Epistle to the Philippians.* Minneapolis: The Harrison Service (1926).

———, *His Very Own, Paul's Epistle to the Ephesians.* Minneapolis: The Harrison Service (1930).

Hendriksen, William, "Exposition of Colossians and Philemon," *New Testament Commentary.* Grand Rapids: Baker Book House (1964).

———, "Exposition of Galatians," *New Testament Commentary.* Grand Rapids: Baker Book House (1968).

———, "Exposition of the Pastoral Epistles," *New Testament Commentary.* Grand Rapids: Baker Book House (1957).

Hervey, A. C., "The Pastoral Epistles—I Timothy," *The Pulpit Commentary.* Grand Rapids: Wm. B. Eerdmans Pub. Co. (1950 reprint).

Hiebert, D. Edmond, *The Thessalonians Epistles. A Call to Readiness.* Chicago: Moody Press (1971).

Hinson, E. Glenn, "1-2 Timothy and Titus," *The Broadman Bible Commentary.* Vol. 11. Nashville: Broadman Press (1971).

Howson, J. S., "Galatians," *The Speaker's Commentary, New Testament. Vol. III.* London: John Murray (1881).

Hughes, Philip Edgcumbe, "Paul's Second Epistle to the Corinthians," *The New International Commentary on the New Testament.* Grand Rapids: Wm. B. Eerdmans Pub. Co. (1962).

Humphreys, A. E., "The Epistles to Timothy and Titus," *Cambridge Bible for Schools and Colleges.* Cambridge: University Press (1925 reprint).

Kelly, J. N. D., "A Commentary on the Pastoral Epistles, I Timothy, II Timothy, Titus," *Harper's New Testament Commentaries.* New York: Harper & Row (1963).

Kennedy, H. A., "The Epistle of Paul to the Philippians," *The Expositor's Greek Testament.* Vol. III. Grand Rapids: Wm. B. Eerdmans Pub. Co. (reprint, n.d.).

Knox, John, and Buttrick, George A., "The Epistle to Philemon," *The Interpreter's Bible.* Vol XI. New York: Abingdon Press (1955).

Knox, John, and Cragg, Gerald R., "The Epistle to the Romans," *The Interpreter's Bible.* Vol. IX. New York. Abingdon Press (1954).

Lange, John Peter, "The Epistle of Paul to the Romans," *Commentary on the Holy Scriptures.* Grand Rapids: Zondervan Publishing House (1950 reprint).

Lenski, R. C. H., *The Interpretation of the Acts of the Apostles.* Columbus, Ohio: Lutheran Book Concern (1934).

———, *The Interpretation of St. Paul's Epistles to the Colossians, to the Thessalonians, to Timothy, to Titus, and to Philemon.* Columbus, Ohio: Lutheran Book Concern (1937).

———,*The Interpretation of St. Paul's Epistles to the Galatians, to the Ephesians, and to the Philippians.* Columbus, Ohio: Lutheran Book Concern (1937).

———, *The Interpretation of St. Paul's Epistle to the Romans.* Columbus, Ohio: Lutheran Book Concern (1936).

———, *The Interpretation of St. Paul's First and Second Epistle to the Corinthians.* Columbus, Ohio: Lutheran Book Concern (1935).

Lightfoot, J. B., *Saint Paul's Epistles to the Colossians and to Philemon.* London: Macmillan and Co. (1900 reprint).

———, *Saint Paul's Epistle to the Galatians.* London: Macmillan and Co. (1910 reprint).

———, *Saint Paul's Epistle to the Philippians.* London: Macmillan and Co. (1898 reprint).

Lock, Walter, "A Critical and Exegetical Commentary on the Pastoral Epistles," *The International Critical Commentary.* Edinburgh: T. & T. Clark (1924).

Lohse, Eduard, "Colossians and Philemon," *Hermenia—A Critical and Historical Commentary on the Bible.* Translated by William R. Poehlmann and Robert J. Karris. Philadelphia: Fortress Press (1971).

MacKenzie, W. Douglas, "Galatians and Romans," *The Westminster New Testament.* London: Andrew Melrose (1912).

Maclaren, Alexander, "The Epistles of St. Paul to the Colossians and to Philemon," *The Expositor's Bible.* Vol. VI. New York: A. C. Armstrong and Son (1903).

Martin, Ralph P., "Colossians and Philemon," *New Century Bible Based on the Revised Standard Version.* Greenwood, S.C.: The Attic Press (1974).

Meyer, Heinrich August Wilhelm, *Critical and Exegetical Hand-Book to the Epistles to the Corinthians.* New York: Funk and Wagnalls (1884).

———, *Critical and Exegetical Hand-Book to the Epistle to the Ephesians.* New York: Funk and Wagnalls (1892).

———, *Critical and Exegetical Hand-Book to the Epistles to the Philippians and Colossians, and to Philemon.* New York: Funk and Wagnalls (1885).

———, *Critical and Exegetical Hand-Book to the Epistle to the Romans.* New York: Funk and Wagnalls (1884).

Milligan, George, *St. Paul's Epistles to the Thessalonians.* Grand Rapids: Wm. B. Eerdmans Pub. Co. (1952 reprint).

Moffatt, James, "The First and Second Epistles of Paul the Apostle to the Thessalonians," *The Expositor's Greek Testament.* Vol. IV. Grand Rapids: Wm. B. Eerdmans Pub. Co. (reprint, n.d.).

———, "The First Epistle of Paul to the Corinthians," *The Moffatt New Testament Commentary.* New York: Harper & Brothers (n.d.).

Morris, Leon, "The First and Second Epistles to the Thessalonians," *The New International Commentary on the New Testament.* Grand Rapids: Wm. B. Eerdmans Pub. Co. (1959).

Moule, C. F. D., "The Epistles of Paul the Apostle to the Colossians and to Philemon," *Cambridge Greek Testament Commentary.* Cambridge: University Press (1957).

Moule, H. C. G., "The Epistles of Paul the Apostle to the Colossians and to Philemon," *Cambridge Bible for Schools and Colleges.* Cambridge: University Press (1932 reprint).

———, "The Epistle of Paul the Apostle to the Romans," *Cambridge Bible for Schools and Colleges.* Cambridge: University Press (1881).

———, "The Second Epistle to Timothy. Short Devotional Studies on the Dying Letter of St. Paul," *The Devotional Commentary.* London: The Religious Tract Society (1905).

Neil, William, "The Epistle of Paul to the Thessalonians," *The Moffatt New Testament Commentary.* London: Hodder and Stoughton (1950).

Ockenga, Harold J., *The Comfort of God, Preaching in Second Corinthians.* New York: Fleming H. Revell Co. (1944).

Olshausen, Herman, *Biblical Commentary on the New Testament—The Epistle to the Romans.* Edinburgh: T. & T. Clark (1849).

Pearce, E. H., and Garvie, A. E., *The Study Bible—Galatians.* Garden City, N.Y.: Doubleday, Doran and Co. (n.d.).

Plummer, A., "The Epistles of St. John," *Cambridge Bible for Schools and Colleges.* Cambridge: University Press (1883; 1938 reprint).

———, "The Pastoral Epistles," *The Expositor's Bible.* New York: A. C. Armstrong and Son (1903).

———, "The Second Epistle of Paul the Apostle to the Corinthians," *Cambridge Greek Testament.* Cambridge: University Press (1912 reprint).

Ramsay, W. M., *The Letters to the Seven Churches of Asia.* New York: George H. Doran Co. (n.d.).

Rendall, Fredric, "The Epistle of Paul to the Galatians," *The Expositor's Greek Testament.* Vol. III. Grand Rapids: Wm. B. Eerdmans Pub. Co. (n.d.).

Robertson, A. T., *Paul's Joy in Christ.* New York: Fleming H. Revell Co. (1917).

Salmond, S. D. F., "The Epistle of Paul to the Ephesians," *The Expositor's Greek Testament.* Vol. III. Grand Rapids: Wm. B. Eerdmans Pub. Co. (n.d.).

Sanday, William, and Headlam, Arthur C., "A Critical and Exegetical Commentary on the Epistle to the Romans," *The International Critical Commentary.* New York: Charles Scribner's Sons (1902 reprint).

Scott, E. F., "The Pastoral Epistles," *The Moffatt New Testament Commentary.* London: Hodder and Stoughton (1948 reprint).

Stagg, Frank, "Philippians," *The Broadman Bible Commentary.* Vol. 11. Nashville: Broadman Press (1971).

Stifler, James M., *The Epistle to the Romans.* New York: Fleming H. Revell Co. (1897; reprint, n.d.).

Stoeckhardt, G., *Commentary on St. Paul's Letter to the Ephesians.* Translated into English by Martin S. Sommer. St. Louis: Concordia Publishing House (1952).

Strachan, R. H., "The Second Epistle of Paul to the Corinthians," *The Moffatt New Testament Commentary.* New York: Harper and Brothers (1935).

Thomas, W. H. Griffith, "St. Paul's Epistle to the Romans," *Devotional Commentary.* Grand Rapids: Wm. B. Eerdmans Pub. Co. (1946 reprint).

Thrall, Margaret E., "The First and Second Letters of Paul to the Corinthians," *The Cambridge Bible Commentary, New English Bible.* Cambridge: University Press (1965).

Van Oosterzee, J. J., "The Epistle of Paul to Titus," J. P. Lange's *Commentary on the Holy Scriptures.* Grand Rapids: Zondervan Publishing House (1950 reprint).

———, "The Two Epistles of Paul to Timothy," Lange's *Commentary on the Holy Scriptures.* Grand Rapids: Zondervan Publishing House (1950 reprint).

Vincent, Marvin R., "A Critical and Exegetical Commentary on the Epistles to the Philippians and to Philemon," *The International Critical Commentary.* Edinburgh: T. & T. Clark (1897; 1950 reprint).

White, Newport J. D., "The First and Second Epistles to Timothy and the Epistle to Titus," *The Expositor's Greek Testament.* Vol. IV. Grand Rapids: Wm. B. Eerdmans Pub. Co. (reprint, n.d.).

Williams, A. Lukyn, "The Epistles of Paul the Apostle to the Colossians and to Philemon," *Cambridge Greek Testament.* Cambridge: University Press (1928 reprint).

———, "The Epistle of Paul the Apostle to the Galatians," *Cambridge Greek Testament.* Cambridge: University Press (1910).

## IV. OTHER BOOKS

Adams, J. McKee, *Biblical Backgrounds, A Geographical Survey of Bible Lands in the Light of the Scriptures and Recent Research.* Nashville: Broadman Press (7th printing, 1943; Revised Ed., 1965).

Angus, S., *The Environment of Early Christianity.* New York: Charles Scribner's Sons (1932).

*The Ante-Nicene Fathers, Volume I. The Apostolic Fathers—Justin Martyr—Irenaeus.* Grand Rapids: Wm. B. Eerdmans Pub. Co. (1950 reprint).

Barrett, C. K., *The New Testament Background: Selected Documents.* New York: Harper & Row (1956; 1961 reprint).

Bernard, Thomas Dehany, *The Progress of Doctrine in the New Testament.* Introduction by Wilbur M. Smith. Grand Rapids: Zondervan Publishing House (reprint, n.d.).

Bruce, F. F., *The Books and the Parchments.* London: Pickering & Inglis (1950).

Carcopino, Jerome, *Daily Life in Ancient Rome.* New Haven, Conn.: Yale University Press (1940).

Cary M.; Denniston, J. D.; Duff, J. Wright; Nock, A. D.; Ross, W. D.; and Scullard, H. H., eds., *The Oxford Classical Dictionary.* Oxford: Clarendon Press (1949; 1957 reprint).

Conybeare, W. J., and Howson, J. S., *The Life and Epistles of St. Paul.* Grand Rapids: Wm. B. Eerdmans Pub. Co. (1949 reprint).

Deissman, G. Adolph, *Bible Studies.* Edinburgh: T. & T. Clark (1909).

———, *The New Testament in the Light of Modern Research. The Haskell Lectures, 1929.* Garden City, N.Y.: Doubleday, Doran & Co. (1929).

Farrar, F. W., *The Life and Work of St. Paul.* New York: E. P. Dutton and Co. (1889).

Finegan, Jack, *Light from the Ancient Past.* Princeton, N.J.: Princeton University Press (1946; Revised Ed., 1959).

Frank, Tenney, *A History of Rome.* New York: Holt, Rinehart and Winston (1923; 1964 reprint).

Gasque, W. Ward, and Martin, Ralph P., eds., *Apostolic History and the Gospel. Biblical and Historical Essays presented to F. F. Bruce on his 60th Birthday.* Grand Rapids: Wm. B. Eerdmans Pub. Co. (1970).

Goodspeed, Edgar J., *The Key to Ephesians.* Chicago: University of Chicago Press (1956).

———, *The Meaning of Ephesians.* Chicago: University of Chicago Press (1933).

———, *New Solutions of New Testament Problems.* Chicago: University of Chicago Press (1927).

Harrison, Everett F., ed., *Baker's Dictionary of Theology.* Grand Rapids: Baker Book House (1960).

Harrison, Norman B., *His Book, or Structure in Scripture.* Chicago: Moody Press (Revised, 1936).

Hiebert, D. Edmond, *Personalities Around Paul.* Chicago: Moody Press (1973).

Jackson, F. J. Foakes, and Lake, Kirsopp, eds., *The Beginnings of Christianity.* Vol. 5. Grand Rapids: Baker Book House (1966 reprint).

Josephus, Flavius, *The Life and Works of Flavius Josephus.* Translated by William Whiston. Philadelphia: John C. Winston Co. (n.d.).

Knowling, R. J., *The Testimony of St. Paul to Christ.* London: Hodder and Stoughton (1905).

Ladd, George E., *The Blessed Hope.* Grand Rapids: Wm. B. Eerdmans Pub. Co. (1956).

Lewin, Thomas, *The Life and Epistles of St. Paul.* Two vols. London: George Bell and Sons (1878).

Lockyer, Herbert, *Selected Scripture Summaries. Volume Two.* Grand Rapids: Baker Book House (1975).

Loetscher, Lefferts A., ed., *Twentieth Century Encyclopedia of Religious Knowledge. An extension of the New Schaff-Herzog Encyclopedia of Religious Knowledge.* Two vols. Grand Rapids: Baker Book House (1955).

Longenecker, Richard N., and Tenney, Merrill C., eds., *New Dimensions in New Testament Study.* Grand Rapids: Zondervan Publishing House (1974).

Luther, Martin, *Works of Martin Luther.* Philadelphia: Muhlenberg Press (1932).

MacDonald, William, *What's the Difference? A Study of Important Biblical Distinctions.* Kansas City, Kans.: Walterick Publishers (1975).

Manson, T. W., *Studies in the Gospels and Epistles.* Philadelphia: The Westminster Press (1962).

Martin, R. P., *Carmen Christi. Philippians ii. 5-11 in Recent Interpretation and in the Setting of Early Christian Worship.* Cambridge: University Press (1967).

——, *An Early Christian Confession. Philippians II. 5-11 in Recent Interpretation.* London: The Tyndale Press (1960).

Merivale, Charles, *St. Paul at Rome.* London: Society for Promoting Christian Knowledge (n.d.).

Moe, Olaf, *The Apostle Paul, His Life and His Work.* Translated by L. A. Vigness. Minneapolis: Augsburg Publishing House (1950).

Morgan, Jill, *A Man of the Word, Life of G. Campbell Morgan.* London: Pickering & Inglis (1951).

Myers, J. M.; Reimherr, O.; and Bream, H. N., *Search the Scriptures. New Testament Studies in Honor of Raymond T. Stamm.* Leiden: E. J. Brill (1969).

Paley, William, *Horae Paulinae; or The Truth of the Scripture History of St. Paul Evinced.* New York: Robert Carter and Brothers (n.d.).

Purves, George T., *Christianity in the Apostolic Age.* Grand Rapids: Baker Book House (1900; 1955 reprint).

Ramsay, W. M., *The Church in the Roman Empire Before A.D. 170.* New York: G. P. Putnam's Sons (1919).

———, *St. Paul the Traveller and the Roman Citizen.* New York: G. P. Putnam's Sons (14th impression, n.d.).

Reicke, Bo, "Caesarea, Rome, and the Captivity Epistles," in *Apostolic History and the Gospel,* W. Ward Gasque and Ralph P. Martin, eds. Grand Rapids: Wm. B. Eerdmans Pub. Co. (1970).

Schaff, Philip, *History of the Christian Church.* Vol. I. New York: Charles Scribner's Sons (3rd revision, 1910).

Smith, David, *The Life and Letters of St. Paul.* New York: Harper and Brothers (n.d.).

Stirewalt, M. Luther, Jr., "Paul's Evaluation of Letter-Writing," in *Search The Scriptures, New Testament Studies in Honor of Raymond T. Stamm.* J. M. Myers; O. Reimherr; and H. N. Bream, eds. Leidon: E. J. Brill (1969).

Thayer, Joseph Henry, *A Greek-English Lexicon of the New Testament.* New York: American Book Co. (1889; reprint, n.d.).

Tucker, T. G., *Life in the Roman World of Nero and St. Paul.* London: Macmillan and Co. (1910).

Unger, Merrill F., *Archaeology and the New Testament.* Grand Rapids: Zondervan Publishing House (1962).

Walvoord, John F., *The Rapture Question.* Grand Rapids: Zondervan Publishing House (1957; 1972 reprint).

## V. DICTIONARY AND ENCYCLOPEDIA ARTICLES

Aherne, C., "Timothy and Titus, Epistles to," in *The Catholic Encyclopedia.* New York: The Gilmary Society (1940), Vol. XIV, pp. 727-733.

Baker, G. W., "Ephesians, Letter of Paul to the," in *The Zondervan Pictorial Encyclopedia of the Bible,* Merrill C. Tenney, ed. Grand Rapids: Zondervan Publishing House (1975), Vol. II, pp. 316-324.

Bruce, F. F., "Corinthians, First Epistle to the," in *The Zondervan Pictorial Encyclopedia of the Bible,* Merrill C. Tenney, ed. Grand Rapids: Zondervan Publishing House (1975), Vol. I, pp. 964-972.

Castelot, J. J., "Peter, Apostle, St." in *New Catholic Encyclopedia.* New York: McGraw-Hill Book Co. (1967), Vol. XI, pp. 200-205.

Davis, William David, "Paul the Apostle," in *Twentieth Century Encyclopedia.* Lefferts A. Loetscher, ed. Grand Rapids: Baker Book House (1955), Vol. II, pp. 854-856.

Drum, Walter, "Thessalonians, Epistles to the," in *The Catholic Encyclopedia.* New York: The Gilmary Society (1940), Vol. XIV, pp. 629-633.

Fausset, A. R. "Epistle," *Bible Cyclopaedia, Critical and Expository.* Hartford, Conn.: The S. S. Scranton Co. (1902), pp. 210-211.

———, "Paul," *Bible Cyclopaedia, Critical and Expository*. Hartford, Conn.: The S. S. Scranton Co. (1902), pp. 543-551.

Findlay, George G., "Galatians, Epistle to the," in *The International Standard Bible Encyclopaedia,* James Orr, ed. Grand Rapids: Wm. B. Eerdmans Pub. Co. (1939), Vol. 2, pp. 1155-1163.

Harrison, Everett F., "Rapture," in *Baker's Dictionary of Theology,* Everett F. Harrison, ed. Grand Rapids: Baker Book House (1960), pp. 433-434.

Hayes, Doremus Almy, "Philippians, The Epistle to," in *The International Standard Bible Encyclopaedia*. James Orr, ed. Grand Rapids: Wm. B. Eerdmans Pub. Co. (1939), Vol. IV, pp. 2372-2376.

Hiebert, D. Edmond, "Philippians, Letter to the," in *The Zondervan Pictorial Encyclopedia of the Bible,* Merrill C. Tenney, ed. Grand Rapids: Zondervan Publishing House (1975), Vol. IV, pp. 762-767.

Pratt, Dwight M., "Epistle," in *The International Standard Bible Encyclopaedia*. James Orr, ed. Grand Rapids: Wm. B. Eerdmans Pub. Co. (1939), Vol. II, pp. 966-967.

Ramsay, W. M., "Galatia," in *The International Standard Bible Encyclopaedia*. James Orr, ed. Grand Rapids: Wm. B. Eerdmans Pub. Co. (1939), Vol. II, pp. 1154-1155.

Rutherfurd, John, "Pastoral Epistles, The," in *The International Standard Bible Encyclopaedia*. James Orr, ed. Grand Rapids: Wm. B. Eerdmans Pub. Co. (1939), Vol. IV, pp. 2258-2262.

Stevenson, George Hope, "Postal Service (Roman)," in *The Oxford Classical Dictionary*. Oxford: Clarendon Press (1949; 1957 reprint), p. 723.

Tod, M. N., "Illyricum," in *The International Standard Bible Encyclopaedia*. James Orr, ed. Grand Rapids: Wm. B. Eerdmans Pub. Co. (1939), Vol. III, pp. 1149-1150.

———, "Philippi," in *The International Standard Bible Encyclopaedia*. James Orr, ed. Grand Rapids: Wm. B. Eerdmans Pub. Co. (1939), Vol. IV, pp. 2369-2371.

———, "Thessalonica," in *The International Standard Bible Encyclopaedia*. James Orr, ed. Grand Rapids: Wm. B. Eerdmans Pub. Co. (1939), Vol. V, pp. 2970-2971.

Turner, C. H., "Chronology Of The New Testament," in Hastings *Dictionary of the Bible,* James Hastings, ed. New York: Charles Scribner's Sons (1908), Vol. I, pp. 403-425.

Walker, Rollin Hough, "Thessalonians, The First Epistle of Paul to the," in *The Internaional Standard Bible Encyclopaedia*. James Orr, ed. Grand Rapids: Wm. B. Eerdmans Pub. Co. (1939), Vol. V, pp. 2966-2968.

———, "Thessalonians, The Second Epistle of Paul to the," in *The International Standard Bible Encyclopaedia.* James Orr, ed. Grand Rapids: Wm. B. Eerdmans Pub. Co. (1939), Vol. V, pp. 2968-2970.

## VI. PERIODICAL ARTICLES

Anderson, Charles P., "Who Wrote 'The Epistle from Laodicea'?" *Journal of Biblical Literature,* Vol. 85, No. 4, 1966, pp. 436-440.

Broneer, Oscar, "The Apostle Paul and the Isthmian Games," *The Biblical Archaeologist,* Vol. XXV, No. 1, Feb. 1962, pp. 2-31.

———, "Corinth; Center of St. Paul's Missionary Work in Greece," *The Biblical Archaeologist,* Vol. XIV, No. 4, Dec. 1951, pp. 78-96.

Burton, Ernest DeWitt, "The Politarchs," *The American Journal of Theology,* Vol. 2, 1898, pp. 598-632.

Cadbury, H. J., "The Dilemma of Ephesians," *New Testament Studies,* Vol. 2, Jan. 1959, pp. 91-102.

Gregson, R., "A Solution to the Problems of the Thessalonian Epistles," *The Evangelical Quarterly,* Vol. XXXVIII, No. 2, April-June 1966, pp. 76-80.

Hitchcock, F. R. Montgomery, "The Latinity of the Pastorals," *Expository Times,* Vol. XXXIX, May 1928, pp. 347-352.

Hoerber, Robert G., "Galatians 2:1-10 and the Acts of the Apostles," *Concordia Theological Monthly* 31, Aug. 1960, pp. 482-491.

Johnson, Sherman E., "Laodicea and Its Neighbors," *The Biblical Archaeologist,* Vol. XIII, No. 1, Feb. 1950, pp. 1-18.

Lockyer, Herbert, "The Second Advent in the Thessalonian Epistles," *Our Hope,* Vol. LIX, No. 4, Oct. 1952, pp. 229-236.

Stein, Robert H., "The Relationship of Galatians 2:1-10 and Acts 15:1-35: Two Neglected Arguments," *Journal of the Evangelical Theological Society,* Vol. 17, No. 4, Fall 1974, pp. 239-242.

# INDEX

NOTE: The detailed contents of the outlines of the epistles have not been entered in this index. See the individual outlines for the various subjects dealt with in each epistle.


Authenticity
  Colossians, 220-22
  Ephesians, 256-60
  Philemon, 242-43
  Philippians, 288-90
  2 Thessalonians 54-58
Authorship of the Pastoral Epistles, 308-318

Bearer
  Colossians, 223-24
  1 Corinthians, 113
  2 Corinthians, 147
  Romans, 176
  Philemon, 244
  Philippians, 292
  1 Thessalonians, 40
  2 Timothy, 354
  Titus, 344-45
Book List
  Colossians, 235-39
  1 Corinthians, 131-34
  2 Corinthians, 159-62
  Ephesians, 277-81
  Galatians, 96-101
  Pastoral Epistles, 335-39
  Philemon, 250-52
  Philippians, 300-303
  Romans, 196-201
  1 and 2 Thessalonians, 49-53
  1 Timothy. *See* Book List, Pastoral Epistles
  2 Timothy, 362-63
  Titus, 349

Characteristics
  Colossians, 226-28
  1 Corinthians, 114-16
  2 Corinthians, 149-51
  Ephesians, 266-69
  Galatians, 88-90
  Philemon, 245-49
  Philippians, 294-96
  Romans, 179-81
  1 Thessalonians, 43-45
  2 Thessalonians, 61-64
  1 Timothy, 329-30
  2 Timothy, 355-58
  Titus, 346-47
Christological group, introduction to the, 205-213
Church, the, in
  Colossae, 218-20
  Corinth, 107-110
  Ephesus, 255-56
  Philippi, 285-88
  Rome, 166-70
  Thessalonica, 35-39
Churches, the, in
  Crete, 342-43
  Galatia, 71-72, 77-80
City, the, of
  Colossae, 214-18
  Corinth, 102-7
  Ephesus, 253-55
  Philippi, 282-85
  Rome, 163-65
  Thessalonica, 33-34
Colossae
  Church, 218-20
  City, 214-18
Colossians, Epistle to the
  Authenticity, 220-22
  Bearer, 223-24
  Book List, 235-39
  Characteristics, 226-28
  Date, 223
  Introduction, 214-30
  Occasion, 222
  Outline, 230-35
  Place of composition, 223
  Purpose, 224-26
Corinth
  Church, 107-110
  City, 102-7
  Relations of Paul to Church, 144-45
Corinthians, First Epistle to the
  Bearer, 113
  Book List, 131-34
  Characteristics, 114-16
  Date, 112-13
  Introduction, 102-116

Occasion, 110-12
Outline, 116-31
Place of composition, 112
Purpose, 113-14
Corinthians, Second Epistle to the
Bearer, 147
Book List, 159-62
Characteristics, 149-51
Date, 146-47
Introduction, 135-51
Occasion, 145-46
Outline, 151-59
Place of composition, 146
Purpose, 147-49
Unity, 135-44
Crete, Churches in, 342-43

Date
Colossians, 223
1 Corinthians, 112-13
2 Corinthians, 146-47
Ephesians, 265
Galatians, 82-87
Philemon, 244
Philippians, 291-92
Romans, 175-76
1 Thessalonians, 39-40
2 Thessalonians, 59-60
1 Timothy, 328
2 Timothy, 354
Titus, 344-45
Destination
Ephesians, 260-65
2 Timothy, 353-54

Ecclesiological group, introduction to the, 307-323
Ephesians, Epistle to the
Authenticity, 256-60
Book List, 277-81
Characteristics, 266-69
Date, 265
Destination, 260-65
Introduction, 253-69
Occasion, 265
Outline, 270-77
Place of composition, 265
Purpose, 265-66
Ephesus
Church, 255-56
City, 253-55
"Epistle from Laodicea, The," 228-30
Epistles, did Paul write?, 15-16
Epistles, New Testament
Fitness of for revelation, 14-15
Uniqueness, 13-14
Epistles, Pauline, as a group
General introduction, 13-24
Grouping, 22-24
Method of composition and transmission, 19-20
Number, 17-18
Order, 20-22
Origin, 18
Value, 24
Eschatological group, introduction to the, 31-32

Galatia
Churches in, character of the, 71-72
Meaning, 72-75
Visits of Paul to, 75-77
Galatians Churches, The
Character, 71-72
Location, 77-80
Galatians, Epistle to the
Book List, 96-101
Characteristics, 88-90
Date, 82-87
Introduction, 71-90
Occasion, 80-82
Outline, 90-96
Place of composition, 87-88
Purpose, 88
Groups of Pauline Epistles, introductions to
Group 1 (Eschatological), 31-32
Group 2 (Soteriological), 69-70
Group 3 (Christological), 205-213
Group 4 (Ecclesiological), 307-323

Introduction
Colossians, 214-30
1 Corinthians, 102-116
2 Corinthians, 135-51
Ephesians, 253-69
Galatians, 71-90
Pastoral Epistles, 307-323
Pauline Epistles, 13-24
Philemon, 240-49
Philippians, 282-96
Prison Epistles, 205-213
Romans, 163-82
1 Thessalonians, 33-45
2 Thessalonians, 54-64
1 Timothy, 324-30
2 Timothy, 350-58
Titus, 340-47

Journeys of Paul in the Pastoral Epistles, 318-23

"Laodicea, The Epistle from," 228-30

Occasion
Colossians, 222
1 Corinthians, 110-12
2 Corinthians, 147
Ephesians, 265
Galatians, 80-82
Philemon, 243-44
Philippians, 290
Romans, 176
1 Thessalonians, 38-39

2 Thessalonians, 58-59
1 Timothy, 327-28
2 Timothy, 352-53
Titus, 343-44
Order
The Pastoral Epistles, 323
The Prison Epistles, 211-13
Outline
Colossians, 230-35
1 Corinthians, 116-31
2 Corinthians, 151-59
Ephesians, 270-77
Galatians, 90-96
Philemon, 249-50
Philippians, 296-300
Romans, 182-96
1 Thessalonians, 45-49
2 Thessalonians, 64-66
1 Timothy, 330-35
2 Timothy, 359-62
Titus, 347-49

Pastoral Epistles, the
Authorship of, 308-318
Book List, 335-39
Introduction, 307-323
Journeys of Paul, 318-23
Order, 323
Pauline Epistles as a group. *See* Epistles, Pauline
Philemon, home of, 240-42
Philemon, Epistle to
Authenticity, 242-43
Bearer, 244
Book List, 250-52
Characteristics, 245-49
Date, 244
Introduction, 240-49
Occasion, 243-44
Outline, 249-50
Place of composition, 244
Purpose, 244-45
Philippi
Church, 285-88
City, 282-85
Philippians, Epistle to the
Authenticity, 288-90
Bearer, 292
Book List, 300-303
Characteristics, 294-96
Date, 291-92
Introduction, 282-96
Occasion, 290
Outline, 296-300
Place of composition, 290-91
Purpose, 292-94
Unity, 289-90
Place of composition
Colossians, 223
1 Corinthians, 112
2 Corinthians, 146
Ephesians, 265
Galatians, 87-88
Philemon, 244
Philippians, 290-91
Prison Epistles, 206-211
Romans, 175
1 Thessalonians, 39
2 Thessalonians, 59
1 Timothy, 328
2 Timothy, 354
Titus, 344
Prison Epistles
Introduction, 205-213
Order of composition, 211-13
Place of composition, 206-211
Purpose
Colossians, 224-26
1 Corinthians, 113-14
2 Corinthians, 147-49
Ephesians, 265-66
Galatians, 88
Philemon, 244-45
Philippians, 292-94
Romans, 176-79
1 Thessalonians, 40-43
2 Thessalonians, 60-61
1 Timothy, 328-29
2 Timothy, 354-55
Titus, 345-46

Romans, Epistle to the
Bearer, 176
Book List, 196-201
Characteristics, 179-81
Date, 175-76
Introduction, 163-82
Occasion, 176
Outline, 182-96
Place of Composition, 175
Purpose, 176-79
Tributes, 181-82
Unity, 170-75
Rome
Church, 166-70
City in A.D. 58, 163-65

Soteriological Group, Introduction to the, 69-70
Study procedure, suggested, 25-28

Thessalonians, First Epistle to the
Bearer, 40
Book List, 49-53
Characteristics, 43-45
Introduction, 33-45
Occasion, 38-39
Outline, 45-49
Place of Composition, 39
Purpose, 40-43
Thessalonians, Second Epistle to the
Authenticity, 54-58
Characteristics, 61-64
Introduction, 54-64

Occasion, 58-59
Outline, 64-66
Place and date of composition, 59-60
Purpose, 60-61
Thessalonica
Church, 35-39
City, 33-34
Timothy, the addressee, 324-27
Timothy, First Epistle to
Book List. *See* Book List, Pastoral Epistles
Characteristics, 329-30
Date, 328
Introduction, 324-30
Occasion, 327-28
Outline, 330-35
Place of composition, 328
Purpose, 328-29
Timothy, Second Epistle to
Bearer, 354
Book List, 362-63
Characteristics, 355-58
Date, 354
Destination, 353-54
Historical situation, 350-52
Introduction, 350-58
Occasion, 352-53
Outline, 359-62
Place of composition, 354
Purpose, 354-55
Titus, the addressee, 340-42
Titus, Epistle to
Bearer, 344-45
Book List, 349
Characteristics, 346-47
Date, 344-45
Introduction, 340-47
Occasion, 343-44
Outline, 347-49
Place of composition, 344
Purpose, 345-46

Unity
2 Corinthians, 135-44
Philippians, 289-90
Romans, 170-75

Value of the Pauline Epistles, 24